T0276555

Latest Research in Computational Intelligence and Soft Computing

Volume II

Latest Research in Computational Intelligence and Soft Computing Volume II

Edited by **Tom Halt**

LANRYE
INTERNATIONAL

New Jersey

Published by Clanrye International,
55 Van Reypen Street,
Jersey City, NJ 07306, USA
www.clanryeinternational.com

Latest Research in Computational Intelligence and Soft Computing
Volume II
Edited by Tom Halt

International Standard Book Number: 978-1-63240-330-8 (Hardback)

Contents

Preface

Soft computing is a subject that is used in the science of computers. It is basically used to refer to the problems in the field of computer science whose solutions are mostly unpredictable and always have a probability value of zero to one. This field came into existence in early 1990s with a huge impact on computer sciences. The perfect example of a soft computing model is the human mind. It becomes pertinent to note here, that soft computing is absolutely tolerant of approximation and uncertainty, unlike hard computing. Moreover, there's a huge difference between possibility and soft computing.

Earlier applied computational approaches were used to model and analyze only simple systems. But due to advancement in the fields of biology, medical science, humanities, management, and numerous others, the need for soft computing and applied computations gained significant attention. Applied computation and soft computing deals with problems like imprecision, uncertainty, partial truth, and approximated values to achieve practicability, robustness, and above all low solution cost. The soft computing process is mostly used when the information about the problem is highly limited and not even available sometimes.

Instead of organizing the book into a pre-formatted table of contents with chapters, sections and then asking the authors to submit their respective chapters based on this frame, the authors were encouraged by the publisher to submit their chapters based on their area of expertise. The editor was then commissioned to examine the reading material and put it together as a book.

I especially wish to acknowledge the contributing authors, without whom a work of this magnitude would definitely not be realizable. I thank them for allocating their very scarce time to this project. Not only do I appreciate their participation, but also their adherence as a group to the time parameters set for this publication.

Editor

Tuning PID Controller Using Multiobjective Ant Colony Optimization

Ibtissem Chiha,[1] Noureddine Liouane,[2] and Pierre Borne[3]

[1] Ensi Enim, Monastir, Rabat, Tunisia
[2] Ensi Enim, Tunisia
[3] National Cancer Institute, 92513 Boulogne Billan Court Cedex, France

Correspondence should be addressed to Ibtissem Chiha, chiha.ibtissem@yahoo.fr

Academic Editor: F. Morabito

This paper treats a tuning of PID controllers method using multiobjective ant colony optimization. The design objective was to apply the ant colony algorithm in the aim of tuning the optimum solution of the PID controllers (K_p, K_i, and K_d) by minimizing the multiobjective function. The potential of using multiobjective ant algorithms is to identify the Pareto optimal solution. The other methods are applied to make comparisons between a classic approach based on the "Ziegler-Nichols" method and a metaheuristic approach based on the genetic algorithms. Simulation results demonstrate that the new tuning method using multiobjective ant colony optimization has a better control system performance compared with the classic approach and the genetic algorithms.

1. Introduction

Proportional-integral-derivative (PID) controllers are frequently used in the control process to regulate the time domain behavior of many different types of dynamic plants. These controllers are extremely popular because of their simple structure and they can usually provide a good closed loop response characteristic. Despite its simple structure it seems so hard to find a proper PID controller [1]. Considering this problem, various methods have been proposed to tune these parameters.

Ziegler-Nichols tuning method is the most standard one but it is often difficult to find optimal PID parameters with these methods. Therefore many optimization methods are developed to tune the PID controllers such as fuzzy logic [2, 3], neural network [4], neural-fuzzy logic [5], immune algorithm [6], simulated annealing [7], and pattern recognition [8]. In addition, we have many other optimum tuning PID methods based on many random search methods such as genetic algorithm (GA) [9, 10], particle swarm optimization [11], and ant colony optimization [12].

In this work, we developed the problem of design PID controllers as a multiobjective optimization problem taking in consideration the ant colony optimization algorithm (ACO). Researchers have reported the capacity of ACO to efficiently search for and locate an optimum solution. This method was mainly inspired by the fact that ants are able to find the shortest route between their nest and a food source.

Ant colony optimization (ACO) [13, 14] is a recently developed metaheuristic approach for solving hard combinatorial optimization problems such as the travelling salesman problem TSP [15], quadratic assignment problem [16], graph coloring problems [17], hydroelectric generation scheduling problems [18], vehicle routing [19], sequential ordering, scheduling [20], and routing in Internet-like networks [21].

Ant colony optimization algorithms are especially suited for finding solutions to difficult optimization problems. A colony of artificial ants cooperates to find good solutions, which are an emergent property of the ants' cooperative interaction. Based on their similarities with ant colonies in nature, ant algorithms are adaptive and robust and can be applied to different versions of the same problem as well as to different optimization problems.

The main traits of artificial ants are taken from their natural model. These main traits are as follows: (1) artificial ants exist in colonies of cooperating individuals, (2) they communicate indirectly by depositing (artificial) pheromone

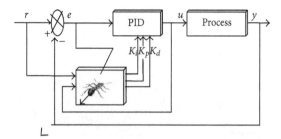

FIGURE 1: PID control system.

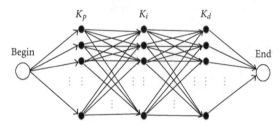

FIGURE 2: Ant colony optimization graph.

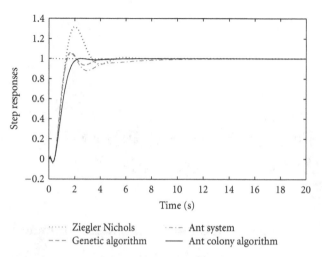

FIGURE 3: Comparison of step responses of the $G_1(s)$ plant.

(stigmergic communication), (3) they use a sequence of local moves to find the shortest path from a starting position, to a destination point (i.e., the optimal solution to a given problem), and (4) they apply a stochastic decision policy using local information only (i.e., they do not look ahead) to find the best solution. If necessary in order to solve a particular optimization problem, artificial ants have been enriched with some additional capabilities not present in real ants.

An ant colony of finite size searches collectively for a good solution to a given optimization problem. Each individual ant can find a solution or at least part of a solution to the optimization problem on its own but only when many ants work together they can find the optimal solution. Since the optimal solution can only be found through the global co-operation of all the ants in a colony, it is an emergent result of such this cooperation. While searching for a solution the ants do not communicate directly but indirectly by adding pheromone to the environment. Based on the specific problem an ant is given a starting state and moves through a sequence of neighboring states trying to find the shortest path. It moves based on a stochastic local search policy directed by its internal state (private information), the pheromone trails, and local information encoded in the environment (together public information). Ants use this private and public information in order to decide when and where to deposit pheromones. In most applications the amount of pheromone deposited is proportional to the quality of the move an ant has made. Thus, the more pheromone, the better the solution found. After an ant has found a solution, it dies, that is, it is deleted from the system.

This paper is organized as follows: the implementation of ACO to design multiobjective optimization is developed in Section 2. In Section 3, the effectiveness of this approach is tested, compared with other methods which are the standard method (Ziegler-Nichols), metaheuristique method (Genetic Algorithm), and ant system in the same section the

construction of a Pareto optimal set of solutions, and the convergence graph in the ACO method are shown. Finally, some conclusions are given in Section 4.

2. Design PID Controller Using Multiobjective Ant Colony Algorithm

The series controllers are very frequent because of higher order systems. The transfer function of PID controller is defined for a continuous system as:

$$G_c(p) = K_p + \frac{K_i}{s} + K_d s. \tag{1}$$

The design implies the determination of the values of the constants K_p, K_i, and K_d, meeting the required performance specifications.

The textbook version of the PID controller in continuous time is

$$e(t) = r(t) - y(t),$$

$$u(t) = K_p e(t) + K_i \int_0^t e(\tau) d\tau + K_d e(t) = u_p(t) + u_i(t) + u_d(t), \tag{2}$$

where $e(t) = r(t) - y(t)$ is the difference between the reference signal $r(t)$ and the output, $y(t)$ of the controlled process.

The PID controller is implemented to improve the dynamic response in addition to reduce or eliminate the steady-state error. To characterise the performance of the PID controller systems, we compute the indexes' performance of the transient response such as rise time (t_r), overshoot (O_s), settling time (t_s), the integral square error (ISE)....

The problem is how to tune the parameters of the PID controllers using the multiobjective ant colony optimization as indicated in Figure 1.

As shown in Figure 3, the gains K_p, K_i, and K_d of the PID controller are generated by the multiobjective ACO algorithm for a given plant.

In order to exploit the ACO algorithm, it would be better to represent our optimization problem by a direct way in the form of construction graph.

The population is represented by $100 * 3$ matrix, where the ant select the optimum parameters K_p, K_i, and K_d of the PID control system by minimizing the objective function L^A. The graph shown in Figure 2 illustrates the design PID problem using ant colony algorithm.

In this study, each parameter of K_p, K_i, and K_d is coded by 100 numbers (nodes), respectively. Therefore, only one node represents the optimum solution values of the parameters K_p, K_i, and K_d.

The basic step in applying optimization method is to choose the optimization criteria that are used to evaluate fitness. Since the PID controller has many indexes performance of the transient response, then we can combine them into one objective function composed of the weighted sum of objectives.

The objective function must be set:

$$L^A = \min(\Phi F), \qquad (3)$$

where $F = [f_1 \ f_2 \ f_3 \ f_4 \ f_5 \ f_6 \ f_7]^T$: vector of objective functions, f_1: setting time (t_s), f_2: overshoot (OS), f_3: rise time (t_r), f_4: integral absolute error (IAE), f_5: integral square error (ISE), f_6: integral time absolute error (ITAE), f_7: integral time square error (MSE), and $\Phi = [\lambda_1 \ \lambda_2 \ \lambda_3 \ \lambda_4 \ \lambda_5 \ \lambda_6 \ \lambda_7]$: vector of nonnegative weights.

The goal of multiobjective optimization problems is to find the best compromise between multiple and conflicting objectives. Considering all objectives in these problems, there will be more than one solution that optimizes simultaneously all the objectives and there is no distinct superiority between these solutions. Usually there is not a single best solution being better than the remainder with respect to every objective. Therefore, we face with a set of solutions which are better than remainder solutions called the Pareto front. Among the feasible solutions, solutions belonging to the Pareto front are known as nondominated solutions, while the remainder solutions are known as dominated. Since none of the Pareto set solutions is absolutely better than the other nondominated solutions, all of them are equally acceptable as regards the satisfaction of all the objectives [22].

ACO uses a pheromone matrix $\tau = \{\tau_{ij}\}$ for the construction of potential good solutions. The initial values of τ are set $\tau_{ij} = \tau_0$ for all (i, j), where $\tau_0 > 0$.

The probability $P_{ij}^A(t)$ of choosing a node j at node i is defined in (4). At each generation of the algorithm, the ant constructs a complete solution using (4), starting at source node.

$$P_{ij}^A(t) = \frac{\left[\tau_{ij}(t)\right]^\alpha \left[\eta_{ij}\right]^\beta}{\sum_{i,j \in T^A} \left[\tau_{ij}(t)\right]^\alpha \left[\eta_{ij}\right]^\beta}, \qquad \text{if } i, j \in T^A, \qquad (4)$$

where η_{ij} representing heuristic functions, α and β are constants that determine the relative influence of the pheromone values and the heuristic values on the decision of the ant, and T^A: is the path effectuated by the ant A at a given time.

The pheromone evaporation is a way to avoid unlimited increase of pheromone trails. Also it allows the forgetfulness of the bad choices:

$$\tau_{ij}(t) = \rho \tau_{ij}(t - 1) + \sum_{A=1}^{NA} \Delta \tau_{ij}^A(t), \qquad (5)$$

where $\Delta \tau_{ij}^A$ the quantity of pheromone on each path, NA: number of ants, ρ: the evaporation rate $0 < \rho \leq 1$.

Implementation Algorithm. The proposed algorithm can be described by the following general algorithm.

Begin

Step 1. Initialize randomly a potential solutions of the parameters (K_p, K_i, K_d) by using uniform distribution.
  Initialize the pheromone trail, and the heuristic value.
  Initialize the Pareto set to an empty set.

Step 2. Place the Ath ant on the node.
Compute the heuristic value associated in the multiobjective L^A.

  Choose the successive node with probability:

$$P_{ij}^A(t) = \frac{\left[\tau_{ij}(t)\right]^\alpha \left[\eta_{ij}\right]^\beta}{\sum_{i,j \in T^A} \left[\tau_{ij}(t)\right]^\alpha \left[\eta_{ij}\right]^\beta}, \qquad \text{if } i, j \in T^A, \qquad (6)$$

where $\eta_{ij} = 1/K_j$, $j = [p, i, d]$: representing heuristic functions, T^A: is the path effectuated by the ant A at a given time.

  The quantity of pheromone $\Delta \tau_{ij}^A$ on each path may be defined as:

$$\Delta \tau_{ij}^A = \begin{cases} \dfrac{L^{\min}}{L^A}, & \text{if } i, j \in T^A, \\ 0, & \text{else,} \end{cases} \qquad (7)$$

where L^A is the value of the objective function found by the ant A. $L^{\min}$ is the best solution carried out by the set of the ants until the current iteration.

Step 3. Use pheromone evaporation given by (5) to avoid unlimited increase of pheromone trails and allow the forgetfulness of bad choices:

$$\tau_{ij}(t) = \rho \tau_{ij}(t - 1) + \sum_{A=1}^{NA} \Delta \tau_{ij}^A(t), \qquad (8)$$

where NA: number of ants, and ρ: the evaporation rate $0 < \rho \leq 1$.

Step 4. Evaluate the obtained solutions according to the different objectives.
  Update the Pareto archive with the nondominated ones.
  Reduce the size of the archive if necessary.

Step 5. Display the optimum values of the optimization parameters.

Step 6. Globally update the pheromone, according to the optimum solutions calculated at Step 5.
  Iterate from Step 2 until the maximum of iterations is reached.
End

TABLE 1: Simulation results.

	Ziegle-Nichols [23]	Genetic algorithm [24]	Ant system [12]	Multiobjective ant colony optimization
$G_1(s) = e^{-0.5s}/(s+1)^2$	$K_p = 2.808$ $K_i = 1.712$ $K_d = 1.151$ $f_1: t_s = 4.78$ $f_2:$ OS $= 31.59\%$ $f_3: t_r = 0.664$ $f_5:$ ISE $= 0.854$	$K_p = 2.391$ $K_i = 1.072$ $K_d = 1.458$ $f_1: t_s = 3.63$ $f_2:$ OS $= 5.84\%$ $f_3: t_r = 0.676$ $f_5:$ ISE $= 0.797$	$K_p = 2.4911$ $K_i = 0.8158$ $K_d = 1.3540$ $f_1: t_s = 5.9$ $f_2:$ OS $= 4.95\%$ $f_3: t_r = 0.701$ $f_5:$ ISE $= 0.809$	$K_p = 1.905$ $K_i = 0.903$ $K_d = 0.989$ $f_1: t_s = 3$ $f_2:$ OS $= 0\%$ $f_3: t_r = 0.7$ $f_5:$ ISE $= 0.772$
$G_2(s) =$ $4.228/(s+0.5)(s^2+1.64s+8.456)$	$K_p = 2.190$ $K_i = 2.126$ $K_d = 0.565$ $f_1: t_s = 6.6$ $f_2:$ OS $= 16.46\%$ $f_3: t_r = 0.8$ $f_5:$ ISE $= 0.785$	$K_p = 1.637$ $K_i = 0.964$ $K_d = 0.387$ $f_1: t_s = 5.97$ $f_2:$ OS $= 3\%$ $f_3: t_r = 2.45$ $f_5:$ ISE $= 0.588$	$K_p = 2.517$ $K_i = 2.219$ $K_d = 1.151$ $f_1: t_s = 6.51$ $f_2:$ OS $= 16\%$ $f_3: t_r = 0.627$ $f_5:$ ISE $= 0.684$	$K_p = 2.1604$ $K_i = 1.8546$ $K_d = 1.6920$ $f_1: t_s = 5.22$ $f_2:$ OS $= 0.09\%$ $f_3: t_r = 2.54$ $f_5:$ ISE $= 0.448$
$G_3(s) = 27/(s+1)(s+3)^3$	$K_p = 3.072$ $K_i = 2.272$ $K_d = 1.038$ $f_1: t_s = 8.2473$ $f_2:$ OS $= 51.47\%$ $f_3: t_r = 22.5$ $f_5:$ ISE $= 0.66$	$K_p = 1.772$ $K_i = 1.061$ $K_d = 0.772$ $f_1: t_s = 7.3959$ $f_2:$ OS $= 30.7\%$ $f_3: t_r = 15.3$ $f_5:$ ISE $= 0.7311$	$K_p = 2.058$ $K_i = 1.137$ $K_d = 0.746$ $f_1: t_s = 7.0311$ $f_2:$ OS $= 19.82\%$ $f_3: t_r = 8.9$ $f_5:$ ISE $= 0.708$	$K_p = 1.702$ $K_i = 1.061$ $K_d = 0.772$ $f_1: t_s = 6.973$ $f_2:$ OS $= 6\%$ $f_3: t_r = 6.2$ $f_5:$ ISE $= 0.501$

3. Simulation Results

In this section, we presented the numerical results to improve the performance of the proposed solution algorithm.

All the computation is implemented with Matlab/Simulink. The values of the parameters in ACO are $m = 500$ (numbers of ants), $\alpha = 0.5$, $\beta = 0.5$, $\rho = 0.5$, and maximum generation = 300.

In this study, we utilised two examples in order to illustrate the efficiency of the proposed algorithm.

Example 1. The performance of the algorithm developed was tested with three transfer functions with different order. The chosen performance criterion is often a weighted combination of various performance characteristics such as rise time, settling time, overshoot, and integral of the square of the error [24].

We chose the following objective function:

$$L^A = \min(\lambda_1 f_1 + \lambda_2 f_2 + \lambda_5 f_5). \tag{9}$$

The objective function here is f_1: the setting time to measure the performance of the closed-loop system, f_2: the overshoot, and f_5: the integral square error that should be minimized.

Therefore the vector of weights is $\Phi = [1\ 1\ 0\ 0\ 1\ 0\ 0]$.

The closed loop PID controller cascaded with the process was tuned for the values K_p, K_i, and K_d first by using the Ziegler-Nichols method [23], genetic algorithm [24], ant system [12] and then by our multiobjective ant colony algorithm. So that, the percent maximum overshoot, the settling time, the rise time, and the integral of the squared error were computed in both cases and given in Table 1.

In this table OS represents the percent maximum overshoot, t_s is the 5 percent settling time, t_r is the rise time, and ISE is the integral of the squared error.

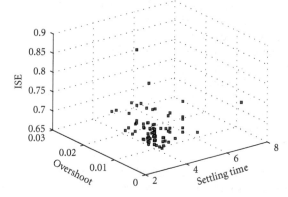

FIGURE 4: Multiobjective optimization Pareto-sets of the $G_1(s)$ plant.

The objective function used in [24] and [12] is defined using the performance indices: the response overshoot (OS), the 5% settling time t_s, and integral of the square of the error (ISE).

As shown in results of Table 1 and in all the cases tested, the value of the maximum overshoot is quite small, nearly zero percent and the values of the settling times, the rise time, and the integral of the squared error obtained by multiobjective ant colony optimization were much less than those values by the other methods.

The graphs of the obtained three-dimensional Pareto optimal fronts (the settling times, the overshoot, and the squared error) for the generated problem corresponding in each transfer function are depicted in Figures 4, 7, and 10. So that, it is possible to find a well-distributed set of nondominated solutions along the Pareto optimal front.

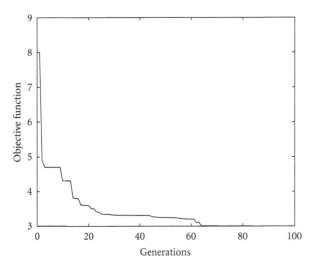

FIGURE 5: Convergence graph in the ACO method of the $G_1(s)$ plant.

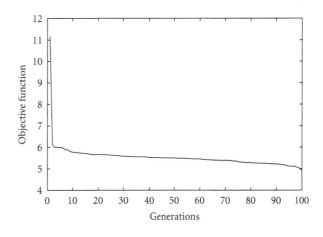

FIGURE 8: Convergence graph in the ACO method of the $G_2(s)$ plant.

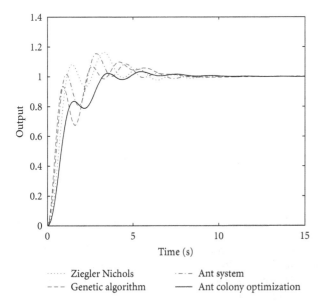

Ziegler Nichols .... Ant system –·–
Genetic algorithm – – – Ant colony optimization ——

FIGURE 6: Comparison of step responses of the $G_2(s)$ plant.

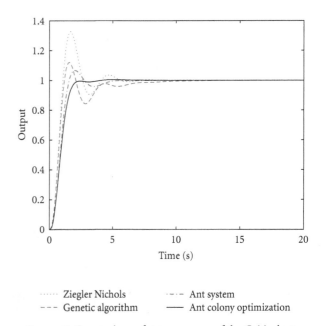

Ziegler Nichols .... Ant system –·–
Genetic algorithm – – – Ant colony optimization ——

FIGURE 9: Comparison of step responses of the $G_3(s)$ plant.

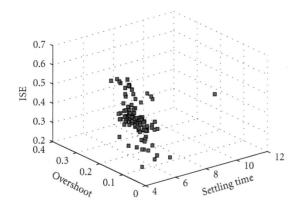

FIGURE 7: Multiobjective optimization the Pareto sets of the $G_2(s)$ plant.

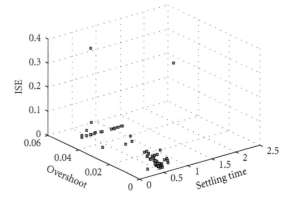

FIGURE 10: Multiobjective optimization Pareto sets of the $G_3(s)$ plant.

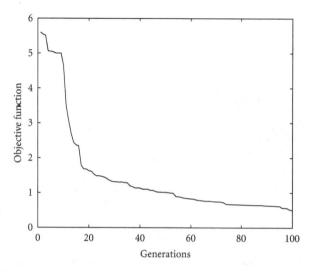

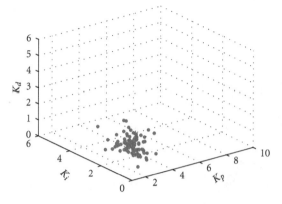

FIGURE 13: The Intermediate search space of parameters (K_p^{best}, K_i^{best}, K_d^{best}).

FIGURE 11: Convergence graph in the ACO method of the $G_3(s)$ plant.

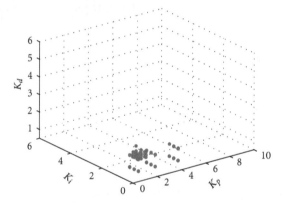

FIGURE 14: The final search space of parameters (K_p^{opt}, K_i^{opt}, K_d^{opt}).

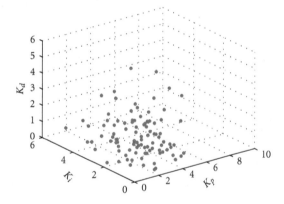

FIGURE 12: The initial search space of parameters (K_p, K_i, K_d).

Figures 3, 6, and 9 show the step responses of $G_1(s)$, $G_2(s)$, and $G_3(s)$, respectively, which are ploted with the optimum values of the parameters K_p, K_i, and K_d obtained by the proposed algorithm. the results obtained by using Ziegler-Nichols, genetic algorithm, and ant system algorithm are presented for comparison.

In all cases, the proposed algorithm produces better responses than that obtained using the other methods. So, we can say that the multiobjective ant colony algorithm well improves the performance of the PID controllers.

Figures 5, 8, and 11 report the evaluation of the objective function on the above three transfer functions. It is observed that the objective function value decreases substantially.

Initially, each parameter (K_p, K_i, K_d) is randomly and uniformly distributed with an average value which is equal to the value founded by Ziegler-Nichols of the transfer function $G_1(s)$, the search space of these parameters is shown in Figure 12.

After several iterations, the multiobjective ant colony algorithm generated the best solutions of the PID parameters ($K_p^{best}, K_i^{best}, K_d^{best}$), the search space of these parameters is

shown in Figure 13, it may be noted that these solutions are somewhat condensed.

After that, each parameter ($K_p^{best} K_i^{best} K_d^{best}$) is randomly and uniformly distributed with an average value which is equal to the value founded in the last generation, the multiobjective ant colony algorithm generated the optimal solutions ($K_p^{opt} K_i^{opt} K_d^{opt}$), as shown in the Figure 14, and these solutions are more condensed than that found in the last generation.

4. Conclusions

In this study, a tuning PID method based on the multiobjective ant colony optimization is developed for getting good performances and tunes the optimal PID parameters. In contrast to the single-objective algorithms, which try to find a single solution of the problem, the multiobjective technique searches for the optimal Pareto set directly. The aim of the multiobjective ACO algorithm is to determine the optimal solutions of the PID controller parameters by minimization the multiobjective function and to identify the Pareto optimal solution. This method is able to ind the optimum solution of the PID controller's parameters (K_p, K_i, and K_d) that they allow to guarantee the performance of the system.

Simulation results demonstrate that the new tuning method using multiobjective ant colony optimization has a better control system performance compared with classic approach, the genetic algorithms and ant system. The multiobjective ACO algorithm is able to undertake local search with a fast convergence rate. From the simulation study it has been found that this method converges to the global optimum.

References

[1] A. Oonsivilai and P. Pao-La-Or, "Application of adaptive tabu search for optimum PID controller tuning AVR system," *WSEAS Transactions on Power Systems*, vol. 3, no. 6, pp. 495–506, 2008.

[2] S. Tzafestas and N. P. Papanikolopoulos, "Incremetal fuzzy expert PID control," *IEEE Transactions on Industrial Electronics*, vol. 37, no. 5, pp. 365–371, 1990.

[3] A. Visioli, "Tuning of PID controllers with fuzzy logic," *IEE Proceedings: Control Theory and Applications*, vol. 148, no. 1, pp. 1–8, 2001.

[4] C. Cao, X. Guo, and Y. Liu, "Research on ant colony neural network PID controller and application," in *Proceedings of the 8th ACIS International Conference on Software Engineering, Artificial Intelligence, Networking, and Parallel/Distributed Computing (SNPD '07)*, pp. 253–258, 2007.

[5] T. L. Seng, M. B. Khalid, and R. Yusof, "Tuning of a neuro-fuzzy controller by genetic algorithm," *IEEE Transactions on Systems, Man, and Cybernetics Part B*, vol. 29, no. 2, pp. 226–236, 1999.

[6] D. H. Kim, "Tuning of a PID controller using a artificial immune network model and local fuzzy set," in *Proceedings of the Annual Conference of the North American Fuzzy Information Processing Society (NAFIPS '01)*, vol. 5, pp. 2698–2703, 2001.

[7] G. Zhou and J. D. Birdwell, "Fuzzy logic-based PID autotuner design using simulated annealing," in *Proceedings of the IEEE/IFAC Joint Symposium on Computer-Aided*, pp. 67–72, 1994.

[8] P. Wang and D. P. Kwok, "Optimal design of PID process controllers based on genetic algorithms," *Control Engineering Practice*, vol. 2, no. 4, pp. 641–648, 1994.

[9] P. Wang and D. P. Kwok, "Optimal design of PID process controllers based on genetic algorithms," *Control Engineering Practice*, vol. 2, no. 4, pp. 641–648, 1994.

[10] Y. Mitsukura, T. Yamamoto, and M. Kaneda, "A design of self turning PID controllers'using a genetic algorithm," in *Proceedings of the American Control Conference*, pp. 1361–1365, San Diego, Calif, USA, 1999.

[11] S. E. Selvan, S. Subramanian, and S. T. Solomon, "Novel technique for PID tuning by particle swarm optimization," in *Proceedings of the 7th Annual Swarm Users/Researchers Conference (SwarmFest '03)*, 2003.

[12] Y. T. Hsiao, C. L. Chuang, and C. C. Chien, "Ant colony optimization for designing of PID controllers," in *Proceedings of the IEEE International Symposium on Computer Aided Control Systems Design*, Taipei, Taiwan, 2004.

[13] M. Dorigo and G. Di Caro, "The ant colony optimization meta-heuristic," in *New Ideas in Optimization*, D. Corne, M. Dorigo, and F. Glover, Eds., pp. 11–32, McGraw Hill, London, UK, 1999.

[14] M. Dorigo, G. Di Caro, and L. M. Gambardella, "Ant algorithms for discrete optimization," *Artificial Life*, vol. 5, no. 2, pp. 137–172, 1999.

[15] G. Reinelt, *The Traveling Salesman: Computational Solutions for TSP Applications*, vol. 840 of *Lecture Notes in Computer Science*, Springer, Berlin, Germany, 1994.

[16] T. Stützle and M. Dorigo, "ACO algorithms for the quadratic assignment problem," in *New Ideas in Optimization*, D. Corne, M. Dorigo, and F. Glover, Eds., pp. 33–50, McGraw Hill, London, UK, 1999.

[17] D. Costa and A. Hertz, "Ants can colour graphs," *Journal of the Operational Research Society*, vol. 48, no. 3, pp. 295–305, 1997.

[18] S. J. Huang, "Enhancement of hydroelectric generation scheduling using ant colony system based optimization approaches," *IEEE Transactions on Energy Conversion*, vol. 16, no. 3, pp. 296–301, 2001.

[19] L. M. Gambardella, E. D. Taillard, and G. Agazzi, "MACS-VRPTW: a multiple ant colony system for vehicle routing problems with time windows," in *New Ideas in Optimization*, D. Corne, M. Dorigo, and F. Glover, Eds., pp. 63–76, McGraw Hill, London, UK, 1999.

[20] L. M. Gambardella and M. Dorigo, "An ant colony system hybridized with a new local search for the sequential ordering problem," *INFORMS Journal on Computing*, vol. 12, no. 3, pp. 237–255, 2000.

[21] G. Di Caro and M. Dorigo, "Ant colonies for adaptive routing in packetswitched communications networks," in *Proceedings of the Proceedings of 5th International Conference on Parallel Problem Solving from Nature (PPSN '98)*, A. E. Eiben, T. Bäck, M. Schoenauer, and H.-P. Schwefel, Eds., vol. 1498 of *Lecture Notes in Computer Science*, pp. 673–682, Springer, Berlin, Germany, 1998.

[22] A. Afshar, A. Kaveh, and O. R. Shoghli, "Multi-objective optimization of time-cost-quality using multi-colony ant algorithm," *Asian Journal Of Civil Engineering*, vol. 8, no. 2, pp. 113–124, 2007.

[23] J. G. Ziegler and N. B. Nichols, "Optimum settlings for automatic controllers," *Transactions of the ASME*, vol. 64, pp. 759–768, 1942.

[24] A. Bagis, "Determination of the PID controller parameters by modified genetic algorithm for improved performance," *Journal of Information Science and Engineering*, vol. 23, no. 5, pp. 1469–1480, 2007.

Using Genetic Algorithms for Navigation Planning in Dynamic Environments

Ferhat Uçan[1,2] and D. Turgay Altılar[2]

[1] Center of Research for Advanced Technologies of Informatics and Security (TÜBİTAK BILGEM), 41470 Kocaeli, Turkey
[2] Computer Engineering Department, Istanbul Technical University, 34469 Istanbul, Turkey

Correspondence should be addressed to Ferhat Uçan, ferhat.ucan@bte.tubitak.gov.tr

Academic Editor: Tzung P. Hong

Navigation planning can be considered as a combination of searching and executing the most convenient flight path from an initial waypoint to a destination waypoint. Generally the aim is to follow the flight path, which provides minimum fuel consumption for the air vehicle. For dynamic environments, constraints change dynamically during flight. This is a special case of dynamic path planning. As the main concern of this paper is flight planning, the conditions and objectives that are most probable to be used in navigation problem are considered. In this paper, the genetic algorithm solution of the dynamic flight planning problem is explained. The evolutionary dynamic navigation planning algorithm is developed for compensating the existing deficiencies of the other approaches. The existing fully dynamic algorithms process unit changes to topology one modification at a time, but when there are several such operations occurring in the environment simultaneously, the algorithms are quite inefficient. The proposed algorithm may respond to the concurrent constraint updates in a shorter time for dynamic environment. The most secure navigation of the air vehicle is planned and executed so that the fuel consumption is minimum.

1. Introduction

Navigation planning requires producing a flight plan to describe a proposed aircraft flight. It involves two safety-critical aspects: minimum fuel consumption and compliance with air traffic control requirements. Navigation planning involves creating a flight plan to guide a point-like object from its initial position to a destination waypoint [1]. Along the way, there may be a set of regions to visit and a set of regions to avoid. Planners wish to reach the destination economically and by minimum risk of mid-air collision. Fuel consumption involves fuel flow rate estimations, so that the relation of fuel flow with air temperature, flight altitude, true airspeed, and gross weight can be defined with an accurate formula [2]. Safety regulations require aircraft to carry fuel beyond the minimum needed to fly from origin to destination, allowing for unforeseen circumstances or for diversion to another airport if the planned destination becomes unavailable. Furthermore, under the supervision of air traffic control, aircraft flying in controlled airspace must follow predetermined routes known as airways, even if such routes are not as economical as a more direct flight [3, 4]. The basis of the flight profile is the route that the aircraft is to fly from the departure airport to the destination airport. Flight planning function provides for the assembly, modification, and activation of this route data known as a flight plan. Flight plans are normally constructed by linking data stored in the navigation database.

In this paper, by using the flight map and waypoint information, the aim is to calculate the most secure, shortest flight path and the guidance information in order to execute the flight plan by using flight data. For the real-time navigation planning problem, the change in the cost criteria like distance and security is related with the flight level. Flight level is a standard nominal altitude of the air vehicle [4]. This altitude is calculated from the international standard pressure datum, the average sea-level pressure, and therefore is not necessarily the same as the aircraft's true altitude either above mean sea level or above ground level.

Traditional methods used for the standard route planning problem are Dijkstra, Floyd Warshall, A-Star, and

Bellman Ford's algorithm [5]. When the constraints of the problem are dynamic and the environment is not stable, these methods are not valid. The effect of the constraints like security and distance may be modeled with the classical optimization techniques, but in a dynamic environment, restarting to find the solution at each graph update increases the operation complexity. Moreover, when new waypoints or routes are inserted or some of the existing routes are deleted, the classical algorithms cannot compensate this situation without starting the solution from the beginning. The proposed evolutionary method considers multiobjectives and compensate dynamic conditions due to the evolutionary operators and the problem-specific fitness function. The proposed evolutionary navigation planning approach reduces the number of operations in dynamic environments; because it does not restart the solution at each update, it trends to extend best-fit individuals into the new generations.

2. Evolutionary Methods Used for Path Planning in Literature

In recent years, evolutionary algorithms have been successfully applied to real-time task and path planning problems. The evolutionary based techniques are attractive for solving large-scale complex path planning problems because gradient information about objective functions and constraints are not needed during search for optimal solutions. Gradients usually do not exist for all feasible solutions in the search space. Another crucial advantage of evolutionary techniques is that they can eventually give the global optimal solutions for large-scale path planning problems.

Nikolos et al. made a research for 3D path planning of unmanned air vehicles [6]. In their study they used evolutionary algorithms for calculating the path curve according to the earth's surface in a 3-D environment. They realized that, in order to obtain better results, the route must be curved instead of the combination of the straight lines. This may be a good idea, but in some cases especially if you provide guidance, the route must be divided into parts of segments.

Hui et al. studied the importance of artificial intelligence in game playing [7]. In their paper, they investigated the use of artificial intelligence in game development. Research is done on how artificial intelligence can be applied in games and the advantages it brings along. As the fields of artificial intelligence in game development are too wide to be covered, the focus of their project is placed on certain areas. Two programs are implemented through this project: an intelligent camera system and path finding in a 3D application. The path-finding problem in game theory is very different from the path-planning problem in the avionics, because security concept is essential in the dynamic navigation problem.

Misra and Oommen presented the first learning-automaton based solution to the dynamic single-source shortest-path problem [8]. It involves finding the shortest path in a single-source stochastic graph topology where there are continuous probabilistic updates in the edge-weights. The important contribution of their algorithm was that all the edges in a stochastic graph are not probed, and even if they are, they were not all probed equally often.

Li et al. developed an improved genetic algorithm of optimum path planning for mobile robots [9]. They introduced an obstacle avoidance algorithm to generate the initial population in order to improve the path planning efficiency. Domain heuristic knowledge-based crossover, mutation, refinement, and deletion operators are specifically designed to fit path planning for mobile robots.

Tu and Yang proposed a novel genetic algorithm-based approach to path planning of a mobile robot [10]. The major characteristic of the proposed algorithm was that the chromosome has a variable length. The locations of target and obstacles were included to find a path for a mobile robot in an environment that was a 2D workplace discredited into a grid net.

Wei et al. proposed a gene-constrained genetic algorithm to solve shortest-path problem [11]. In this genetic algorithm, gene was constrained to ensure that each chromosome represents a feasible path without loop during the whole process of search. Contrasting with other genetic algorithm for shortest-path problem, their algorithm improved the searching capacity with a more accurate solution and more rapid speed of convergence.

Mahjoubi et al. proposed a path planning-method which uses genetic algorithm to find the feasible and suitable paths in an environment with static and dynamic obstacles [12]. To increase the speed of calculations, dimension of the search space was reduced by developing a new method to represent the environment. Their representation method was based on detecting the corners of circumferential polygons of all obstacles as representatives of the environment.

Inagaki et al. proposed an algorithm that employs fixed-length chromosomes [13]. The chromosomes in the algorithm are sequences of integers, and each gene represents a node identifier that is selected randomly from the set of nodes connected with the node corresponding to its locus number.

The most familiar dynamic path-planning solution techniques are Ramalingam Reps [14], Franciosa et al. [15], and Frigioni et al. [16]. The solution by Franciosa et al. can be used only for semidynamic case. The Ramalingam Reps solution was found successful concerning run-time; Frigioni's is better when the number of segments to be updated had to be minimized. The existing fully dynamic algorithms process unit changes to topology one modification at a time, but when there are several such operations occurring in the environment simultaneously, the algorithms are quite inefficient. The problems are worse in large topologies which have a large number of nodes and edges, where a large number of topology modifications occur continuously at all times. In such cases, the existing algorithms may fail to determine the shortest path information in a time critical manner. The proposed algorithm may respond to the concurrent weight updates in a shorter time especially for dynamic environments [17].

There are four possible edge operations (insertion/deletion and increase/decrease); it has been shown that edge-insertion is equivalent to edge-weight decrease and edge-deletion is equivalent to edge-weight increase. If all edge operations are allowed, the problem is referred to as the fully dynamic problem. If only edge insertion/weight decrease or edge deletion/weight increase is allowed, the problem is referred to as the semi-dynamic problem. The solution by Franciosa et al. can be used only for semi-dynamic case. The Ramalingam-Reps algorithm processes only one change at a time. But in the dynamic navigation problem, a large number of topology modifications occur continuously and this case is not handled by Ramalingam Reps algorithm. Frigioni algorithm cannot be used for the environments where the edge-weights change stochastically. The proposed algorithm should work with uncertain graphs by means of multi objective fitness function. All these three algorithms (Franciosa, Ramalingam Reps and Frigioni) solve dynamic, single-source shortest path problem. They do not consider path security or fuel consumption parameters, since none of these algorithms solve the dynamic flight navigation problem.

In order to model and solve the path planning problem for different environments, many researches have been done recently [18]. If the domain is air vehicle routing and navigation planning-usually 3D graph-based methods are used. Genetic and evolutionary computation algorithms can be used to solve dynamic navigation planning problem [19, 20]. Particle swarm optimization algorithm also can be used to find optimal path planning in 3D [21, 22]. All of these algorithms could not solve uncertain and stochastically changing graph problem in navigation. This is due to problem-specific multiobjective constraints for navigation planning. Minimum fuel consumption is the main aim in order to achieve this, the flight route for the air vehicle must be short and secure. The flight route segments are defined with flight altitude levels the vertical navigation should also be considered for the minimum fuel consumption. Dubins, Pythagorean hodograph, and Cornu-spiral are all algorithms which are based on curve to solve path planning problem [23–26]. The most advantage of those algorithms is non-discontinuous path planning because of curve path construction [24]. But all these algorithms fail to solve edge insertion and deletion issues for stochastically changing topologies and they do not propose solution for minimum fuel consumption calculation under distance, security, and altitude constraints.

The path-planning strategy could be either static or dynamic depending on whether the path-planning problem is to create a path in static or in dynamic environment [27]. Navigation planning solutions will attempt to for flight routes that are minimum in length, maximum in security and fully consistent with the physical constraints of the aircraft. Navigation planning can be divided in two forms. Former is pregenerated to show the flight route between source and destination waypoints that will be taken by the aircraft while it navigates between two waypoints and the latter is the controller that guides the aircraft between two waypoints while tracking a route that was pregenerated.

In [28] a concurrent constraint programming was used as the main tool for the design and the implementation of a navigation planner. It is a very high level and complex heuristic path planner that takes into account the obstacle avoidance, shortest and best flight path, and weighed regions. But it fails to solve fully dynamic navigation problem. Most path planning follows an approach where the path planning, trajectory smoothing, and flight stability are separated into separate layers [29–31]. However, most of these do not deal with three-dimensional path planning. It is not an easy task to control the aircraft in a three-dimensional environment while at the same time executing the path algorithm. Our proposed method solves three-dimensional fully dynamic navigation planning problem, and our flight execution subsystem provides guidance in following the desired flight path under changing wind and speed conditions and platform dynamics.

Lin et al. designed a route guidance system for finding the shortest driving time which is their application on virtual maps of square matrix with appropriate to be used on handheld devices [32]. But their proposed solution fails to solve multiobjective navigation problem of air vehicles. Hasan et al. produced a different solution for the shortest-path problem using genetic algorithm [33]. They employed a chromosome-coding scheme using node indices and distance weights. Our proposed study presents a route guidance system and an evolutionary approach applied on this routing system to find the most secure flight path with minimum fuel consumption and shortest arrival time to the destination waypoint. The proposed guidance system provides the driving advice for the drivers considering not only the distances, but also the altitude and security values of the roads. Thus, it computes the optimum flight path instead of the shortest path.

Several approaches have been developed for evolutionary algorithms to address dynamic environments such as maintaining diversity during the run, increasing diversity after a change, using memory schemes to reuse stored useful information, and applying multipopulation and speciation schemes to search in different regions of the search space applying multipopulation and speciation schemes to search in different regions of the search space [34, 35]. The proposed evolutionary method considers multiobjectives like distance, security, and traffic, due to the objective function. The method responds to the dynamic environment situations and may offer an appropriate solution approach. It reduces the number of operations in dynamic environments; because it does not restart the solution at each update, it trends to protect and extend best-fit individuals according to the changed conditions.

3. System Definition

The evolutionary navigation planning system consists of two subsystems: mission planning subsystem and mission execution subsystem. In the mission planning subsystem, the flight transition of the air vehicle from a departure waypoint to a descent waypoint is planned by the dynamic evolutionary algorithm. The constraints of the mission planning subsystem are distance, security, and altitude. The mission execution subsystem provides lateral and vertical guidance algorithms and fuel flow rate calculations so that the air vehicle passes through the flight legs and desired route in a real-time environment. Real-time flight data is taken from the Aerosim flight simulator. Mission execution subsystem uses these real-time data in order to calculate pitch and bank angle commands that feed the pilot. Mission execution subsystem executes the planned flight path from the desired departure waypoint to the each arrival waypoint owing to the lateral and vertical navigation guidance functions. The constraints of the fuel flow-rate calculation problem are gross weight, air temperature, flight altitude, and true airspeed. The two subsystems developed use 3-D graphs for the solution. The block diagram of the system and the data flow is shown in Figure 1.

4. Navigation System

Flight management system (FMS) is a computer system which handles all the navigation and flight functions of the air vehicle. FMS gathers all of the information generated by electronic equipments and sensors on a screen. So the workload of the pilot decreases. FMS provides autonomous guidance by means of inertial navigation unit and global positioning system [36]. The navigation functions of the FMS may be used to fly published airways, to route directly to a waypoint, to follow a flight plan, or to execute a mission pattern. FMS permits loading of flight plan database and it also permits the pilot to generate a new flight plan by using the waypoint database or modifying the existing plan due to the dynamic environment.

The navigation planning system takes the position coordinates of the waypoints as an input. Coordinate values are given as longitude and latitude. Latitude is the angle from a point on the earth's surface to the equatorial plane, measured from the center of the sphere. Longitude is the angle between the two geographical poles to another meridian that passes through an arbitrary point. The longitude and latitude components specify the position of any location on the planet but do not consider altitude or depth. The altitude constraint is considered for the legs of the flight plan. A flight leg is a route between two combined waypoints. The constraints of the flight leg are defined as a vector consists of the distance, the security value, and the altitude of the flight leg.

A primary flight display provides flight and navigation information. The primary flight display contains an attitude indicator, which gives the pilot information about the aircraft's attitude information, pitch and roll angles, and the orientation of the aircraft with respect to the horizon. The mechanical gyroscope is a separate device whose information is simply displayed on the primary flight display. Unlike mechanical instruments, this information can be dynamically updated as required; the stall angle, for example, can be adjusted in real time to reflect the calculated critical angle of attack of the aircraft in its current configuration. The primary flight display may also show an indicator of the aircraft's future path, as calculated by the proposed dynamic

navigation planning algorithm, making it easier for pilots to anticipate aircraft movements and reactions. There are airspeed and altitude indicators next to the pitch and roll indicators. The airspeed indicator displays the speed of the aircraft in knots, while the altitude indicator displays the aircraft's altitude above sea level. These measurements are conducted through the aircraft's pitot system, which tracks air pressure measurements. The vertical speed indicator, next to the altitude indicator, indicates to the pilot how fast the aircraft is ascending or descending or the rate at which the altitude changes. This is usually represented with numbers in "thousands of feet per minute." At the bottom of the primary flight display is the heading display, which shows the pilot the magnetic heading of the aircraft. This functions much like a standard magnetic heading indicator, turning as required.

The most critic parameters of a primary flight display are pitch, roll, heading indicators, speed, and altitude indicators. The proposed algorithm and control system uses these data in order to find the best route for the air vehicle. The primary flight display consists of a vertical situation display with flight instruments, a flight director, and essential engine instruments and mode-selectable horizontal situation displays. The flight director commands calculated by the proposed control system show steering commands to capture desired aircraft roll and pitch. Flight director commands are satisfied by flying the aircraft into the intersection formed by the command bars.

For the execution test of the developed algorithm, air navigation process of the air vehicles from a departure waypoint to a descent waypoint is simulated. The simulation environment used to verify the navigation algorithms is shown in Figure 2.

The simulator represents a simulation of the aircraft in open-loop flight [37]. That is, all aircraft control inputs are set to fixed values, independent of the aircraft states. The lateral dynamics of the aircraft is stabilized by adding a wing leveler. This is implemented using proportional and integral feedback from bank angle to ailerons. The flight path guidance law is tested with an accurate nonlinear dynamic model of the Aerosonde [37, 38]. In the assessment of this work, both vehicle guidance and camera pointing algorithms are based on GPS data; the camera-pointing algorithm relies on aircraft attitude information. Some navigation algorithms are used for the guidance of air vehicles. These algorithms include the distance between two waypoints, the course angle between two waypoints, the intersection point of two radials, the cross-track error, and along-track distance calculations. The air vehicle is supposed to approach the desired flight path on a smoothly bank to capture the desired path without overshoot and exceeding the maximum bank angle. This may be achieved by modelling of the Helmsman behavior [39, 40].

The parameters like initial position, wind speed, initial velocity, initial altitude, initial engine speed, and sample time can be modified before the navigation simulation. The algorithm developed here can save the flight state information and current position and can continue to the flight to a different waypoint.

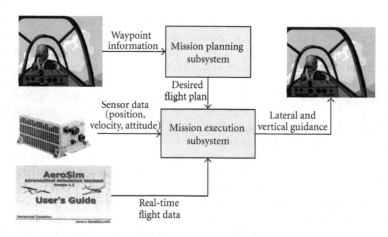

FIGURE 1: System block diagram.

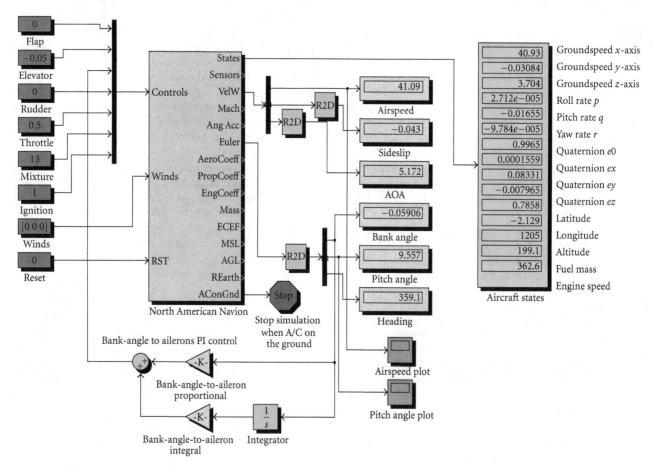

FIGURE 2: Aerosim smulator block diagram.

The AeroSim blockset provides a complete set of tools for developing nonlinear 6-degree-of-freedom aircraft dynamic models. The Simulink blocks include the nonlinear equations of motion, linear aerodynamics based on component buildup, piston-engine propulsion, aircraft inertia model including weight variation due to fuel consumption, atmosphere models including standard atmosphere, wind gusts and von Karman turbulence, and Earth models which provide Earth radius, gravity, and magnetic field components at current aircraft location. In addition the AeroSim blockset provides basic analog sensor and nonlinear actuator models and unit conversion blocks for translation between metric and English units, as well as transformations between various reference frames (wind, body, navigation, and Earth-centered frame). In addition to the individual blocks, several prebuilt aircraft models are available, which can be customized through parameter files.

5. Lateral and Vertical Guidance

The general functions used in lateral and vertical navigation are geometric distance, bearing, and coordinate calculation functions. The first basic function calculates the distance between two waypoints and bearing angle of the flight route formed by the combination of two waypoints.

The inputs of the basic function of navigation are the longitude and latitude values of the source and destination waypoints. The outputs of the function are the distance of the flight leg and bearing angle of the flight route. The function calculates the distance value in radians. In order to convert the distance to units of length, the distance value is multiplied by the radius of the Earth. According to the WGS-84 ellipsoid model, the radius of the earth is 6378.137 kilometers. The function initially calculates the unit position vectors of two waypoints in Earth-centered Earth-fixed coordinate system. Then the cross-multiplication of two vectors is taken. So the angle and distance between two position vectors can be calculated.

The navigation planning system takes the position coordinates of the waypoints as an input. Coordinate values are given as longitude and latitude. Latitude is the angle from a point on the earth's surface to the equatorial plane, measured from the center of the sphere. Longitude is the angle between the two geographical poles to another meridian that passes through an arbitrary point. The longitude and latitude components specify the position of any location on the planet but do not consider altitude or depth. The altitude constraint is considered for the legs of the flight plan. A flight leg is a route between two combined waypoints. The constraints of the flight leg are defined as a vector consists of the distance, the security value, and the altitude of the flight leg:

$$\mathbf{P}_1 = \cos(L_1)\cos(\lambda_1)\mathbf{i} + \cos(L_1)\sin(\lambda_1)\mathbf{j} + \sin(L_1)\mathbf{k},$$
$$\mathbf{P}_2 = \cos(L_2)\cos(\lambda_2)\mathbf{i} + \cos(L_2)\sin(\lambda_2)\mathbf{j} + \sin(L_2)\mathbf{k}. \qquad (1)$$

By using the two equations above, the distance between source and target waypoints is calculated as shown below:

$$\text{dist } 12 = \tan^{-1}\left(\frac{|\mathbf{P}_1 \times \mathbf{P}_2|}{\mathbf{P}_1 \cdot \mathbf{P}_2}\right). \qquad (2)$$

The bearing angle between the source and destination waypoints is calculated by using the formula below:

$$\boldsymbol{\eta}_{P_1P_2} = \frac{\mathbf{P}_1 \times \mathbf{P}_2}{|\mathbf{P}_1 \times \mathbf{P}_2|}, \qquad \boldsymbol{\eta}_{P_2P_1} = \frac{\mathbf{P}_2 \times \mathbf{P}_1}{|\mathbf{P}_2 \times \mathbf{P}_1|},$$
$$\psi_{12} = \tan^{-1}\left(\frac{-\boldsymbol{\eta}_{P_1P_2}}{P_1\boldsymbol{\eta}_{P_1P_2} - P_1\boldsymbol{\eta}_{P_1P_2}}\right). \qquad (3)$$

The distance and bearing angle of a flight leg are shown in Figure 3.

Another function used for lateral guidance is the position calculation function. This function calculates the longitude

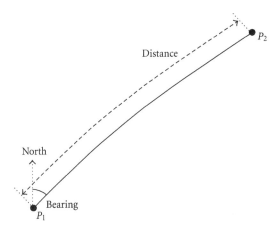

FIGURE 3: Distance and bearing of a flight leg.

and latitude of the waypoint from a given position vector, distance, and bearing values. In order to find the second waypoint's position, firstly tangent unit vector in the bearing angle direction to great circle is calculated. L_1 is the latitude; λ_1 is the longitude of the first waypoint. ψ_{12} is the input bearing angle. The coordinates of the new waypoint are calculated by the rotation of the first waypoint and the unit vector:

$$\mathbf{U}_\psi = -\sin(L_1)\cos(\lambda_1)\cos(\psi_{12}) - \sin(\lambda_1)\sin(\psi_{12})\mathbf{i}$$
$$- (\sin(L_1)\sin(\lambda_1)\cos(\psi_{12}) - \cos(\lambda_1)\sin(\psi_{12}))\mathbf{j}$$
$$+ \cos(L_1)\cos(\psi_{12})\mathbf{k},$$
$$\mathbf{P}_2 = \cos(\text{dist }12)\mathbf{P}_1 + \sin(\text{dist }12)\mathbf{U}_\psi,$$
$$L_2 = \tan^{-1}\left(\frac{P_2}{\sqrt{1 - (P_2)^2}}\right), \qquad \lambda_2 = \tan^{-1}\left(\frac{P_2}{P_2}\right). \qquad (4)$$

Third basic function for lateral navigation is the calculation of the coordinates of the intersection of two flight legs. For lateral navigation, when the air vehicle is routed by parallel deviation from a flight plan, the intersection point of two segments is calculated for navigation planning. An intersection point of two flight segments is shown in Figure 4. P_0 is the intersection of the P_1-P_2 route and P_3-P_4 route.

L_1, λ_1 are the coordinates of P_1, similarly L_2, λ_2 are the coordinates of P_2, L_3, λ_3 are the coordinates of P_3, and L_4, λ_4 are the coordinates of P_4. The longitude and latitude values of the intersection point P_0 are L_0, λ_0.

$$\boldsymbol{\eta}_{P_1P_2} = \mathbf{P}_1 \times \mathbf{P}_2, \qquad \boldsymbol{\eta}_{P_3P_4} = \mathbf{P}_3 \times \mathbf{P}_4,$$
$$\mathbf{P}_{01} = \frac{\boldsymbol{\eta}_{P_1P_2} \times \boldsymbol{\eta}_{P_3P_4}}{\left|\boldsymbol{\eta}_{P_1P_2} \times \boldsymbol{\eta}_{P_3P_4}\right|}, \qquad \mathbf{P}_{02} = \frac{\boldsymbol{\eta}_{P_3P_4} \times \boldsymbol{\eta}_{P_1P_2}}{\left|\boldsymbol{\eta}_{P_3P_4} \times \boldsymbol{\eta}_{P_1P_2}\right|}. \qquad (5)$$

In order to calculate the coordinates of the intersection point, firstly the normal vectors of the two surfaces are found. These two surfaces intersect at two points. These two points are found by the formula shown above. By using Pnk(i),

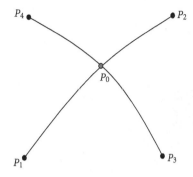

FIGURE 4: Intersection of two flight paths.

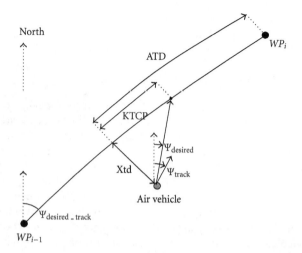

FIGURE 5: Track and bearing angles.

the latitude and the longitude of the intersection point are calculated. Pnk(i) shows the ith element of the Pnk vector:

$$L_0 = \tan^{-1}\left(P_{01}(3), \sqrt{1 - (P_{01}(3))^2}\right),$$
$$\lambda_0 = \tan^{-1}(P_{01}(2), P_{01}(1)). \tag{6}$$

When a deviation from the flight plan occurs, the pitch and bank angle commands are calculated in order to fit the desired flight leg. Beside this, when the route switching points are reached, these angles are again calculated in order to put the air vehicle in the next flight route. For the calculation of the lateral guidance command, firstly the projection of the air vehicle on the desired route is found. KTCP distance shown in Figure 5 is the distance between the projection of the air vehicle and the point that the air vehicle will pass on the route. The coordinates of the point that the air vehicle will pass on the flight leg are found by (7). The bearing angle between the current position of the air vehicle and the point RP is calculated by (3). This angle is called desired track angle. ATD is the along-track distance, the distance between the vertical projection of the air vehicle and the waypoint to be reached. Xtd is the vertical distance to the flight leg:

$$\psi_{\text{track}} = \tan^{-1}\left(\frac{V_{\text{GS\_E}}}{V_{\text{GS\_N}}}\right). \tag{7}$$

Then the track angle is found by calculating the angle between the ground speed components, east and north. The track angle error is found by subtracting track angle from the desired track:

$$\psi_{\text{error}} = \psi_{\text{desired}} - \psi_{\text{track}}. \tag{8}$$

By using the track angle error found by (8), lateral-rotation speed command is found. The fd_lat parameter is chosen according to the simulations. And finally by using

(10), the lateral navigation bank-angle command is calculated. This command provides holding the air vehicle in the desired route:

$$\dot{\psi}_{\text{commanded}} = (2\pi f_{\text{d\_lat}})\,\psi_{\text{error}}, \tag{9}$$

$$\phi_{\text{commanded}} = \tan^{-1}\left(\frac{(V_{\text{GS\_N}}^2 + V_{\text{GS\_E}}^2)^{1/2} \cdot \dot{\psi}_{\text{commanded}}}{g}\right). \tag{10}$$

6. Mission Planning Subsystem

Route planning and navigation control based on evolutionary programming concepts can be designed as a general, flexible and adaptive technique. By integrating the planning process in evolutionary algorithms, definition of the different optimization criteria, dynamic update of the constraints, domain specific evolutionary operators, and control of the dynamic obstacles may be handled. Evolutionary algorithms, in comparison to the classical optimization methods, are more effective for discontinuous and noisy objective functions [41].

Genetic algorithms imitate the evolutionary process in order to solve the optimization problems. Instead of developing one solution candidate, genetic algorithms form a set of individuals. The set, which contains probable solution candidates, is defined as population in genetic algorithm terminology. Population occurs from arrays called vector, chromosome, or individual. Each element of an individual is called gene. In evolutionary programming method, individuals in the population are determined by the operators of the evolutionary algorithm. In the problems like path planning, the permutation representation is used and the operators differ from the operators of the basic genetic algorithm. The most important parameters of the genetic algorithm are cross-over rate, mutation rate, and the number of individuals in a population. In order to declare cross-over and mutation rates, different values are tested, and by this way the most appropriate values are found for these parameters. Chromosome number in the population is determined according to the nodes of the graph topology.

In the proposed heuristic approach, variable-length chromosomes are used for representing the routes. Variable-length chromosomes are used in dynamic path-planning systems in order to cover the whole search space [42]. Chromosomes are encoded by permutation-encoding method. Each gene of a chromosome represents a node in the graph. Evolutionary parameters of the mission planning system are listed in Table 1.

In a genetic algorithm, crossover takes two parents and replaces a randomly chosen part of one parent with another, randomly chosen part of the other. This is often very destructive to the structure and functionality of the child program. It is, however, the means by which valuable code can be transferred between programs and is also the theoretical reason why genetic programming is an efficient and successful search strategy. Even though it often produces unfit children, it does produce parent-superior fitness occasionally and those individuals often possess the critical improvements that allow evolution to progress to the next round of fitness improving generations. Mutation takes one parent and replaces a randomly selected chunk of that parent with a randomly generated sequence of code. One of the advantages of this operator is that it maintains diversity in the population, since any of the function/terminal set can be inserted into the program, whereas crossover can only insert code present in the current generation's population. Through the repeated application of these operators to the selected parents of the old generation, a new generation is formed, some of the members of which will hopefully be more fit than the best of the last generation. At this point a new population is available to be evaluated for fitness. The cycle will continue, until either a single member of the population is found which satisfies the problem within the level of error designated as acceptable by the success criteria or the number of generations exceeds the limit specified.

Cross-over operator developed for navigation planning problem exchanges pieces of routes. An identical intermediate node is chosen. The first part of the route connects the initial node to the intermediate node. The second part of the route connects the intermediate node to the target node. Crossover may generate infeasible chromosomes that violate the loop constraint. Repair operator makes a postprocessing operation and removes the cycles from the infeasible individuals [43].

Mutation operator increases the variation in the population. Mutation avoids local optima by changing the genes of the potential chromosome. Two-point mutation is applied. The genes in the region between the mutation points are modified with a different route. Finally two new individuals with different genotype are formed. The fitness of the individual chromosome is calculated by using the distance, height difference, and security values of the segments in the path. Height difference is the difference of altitudes of a segment and the altitude of the previous segment. The height difference is not considered for the first segment of the route. The sample crossover and repair operations are shown in

TABLE 1: Evolutionary algorithm parameters.

Selection method	Roulette wheel
Chromosome length	Variable
Cross-over rate	70–80%
Mutation rate	5–10%
Representation	Permutation based
Stopping criteria	Individual similarity
Population size	Proportional with the number of edges

Figures 6 and 7. For postprocessing local search is included in the procedure in order to eliminate the individual that have very low fitness values.

The flowchart of the mission planning subsystem is shown in Figure 8. At the first step the initial individuals are generated randomly and represented by chromosomes. In order to evaluate the initial population, the multi-objective fitness function is used. The individuals are divided into pairs in the parent selection phase. Cross-over operator is applied to the pairs. After crossover if necessary the repair operator is applied in order to remove the cycles in the flight path. Mutation operator is applied to some of the individuals for diversity. After recombination phase, the fitness function is used again to evaluate the parents and individuals. The individuals which have higher fitness values are kept alive. This procedure is continued again till the stopping criterion is satisfied.

7. Experimental Results

Three most important parameters of the proposed evolutionary method are cross-over rate, mutation rate, and number of generations. For each parameter different flight simulations are planned and executed, and the following graphs are formed by the average values of the experimental results. The experiments are done with 50 waypoints city map. We produced a connected graph and selected a source waypoint for the start of the flight and a destination waypoint for arrival. The experiments are repeated with updated constraints and edges. At each measurement, different edges are added to the graph or some edges are removed from the graph. The experiments are repeated for 100 different maps in the same topology.

A first set of experiments is done for determining the appropriate cross-over rate. The mutation rate, number of individuals, and the stop criteria are fixed in this set. The mutation rate in this set is 10%. The stopping criterion is individual similarity. The result of the first experiment set is shown in Figure 9. As cross-over rate increases up to 80%, the error percentage decreases. Error percentage is calculated by finding the ratio of the fitness of the proposed solution and the real most secure, shortest path solution. Experimental results show that for this kind of navigation planning problem, the most suitable cross-over rate is 70%.

A second set of experiments is done for determining the appropriate mutation rate. The cross-over rate, number of individuals, and the stop criteria are fixed in this set. The cross-over rate in this set is 70%. The stopping criterion is

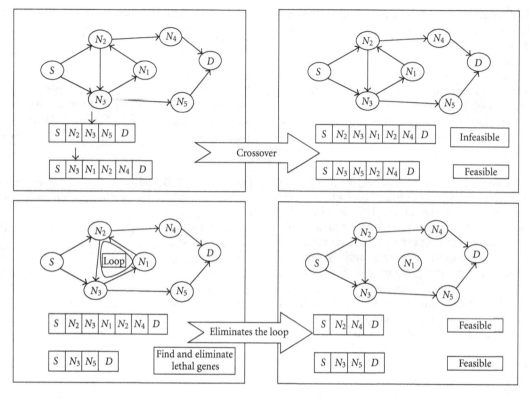

↓ Crossing site

FIGURE 6: Crossover and repair operators.

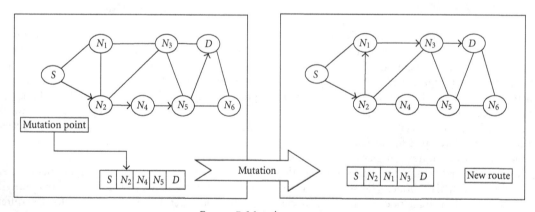

FIGURE 7: Mutation operator.

individual similarity. The result of the second experiment set is shown in Figure 10. As mutation rate increases up to 10%, the error percentage decreases. Experimental results show that for this kind of navigation planning problem, the most suitable mutation rate is 10%. If mutation rate is chosen at higher values, it may lead to loss of good solutions. If mutation rate is too small, then it is more difficult to reach different points of the search space, and usually the algorithm may converge to local optima in these cases.

In order to show the best candidate of each generation, a third set of experiments is done. The cross-over rate is fixed to 70%; the mutation rate is fixed to 10%. For each

population number of individuals is 100 in this set. The result of the third experiment set is shown in Figure 11. In each generation the individual, who has highest fitness value, becomes nearer to the real solution, but when the global optimum is reached, further generations do not produce better individuals, and by means of the stopping criteria, genetic algorithm reproduction loop is terminated.

The run-time performance and the complexity of the proposed algorithm are compared with deterministic methods. When segment insertion/deletion/cost update operations occur, the proposed algorithm does not start calculations from scratch, and it converges to the solution in a

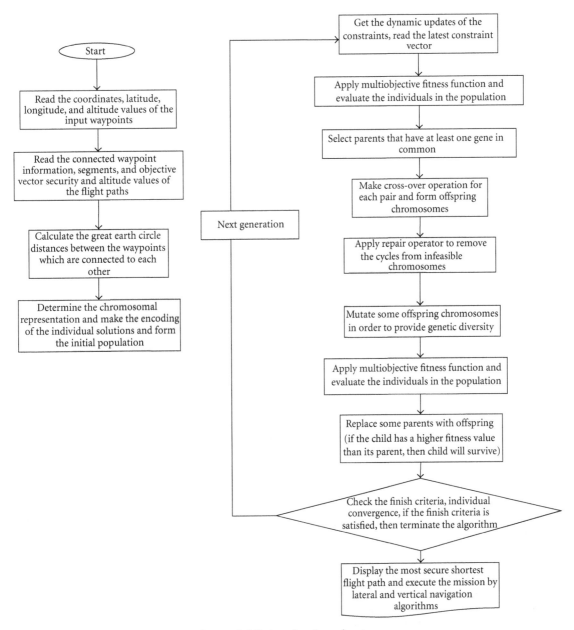

FIGURE 8: Mission planning subsystem.

shorter time than Dijkstra. Figure 12 shows the performance of the proposed algorithm at each dynamic change. Figure 12 also shows the higher performance of the proposed algorithm especially for strongly connected graphs. When the number of nodes increases, the computation time difference between the Dijkstra algorithm and the proposed algorithm in dynamic scheme also increases.

8. Navigation Simulations

In the simulations a part of USA waypoint database, including the longitude and latitude coordinates of the south region states, is used. Transition of the air vehicles between waypoints is planned. For the visual simplicity, the numbers

are used instead of the names of the states, and only 15 states are chosen. Finding the most secure, smoothest and the fastest transition of the air vehicles from an initial waypoint to a target waypoint is aimed. In the city map shown in Figure 13, the links between the cities are represented by vectors of distance, security, and altitude. As the flight plan is generated, the altitudes of the waypoints are also considered and 3-D graph solution is planned.

The proposed evolutionary method aims to find the shortest, most secure and the smoothest route for the initial constraints. As the problem considers distance, height, and security conditions, the problem is multi-objective optimization problem. The initial solution of the dynamic system for the initial conditions is shown in Figure 14.

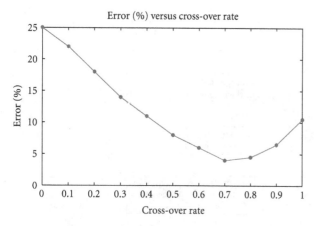

FIGURE 9: Effect of the cross-over rate.

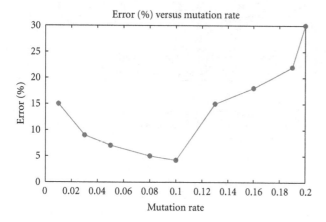

FIGURE 10: Effect of the mutation rate.

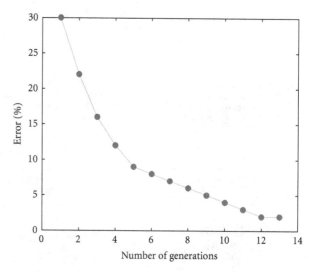

FIGURE 11: Effect of the number of generation count.

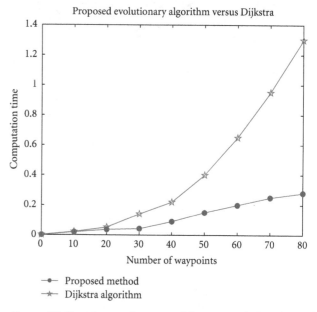

FIGURE 12: Run-time performance of the proposed algorithm.

When the links between City 8-City 9 and City 8–City 11 are disabled dynamically, the new transition flight plan for the air vehicle is shown in Figure 15.

When the link between City 1–City 3 is disabled dynamically, the proposed route computed by the algorithm is shown in Figure 16. The algorithm proposes that a flight plan passes through City 8 considering smoothness and security. The link between the cities, City 4–City 8, is suitable for security and distance metrics.

The system converges to the solution in the dynamic environments without processing from scratch. Analytical approaches repeat the calculations from scratch because an update in the constraints change the matrix used to find the solution [44, 45]. This property is an important characteristic of the proposed algorithm. Evolutionary methods may succeed this by problem specific fitness function and selection operators [46]. The fitness function used in the proposed algorithm is

$$\sum_{i=1}^{segmentcount} \left(\frac{A}{distance} + \frac{B}{(100-security)} + \frac{C}{altitude\_difference} \right). \quad (11)$$

The fitness of the individual chromosome is calculated by using the distance, height difference, and security values of the segments in the path. Height difference is the difference of altitudes of a segment and the altitude of the previous segment. The height difference is not considered for the first segment of the route. The problem is multi-objective in our case, because security objective may subject to distance constraints, and distance constraint depends on a statistical distribution function. The effects of metrics like security and distance to the solution may be modeled with the classical optimization techniques, but in the dynamic environments like battle scenarios, at each condition change, the algorithm starts the solution from the scratch and increase the operation complexity and calculation time, so they are infeasible [47]. Furthermore, the insertion/deletion of the nodes or segments from the graph changes the matrix of the topology, so they have to start the solution from scratch. The proposed

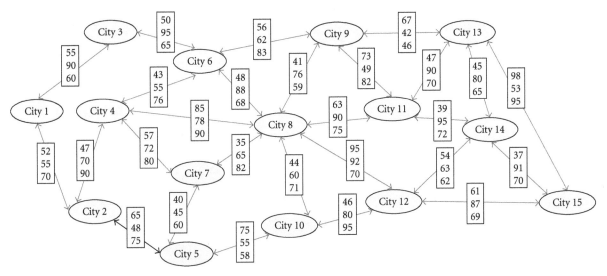

FIGURE 13: Initial city map.

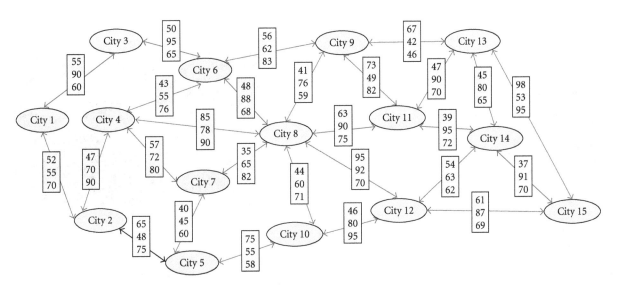

FIGURE 14: Initial transition plan.

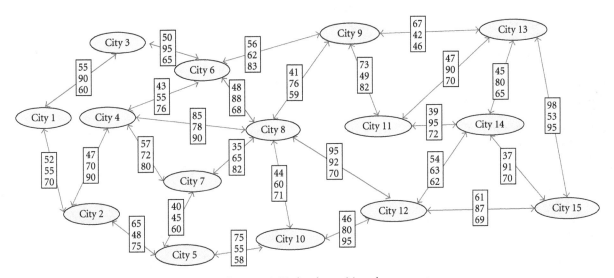

FIGURE 15: Updated transition plan.

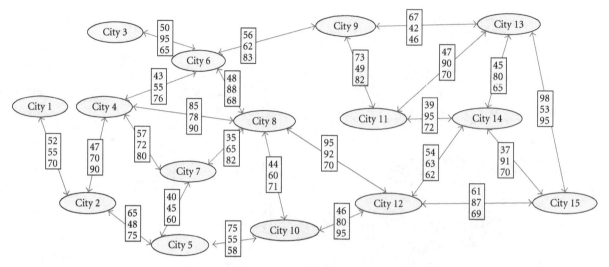

FIGURE 16: Dynamic transition plan.

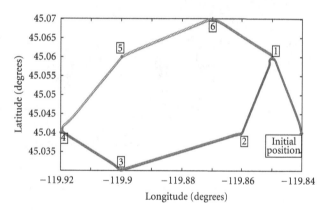

FIGURE 17: Flight route execution simulation.

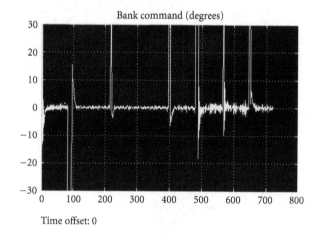

Time offset: 0

FIGURE 18: Lateral navigation bank-angle command simulation result.

algorithm responds to the concurrent modifications and the best-fit individuals according to the modified conditions are spread over the population. Military transition is a mission critic problem, and in dynamic environments the aim is to reach the best solution in an acceptable time. This time changes according to the graph density and the number of nodes. The coefficients A, B, and C may be modified according to which objective will have more effect on the calculation of the flight path. These coefficients may be given as an input to the algorithm.

By the execution of the flight plan formed by the mission planning subsystem, the most secure, shortest navigation path is processed by mission execution subsystem. The simulation results of the flight plan with six waypoints are shown in the Figures 17 and 18. The graph related with the execution of the flight plan is shown in Figure 17; the commanded bank angle for the execution of this flight path is shown in Figure 18. In this example, the air vehicle follows the desired flight path under (north 10 meters/second, east 10 meters/second) wind. The wind speed is 14.14 meters/second. The initial position is 45° 04′ 47″ latitude

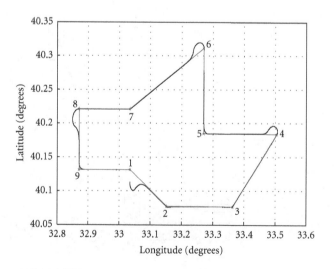

FIGURE 19: Mission execution 2D graph with nine waypoints.

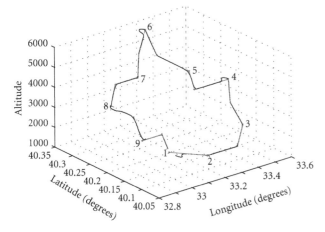

FIGURE 20: Mission execution 3D graph with nine waypoints.

TABLE 2: Coordinate and altitude values of the second flight plan waypoints.

WP number	Latitude (°)	Longitude (°)	Altitude (meters)
1	40,1310	33,0351	1985,7
2	40,0768	33,1524	1985,7
3	40,0764	33,3635	2985,7
4	40,1840	33,5050	3985,7
5	40,1847	33,2701	4985,7
6	40,3109	33,2706	5985,7
7	40,2211	33,0352	4985,7
8	40,2210	32,8706	3985,7
9	40,1309	32,8708	2985,7

and 19° 84′ 06″ longitude. The initial ground speed is 70 meters/second, and the initial altitude is 1985 meters.

Another flight plan execution simulation is shown in the Figures 19 and 20. For the second example simulation, the flight plan for nine waypoints is found by evolutionary mission planning subsystem (see Table 2). In this example, the air vehicle follows the desired flight path under (north 10 meters/second, east 10 meters/second) wind. The wind speed is 14.14 meters/second. The initial position is 40° 06′ 47″ latitude and 33° 02′ 06″ longitude. The initial ground speed is 70 meters/second, and the initial altitude is 1985 meters.

In Figure 19, the flight path of the air vehicle is shown by the 2-D graph. 3-D graph structure of this simulation is shown in Figure 20.

9. Conclusion

Navigation planning is an optimization problem that requires finding and executing the most feasible flight path between source and destination waypoints. Deterministic algorithms like Floyd, Dijkstra, or heuristic methods like neural network and A-Star may be used for the solution of navigation planning problem in static schemes. Dynamic path planning algorithms like Frigioni, Franciosa, and Rama-lingam Reps may be used in dynamic environments, but they are constrained by some limitations. When several concurrent changes occur in the environment simultaneously, these algorithms are quite inefficient. When the segment costs and conditions change stochastically and continuously, these algorithms fail to reach the actual underlying average solution. And these algorithms run when the costs of the links in the graph are clear. But in a flight plan scenario, the altitude of the paths and the security of the links may be approximately known. So the algorithm should work with uncertain graphs.

The flight and mission planning is a fault-tolerant real-time system, so the algorithm should attach more importance to a constraint, like distance, time, security, or altitude. In the algorithms like Floyd and Dijkstra, the graph is represented by a matrix. But the proposed solution is not matrix-based. Owing to the reproduction loop, selection

mechanism and the fitness function, the algorithm finds better results in a shorter computation time compared with the analytical algorithms. The proposed algorithm provides advanced search speed, quality, and flexibility in dynamic schemes. In addition to the flight planning algorithm, a flight execution algorithm is developed to guide the pilot follow the mission plan. The execution algorithm provides flight commands like pitch, bearing, track and bank angles, and desired ground speed to arrive the next waypoint on time and fuel flow rate.

The results support the view that evolutionary algorithms are an effective, robust search procedure for NP complete problems in the sense that, although they may not outperform highly tuned, problem-specific algorithms. Evolutionary algorithms can be easily applied to a broad range of NP-complete problems with performance characteristics no worse than the theoretical lower bound of an N^3 speedup.

References

[1] M. A. Al-Jarrah and M. M. Hasan, "HILS setup of dynamic flight path planning in 3D environment with flexible mission planning using Ground Station," *Journal of the Franklin Institute*, vol. 348, no. 1, pp. 45–65, 2011.

[2] Joint Planning and Development Office, "Concept of operations for the next generation air transportation system," Version 3.0, 2009.

[3] M. T. De Garmo, "Issues concerning integration unmanned aerial vehicles in civil airspace," Tech. Rep. MP 04W0000323, MITRE, Va, USA, 2004.

[4] R. Weibel and R. J. Hansman, "Safety considerations for operation of unmanned aerial vehicles in the national airspace system," MIT International Center for Air Transportation Report ICAT, 2005-01, ICAT, 2005.

[5] B. M. Sathyaraj, L. C. Jain, A. Finn, and S. Drake, "Multiple UAVs path planning algorithms: a comparative study," *Fuzzy Optimization and Decision Making*, vol. 7, no. 3, pp. 257–267, 2008.

[6] I. K. Nikolos, N. Tsourveloudis, and K. P. Valavanis, "Evolutionary algorithm based 3-D path planner for UAV navigation," in *Proceedings of the 9th Mediterranean Conference on Control and Automation (CDROM'10)*, Dubrovnik, Croatia, 2001.

[7] Y. C. Hui, E. C. Prakash, and N. S. Chaudhari, "Game AI: artifical intelligence for 3D path finding," in *Proceedings of*

the IEEE Region 10 Conference: Analog and Digital Techniques in Electrical Engineering (TENCON'04), pp. B306–B309, tha, November 2004.

[8] S. Misra and B. J. Oommen, "Stochastic learning automata-based dynamic algorithms for the single source shortest path problem," in *Proceedings of the 17th International Conference on Industrial and Engineering Applications of Artificial Intelligence and Expert Systems (IEA/AIE'04)*, pp. 239–248, May 2004.

[9] Q. Li, W. Zhang, Y. Yin, Z. Wang, and G. Liu, "An improved genetic algorithm of optimum path planning for mobile robots," in *Proceedings of the 6th International Conference on Intelligent Systems Design and Applications (ISDA'06)*, pp. 637–642, October 2006.

[10] J. Tu and S. X. Yang, "Genetic algorithm based path planning for a mobile robot," in *Proceedings of the IEEE International Conference on Robotics and Automation*, pp. 1221–1226, Taiwan, September 2003.

[11] W. Wu and Q. Ruan, "A gene-constrained genetic algorithm for solving shortest path problem," in *Proceedings of the 7th International Conference on Signal Processing Proceedings (ICSP'04)*, pp. 2512–2515, September 2004.

[12] H. Mahjoubi, F. Bahrami, and C. Lucas, "Path planning in an environment with static and dynamic obstacles using genetic algorithm: a simplified search space approach," in *Proceedings of the IEEE Congress on Evolutionary Computation (CEC'06)*, pp. 2483–2489, Vancouver, Canada, July 2006.

[13] J. Inagaki, M. Haseyama, and H. Kitajima, "Genetic algorithm for determining multiple routes and its applications," in *Proceedings of the 1999 IEEE International Symposium on Circuits and Systems (ISCAS '99)*, pp. I-137–I-140, June 1999.

[14] G. Ramalingam and T. Reps, "On the computational complexity of dynamic graph problems," *Theoretical Computer Science*, vol. 158, no. 1-2, pp. 233–277, 1996.

[15] P. G. Franciosa, D. Frigioni, and R. Giaccio, "Semi-dynamic shortest paths and breadth first search in digraphs," in *Proceedings of the 14th Annual Symposium on Theoretical Aspects of Computer Science*, pp. 33–46, Lübeck, Germany, 1997.

[16] D. Frigioni, A. Marchetti-Spaccamela, and U. Nanni, "Fully dynamic algorithms for maintaining shortest paths trees," *Journal of Algorithms*, vol. 34, no. 2, pp. 251–281, 2000.

[17] A. Elshamli, H. A. Abdullah, and S. Areibi, "Genetic algorithm for dynamic path planning," in *Proceedings of the Canadian Conference on Electrical and Computer Engineering*, pp. 677–680, May 2004.

[18] D. Catanzaro, M. Labbé, and M. Salazar-Neumann, "Reduction approaches for robust shortest path problems," *Computers and Operations Research*, vol. 38, no. 11, pp. 1610–1619, 2011.

[19] C. Zheng, L. Li, F. Xu, F. Sun, and M. Ding, "Evolutionary route planner for unmanned air vehicles," *IEEE Transactions on Robotics*, vol. 21, no. 4, pp. 609–620, 2005.

[20] G. Xiao, F. Xiao, and C. Da, "A genetic-algorithm-based approach to UA V path planning problem," in *Proceedings of the 5th WSEAS International Conference on Simulation, Modelling and Optimization*, pp. 17503–19507, Corfu, Greece, August 2005.

[21] S. Li, X. Sun, and Y. Xu, "Particle swarm optimization for route planning of unmanned aerial vehicles," in *Proceedings of the IEEE International Conference on Information Acquisition (ICIA'06)*, pp. 1213–1218, Shandong, China, August 2006.

[22] G. Wang, Q. Li, and L. Guo, "Multiple UAVs routes planning based on particle swarm optimization algorithm," in *Proceedings of the 2nd International Symposium on Information Engineering and Electronic Commerce (IEEC'10)*, pp. 150–154, July 2010.

[23] H. Chitsaz and S. M. LaValle, "Time-optimal paths for a dubins airplane," in *Proceedings of the 46th IEEE Conference on Decision and Control (CDC'07)*, pp. 2379–2384, New Orleans, La, USA, December 2007.

[24] R. Dai and J. E. Cochran, "Path planning for multiple unmanned aerial vehicles by parameterized cornu-spirals," in *Proceedings of the American Control Conference (ACC'09)*, pp. 2391–2396, St. Louis, Mo, USA, June 2009.

[25] M. Shanmugavel, A. Tsourdos, and B. A. White, "Collision avoidance and path planning of multiple UAVs using flyable paths in 3D," in *Proceedings of the 15th International Conference on Methods and Models in Automation and Robotics (MMAR'10)*, pp. 218–222, August 2010.

[26] M. Shanmugavel, A. Tsourdos, B. White, and R. Zbikowski, "Co-operative path planning of multiple UAVs using Dubins paths with clothoid arcs," *Control Engineering Practice*, vol. 18, no. 9, pp. 1084–1092, 2010.

[27] S. P. Bhat and P. Kumar, "A feedback guidance strategy for an autonomous mini-air vehicle," in *Proceedings of the National Conference on Control and Dynamical Systems*, IIT Bombay, Bombay, India, January 2005.

[28] S. Gualandi and B. Tranchero, "Concurrent constraint programming-based path planning for uninhabited air vehicles," in *Proceedings of the SPIE/Defense and Security Symposium on Unmanned Ground, Ocean, and Air Technologies*, pp. 12–16, April 2004.

[29] W. Ren and R. W. Beard, "Constrained nonlinear tracking control for small fixed-wing unmanned air vehicles," in *Proceedings of the American Control Conference (AAC'04)*, pp. 4663–4668, Boston, Mass, USA, July 2004.

[30] D. Kingston, *Implementation issue of real-time trajectory generation of small UAV [M.S. thesis]*, Birmingham Young University, 2004.

[31] R. Beard, D. Kingston, M. Quigley et al., "Autonomous vehicle technologies for small fixed-wing UAVs," *Journal of Aerospace Computing, Information and Communication*, pp. 92–108, 2005.

[32] C. H. Lin, J. L. Yu, J. C. Liu, and C. J. Lee, "Genetic algorithm for shortest driving time in intelligent transportation systems," in *Proceedings of the International Conference on Multimedia and Ubiquitous Engineering (MUE'08)*, pp. 402–406, Busan, Korea, April 2008.

[33] B. S. Hasan, M. A. Khamees, and A. S. H. Mahmoud, "A heuristic genetic algorithm for the single source shortest path problem," in *Proceedings of the IEEE/ACS International Conference on Computer Systems and Applications (AICCSA'07)*, pp. 187–194, May 2007.

[34] S. Yang, H. Cheng, and F. Wang, "Genetic algorithms with immigrants and memory schemes for dynamic shortest path routing problems in mobile ad hoc networks," *IEEE Transactions on Systems, Man and Cybernetics Part C*, vol. 40, no. 1, pp. 52–63, 2010.

[35] S. Yang, "Population-based incremental learning with memory scheme for changing environments," in *Proceedings of the Genetic and Evolutionary Computation Conference (GECCO'05)*, pp. 711–718, June 2005.

[36] J. A. Farrell and M. Barth, *The Global Positioning System & Inertial Navigation*, McGraw Hill, 1999.

[37] "Aerosim Blockset," Version 1.2, User's Guide, Unmanned Dynamics, LLC.

[38] S. Stolle and R. Rysdyk, "Flight path following guidance for unmanned air vehicles with pan-tilt camera for target observation," in *Proceedings of the 22nd Digital Avionics Systems Conference*, pp. 8.B.3/1–8.B.3/12, Indianapolis, Ind, USA, October 2003.

[39] K. Y. Pettersen and E. Lefeber, "Way-point tracking control of ships," in *Proceedings of the 40th IEEE Conference on Decision and Control (CDC'01)*, pp. 940–945, Orlando, Fla, USA, December 2001.

[40] R. Rysdyk, "UAV Path Following for constant line-of-sight," in *Proceedings of the 2nd AIAA "Unmanned Unlimited" Systems, Technologies, and Operations Aerospace, Land, and Sea Conference*, paper no. 6626, San-Diego, Calif, USA, September 2003.

[41] T. Back, D. B. Fogel, and Z. Michalewicz, *Handbook of Evolutionary Computation*, Oxford University Press, London, UK, 1997.

[42] G. Harik, E. Cantu-Paz, D. E. Goldberg, and B. L. Miller, "The Gambler's ruin problem, genetic algorithms, and the sizing of populations.," *Evolutionary Computation*, vol. 7, no. 3, pp. 231–253, 1999.

[43] C. W. Ahn and R. S. Ramakrishna, "A genetic algorithm for shortest path routing problem and the sizing of populations," *IEEE Transactions on Evolutionary Computation*, vol. 6, no. 6, pp. 566–579, 2002.

[44] I. Hatzakis and D. Wallace, "Dynamic multi-objective optimization with evolutionary algorithms: a forward-looking approach," in *Proceedings of the 8th Annual Genetic and Evolutionary Computation Conference (GECCO'06)*, pp. 1201–1208, July 2006.

[45] P. A. N. Bosman, "Learning, anticipation and time-deception in evolutionary online dynamic optimization," in *Proceedings of the Workshop on Evolutionary Algorithms for Dynamic Optimization (GECCO'05)*, Washington, DC, USA, 2005.

[46] C. Chitra and P. Subbaraj, "Multiobjective optimization solution for shortest path routing problem," *International Journal of Computer and Information Engineering*, vol. 4, no. 2, pp. 77–85, 2010.

[47] R. W. Morrison, *Designing Evolutionary Algorithms for Dynamic Environments*, Springer, Berlin, Germany, 2004.

An Application of Improved Gap-BIDE Algorithm for Discovering Access Patterns

Xiuming Yu,[1] Meijing Li,[1] Taewook Kim,[1] Seon-phil Jeong,[2] and Keun Ho Ryu[1, 2, 3]

[1] *Database and Bioinformatics Laboratory, Chungbuk National University, Cheongju 361-763, Republic of Korea*
[2] *Division of Science and Technology, BNU-HKBU United International College, Zhuhai 519-085, China*
[3] *Multimedia Systems Laboratory, School of Computer Science and Engineering, The University of Aizu, Aizu-Wakamatsu, Fukushima 965-8580, Japan*

Correspondence should be addressed to Xiuming Yu, yuxiuming@dblab.chungbuk.ac.kr

Academic Editor: Qiangfu Zhao

Discovering access patterns from web log data is a typical sequential pattern mining application, and a lot of access pattern mining algorithms have been proposed. In this paper, we propose an improved approach of Gap-BIDE algorithm to extract user access patterns from web log data. Compared with the previous Gap-BIDE algorithm, a process of getting a large event set is proposed in the provided algorithm; the proposed approach can find out the frequent events by discarding the infrequent events which do not occur continuously in an accessing time before generating candidate patterns. In the experiment, we compare the previous access pattern mining algorithm with the proposed one, which shows that our approach is very efficient in discovering access patterns in large database.

1. Introduction

The web has become an important channel for conducting business transactions and e-commerce. Also, it provides a convenient means for us to communicate with each other worldwide. With the rapid development of web technology, the web has become an important and preferred platform for distributing and acquiring information. The data collected automatically by the web and application web servers represent the navigational behavior of web users, and such data is called web log data.

Web mining is a technology to discover and extract useful information from web log data. Because of the tremendous growth of information sources, increasing interest of various research communities, and the recent interest in e-commerce, the area of web mining has become vast and more interesting. It deals with data related to the web, such as data hidden in web contents, data presented on web pages, and data stored on web servers. Based on the kinds of data, there are three categories of web mining: web content mining, web structure mining, and web usage mining [1]. The Web usage data includes the data from web server access logs, proxy server logs, and browser logs. It is also known as

web access patterns. Web usage mining tries to discover the access patterns from web log files. Web access tracking can be defined as web page history [2]; the mining task is a process of extracting interesting patterns in web access logs. There are so many techniques of mining web usage data including statistical analysis [3], association rules [4], sequential patterns [5–7], classification [8–10], and clustering [11–13]. Access pattern mining is a popular approach of sequential pattern mining, which extracts frequent subsequences from a sequence database [14]. Further, discovering access patterns is an important challenge in the field of web mining. And the popular applications of access patterns mining are obtaining useful information of web users' behavior.

A lot of studies have been proposed on access pattern mining for finding valuable knowledge from web log data, such as AprioriAll algorithm [15, 16] and GSP (generalized sequential pattern) algorithm [17]. All of above algorithms mine sequential patterns using a paradigm of candidate generate-and-test maintain a candidate set of already mined patterns in the mining process. When the data set is huge, it will generates a lot of candidate patterns. In other words, GSP algorithm needs much memory while the data set is large. The BIDE algorithms [18] mine frequent patterns without

---

ALGORITHM: gap-Bide (SDB, t_session, min_sup_les, min_sup, M, N)

INPUT: (1) SDB: An input sequence database with time, (2) t_session: the time user session, (3) min_sup_les: the minimum support threshold of getting large event set, (4) min_sup: the minimum support threshold of getting closed sequential pattern, (5) M and N: the parame-ters of a gap constraint.

OUTPUT: the set of gap-constrained closed sequential patterns.

(1) call getLargeEventSet (SDB, t_session, min_sup_les);
(2) select sequence from input database only contained in LES
(3) find the set of length-1 frequent sequential patterns, $L1$;
(4) for each item i in $L1$
(5) call patternGrowth(i);
(6) return

ALGORITHM 1: Improved Gap-BIDE algorithm.

---

keeping the candidate pattern sets, therefore it needs less space during the mining task. And above algorithms focus on finding out the patterns which are adjacent and that may miss some hidden relationships among noncontinuous patterns. So the constraint of gap should be considered. In the paper [19], the author proposed an improved BIDE algorithm (Gap-BIDE) for mining closed sequential patterns with gap constraint and considers the patterns that are not only adjacent but also noncontiguous; Gap-BIDE algorithm had been applied to web mining in [20]. And in the previous work [21], we have improved the Gap-BIDE algorithm by discarding infrequent events before generating frequent candidate events and applying the improved algorithm to access pattern mining and discussed the efficient of parameter of the values of gap. In this paper, we perform the improved algorithm and compare the efficiency with previous access pattern mining algorithms, such as GSP algorithm.

The rest of this paper is organized as follows. Section 2 presents the precedent of our algorithm compared with the original algorithm. Section 3 focuses on discovering access patterns, namely, preprocessing, pattern discovery, and result analysis, and it focuses on the efficiency of the proposed approach in terms of access pattern mining. In Section 4, we present an extensive performance study. Finally, we conclude this study in Section 5.

2. Algorithm of Improved Gap-BIDE

2.1. Gap-BIDE Algorithm. Gap-BIDE algorithm is presented in paper [19], and it inherits the same design philosophy as BIDE algorithm. It shares the same merit, that is, it does not need to maintain a candidate pattern set, which saves space consumption, and it can find some hidden relationships among the patterns that contend for the gap constraint.

The algorithm first finds the set of all frequent patterns, and it then mines the gap-constrained closed sequential patterns with pattern P as the prefix. In this process, it first scans the backward spaces of prefix pattern P, uses the gap-constrained backscan pruning method to prune search space, scans the forward spaces of prefix P, and uses the

gap-constrained pattern closure checking scheme to check whether or not pattern P is closed; finally, it scans each forward space of all appearances of pattern P and finds the set of all locally frequent items, L, uses each item in L to extend P, and mines the gap-constrained closed sequential patterns for the new prefix by calling subroutine again.

In the algorithm, forward space is defined as that given an appearance of pattern $P[M, N]$ with triple (sid, beginPos, and endPos). The forward space of appearance is part of the sequence of range [endPos + M, endPos + N] ∩ [endPos, l), where l is the length of sequence sid. Here, the definition of forward space (FS) is induced for getting frequent subsequence patterns. We can get the sequence support of every subsequence by scanning the forward spaces of the appearances of a prefix pattern. The sequences whose supports are greater than or equal to the minimal support threshold Minsup will be the frequent subsequences patterns of a prefix pattern.

The definition of backward space (BS) is important, and it is defined as that given an appearance of pattern $P[M, N]$ with triple (sid, beginPos, and end-Pos). The backward space of appearance is part of the sequence sid that is of the range [beginPos $-N$, beginPos $-M$] ∩ [0, beginPos).

Performance of proposed approach shows that Gap-BIDE is both runtime and space efficient in mining frequent, closed sequences with gap constraints.

2.2. Improved Gap-BIDE Algorithm. Although Gap-BIDE algorithm is advanced in the algorithms of sequential pattern mining, there are still a lot of fool's errands are done during the mining task, such as generating some candidate patterns for infrequent events in the original data set. To avoid the unnecessary memory use, an improved algorithm is proposed. Our algorithm is designed based on the Gap-BIDE algorithm; the main idea is to discard infrequent events before generating frequent candidate events; we call this process as getting a large event set.

Algorithm 1 is the main algorithm. The Algorithm 2 is a subroutine of Algorithm 1; it proposes the process of

---

ALGORITHM: getLargeEventSet (SDB, $t\_session$, min_sup_les)
INPUT: (1) SDB: An input sequence database with time, (2) $t\_session$: the time user session, (3) min_sup_les: the minimum support threshold of getting large event set.
OUTPUT: LES: large event set.
(7) scan sequence database; find all candidate events $[\langle E1 \rangle$, $\langle E2 \rangle, \ldots, \langle Ej \rangle]$
(8) group sequences by IP address and t-session; find all sessions $[S1, S2, \ldots, Sm]$
(9) for each candidate event Ej in session Sm
(10) calculate support for Ej
(11) if (support of $Ej \geq$ min_sup_les)
(12) output event Ej to LES
(13) return

ALGORITHM 2: Get large event set.

ALGORITHM: patternGrowth (P)
INPUT: (1) P: prefix sequence pattern.
OUTPUT: the set of gap-constrained closed sequential patterns with prefix P.
(14) backward_check (P needPruning, hasBackwardExtension)
(15) if (needPruning)
(16) return;
(17) forward_check(P, hasForwardExtension);
(18) if ! (hasBackwardExtension || hasForwardExtension)
(19) output pattern P;
(20) search each forward space of all appearances of P, and find the set of all local frequent items, L;
(21) for each item i in L
(22) build new pattern $P_{new} = P + i$;
(23) call patternGrowth (P_{new});
(24) return.

ALGORITHM 3: Generate closed sequential patterns.

getting a large event set. A large event set (LES) is an event set that contains the events that satisfy a user specified minimum support threshold. The events in LES represent the transactions or objects with large proportion in the entire data set. In this paper, a web log file denotes the data set, and one web page is defined as an event; thus, LES denotes the set of web pages that are accessed by web users with enough frequency in a period of time. In this mining process, the generation sequence through LES can reduce the number of test data to improve the efficiency and accuracy of the mining task. After obtaining large event set, sequence data with only large events are generated. Then the algorithm scans the generated database, finds the set of all frequent items with length (length-1), and calls Algorithm 3 iteratively. Algorithm 3 patternGrowth (P) is the other subroutine of Algorithm 1; it proposes the process to mine the gap-constrained closed sequential patterns with pattern P as the prefix.

An important definition for generating LES is the user session. The user session is an activity that a user with a unique IP address spends on a web page during a specified period of time. It can be used to identify a continuous access to user statistics visits by this measure. The specified period of time is determined via a cookie, also known as web cookie and HTTP cookie, which can be set by the server with or without an expiration date, modified by web designer and is set to a default value of 600 seconds. Within the expiration date, the access of web user is effective.

3. Discovery of Access Patterns

In this section, the process of mining task is discussed.

3.1. Data Preprocessing. Web log files reside on the web servers that record the activities of clients who access the web server via a web browser. Traditionally, there have been many types of web log files including error logs, access logs, and referrer logs. In this paper, data in the web access log is defined as the raw data. The web access log records all requests that are processed by the web server. Data in the log file contains some missing value data and irrelevant attributes; it cannot be directly used for the mining task. In this section, we describe the process of data cleaning and attribute selection to remove unwanted data.

(1) *Data cleaning*: removing irrelevant data.

    (a) *Remove the records with URLs of jpg, png, gif, js, css, and so on, which are automatically generated when a web page is requested.*

    (b) *Remove the data with wrong statue numbers that start with the numbers 4 or 5.* These wrong records are caused by the error of requests or server. For example, the HTTP client error: 400 Bad Request and 404 Not Found and HTTP server error: 500 Internal Server Error and 505 HTTP Version Not Supported.

    (c) *Discard missing value data that are caused by breaking a web page while loading.*

(2) *Attribute selection*: removing the irrelevant attributes. There are many attributes in one record of web log file. In this paper, we need the attributes of IP Address, Time, and URL; thus, the rest of attributes of method, status, size, and so on, need to be discarded.

(3) *Transformed URLs into code numbers.*

It is difficult to distinguish the requested URLs of web log data in thousands of records. There are typically dozens of kinds of web pages in thousands of records. So, the URLs can be transformed into code numbers for simplicity. For example, a web log data that comes from the server of website http://www.vtsns.edu.rs/, and there are 31 different kinds of web pages that have been accessed. We transform their URLs into code numbers, such as galerija.php → 1, nenastavno_osoblje.php → 15, and rezultati_ispita.php → 21.

We choose a set of data from a web log file as an example data. After data preprocessing, we get the clean data shown in Table 1.

3.2. Process of Discovering Access Patterns. In this section, we present the process of discovering access patterns with an example.

After data preprocessing, we apply the algorithm to web log data. Then, LES is generated with sorting the data in Table 1 by the attributes of IP Address and Time; here, the time of user session is defined as one hour for simplicity. Then, these data are grouped by one hour for each web user; finally, the sorted data is shown in Table 2.

Then, we calculate the support of each event. For example, for the event ⟨2⟩, it occurs three times, which are in "82.117.202.158" at time 2, in "82.208.207.41" at time 2, and in "82.208.255.125" at time 2. After calculating of events support, the candidate event set is obtained as shown in Table 3.

Finally, a user specified minimum support threshold (MinSup) must be defined. MinSup denotes a kind of abstract level that is a degree of generalization. Choosing

TABLE 1: Example data.

No.	IP address	Time	URL
1	82.117.202.158	01:12:18	4
2	82.117.202.158	01:12:22	1
3	82.208.207.41	01:12:43	4
4	83.136.179.11	01:22:43	4
5	83.136.179.11	01:23:43	3
6	82.208.207.41	02:12:23	4
7	82.208.207.41	02:12:25	7
8	82.208.207.41	02:13:43	2
9	82.117.202.158	02:17:26	6
10	82.117.202.158	02:17:39	2
11	83.136.179.11	02:17:41	6
12	82.208.255.125	02:17:44	6
13	82.208.255.125	02:17:53	2
14	82.117.202.158	03:12:42	7
15	83.136.179.11	03:27:23	4
16	83.136.179.11	03:37:32	5
17	82.208.255.125	03:37:44	7
18	83.136.179.11	04:13:43	7
19	82.117.202.158	04:17:26	4
20	82.208.255.125	05:17:39	6
21	82.208.255.125	05:17:41	7
22	82.208.207.41	05:18:40	7
23	82.117.202.158	05:37:53	6
24	82.117.202.158	05:39:42	7
25	83.136.179.11	06:27:23	6
26	83.136.179.11	06:37:32	7
27	82.117.202.158	01:12:18	4

TABLE 2: Sorted data.

IP address	Time	Event
82.117.202.158	1	4, 1
82.117.202.158	2	6, 2
82.117.202.158	3	7
82.117.202.158	4	4
82.117.202.158	5	6, 7
83.136.179.11	1	4, 3
83.136.179.11	2	6
83.136.179.11	3	4, 5
83.136.179.11	4	7
83.136.179.11	6	6, 7
82.208.207.41	1	4
82.208.207.41	2	4, 7, 2
82.208.207.41	3	7
82.208.255.125	2	6, 2
82.208.255.125	3	7
82.208.255.125	5	6, 7

MinSup is very important; if it is low, then we can get a detailed event. If it is high, then we can get general events. In this example, MinSup is defined as 75%. In other words, if a web page is accessed by greater than or equal to 75% web users, then this web page can be denoted as a large event. After the process of getting large event set, the LES is obtained as shown in Table 4.

TABLE 3: Candidate event set.

Event	Support
1	1
2	3
3	1
4	3
5	1
6	3
7	4

TABLE 4: Large event set.

Event	Support
2	3
4	3
6	3
7	4

TABLE 5: Sequence set.

Sequence identifier	Sequence
82.117.202.158	4
82.117.202.158	6, 2
82.117.202.158	7
82.117.202.158	4
82.117.202.158	6, 7
83.136.179.11	4
83.136.179.11	6
83.136.179.11	4
83.136.179.11	7
83.136.179.11	6, 7
82.208.207.41	4
82.208.207.41	4, 7, 2
82.208.207.41	7
82.208.255.125	6, 2
82.208.255.125	7
82.208.255.125	6, 7

TABLE 6: Closed patterns.

No.	Pattern	Support
1	[4, 7]	3
2	[6, 7]	3
3	[6, 7, 7]	3
4	[7, 7]	4

After obtaining LES, the infrequent events ⟨1⟩, ⟨3⟩, and ⟨5⟩ are removed from Table 2, and the events are then transformed into a set of tuples (sequence identifier, sequence). We define the IP Address as the sequence identifier and define the event as a sequence. The sequence set is shown in Table 5.

Then, we call the original Gap-BIDE algorithm to find the frequent sequential pattern and prune the patterns. Here, gap is defined as $g(M, N)$, where M is the value of minimum gap, and N is the value of the maximum gap. Assume a pattern P with $g(M, N)$, which can be expressed as $P[M, N]$. This approach is presented like the description of timing constrains with the mingap and maxgap. If the value of M-N is D, then the events in a sequence must occur within D of the events occurring in the previous event.

After calling our improved algorithm, we get the closed patterns as shown in Table 6.

Useful information can be found from the experimental result. The relationships of web pages are known easily, and user behavior information is shown directly. Each number in the output sequential patterns represents a website or a web user request. For example, the numbers 6 and 7 represent web pages ispit_raspored_god.php and upis_prva.php, respectively. For the closed sequential pattern [6, 7] shown in Table 6, it means 75% (3 out of 4 user sessions) of the web users who access web page upis_prva.php tend to always visit web page ispit_raspored_god.php first. According to the relationship between these two web pages, the design of web pages can be improved. For example, the web designer can add a hyperlink into web page ispit_raspored_god.php that points to web page upis_prva.php. This approach can be applied in many areas. For instance, in the electronic shopping cart, when customers complete their shopping, there can be some hyperlinks in the finished web page that point to some related web pages according to the mining result of purchase history. When web users watch a movie, some hyperlinks that point to some web pages of related movies on the site must be present.

4. Experimental Result and Analysis

4.1. Effect of Parameter in the Process of Getting Large Event Set. The process of getting a large event set aims at extracting the events that satisfy a user defined minimum support of large event set. It can discard the infrequent events to reduce the size of experimental database for reducing the search space and time and maintaining the accuracy of the whole process of mining task. To evaluate the parameter effect, we compare the numbers of large events by changing the values of the minimum support of large event set (MSLE). In this experiment, the experimental data records the access information of website (http://www.vtsns.edu.rs/), which is an institution's official website. The number of original records in the web log file is 5999, and after data preprocessing, there are 269 user sessions in the records. The experimental result is shown in Figure 1. We can see that the smaller the minimum support are, the more generalized the obtained LES becomes. There always exists a value of minimum support, and from the value, the number of large events will not change, or will change very little. This value is always selected to be used as the value of minimum support in the experiment.

4.2. Comparing with Original Gap-BIDE Algorithm. In this section, we compare our algorithm with the original Gap-BIDE algorithm [19]. The experimental data come from internet information server (IIS) logs for msnbc.com and

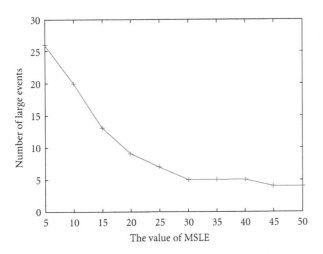

FIGURE 1: Effect of parameter in the process of getting large event set.

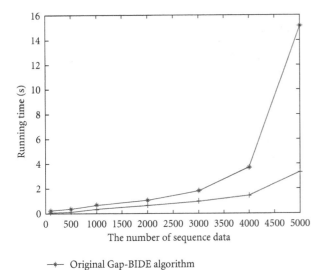

FIGURE 2: Comparing with original Gap-BIDE.

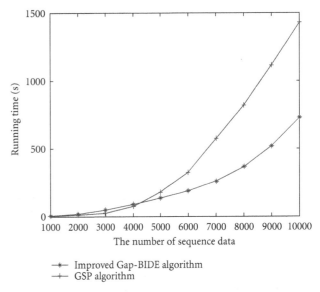

FIGURE 3: Comparing with GSP algorithm.

4.3. Comparing with GSP Algorithm. Previous studies have shown that our proposed algorithm is more effective than original Gap-BIDE algorithm when we apply the algorithms on discovering access patterns. In this section, we want to prove that our proposed algorithm is more effective than previous access pattern mining algorithm. To validate it, we compare our algorithm and GSP algorithm proposed in [17] with an experiment. The experimental data come from Internet information server (IIS) logs for msnbc.com and news-related portions of msn.com for the entire day of September 28, 1999, and we choose the test data by the approach of simple random sampling without replacement from these data. In the experiment, we define minimum support of closed sequential pattern as 10 and the experimental result is shown in Figure 3. It shows that when applying our proposed algorithm to large database, the cost of time is less than that GSP algorithm.

5. Conclusion

In this paper, we presented the application of improved Gap-BIDE algorithm for discovering closed sequential patterns in web log data. We improve the algorithm by discarding all infrequent events before generating the frequent candidate events. In the process of data preprocessing, we removed the irrelevant attributes and transformed URLs into code numbers for simplicity, and we removed the missing value data to improve the quality of data. For getting experimental data for the mining task, we transformed the web log data into sequences based on the time constraint. The value of time is determined by an expiration date of the cookies. As a result, we obtained new web access patterns that expressed the order in which websites were access based on the Gap-BIDE algorithm. Compared with the previous web mining approaches, the proposed approach achieves the best performance in terms of getting a large event set of sequence. It reduces the sequences to get more effective and accurate

news-related portions of msn.com for the entire day of September 28, 1999. Each sequence in the dataset corresponds to page views of a user during that twenty-four hour period. Each event in the sequence corresponds to a user's request for a page. There are 989818 anonymous user sessions; we choose the test data by the approach of simple random sampling without replacement from these data. In the experiment, we define minimum support threshold of large event set as 20, minimum support of closed sequential pattern as 10, and the value of gap as [0, 2]. We implemented the experiment on a 2.40-GHz Pentium PC machine with 4.00 GB main memory and ran the algorithm in Python 2.7 with JDK 1.6.0. Then, the experimental result is shown in Figure 2. It shows that when applying our proposed algorithm, the cost of time is less than that of the original Gap-BIDE algorithm.

results. We performed some experiments to compare our algorithm with previous algorithms. The experiments show that our algorithm uses less time than the original Gap-BIDE algorithm and cost less time than GSP algorithm in discovering access patterns in large database. In future work, we will try to find a more efficient algorithm for mining the closed gap constraint sequential patterns and will try to achieve a more efficient way for transforming web log files into sequence patterns.

Acknowledgment

This work was supported by the National Research Foundation of Korea (NRF) grant funded by the Korea government (MEST) (no. 2012-0000478).

References

[1] L. K. J. Grace, V. Maheswari, and D. Nagamalai, "Analysis of web logs and web user in web mining," *International Journal of Network Security & Its Applications*, vol. 3, no. 1, 2011.

[2] K. Saxena and R. Shukla, "Significant interval and frequent pattern discovery in web log data," *International Journal of Computer Science Issue*, vol. 7, no. 1, 2010.

[3] K. Suresh and S. Paul, "Distributed linear programming for weblog data using mining techniques in distributed environment," *International Journal of Computer Applications (0975-8887)*, vol. 11, no. 7, 2010.

[4] Y. Wang, J. Le, and D. Huang, "A method for privacy preserving mining of association rules based on web usage mining," in *International Conference on Web Information Systems and Mining (WISM '10)*, vol. 1, pp. 33–37, IEEE Computer Society Washington, Washington, DC, USA, 2010.

[5] C. Wei, W. Sen, Z. Yuan, and L. C. Chang, "Algorithm of mining sequential patterns for web personalization services," *ACM SIGMIS Database*, vol. 40, no. 2, pp. 57–66, 2009.

[6] J. Zhu, H. Wu, and G. Gao, "An efficient method of web sequential pattern mining based on session filter and transaction identification," *Journal of Networks*, vol. 5, no. 9, pp. 1017–1024, 2010.

[7] X. Yu, M. Li, and H. Kim, "Mining access patterns using temporal interval relational rules from web logs," in *Proceedings of the 4th International Conference (FITAT/DBMI '11)*, pp. 80–83, 2011.

[8] M. Santini, "Cross-testing a genre classification model for the web," *Genres on the Web*, vol. 42, Part 3, pp. 87–128, 2011.

[9] J. J. Rho, B. J. Moon, Y. J. Kim, and D. H. Yang, "Internet customer segmentation using web log data," *Journal of Business & Economics Research*, vol. 2, no. 11, 2004.

[10] N. Kejžar, S. K. Èerne, and V. Batagelj, "Network analysis of works on clustering and classification from web of science," in *Proceedings of the 11th Conference of the International Federation of Classification Societies (IFCS '10)*, Part 3, pp. 525–536, 2010.

[11] G. Xu, Y. Zong, and P. Dolog, "Co-clustering analysis of weblogs using bipartite spectral projection approach," in *Proceedings of the 14th International Conference on Knowledge-Based and Intelligent Information and Engineering Systems (KES '10)*, vol. 6278, pp. 398–407, 2010.

[12] A. A. O. Makanju, A. N. Zincir-Heywood, and E. E. Milios, "Clustering event logs using iterative partitioning," in *Proceedings of the 15th ACM SIGKDD International Conference on Knowledge Discovery and Data Mining (KDD '09)*, pp. 1255–1263, July 2009.

[13] J. Wang, Y. Mo, B. Huang, and J. Wen, "Web search results clustering based on a novel suffix tree structure," in *Proceedings of the 5th International Conference on Autonomic and Trusted Computing (ATC '08)*, vol. 5060, pp. 540–554, 2008.

[14] J. Chen and T. Cook, "Mining contiguous sequential patterns from web logs," in *Proceedings of the 16th International World Wide Web Conference (WWW '07)*, pp. 1177–1178, May 2007.

[15] M. Saravanan and B. Valaramathi, "Generalization of web log datas using WUM technique," in *Proceedings of the 12th International Conference on Networking, VLSI and signal processing (ICNVS '10)*, pp. 157–165, 2010.

[16] N. R. Mabroukeh and C. I. Ezeife, "A taxonomy of sequential pattern mining algorithms," *ACM Computing Surveys*, vol. 43, no. 1, article 3, 2010.

[17] S. Ramakrishnan and A. Rakesh, "Mining sequential patterns: generalizations and performance improvements," *Lecture Notes in Computer Science*, vol. 1057, pp. 3–17, 1996.

[18] J. Wang, J. Han, and C. Li, "Frequent closed sequence mining without candidate maintenance," *IEEE Transactions on Knowledge and Data Engineering*, vol. 19, no. 8, pp. 1042–1056, 2007.

[19] C. Li and J. Wang, "Efficiently mining closed subsequences with gap constraints," in *Proceedings of International Conference on Data Mining (SIAM '08)*, April 2008.

[20] X. Yu, M. Li, D. G. Lee, K. D. Kim, and K. H. Ryu, "Application of closed gap-constrained sequential pattern mining in web log data," in *Proceedings of the 2nd International Conference of Electrical and Electronics Engineering (ICEEE '11)*, pp. 649–657, 2011.

[21] X. Yu, M. Li, H. Kim, D. G. Lee, and K. H. Ryu, "A novel approach to mining access patterns," in *Proceedings of the 3rd International Conference on Awareness Science and Technology*, pp. 346–352, 2011.

4

Environmental Sound Recognition Using Time-Frequency Intersection Patterns

Xuan Guo,[1] Yoshiyuki Toyoda,[1] Huankang Li,[2] Jie Huang,[1] Shuxue Ding,[1] and Yong Liu[1]

[1] *Graduate Department of Computer and Information Systems, Graduate School of Computer Science and Engineering, The University of Aizu, Aizu-Wakamatsu 965-8580, Japan*
[2] *Department of Computer Science and Engineering, Shanghai Jiaotong University, 200240 Shanghai, China*

Correspondence should be addressed to Jie Huang, j-huang@u-aizu.ac.jp

Academic Editor: Zhishun She

Environmental sound recognition is an important function of robots and intelligent computer systems. In this research, we use a multistage perceptron neural network system for environmental sound recognition. The input data is a combination of time-variance pattern of instantaneous powers and frequency-variance pattern with instantaneous spectrum at the power peak, referred to as a time-frequency intersection pattern. Spectra of many environmental sounds change more slowly than those of speech or voice, so the intersectional time-frequency pattern will preserve the major features of environmental sounds but with drastically reduced data requirements. Two experiments were conducted using an original database and an open database created by the RWCP project. The recognition rate for 20 kinds of environmental sounds was 92%. The recognition rate of the new method was about 12% higher than methods using only an instantaneous spectrum. The results are also comparable with HMM-based methods, although those methods need to treat the time variance of an input vector series with more complicated computations.

1. Introduction

Understanding environmental sounds is an essential function of human hearing. For example, people can recognize the beginning of a rain shower by the rain sound, be cautious when they hear footsteps coming from behind at night, and open the door to welcome visitors after the sound of the door-knocking. Environmental sound recognition is also important for intelligent robots and computer systems. An intelligent robot can be aware of the environments by the audition and use its hearing function to complement its vision [1].

In recent years, environmental sound recognition has received increasing attention, and we have seen some pioneering research in this field. An environmental sound database (RWCP-DB) has been created for research use [2]. The sounds in the database were recorded in an anechoic environment with durations of 250 to 500 ms. In total, there are 105 instances, with each instance including 100 samples. We reclassified this database into 12 types and 45 kinds as listed in Table 1. For many sounds, there are multiple instances with similar but different materials.

An environmental sound recognition method using the instantaneous spectrum at the power peak was proposed [3]. It was reported that the rate of recognition was about 80% for 20 instances of environmental sounds. In this research, the target sounds are limited to impact sounds that have a single power peak followed by exponential attenuation. The instantaneous spectrum $S_p(\omega_m)$ was calculated at the power peak, where ω_m ($m = 1, 2, \ldots, M$) is the frequency. Since the input information was only based on the peak spectrum without time variance, it was not able to capture the environmental sounds and thus the recognition rate was low.

It is natural to consider using existing methods that have proven useful for speech recognition, for example, the hidden Markov Model (HMM) method and the time delay neural network (TDNN) method [4–6], since those methods deal with time variations of an input vector series. Miki and others achieved recognition rate of 95.4% using HMM method for 90 instances of RWCP-DB [5], and Sasou, and

TABLE 1: The RWCP environmental sound database.

Sound type	Kind of materials	Instances
Impact sound	Wood plates	12
	Metal cans, boxes, and so forth	10
	Plastic cases	3
	Glass cups, bottles, and so forth	8
	Bundle of paper	1
	Handclap/handclaps	4
Falling pieces	Grains	2
	Coin/coins	7
	Dice	3
Air jet	Small air pump	1
	Spray	1
	Firecracker	1
	Air bubbles	1
	Dryer	1
Friction sound	File	1
	Sand paper	2
	Saw	2
Musical instruments	Castanets	1
	Cymbals	1
	Drum	1
	Horn	1
	Kara	1
	Maracas	1
	Ring	1
	String	1
	Whistle	3
	Tambourine	1
Phone, buzzer	Buzzer	1
	Clock alarm	2
	Phone	4
	Toys	3
Open	Cap	2
Broken	Chopsticks	1
	Tearing paper	1
	Crumpling paper	1
Release	Clip	2
Shaking	Metal bell/bells	7
Rotation	Coffee mill	1
Others	Doorlock	1
	Leaf through a book	2
	Mech bell	1
	Padlock	1
	Punch	1
	Shaver	1
	Stapler	1

others reported the recognition rate for 59 instances of RWCP-DB using AR-HMM method was 83.0% [6].

The recognition rate of the HMM method was greater than that of the peak-spectrum method. Because the HMM method uses a time series of frequency-feature vectors $[S_n(\omega_m)]$ that includes the time-frequency variance of the signals, where ω_m ($m = 1, 2, \ldots, M$) is the frequency and $S_n(\omega_m)$ indicates the spectrum (or cepstrum) for time frame n ($n = 1, 2, \ldots, N$). However, HMM-based methods may not be the best choice for environmental sound recognition

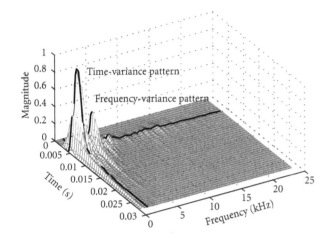

FIGURE 1: The time-frequency intersection pattern refers to the combination of the time-variance patter containing instantaneous powers (or their square roots) for all time frames and the frequency-variance patter with the instantaneous spectrum at power peak. (The time-variance pattern is illustrated as the line along with the spectrum-peaks.)

because environmental sounds differ from human speech. The frequency characteristics of most environmental sounds do not significantly change over time, and therefore it is not necessary to deal with state-transferring in many cases, as the HMM methods for speech signals require.

We can use a simpler method using the combination of a time-variance pattern containing the instantaneous powers (or their square roots) calculated by the sum-of-squares method for all time frames and a frequency-variance pattern with the instantaneous spectrum at the power peak as illustrated in Figure 1. Since this combination contains both time-variance and frequency variance of the signal, it incorporated almost the information needed for environmental sound recognition. We call this input data type a time frequency intersection pattern and refer to the time-variance patter of power as power-variance pattern. Thus, the information can be represented as $[S_p(\omega_m), P(t_n)]$, where ω_m ($m = 1, 2, \ldots, M$) is the frequency, $S_p(\omega)$ indicates the spectrum at the time frame of power peak, and $P(t_n)$ indicates the power of sound for time frame t_n ($n = 1, 2, \ldots, N$). The total information includes two vectors with sizes M and N (total $M + N$), which is less than that of HMM-based methods ($M \times N$ in total). This method can drastically reduce the input data while preserving the main time-frequency characteristics of environmental sounds.

We use perceptron NNs for environmental sound recognition. A multistage classification-recognition strategy is adopted to cover environment sounds with different time lengths. The first stage is the classification part, which classifies environmental sounds into three categories, single bursts, repeated sounds, and continuous sounds, based on their long-term power-variance patterns. The second stage is the recognition part, for individual recognition of each sound. In this stage, three different NN groups are used for different categories of environmental sounds. Two experi-

ments were conducted using an original environment sound database recorded in an ordinary room and the RWCP database recorded in an anechoic chamber to verify the proposed new method.

2. Environmental Sound Database and Preprocessing

Since this research is concerned with a project that aims to develop a security patrol and home-helper robot capable of understanding environmental sounds, the target environmental sounds are chosen to be important for the robot to achieve its tasks. As seen in Table 3, 10 kinds of environmental sounds were selected and recorded in an ordinary room environment, with 30 samples of each kind. The original sampling frequency was 44.1 kHz.

For comparison with the previous methods, we selected 10 kinds of sounds and a total of 45 instances from the RWCP-DB as seen in Table 4.

Since there are unlimited kinds of environmental sounds, no database can cover all of them. Therefore, no system will be able to recognize all environmental sounds. Instead, for a practical system, the target sounds must be limited according to the practical environment and the purpose of tasks. That is, environmental sound recognition is task dependent.

At the preprocessing stage, the environmental sound data were downsampled to 8 kHz. The instantaneous power was calculated for each time frame of 128-point length. While the long-term power-variance patter contains the power data of 48 frames, the short-term power-variance patter is of 16 frames. The peak spectrum was calculated around power peak with a time frame of 64 points. All data were normalized to have a maximum value of one.

3. System Construction

In many cases, environmental sounds can be mainly classified into collision sounds, friction sounds, vibration sounds, electric sound, and other noises. Based on their power-variance patterns, environmental sounds can be roughly classified into single bursts, repeated bursts, continuous sounds, and other noises. It is reasonable to first classify the environmental sounds into different categories based on their long-term power-variance patterns in the classification stage. Recognition based on the combination of short-term power-variance patterns and frequency-variance patterns at the power peak will be performed in the second stage.

The data flow of the environmental sound recognition system is presented in Figure 2. The system consists of a classification part and a recognition part.

A three-layer perceptron NN is used for sound classification and recognition. The construction of the NN is described in Table 2.

3.1. Classification by Long-Term Power-Variance Patterns. The data needed for classification is the long-term power-variance patterns for each input sound. An example of the

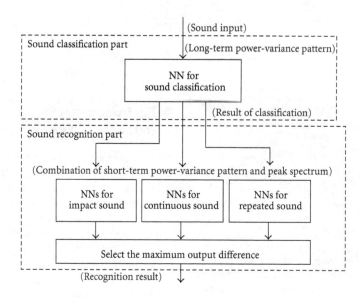

FIGURE 2: System data flow.

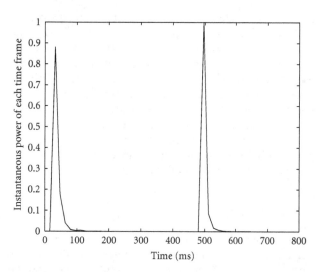

FIGURE 3: A sample of long-term power-variance pattern (a door-knocking sound).

TABLE 2: Construction of NNs for classification and recognition parts.

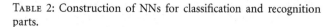

Input layer neuron	48
Intermid layer neuron	32
Output layer neuron	2

long-term power-variance pattern of a door-knocking sound is presented in Figure 3.

This classification stage classifies sounds with short impact sounds as single-impact sounds; sounds of friction, vibration, noises, and electric sounds like phone bells as continuous sounds; some sounds with repetition, for example, hand claps or knocks on a door, as repeated sounds.

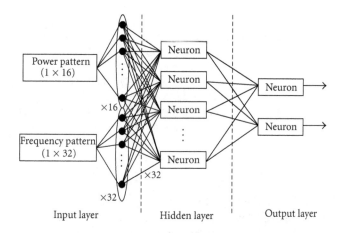

FIGURE 4: NN in the recognition part.

3.2. Construction of the Recognition Part. For almost all kinds of environmental sounds, the time variances of the frequency characteristics are usually rather stable and there are few marked changes during their period compared with speech sounds. The input data for the recognition part assigns the short-term power-variance pattern to the first 16 inputs and the instantaneous spectrum calculated at the power peak to the remaining 32 inputs, as seen in Figure 4. The output layer of each NN has two neurons that correspond to the results of correct and incorrect matching.

The three NNs in the recognition part correspond to the three target sound categories. Each NN, constructed by a three-layered perceptron, is trained for one target sound category. The final recognition result depends on the difference between the two output neurons of each NN. The NN that obtains the maximum difference of correct and incorrect output is dominant and gives the final recognition result (Figure 2).

TABLE 3: Results of recognition experiments for environmental sounds in the original database.

Sound kind	First stage rate	Final recognition rate
Boll impact	100%	100%
Metal impact	100%	95%
Door opening/closing	100%	85%
Lock	100%	95%
Switch on/off	100%	100%
Typing	100%	75%
Repeated typing	80%	80%
Knock	90%	90%
Telephone ringing	100%	100%
Japanese vowels	100%	100%
Average		92.0%

TABLE 4: Results of recognition experiments for environmental sounds in the RWCP database.

Sound kind	First stage rate	Final recognition rate
Wood impact	100%,	96.5%
Metal impact	99.5%,	92.5%
Clap	97.5%,	89.2%
Plastic impact	100%,	100%
Grains falling	100%,	80.0%
Telephone ringing	100%,	88.3%
Metal bell	99.2%,	98.3%
Spray	100%,	95.0%
Whistle	100%,	100%
Drier	100%,	86.0%
Average		92.7%

4. Recognition Experiments

Two experiments using the original prerecorded environmental sound database and the RWCP database were conducted. In all of the experiments, the computer system used was an MS-Windows PC with an Athlone 1600 XP CPU and 512 MB of memory. The NNs were implemented using the MATLAB programming language.

For the original database, 10 samples of each sound kind were used for NN training, and 10 samples of data were used for the recognition tests. The NN training time was about 1 hour in total, and the recognition time for each input data sample was less than 0.1 second. The results of the recognition are listed in Table 3. The average rate of recognition was 92.0%.

From the RWCP database, data for 10 kinds of sounds (total of 45 instances) were selected for the experiments. In the experiments, 10 samples of each sound kind were used for NN training and 20 samples were used for testing. Since there were not enough kinds of repeated sounds in this database, only single-impact and continuous sounds were tested. The required training time was 2 hours, and the recognition time for each data sample was less than 0.1 second. The recognition results are presented in Table 4. The average recognition rate was 92.7%.

5. Conclusion

In this research, we propose a multistage environmental sound recognition method. The method consists of a classification stage and a recognition stage. The classification stage classifies environmental sounds into three categories based on their long-term power-variance patterns, and the recognition stage recognizes the sound kind based on a combination of the short-term power-variance pattern and the instantaneous spectrum at the power peak.

The merit of this method is that it uses a one-dimensional intersectional time-frequency pattern that combines the power-variance pattern and the instantaneous spectrum at the power peak. The recognition rate of the new method was 12% higher than methods using only an instantaneous spectrum at the power peak. The results are also comparable with HMM-based methods, although those methods must accommodate the time variance of the input vector series with more complicated computations.

References

[1] J. Huang, N. Ohnishi, and N. Sugie, "Building ears for rbotos: Sound localization and separation," *Artificial Life and Robotics*, vol. 1, no. 4, pp. 157–163, 1997.

[2] S. Nakamura, K. Hiyane, F. Asano, and T. Endo, "Sound scene data collection in real acoustical environments," *Journal of the Acoustical Society of Japan*, vol. 20, no. 3, pp. 225–232, 1999.

[3] K. Hiyane and J. Iio, "Non-speech sound recognition with microphone array," in *Proceedings of the IEEE International Workshop Hands-Free Speech Communication*, 2001.

[4] K. J. Lang, A. H. Waibel, and G. E. Hinton, "A time-delay neural network architecture for isolated world recognition," *Neural Networks*, vol. 3, pp. 23–43, 1990.

[5] K. Miki, T. Nishiura, S. Nakamura, and G. Kashino, "Environmental sound recognition by HMM," in *Proceedings of the Spring Meet of The Acoustical Society of Japan*, no. 1-8-8, 2000.

[6] A. Sasou and K. Tanaka, "Environmental sound recognition based on AR-HMM," in *Proceedings of the Autumn Meet of The Acoustical Society of Japan*, no. 3-Q-7, 2002.

5

Multiobjective Optimization of Irreversible Thermal Engine Using Mutable Smart Bee Algorithm

M. Gorji-Bandpy and A. Mozaffari

Department of Mechanical Engineering, Babol University of Technology, P.O. Box 484, Babol, Iran

Correspondence should be addressed to A. Mozaffari, amozaffari10@yahoo.com

Academic Editor: Chuan-Kang Ting

A new method called mutable smart bee (MSB) algorithm proposed for cooperative optimizing of the maximum power output (MPO) and minimum entropy generation (MEG) of an Atkinson cycle as a multiobjective, multi-modal mechanical problem. This method utilizes mutable smart bee instead of classical bees. The results have been checked with some of the most common optimizing algorithms like Karaboga's original artificial bee colony, bees algorithm (BA), improved particle swarm optimization (IPSO), Lukasik firefly algorithm (LFFA), and self-adaptive penalty function genetic algorithm (SAPF-GA). According to obtained results, it can be concluded that Mutable Smart Bee (MSB) is capable to maintain its historical memory for the location and quality of food sources and also a little chance of mutation is considered for this bee. These features were found as strong elements for mining data in constraint areas and the results will prove this claim.

1. Introduction

The Atkinson cycle was designed by James Atkinson in 1882 [1]. This engine has two important advantages comparing to other engines; it is one of the most heat efficient as well as high expansion ratio cycles. Generally, four procedures called Intake, Compression, Power, and Exhaust take place in cycle per turn of crankshaft. In fact a classic Atkinson engine is a four-stroke engine and, in a same condition, it can reach a higher efficiency comparing to Otto cycle.

Recently, researchers focused on analyzing and optimizing Atkinson cycle using different optimization techniques and intelligent controlling systems. Leff [2] determined the thermal efficiency of a reversible Atkinson cycle at maximum work output, Al-Sarkhi et al. [3] compared the performance characteristic curves of the Atkinson cycle to Miller and Brayton cycles using numerical examples and simulation techniques. Wang and Hou [4] studied the performance of Atkinson cycle in variable temperature heat reservoirs. Hou [5] investigated the effects of heat leak due to percentage of fuels energy, friction, and variable specific heats of working fluid. Here we proposed a new metaheuristic algorithm to analyze the performance of an air standard Atkinson cycle

with heat transfer losses, friction, and variable specific heats of the working fluid.

Metaheuristic algorithms are population-based methods working with a set of feasible solutions and trying to improve them gradually. These algorithms can be divided into two main parts: evolutionary algorithms (EAs) which attempt to simulate the phenomenon of natural evolution and swarm intelligence base algorithms [6–8]. There are many different variants of evolutionary algorithms. The common ideas behind all of these techniques are the same: defining a population of individuals, selection phase (survival of the fittest according to the theory of evolution) which causes a rise in the fitness of the population. In these methods we randomly create a set of candidate solutions (elements of the function domain) and evaluate the quality of the function through fitness measuring (the higher is better). Based on this fitness, some of the better candidates are chosen to seed the next generation by applying recombination and/or mutation to them. Recombination is an operator applied to two or more selected candidates and result in one or more new candidate. Mutation is applied to one candidate and results in one new candidate. Executing recombination and mutation leads the algorithm to a set of new candidates and this procedure will continue until criteria have been met. Genetic algorithm (GA) which introduced by Holland [9] is one of the most popular algorithms among the EAs. Genetic algorithm (GA) is a powerful numerical optimization algorithm that reaches an approximate global maximum of a complex multivariable function over a wide search space [10]. It always produces high-quality solution because of its independency for selecting the initial configuration of population. But sometimes it may perform inefficient in constraint optimizing problems. In order to make a successful decision in constraint spaces, Tessema and Yen [11] used self adapting penalty function genetic algorithm (SAPF-GA) for optimizing constraint problems which is able to tune some of its characteristics during the optimization and made a powerful algorithm for finding feasible solution in constraint spaces [12].

Other branches of population-based algorithms which are called swarm intelligence focused on collective behavior of some self-organized systems in order to develop some metaheuristics procedures which can mimic such system's problem solution abilities. The interactive behavior between individuals locally with one another and with their environment contributes to the collective intelligence of the social colonies [13, 14] and often leads to convergence of global behavior. There is a wide variety of swarm base algorithms which mimics the natural behavior of insects and animals such as ants, fishes, birds, bees, fireflies, penguins, frogs, and many other organisms. Particle swarm optimization algorithm (PSO) which first developed by Kennedy and Eberhart [15] is one of the most applicable method for optimizing engineering problems which inspired by social behavior of birds flocking or fish schooling [16]. Till now many researchers proposed modified PSO algorithms which have advantages in handling with particular type of problems. Here one of this improved particle swarm algorithms (IPSO) which is strong in optimizing constraint engineering problems [17] is used and also its results compared with proposed modified MSB algorithm.

There are also some algorithms that improved the performance of swarm base algorithms by utilizing some natural concepts. In 2009, Yang and Deb [18] proposed a modern metaheuristic algorithm based on the obligate brood parasitic behavior of some cuckoo species in combination with the Lévy flight behavior of some birds and fruit flies which is called Cuckoo Search (CS).

One of the other improved algorithms which is used in this paper was produced in 2009 by Łukasik and Zak [19] that focused on the characteristics of fireflies and introduced an improved concept of the firefly algorithm (FA) which was strong for constraint continuous optimization tasks. Their improved method was inspired by imitating social behavior of fireflies and the phenomenon of bioluminescent communication [20].

In this paper entropy generation and power output of air standard Atkinson cycle will be analyzed in different situations as a multiobjective problem using MSB algorithm. It will be proved that different types of constraints should be considered to derive to an acceptable engineering solution. Besides, the performance of proposed algorithm will be compared to some other well-known optimization techniques

such as Karaboga's original ABC [21, 22], bees algorithm (BA) [23, 24], improved particle swarm optimization (IPSO) [17], Lukasik fire fly algorithm (LFFA), and self-adaptive penalty function genetic algorithm (SAPF-GA) [11, 12].

2. Bee Colony Optimization Strategies

Recently, many researchers focused on the interactive behavior of bees that occur through a waggle dance during the foraging process. Successful foragers share the information about the direction and the distance to patches of flower and the amount of nectar with their hive mates. Foragers can recruit other bees in their society to search in productive locations for collecting nectars with higher quality. These procedures suggest a successful data mining mechanism.

For the first time Seeley proposed a behavioral model for a colony of honey bees [25]. According to his theory, foraging bees visiting patch of flowers and then return to the hive with their collected nectars. Responding to the quality of the nectar that had been collected, waggle dance take place on the floor where each individual forager can observe the dancing process. The foragers are capable to randomly select a dance to observe and follow the dancer to the flower patch and continuing these processes will lead the colony to optimal food (solution).

Thereafter, many researchers focused on the honey bee organism and several metaheuristics were proposed based on the peculiar intelligent behavior of honey bee swarms. Yonezawa and kikuchi proposed ecological algorithm (EA) which was focused on the description of the collective intelligence based on bees' behavior [26]. Sato and Hagiwara proposed bee system (BS) which was a modified version of genetic algorithm (GA) and reach some acceptable results in optimizing engineering problems [27]. Teodorovic proposed bee colony optimization (BCO) based on forward and backward pass to generate feasible solutions during the searching procedure [28]. In 2001 Abbas [29] inspired mating bee optimization (MBO) for propositional satisfiability problems. Karaboga [30] released the first version of artificial bee colony (ABC) which is one of the most applicable algorithms in numerical optimizing field. Yang [8] concentrated on the virtual bee algorithm (VBA) due to function optimizations with the application in engineering problems. Chong et al. inspired honey bee colony (HBC) for training artificial neural network and job shop scheduling problem [31]. In 2011, Stanarevic et al. [32] introduced a modified artificial bee colony algorithm utilizing smart bees in optimizing constraint problems and demonstrated that this algorithm has better performance for optimizing constraint problems than the Karaboga's artificial bee colony (ABC). There are many other methods in optimizing application that utilized bee's behavior in nature and each one have some advantages for peculiar type of problems.

3. The Mutable Smart Bee Algorithm

Many real-world optimization problems involve inequality and equality constraints. It is hard and also takes a long time to find a feasible solution in searching space which optimizes a constraint problem with traditional strategies. Since one of the crucial problems is to gain a feasible answer in the searching spans, different concepts proposed by researchers and a variety of methods implemented for different optimization situations [33]. Hillier [34] proposed a procedure to predict the chaotic constraints which called linear constraints. Seppälä [35] proposed a set of uniform constraints that replace a single chance constraint and he has also conclude that his method is more accurate, but less efficient than Hiller's procedure. After that, Seppälä and Orpana [36] examined the efficiency of the method which proposed by Seppälä. There are also many other methods and concepts proposed by different researchers for constraint optimization.

Recently, Stanarevic et al. [32] proposed a modified artificial bee colony algorithm (SB-ABC) based on Deb's rule [37] which is really efficient for optimizing the engineering problems that possessed different types of constraints. They improved the performance of artificial bee colony (ABC) algorithm by applying Deb's rule and also defining a penalty function in the structure of ABC algorithm. They also used smart bees in the searching space which were able to maintain their memory. Smart bees are able to compare the new candidate solution to the old one and choose the better one due to their greedy instinct. Results demonstrated that this concept is really useful for optimizing engineering problems with are often multimodal.

Here, we will analyze some features that make this algorithm really strong for optimizing multi-modal problems.

In classical ABC proposed by Karaboga and Basturk [38], the following equation was utilized to produce candidate solution in searching spans (by an employed bee or onlooker bee):

$$v_{ij} = \begin{cases} x_{ij} + \emptyset_{ij} * (x_{ij} - x_{kj}), & R_j < \text{MR} \\ x_{ij}, & \text{otherwise}, \end{cases} \quad (1)$$

where $k \in \{1,2,\ldots,\text{SN}\}$ is a randomly chosen index, x_{ij} is the variable j of the food source, x_k is a neighbor solution around i, R_j is a random number in the range $(0,1)$, and MR is a parameter, which control the modification of parameter x_{ij}. In Karaboga's algorithm, the variable in the candidate solution which exceeds from its spans, takes value of the upper bound or lower bound regarding to its exceeding position. It is obvious that this policy may cause a local convergence.

In SB-ABC algorithm a different style was used to modify the solution:

$$2 * \text{lb}_j - v_{ij}, \quad \text{if } v_{ij} < \text{lb}_j,$$
$$2 * \text{ub}_j - v_{ij}, \quad \text{if } v_{ij} > \text{ub}_j, \quad (2)$$
$$v_{ij}, \quad \text{otherwise},$$

where v_{ij} is the variable j of the candidate solution i and ub_j is the upper bound of variable j.

One of the other advantages in this method is hiring smart bees. These artificial insects can memorize the position

of the best food source and its quality which was found before and replace it to new candidate solution if the new solution is unfeasible or the new solution has a lower fitness than the best-saved solution in the SB memory.

Another important advantage of this method is the time duration for smart bee's data processing procedure. This feature will make the algorithm more durable when high amount of these artificial organisms being hired for searching the solution space. To overcome this problem, we utilized a low amount of smart bees in constraint searching space. Besides, we add a new mutation operator to SB-ABC for overcoming subsequence fast convergence. In each of the iterations, bees that exceed from a finite number of trials will be sent to a container and participate in mutation process based on their mutation probability. The results show that the global solution can be obtained faster and by adapting a dynamic mutation probability (P_m), due to the type of problem, the algorithm escape from local convergence conveniently. In the next parts, the efficient performance of proposed algorithm for optimizing a real life multimodal engineering problem will be shown more closely.

The pseudocode of MSB-ABC is given in the following:

(1) initialize the population of solutions x_{ij};

(2) evaluate the population;

(3) cycle = 1;

(4) repeat;

(5) produce new solutions (food source positions) ϑ_{ij} using (1) and evaluate them;

(6) if cycle $\neq$ 1 use smart bee;

(7) apply selection process based on Deb's method;

(8) calculate the probability values P_{ij} for the solutions x_{ij} using fitness of the solutions and the constraint violations (CV) by:

$$P_i : \begin{cases} 0.5 + \left(\dfrac{\text{fitness}_i}{\sum_{i=1}^{\text{SN}} \text{fitness}_i}\right) * 0.5, \\ \qquad \text{if solution is feasible} \\ \left(1 - \dfrac{\text{CV}}{\sum_{i=1}^{\text{SN}} \text{CV}}\right) * 0.5, \\ \qquad \text{if solution is infeasible}, \end{cases} \quad (3)$$

where CV is defined by:

$$\text{CV} = \sum_{j=1}^{q} g_j(x) + \sum_{j=q+1}^{m} h_j(x), \quad (1)'$$

(9) for each onlooker bee, produce a new solution ϑ_i by (1) in the neighborhood of the solution selected depending on P_i and evaluate it;

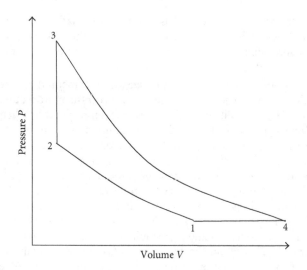

FIGURE 1: P-V diagram of the theoretical air standard Atkinson cycle.

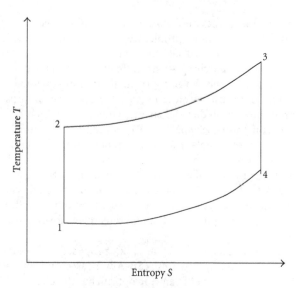

FIGURE 2: T-S diagram of theoretical air standard Atkinson cycle.

(10) apply selection process between ϑ_i and x_i based on Deb's method;

(11) determine the abandoned solutions (source), if exists, and perform mutation on each abandoned solution by following formula:

$$
v'_j : \begin{cases} \begin{cases} v_j + \Delta(t, \mathrm{ub}_j - v_j), \\ \text{or} \\ v_j - \Delta(t, v_j - \mathrm{lb}_j), \end{cases} & \text{rand} < P_m \\ v_j, & \text{rand} > P_m, \end{cases} \tag{4}
$$

where t is current generation number, P_m is mutation probability and $\Delta(t, y)$ is defined by: $\Delta(t, y) = yr(1 - (t/T))^b$; $b > 1$, T is maximum cycle;

(12) memorize the best food source position (solution) achieved so far;

(13) cycle = cycle + 1;

(14) until cycle = maximum cycle number.

4. Atkinson Engine

Here the performance of an air standard Atkinson cycle with heat-transfer loss, friction, and variable specific-heats of the working fluid will be analyzed precisely. According to (P-V) diagram in Figures 1 and 2, process (1-2) is an adiabatic (isentropic) compression then heat is added in process (2-3) at a constant volume. Process (3-4) is an adiabatic (isentropic) expansion, and the last process (4–1) is heat injection which takes place at constant pressure.

According to [39], assume that the specific heat ratio of the working fluid is a function of temperature, so the following linear equation can be considered:

$$
\gamma = \gamma_0 - k_1 T, \tag{5}
$$

where γ is the specific heat ratio and T is the absolute temperature.

It is assumed that air is an ideal gas that consists of 78.1% nitrogen, 20.95% oxygen, 0.92% argon, and 0.03% carbon dioxide.

Heat added to the working fluid in isochoric process $2 \rightarrow 3$ can be derived by:

$$
\begin{aligned}
Q_{\mathrm{in}} &= M \int_{T_2}^{T_3} C_v dT \\
&= M \int_{T_2}^{T_3} \frac{R}{\gamma_0 - k_1 T - 1} dT \\
&= \frac{MR}{k_1} \ln\left(\frac{\gamma_0 - k_1 T_2 - 1}{\gamma_0 - k_1 T_3 - 1} \right),
\end{aligned} \tag{6}
$$

where M is the molar number of the working fluid, R is molar gas constant, and C_v is molar specific heat at constant volume.

Heat rejected by the working fluid in isobaric process $4 \rightarrow 1$ is obtained by:

$$
\begin{aligned}
Q_{\mathrm{out}} &= M \int_{T_1}^{T_4} C_p dT \\
&= M \int_{T_1}^{T_4} \left(\frac{(\gamma_0 - k_1 T)R}{\gamma_0 - k_1 T - 1} \right) dT \\
&= MR \left[T_4 - T_1 + \frac{1}{k_1} \ln\left(\frac{\gamma_0 - k_1 T_1 - 1}{\gamma_0 - k_1 T_4 - 1} \right) \right],
\end{aligned} \tag{7}
$$

where C_p is molar specific heat at constant pressure.

According to [40, 41] the relation between parameters of a reversible adiabatic process with variable specific heat ratio can be considered by following equation:

$$
TV^{\gamma-1} = (T + dT)(V + dV)^{\gamma-1}. \tag{8}
$$

Respecting to (5) and (8), the following equation can be written:

$$T_i(\gamma_0 - k_1 T_j - 1) = T_j(\gamma_0 - k_1 T_i - 1)\left(\frac{V_j}{V_i}\right)^{\gamma_0 - 1}. \quad (9)$$

r_c and r_c^* were defined as specific compression ratio and compression ratio, respectively,

$$r_c = \frac{V_1}{V_2},$$

$$r_c^* = \frac{V_4}{V_2} = \frac{T_4}{T_1} r_c, \quad (10)$$

and two other processes (1-2) and (3-4) can be indicated, respectively, by the following equations:

$$T_1(\gamma_0 - k_1 T_2 - 1)(r_c)^{\gamma_0 - 1} = T_2(\gamma_0 - k_1 T_1 - 1), \quad (11)$$

$$T_3(\gamma_0 - k_1 T_4 - 1) = T_4(\gamma_0 - k_1 T_3 - 1)\left(\frac{T_4}{T_1} r_c\right)^{\gamma_0 - 1}. \quad (12)$$

By combusting an amount of energy received by working fluid that is calculated by following linear equation:

$$Q_{\text{in}} = M[A - B(T_2 + T_3)], \quad (13)$$

where A and B are two constant parameters which they relate to heat transfer and combustion that are function of engine speed. One of the other important aspects of analyzing real cycles is facing with heat leakage loss through the cylinder walls which is proportional to average temperature of the both working fluid and the cylinder wall which can be calculated by following equation [40]:

$$Q_{\text{leak}} = MB(T_2 + T_3 - 2T_0). \quad (14)$$

The power output of the Atkinson cycle engine can be derived by the following equation:

$$\begin{aligned}\dot{W}_{\text{out}} &= \frac{d}{dt}(Q_{\text{in}} - Q_{\text{out}}) \\ &= \frac{MR}{k_1} \ln\left(\frac{(\gamma_0 - k_1 T_2 - 1)(\gamma_0 - k_1 T_3 - 1)}{(\gamma_0 - k_1 T_4 - 1)(\gamma_0 - k_1 T_1 - 1)}\right) \\ &\quad + MR(T_4 - T_1),\end{aligned} \quad (15)$$

where $\dot{W}_{\text{out}}$ represents the power output of cycle during the process.

Now the thermal efficiency of the Atkinson cycle engine can be expressed as following:

$$\eta_{\text{th}} = \frac{W_{\text{out}}}{Q_{\text{in}} - Q_{\text{leak}}}. \quad (16)$$

The amounts of r_c and T are depending on engine initial condition and can be supposed as given data. T_2 determined by (11), after that substituting (6) into (13) concludes T_3 and T_4 calculated by (12). Now these parameters can be placed into (15) and (16) for determining the output power and the thermal efficiency of the Atkinson cycle engine.

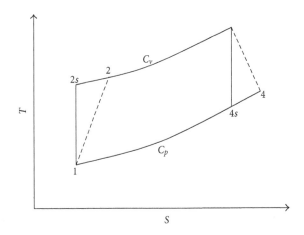

FIGURE 3: T-S diagram of real air standard Atkinson cycle.

After obtaining appropriate equations and data for calculating the power output of the Atkinson cycle, the relations between obtain parameters and entropy generation will be checked. Figure 2 does not represent the real indicated diagram of an internal combustion engine. For example, the actual cooling process between 4 and 1 cannot be compared with that of the theoretical cycle, because real engines are modeled as open systems where mass flows in and out of the system, which leads to a T-S diagram quite different from the theoretical one. Figure 3 indicates the different behavior of an ideal reversible and real irreversible Atkinson cycle.

Process $1 \to 2S$ is an ideal reversible adiabatic compression, while process $1 \to 2$ is an irreversible adiabatic process with high approximation to real compression process in cycle. Heat addition in $2 \to 3$ is an isochoric process. Process $3 \to 4S$ is an ideal reversible adiabatic expansion while process $3 \to 4$ is an irreversible adiabatic process with high approximation to real expansion process in cycle. Heat reject in $4 \to 1$ is an isobaric process.

As it is shown in Figure 3 in real Atkinson cycles, some amount of unexpected entropy generation must be considered. Here we consider two heat transfer units of the hot-and-cold side heat exchangers, ($N_H = N_L = 2$) due to the product of heat-transfer coefficient (α) and heat transfer surface area (F) [42].

And the effectiveness of the hot-and-cold side heat exchangers can be written as following:

$$E_H = 1 - \exp(-N_H),$$

$$E_l = 1 - \exp(-N_l). \quad (17)$$

According to [42] the entropy generation rate for the Atkinson cycle is equal to:

$$\begin{aligned}\sigma &= \frac{Q_L}{T_L} - \frac{Q_H}{T_H} \\ &= m\left[\frac{C_p E_l(G-1)}{1-(1-E_l)G} - \frac{C_v E_H(T_H - T_2)}{T_H + C_i(T_L/T_H)(T_H - T_2)^2}\right],\end{aligned} \quad (18)$$

where G can be written:

$$G = \left(\frac{(1 - E_H)T_2 + E_H T_H}{T_2} \right)^{C_v/C_p}. \quad (19)$$

5. Optimization Process

As it was mentioned before, we have to minimize the unexpected entropy generation and maximize the power output to obtain an efficient performance of the Atkinson cycle. In order to achieve a suitable engineering solution for optimizing the cycle under different situations, we have to face different types of constraints, and under these constraints in searching space it will be harder to find the feasible solution. In this section the efficiency of the Atkinson cycle will be checked using proposed mutable smart bee (MSB-ABC) algorithm and compared to different methods of optimizing and the results will be shown in tables at the end.

The objective functions are defined as following:

$$\dot{W}_{\text{out}} = f(T_1, T_2, T_3, T_4, \gamma_0),$$
$$\sigma = h(T_1, T_2, T_3, E_L, E_H). \quad (20)$$

And signalized objective function can be considered using following approach:

$$\text{Objective function} = \sum_{i=1}^{n} \alpha_i f_i, \quad (21)$$

where α is the weighted coefficient and show the value of a function comparing to another objective functions and $\sum_{i=1}^{n} \alpha_i = 1$.

In this work, $\alpha_1 = 0.6$ for power output and $\alpha_2 = 0.4$ for entropy generation are considered for finding a suitable engineering solution.

Due to (21) the single-objective function will be derived:

$$\text{Objective} = \text{Min}\left\{ \alpha_1 \sigma + \alpha_2 \frac{1}{\dot{W}_{\text{out}}} + \sum_{j=1}^{q} \lambda_j g_j(x) \right\}, \quad (22)$$

where σ is the total entropy generation and $\dot{W}_{\text{out}}$ is the power output of the Atkinson cycle, and according to (1)$'$, $\sum_{j=1}^{q} g_j(x)$ shows the sum of governing constraints which represents the constraint violence (CV) and λ_j indicates the impact of each constraint. These finite numbers of

constraints have been set as following in order to lead the algorithm to a make feasible decision in the searching space:

$C_1: T_2 > T_1 \longrightarrow g_1 = T_1 - T_{2s}$,

$C_{2,3}: T_2, T_{2s} < T_3 \longrightarrow g_2 = T_2 - T_3; \ g_3 = T_{2s} - T_3$,

$C_{4,5}: T_4, T_{4s} > T_1 \longrightarrow g_4 = T_1 - T_4; \ g_5 = T_1 - T_{4s}$,

$C_{6,7}: T_4, T_{4s} < T_2, T_{2s} \longrightarrow g_6 = T_4 - T_2; \ g_7 = T_{4s} - T_{2s}$,

$C_8: T_2 - T_4 > 200 \longrightarrow g_8 = 200 - T_2 + T_4$,

$C_9: T_4 - T_1 < 30 \longrightarrow g_9 = 30 + T_1 - T_4$,

$C_{10}: ||T_2 - T_1| - |T_3 - T_4|| < 200$
$\longrightarrow g_{10} = ||T_2 - T_1| - |T_3 - T_4|| - 200$,

$C_{11}: \left| T_1(\gamma_0 - k_1 T_2 - 1)(r_c)^{\gamma_0 - 1} - T_2(\gamma_0 - k_1 T_1 - 1) \right|$
$\leq \varepsilon; \ \varepsilon = 0.001$
$\longrightarrow g_{11} = \left| T_1(\gamma_0 - k_1 T_2 - 1)(r_c)^{\gamma_0 - 1} \right.$
$\left. - T_2(\gamma_0 - k_1 T_1 - 1) \right| - \varepsilon$,

$C_{12}: \left| \left(\frac{\text{MR}}{k_1} \ln\left(\frac{\gamma_0 - k_1 T_2 - 1}{\gamma_0 - k_1 T_3 - 1} \right) \right) - M[A - B(T_2 + T_3)] \right|$
$\leq \varepsilon; \varepsilon = 0.001$
$\longrightarrow g_{12} = \left| \left(\frac{\text{MR}}{k_1} \ln\left(\frac{\gamma_0 - k_1 T_2 - 1}{\gamma_0 - k_1 T_3 - 1} \right) \right) \right.$
$\left. - M[A - B(T_2 + T_3)] \right| - \varepsilon$,

$C_{13}: \left| T_3(\gamma_0 - k_1 T_4 - 1) - T_4(\gamma_0 - k_1 T_3 - 1)\left(\frac{T_4}{T_1} r_c \right)^{\gamma_0 - 1} \right|$
$\leq \varepsilon; \varepsilon = 0.001$
$\longrightarrow g_{13} = \left| T_3(\gamma_0 - k_1 T_4 - 1) - T_4(\gamma_0 - k_1 T_3 - 1) \right.$
$\left. \times \left(\frac{T_4}{T_1} r_c \right)^{\gamma_0 - 1} \right| - \varepsilon$,

$C_{14}: \dot{W}_{\text{out}} \geq 0 \longleftrightarrow E_{14}:$
if $\{\exists i \mid (\dot{W}_{\text{out}})_i \in (-\infty, 0) \longrightarrow \text{execute the solution}(i)\}$,

$C_{15}: \sigma \geq 0 \longleftrightarrow E_{15}:$
if $\{\exists i \mid (\sigma)_i \in (-\infty, 0) \longrightarrow \text{execute the solution}(i)\}$, $\quad (23)$

where $300 < T_1 < 380$, $1000 < T_2 < 1450$, $1500 < T_3 < 2200$, and $400 < T_4 < 900$. According to [29] the following constants and ranges are set for the analyzing process:

$$T_1 = 360\,\text{k}, \quad A = 60000\,\text{J} \cdot \text{mol}^{-1}, \quad 1.31 < \gamma_0 < 1.41. \quad (24)$$

Once the constraints and the equations are obtained, the essentials for the optimizing withthe mutable smart bee

TABLE 1: Performance of tested algorithm in $\gamma_0 = 1.31$ and $k_1 = 0.00006$.

	Parameters				Entropy generation	Power output	CPU time
	T_1	T_2	T_3	T_4	σ	$\dot{W}$	t (sec)
MSB-ABC	360	1023	2015	755.8	0.0008	0.3912	5.2
ABC	360	1030	2019	701.4	0.0015	0.2331	16.7
BA	360	1029	2081	737.0	0.0011	0.2054	18.4
IPSO	360	1036	2043	799.8	0.0012	0.2759	12.7
LFFA	360	1039	2016	789.3	0.0013	0.2690	12.3
SAPF-GA	360	1041	2090	699.2	0.0009	0.3759	22.2
Optimum performance reported in [40, 42]					0.0012	0.3112	—

algorithm are prepared. This method will find a suitable answer that is enabling to satisfy all of the constraints. Like any other evolutionary computation methods, the answer which is found by mutable smart bee algorithm is not the definite best answer; actually there are slight differences between them. These differences are usually acceptable and in engineering applications these small differences can be disregarded, Moreover in practical works these answers provide a better performance for the systems comparing to answers which are concluding from experimental works.

The difference between the algorithm answer and the real answer can be extended by finding the local optimization instead of global optimization. For avoiding this matter a suitable probability of mutation is necessary. Indeed mutation it can developed the search space for finding the answer and avoid local optimization. Although mutation is necessary to find a global optimization and seek a wide variety of answers but in latest generations can be reduce the convergence rate. Thus, as the algorithm go ahead, the mutation probability should be decreased for a better convergence in answers. A suitable mutation probability is effective on the speed of the algorithm. All the topics that were mentioned in precede will be shown later. Note that all of algorithms and programs are implemented in Matlab software with a computer with 2.21 GHZ and with 1.00 GB RAM memory.

As an initial setting for running mutable smart bee algorithm, the following values for the basic algorithm parameters were selected: maximum cycle number = 2000, number of colony size (NP) = 8, limit = 10, solution number (SN) = NP/2, the modification rate (MR) = 0.8, and P_m = 0.02. As expressed before one of the important advantage of this algorithm comparing to other heuristic algorithm is hiring low amount of population (10 bees in our case) for performing search in the area and also this feature leads the algorithm to perform faster and consuming lower cost.

For bee algorithm (BA) following parameters being set: number of scout bees in hive (n) = 30, number of elite patches (e) = 3, number of best sites (m) = 10, number of bees around elite sites (nep) = 11, number of bees around best sites (nsp) = 7, and neighborhood of sites which scout bees can search (ngh) which experiments show that BA have better performance in searching the local spaces when ngh = (ub − lb)/11.

For Lukasik firefly algorithm the parameters set due to [20] and also for improved particle swarm optimization

algorithms the parameters being set respecting to Bae et al. [43] researches which proved that perform are acceptable in mining data in constraint spaces.

Initial parameters for self-adaptive penalty function genetic algorithm set as P_c = .8, and tunable P_m = 0.04 decrease to 0.02, and the algorithm being implemented with respect to Tessema's method [11] in Matlab.

Arithmetic experiments were repeated 30 times, starting from a random population with different seeds [38]. Also behavior of the cycle has been analyzed in three different states of constant k_1 and γ_0 to find out the effect of these terms on the power output and entropy generation by bee algorithm (BA), improved particle swarm optimization (IPSO), Lukasik firefly algorithm (LFFA), classical artificial bee colony (ABC), and self-adaptive penalty function genetic algorithm (SAPF-GA) for making a compromise.

At the first step the performance of the Atkinson cycle analyzed in $\gamma_0 = 1.31$ and $k_1 = 0.00006$ and the results are shown in Table 1.

It is obvious that the proposed algorithm performs better than others and in some cases we find self-adaptive penalty function genetic algorithm (SAPF-GA) as well as proposed MSB-ABC algorithm after 30 times running but this algorithm use more time (22.2 seconds) for reaching to optimum solution comparing to other algorithms because this algorithm hire more than 60 chromosomes for performing efficient search in constraint spaces. As the table shows the MSB-ABC algorithm reached to fitter maximum power output and lower entropy generated during the performance of the Atkinson cycle and also because of hiring just 8 bees for searching in the constraint area of our problem, it takes acceptable CPU time (just 5.2 seconds) for finding the optimal condition. IPSO and LFFA show similar results and also the results show that they consume equal CPU time. Karaboga's classical artificial bee colony find acceptable solution in this case but as it is shown it takes noticeable time for reaching to fit solution and this matter refers to hiring 30 bees in the searching space. Bee algorithm finds an acceptable amount of entropy generation but it was weak in finding optimum power output and it takes 18.4 seconds for optimizing process. At the end of the first step the power output of the Atkinson cycle and the performance of each algorithms are shown in the following plots and after that the convergence rate of each algorithm and the capability of each of them will be discussed briefly due to obtained plots.

TABLE 2: performance of tested algorithm in $\gamma_0 = 1.41$ and $k_1 = 0.00006$.

	Parameters				Entropy generation	Power output	CPU time
	T_1	T_2	T_3	T_4	σ	$\dot{W}$	t(sec)
MSB-ABC	360	954.9	2126.7	714.6	0.0013	0.3148	10.05
ABC	360	908.9	2067.0	721.6	0.0012	0.3009	15.30
BA	360	1007.6	2200.0	466.7	0.0019	0.2376	13.22
IPSO	360	974.3	2200.0	782.6	0.0017	0.2444	14.12
LFFA	360	991.9	2112.9	689.2	0.0012	0.3070	17.21
SAPF-GA	360	992.4	2008.1	699.1	0.0014	0.2912	44.09
Optimum performance reported in [40, 42]					0.0012	0.3327	—

TABLE 3: performance of tested algorithm in $\gamma_0 = 1.36$ and $k_1 = 0.00009$.

	Parameters				Entropy generation	Power output	CPU time
	T_1	T_2	T_3	T_4	σ	$\dot{W}$	t(sec)
MSB-ABC	360	1100.1	2200.0	779.4	0.0009	0.3253	11.05
ABC	360	1050.1	2138.2	726.5	0.0008	0.3848	17.34
BA	—	—	—	—	—	—	—
IPSO	360	1323.2	2090.1	703.1	0.0015	0.3155	15.01
LFFA	360	1125.7	1823.9	630.0	0.0012	0.2889	14.32
SAPF-GA	360	1253.7	1902.8	570.3	0.0010	0.2773	44.72
Optimum performance reported in [40, 42]					0.0012	0.3202	—

In the first step the performance of each algorithm for finding the maximum power output will be analyzed and the maximum power out will be shown in Figure 4. As it is shown in Table 1 and Figure 4 MSB-ABC and SAPF-GA find more optimum results and IPSO and LFFA act similar; also artificial bee colony (ABC) and bee algorithm (BA) show acceptable results.

In Figure 5, the performance of each algorithm is shown during the iterations. According to results MSB-ABC show better performance in this case and also it escapes from restricted area faster than other algorithms. The capability of each algorithm for escaping from unfeasible regions is shown in Figure 6.

The results indicate that MSB-ABC and SAPF-GA are more capable to escape from constraints and also BA and ABC have lower performance to escape from restricted area and spend more time for this process. L-FFA and I-PSO are very similar in beating the tricks both in quality and duration. According to initial setting of the parameters it seems that MSB-ABC must try harder than other algorithms to escape from local convergence because of its low amount of initial searcher agents, but when we set a fit mutation probability and limit, MSB-ABC performs really efficient for escaping from unfeasible region.

Also the performance of the Atkinson cycle will be shown in different compression ratios in Figures 7 and 8 and it will be indicated that in three states of γ_0 and k_1 the algorithms found fitter power output comparing to experimental data in [39]. As it is shown in $\gamma_0 = 1.31$ and $k_1 = 0.00009$, the Atkinson cycle produces maximum power output. According to Tables 2 and 3, it is obvious that the power output

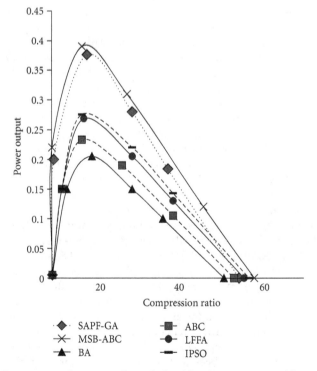

FIGURE 4: Performance of tested algorithm in $\gamma_0 = 1.31$ and $k_1 = 0.00006$.

will rise when the constant γ_0 reduced and the constant k_1 increased.

In the next step, the performance of the Atkinson cycle will be analyzed under $\gamma_0 = 1.36$ and $k_1 = 0.00006$ and the results are shown in Table 4.

TABLE 4: Performance of tested algorithm in $\gamma_0 = 1.36$ and $k_1 = 0.00006$.

	Parameters				Entropy generation	Power output	CPU time
	T_1	T_2	T_3	T_4	σ	$\dot{W}$	$t(\text{sec})$
MSB-ABC	360	953.4	2137.6	751.8	0.0012	0.3740	12.88
ABC	360	881.9	2052.1	766.4	0.0015	0.3490	19.1
BA	360	1615.7	2200.0	481.7	0.0007	0.2052	15.2
IPSO	360	920.9	2052.5	741.1	0.0014	0.3464	22.3
LFFA	360	903.8	2095.8	757.7	0.0012	0.3368	21.9
SAPF-GA	360	892.5	2142.8	792.5	0.0016	0.3584	34.2
Optimum performance reported in [40, 42]					0.0012	0.3165	—

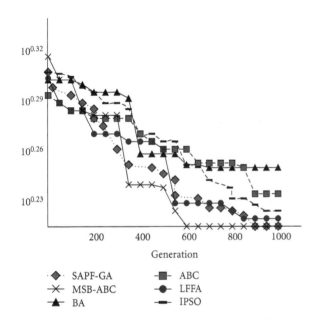

FIGURE 5: Comparison of performance of SPFA-GA, L-FFA, I-PSO, BA, ABC, and MSB-ABC in efficiency analyzing of the Atkinson cycle.

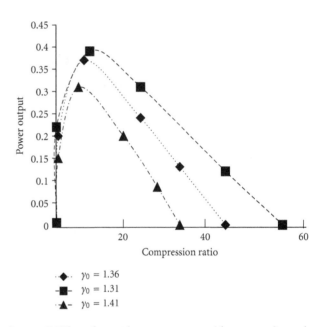

FIGURE 7: Effect of γ_0 on the power output with compression ratio.

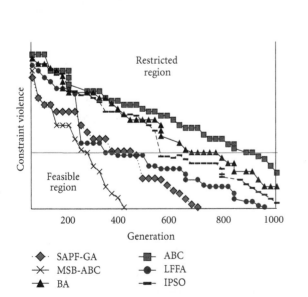

FIGURE 6: Compression of capability of algorithms to escape from restricted area.

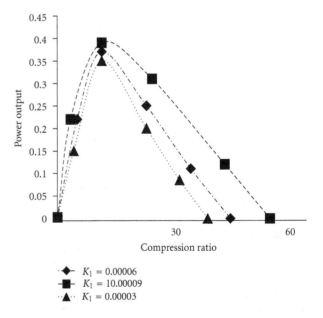

FIGURE 8: Effect of K_1 on the power output with compression ratio.

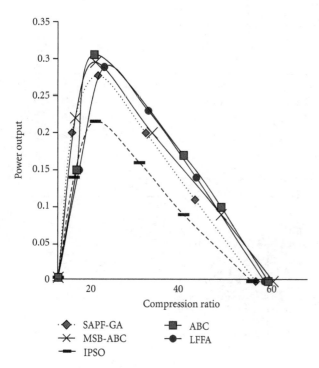

FIGURE 9: Performance of tested algorithm in $\gamma_0 = 1.36$ and $k_1 = 0.00009$.

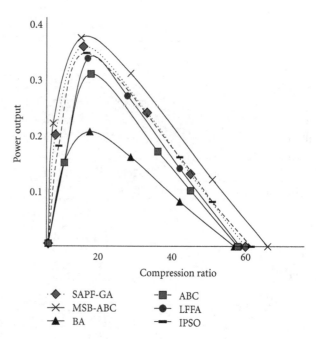

FIGURE 11: Performance of tested algorithm in $\gamma_0 = 1.36$ and $k_1 = 0.00006$.

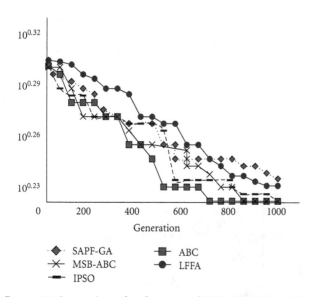

FIGURE 10: Comparison of performance of SPFA-GA, L-FFA, I-PSO, ABC, and MSB-ABC in efficiency analyzing of the Atkinson cycle.

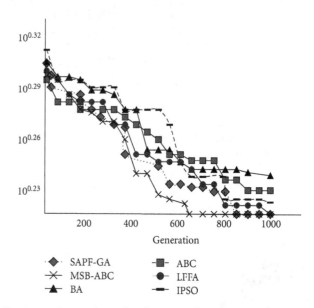

FIGURE 12: Comparison of performance of SPFA-GA, L-FFA, I-PSO, BA, ABC, and MSB-ABC in efficiency analyzing of the Atkinson cycle.

Again the MSB-ABC shows promising results. The time duration for finding optimal solution is acceptable and also it finds better power output. This time bees algorithm (BA) finds the minimum entropy generation rate, but it was not successful in finding maximum power output. SAPF-GA finds near optimal solution but it performs weaker than other algorithms. In fact it reaches to a local optimum solution. Figure 11 shows the performance of the Atkinson cycle and Figure 12 shows the performance of these algorithms in a semilogical plot.

According to Figures 9 and 10, proposed modified algorithm performs more efficiently than other algorithms in most cases. Besides, smart bees are capable to escape from various constraints in a short time, where other algorithms use more time for escaping from all constraints. One of the other important advantages of proposed algorithm is its ability to work with a low population size. This feature makes this algorithm really faster than other algorithms. In addition, mutation phase helps smart bees to escape from local optimums.

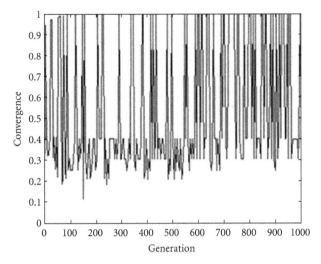

FIGURE 13: Convergence rate of MSB-ABC in the first step.

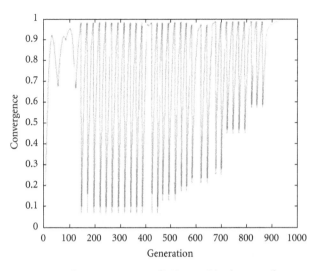

FIGURE 14: Convergence rate of MSB-ABC in the second step.

For the last case, the performance of the Atkinson cycle will be checked in $K = 0.00003$ and $\lambda = 1.36$ and the results will be shown in Table 5.

As it is shown, the Bee Algorithm find lower entropy generation, however, it does not find an acceptable power output. LFFA and MSB-ABC perform promising both in maximizing power output and minimizing the unexpected amount of entropy generation. MSB-ABC consumes lower CPU time to find the optimal solution and this feature leads the MSB-ABC algorithm to perform as s superior algorithm in this case.

6. Analyzing Convergence Rate

One of the other important aspects that prove the advantage of MSB-ABC algorithm is the capability of this algorithm to escape from local optimal values. This claim will be demonstrated in the following plots which indicate the rate of convergence for algorithms during the optimizing process.

For analyzing the convergence ratio of these algorithms this parameter should be defined as:

$$\text{Mean cost} = \frac{\sum_{i=1}^{\text{popsize}} \text{cost}(i)}{\text{popsize}},$$

$$\text{Best cost} = \text{Min}\{\text{cost}\}, \qquad (25)$$

$$\text{Convergence rate} = \frac{\text{best cost}}{\text{Mean cost}}.$$

In the first step the convergence rate of the proposed algorithm will be analyzed under $P_m = 0.08$ and limit = 7 during the optimizing process.

Figure 13 reveals that the algorithm's convergence rate changes very fast and it does not have enough time to perform an acceptable neighbor search during the process.

For that we tune the mutation probability as following:

$$P_m = P'_m - K_{P_m}\frac{t}{T}, \qquad (26)$$

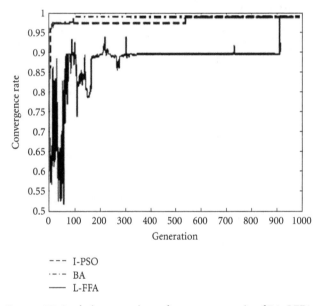

- - - I-PSO
- · - · BA
——— L-FFA

FIGURE 15: Analytic comparison of convergence ratio of BA, LFFA, and IPSO.

where $P'_m = 0.05$, K_{P_m} is a constant number that control P_m, t is current iteration, and T is maximum iteration.

According to Figure 14, the results are acceptable in this case. As it is shown, in the initial iterations, algorithm searches a wide space for finding better regions (food patches) and then it concentrates on neighbor search to reach to the bottom of the valley (global minimum).

At the end the convergence rate of BA, L-FFA, and I-PSO are shown (Figure 15) for make a contrast.

According to the results it is obvious that when we use adaptive parameters, MSB-ABC shows better reaction for escaping from local optimum regions comparing to other algorithms. It seems that bee algorithm (BA) suffers from fast local optimum convergence during optimizing process and again L-FFA and I-PSO have similar behavior. The obtained

TABLE 5: Performance of tested algorithm in $\gamma_0 = 1.36$ and $k_1 = 0.00003$.

	Parameters				Entropy generation	Power output	CPU time
	T_1	T_2	T_3	T_4	σ	$\dot{W}$	t(sec)
MSB-ABC	360	992.3	1889.3	831.1	0.0012	0.3572	10.05
ABC	360	1987.6	1984.8	612.3	0.0009	0.2368	16.23
BA	360	1002.2	1760.5	566.0	**0.0008**	**0.2067**	8.05
IPSO	360	959.9	1730.9	698.9	0.0013	0.3069	12.41
LFFA	360	864.8	2200.0	764.8	0.0014	0.3489	12.79
SAPF-GA	360	1199.5	2112.1	618.3	0.0012	0.3262	35.23
Optimum performance reported in [40, 42]					0.0012	0.3148	—

results demonstrate that MSB-ABC algorithm is one of the most applicable algorithms for optimizing multimodal problems since it is capable to balance the intensive local search strategy and an efficient exploration of the whole search space simultaneously.

7. Conclusions

In this paper, a new method called MSB algorithm proposed for optimizing a well-known multimodal engineering problem, based on the reaction of mutable smart bees during the procedure. Thereafter, proposed algorithm has been compared with some famous optimization methods such as self-adapting penalty function genetic algorithms and improved particle swarm optimization. The results illustrate that MSB algorithm is superior or equal to these existing algorithms for optimizing multimodal problems in most cases. This issue refers to the fine tuning of the parameters that may results efficient searching in feasible space. Furthermore, our simulations indicate that because of adaptive mutation that occurs in smart bee, the algorithm has a suitable convergence rate that leads the algorithm to escape from local optimum solution. Subsequently, it seems that MSB algorithm is more generic and robust for many constraint optimization problems, comparing to other metaheuristic algorithms.

Nomenclature

C_P: Isobaric molar specific heat (kJ/kg K)
C_v: Isochoric specific heat(kJ/kg K)
E_H: Effectiveness of hot heat exchanger
E_L: Effectiveness of cold heat exchanger
F: Heat transfer surface area (m^2)
M: Molar mass of working fluid (kg/mol)
Q_{in}: Heat added to working fluid (kW)
Q_{leak}: Heat leakage (kW)
Q_{out}: Heat rejected from working fluid (kW)
R: Molar gas constant
r_C: Specific compression ratio
r_C^*: Compression ratio
V_1: Volume in state one (m^3)
V_2: Volume in state two (m^3)
V_3: Volume in state three (m^3)
V_4: Volume in state four (m^3)
$\dot{W}$: Output power (kW).

Greek Symbols

γ: Specific heat ratio
α: Heat transfer coefficient (kW/Km^2)
η_{th}: Thermal efficiency
σ: Entropy generation of the cycle.

Acknowledgments

The authors would like to thank S. Noudeh and P. Samadian for their precious collaboration.

References

[1] C. Lyle Cummins, *Internal Fire: The Internal-Combustion Engine 1673–1900*, Carnot Press, Wilsonville, Ore, USA, 2000.

[2] H. S. Leff, "Thermal efficiency at maximum power output: new results for old heat engine," *American Journal of Physics*, vol. 55, pp. 602–610, 1987.

[3] A. Al-Sarkhi, B. A. Akash, J. O. Jaber, M. S. Mohsen, and E. Abu-Nada, "Efficiency of miller engine at maximum power density," *International Communications in Heat and Mass Transfer*, vol. 29, no. 8, pp. 1159–1167, 2002.

[4] P. Y. Wang and S. S. Hou, "Performance analysis and comparison of an Atkinson cycle coupled to variable temperature heat reservoirs under maximum power and maximum power density conditions," *Energy Conversion and Management*, vol. 46, no. 15-16, pp. 2637–2655, 2005.

[5] S. S. Hou, "Comparison of performances of air standard Atkinson and Otto cycles with heat transfer considerations," *Energy Conversion and Management*, vol. 48, no. 5, pp. 1683–1690, 2007.

[6] J. Dréo, P. Siarry, A. Pétrowski, and E. Taillard, *Metaheuristics for Hard Optimization*, Springer, Heidelberg, Germany, 2006.

[7] Z. Michalewicz, "Heuristic methods for evolutionary computation techniques," *Journal of Heuristics*, vol. 1, no. 2, pp. 177–206, 1996.

[8] X. S. Yang, *Nature-Inspired Metaheuristic Algorithms*, Luniver Press, Beckington, UK, 2008.

[9] J. Holland, *Adaptation in Natural and Artificial Systems*, The University of Michigan Press, Ann Arbor, Mich, USA, 1975.

[10] L. Davis, *Handbook of Genetic Algorithms*, Van Nostrand Reinhold, New York, NY, USA, 1991.

[11] B. Tessema and G. G. Yen, "A self adaptive penalty function based algorithm for performing constrained optimization," in *Proceedings of the IEEE Congress on Evolutionary Computation*, G. G. Yen and M. Simon, Eds., pp. 246–253, IEEE Publications, Vancouver, Canada, 2006.

[12] A. C. C. Lemonge and H. J. C. Barbosa, "An adaptive penalty scheme in genetic algorithms for constrained optimization problems," in *Proceedings of the Genetic and Evolutionary Computation Conference*, G. Paun, Ed., pp. 287–294, ACM Press, New York, NY, USA, 2002.

[13] S. M. Saab, N. Kamel, T. El-Omari, and H. Owaied, "Developing optimization algorithm using artificial Bee Colony system," *Ubiquitous Computing and Communication Journal*, vol. 4, pp. 391–396, 2009.

[14] M. Dorigo, V. Maniezzo, and A. Colorni, "The ant system: optimization by a colony of cooperating agents," in *Transactions on Systems Man and Cybernetics*, W. Pedrycz, Ed., pp. 29–41, IEEE Publications, Alberta, Canada, 1996.

[15] J. Kennedy and R. C. Eberhart, "Particle swarm optimization," in *Proceedings of the IEEE International Conference on Neural Networks*, L. M. LeCam and J. Neyman, Eds., pp. 1942–1948, IEEE Publications, Piscataway, NJ, USA, 1995.

[16] J. Kennedy, "Minds and cultures: particle swarm implications, Socially Intelligent Agents," *Ubiquitous Computing and Communication Journal*, vol. 23, pp. 67–72, 1997.

[17] Y.-P. Bu, Z. Wei, and J.-S. You, "An improved PSO algorithm and its application to grid scheduling problem," in *Proceedings of the International Symposium on Computer Science and Computational Technology (ISCSCT '08)*, pp. 352–355, IEEE, 2008.

[18] X. S. Yang and S. Deb, "Cuckoo search via Levy flights," in *Proceedings of the World Congress on Nature & Biologically Inspired Computing (NaBIC '09)*, F. Rothlauf, Ed., pp. 210–214, IEEE Publications, India, December 2009.

[19] S. Łukasik and S. Zak, "Firefly algorithm for continuous constrained optimization tasks," in *Proceedings of the International Conference on Computer and Computational Intelligence*, N. T. Nguyen, R. Kowalczyk, and S. M. Chen, Eds., vol. 5796 of *Lecture Notes in Computer Science*, pp. 97–106, Springer, Wrocław, Poland, 2009.

[20] X.-S. Yang, "Firefly algorithms for multimodal optimization," in *Proceedings of the Stochastic Algorithms: Foundations and Applications*, vol. 5792 of *Lecture Notes in Computer Science*, pp. 169–178, Springer, Sapporo, Japan, 2009.

[21] D. Karaboga and B. Basturk, "A powerful and efficient algorithm for numerical function optimization: artificial Bee Colony (ABC) algorithm," *Journal of Global Optimization*, vol. 39, no. 3, pp. 459–471, 2007.

[22] D. Karaboga and B. Basturk, "On the performance of artificial bee colony (ABC) algorithm," *Applied Soft Computing Journal*, vol. 8, no. 1, pp. 687–697, 2008.

[23] S. Camazine and J. Sneyd, "A model of collective nectar source selection by honey bees: self-organization through simple rules," *Journal of Theoretical Biology*, vol. 149, no. 4, pp. 547–571, 1991.

[24] D. T. Pham, A. Ghanbarzadeh, E. Koc, S. Otri, S Rahim, and M. Zaidi, "The bees algorithm," Technical Note, Manufacturing Engineering Centre, Cardiff University, UK, 2005.

[25] T. D. Seeley, *The Wisdom of the Hive: The Social Physiology of Honey Bee Colonies*, Harvard University Press , 1996.

[26] Y. Yonezawa and T. Kikuchi, "Ecological algorithm for optimal ordering used by collective honey bee behavior," in *Proceedings of the 7th International Symposium on Micro Machine and Human Science*, pp. 249–256, Nagoya, Japan, 1996.

[27] T. Sato and M. Hagiwara, "Bee system: finding solution by a concentrated search," in *Proceedings of the IEEE International Conference on Systems, Man and Cybernetics*, vol. 4, pp. 3954–3959, Orlando, Fla, USA, 1997.

[28] D. Teodorovic, *Bee Colony Optimization (BCO)*, Ministry of Science of Serbia, Belgrade, Serbia, 2001.

[29] H. A. Abbass, "Marriage in honey bee optimization (MBO): a haplometrosis polygynous swarming approach," in *Proceedings of the IEEE Conference on Evolutionary Computation (ICEC '01)*, vol. 1, pp. 207–214, IEEE Publications, Seoul, Korea, 2001.

[30] D. Karaboga, *An Idea Based on Honey Bee Swarm for Numerical Optimization*, Erciyes Universitey, Kayseri, Turkey, 2005.

[31] C. S. Chong, M. Y. H. Low, A. I. Sivakumar, and K. L. Gay, "A Bee Colony Optimization Algorithm to job shop scheduling simulation," in *Proceedings of the Winter Conference*, L. F. Perrone, F. P. Wieland, J. Liu, B. G. Lawson, D. M. Nichol, and R. M. Fujimoto, Eds., pp. 1954–1961, Washington, DC, USA, 2006.

[32] N. Stanarevic, M. Tuba, and N. Bacanin, "Modified Artificial Bee Colony algorithm for constrained problems optimization," *International Journal of Mathematical Models and Methods in Applied Sciences*, vol. 5, no. 3, pp. 644–651, 2011.

[33] S. E. Elmaghraby, H. Soewandi, and M. J. Yao, "Chance-constrained programming in activity networks: a critical evaluation," *European Journal of Operational Research*, vol. 131, no. 2, pp. 440–458, 2001.

[34] F. Hillier, "Chance-constrained programming with 0-1 or bounded continuous decision variables," *Journal of Management Science*, vol. 14, pp. 34–57, 1967.

[35] Y. Seppala, "Constructing sets of uniformly tighter linear approxima-tions for a chance-constraint," *Journal of Management Science*, vol. 17, pp. 736–749, 1971.

[36] Y. Seppälä and T. Orpana, "Experimental study on the efficiency and accuracy of a chance-constrained programming algorithm," *European Journal of Operational Research*, vol. 16, no. 3, pp. 345–357, 1984.

[37] K. Deb, "An efficient constraint handling method for genetic algorithms," *Computer Methods in Applied Mechanics and Engineering*, vol. 186, no. 2–4, pp. 311–338, 2000.

[38] D. Karaboga and B. Basturk, "Artificial Bee Colony (ABC) optimization algorithm for solving constrained optimization problems," in *Advances in Soft Computing: Foundations of Fuzzy Logic and Soft Computing*, C. Ozturk, Ed., pp. 789–798, Springer, Berlin, Germany, 2007.

[39] R. Ebrahimi, "Performance of an Endoreversible Atkinson cycle with variable specific heat ratio of working fluid," *American Journal of Science*, vol. 6, pp. 12–17, 2010.

[40] Y. Ge, L. Chen, and F. Sun, "Finite time thermodynamic modeling and analysis for an irreversible atkinson cycle," *Thermal Science*, vol. 14, no. 4, pp. 887–896, 2010.

[41] A. Al-Sarkhi, B. Akash, E. Abu-Nada, and I. Al-Hinti, "Efficiency of atkinson engine at maximum power density using temperature dependent specific heats," *Jordan Journal of Mechanical and Industrial Engineering*, vol. 2, pp. 71–75, 2005.

[42] C. Lingen, Z. Wanli, and S. Fenguri, "Power, efficiency, entropy-generation rate and ecological optimization for a class of generalized irreversible universal heat-engine cycles," *Applied Energy*, vol. 84, no. 5, pp. 512–525, 2007.

[43] J. Bae J, P. Y. Won, J. J. Rin, and K. Y. S. Lee, "An improved particle swarm optimization for nonconvex economic dispatch problems," *IEEE*, vol. 25, pp. 156–166, 2010.

6

Asymmetrical Gating with Application on Maneuvering Target Tracking

Farzad Hashemzadeh

Faculty of Electrical Engineering, Sarab Islamic Azad University, Sarab 54716-376, Iran

Correspondence should be addressed to Farzad Hashemzadeh, farzad.hashemzadeh@ualberta.ca

Academic Editor: Anyong Qing

A new asymmetrical gate with application in target tracking is proposed. Proposed gate has asymmetric shape that has large probability of target detection in the gate and has more advantages compared with elliptical gate. The gate is defined as the region in which the tracked target is expected to exist and just observation vectors in the gate are used as target detection. An analytical method to compute optimal size of gate is proposed and recursive estimation of asymmetric parameters of gate are studied. Comparison between proposed gate and conventional elliptical gate showed the efficiency of the proposed method in maneuvering target tracking applications and simulation results showed the proficiency of the proposed method.

1. Introduction

Tracking is meant to be the estimation of the true values of specifications of target motion, such as the position and velocity, based on the n-dimensional observational vector by the sensors [1–3]. One-dimensional observation vectors are obtained in a direction-finding setup observing just the azimuth angle [4]. Two-dimensional observation vectors are obtained in optical sensors observing the azimuth angle and elevation angle, or in radars observing the range and azimuth angle. Historically, PDA (Probabilistic Data Association) [5], JPDA (Joint PDA) [6], and MHT (Multiple Hypothesis Tracking) [7–9] have drawn attention as target tracking methods in an environment in which false signals from objects other than the target such as clutter exist [10, 11]. In target tracking in such an environment, just the region is considered for each target in which the target is expected to exist at the next sampling time [12]. This region is called the gate. The observation data within the gate are used for tracking. Various gate shapes are conceivable, such as a rectangle, circle, and ellipse. However, it is not known which shape of gate is optimum. If the gate is enlarged, many observation vectors from clutter or objects other than the target fall within the gate, resulting in some difficulties in target tracking. On the other hand, if the gate is made smaller, there is a danger that the observation data from the target to be tracked may not fall within the gate. It is more desirable that the position of the observation vector detected from the target be closer to the center of the gate compared with location of the false signals in the gate [13]. A method of determining the in-gate probability has been proposed in [10].

In this paper, asymmetrical gaussian distribution is introduced. Cross-surface of asymmetrical gaussian distribution is considered as asymmetrical gate. Parameters of asymmetrical Gaussian distribution should be estimated to estimate parameters of asymmetrical gate. Kalman filter as a standard method to estimate parameters of symmetrical distribution is used to estimate parameters of asymmetrical distribution. Standard deviation of asymmetrical distribution in opposite to the movement direction is estimated using estimation of acceleration in movement direction in centric coordinate system. In this paper, analytical preference of asymmetrical gate compared with the elliptical gate is studied. In this analytical study, volumes of gates are considered as a comparison criteria subjected to the assumption that in-gate probability of distribution for both asymmetric and elliptical gates are equal.

In the following of this paper, Section 2 introduces asymmetrical gaussian distribution. Section 3 is about estimation of parameters of gate. In Section 4, analytical comparison between asymmetrical gate and elliptical gate is considered. In Section 5, optimal size of gate is calculated and in Section 6, preference of this new method is shown by simulation result.

2. Asymmetric Gaussian Gate

Maneuvering target that has nonzero acceleration in direction of movement could be modeled with almost-constant-acceleration target motion model in which process and measurement noise on direction of movement have asymmetric distribution and process and measurement noises on orthogonal to the movement direction have gaussian distribution.

In this paper, it is assumed that distribution of location of maneuvering target in the next time is asymmetric gaussian in centric coordinate system. Center of centric coordinate system is in the location of target and directions of axis of it are in the movement direction and orthogonal to the movement direction.

One-dimensional asymmetric Gaussian distribution in direction of movement is illustrated as follows:

$$f(x_t) = \begin{cases} \dfrac{1}{k} \exp\left(-\dfrac{1}{2}\dfrac{(x_t - m)^2}{\sigma_{x_1}^2}\right) & x_t > m, \\ \dfrac{1}{k} \exp\left(-\dfrac{1}{2}\dfrac{(x_t - m)^2}{\sigma_{x_2}^2}\right) & x_t < m, \end{cases} \tag{1}$$

where k is normalization factor and can be calculated as follow:

$$\begin{aligned} k &= \int_{-\infty}^{m} \exp\left(-\frac{1}{2}\frac{(x_t - m)^2}{\sigma_{x_1}^2}\right) + \int_{m}^{+\infty} \exp\left(-\frac{1}{2}\frac{(x_t - m)^2}{\sigma_{x_2}^2}\right) \\ &= \frac{\sqrt{2\pi\sigma_{x_1}^2}}{2} + \frac{\sqrt{2\pi\sigma_{x_2}^2}}{2} = \sqrt{2\pi}\left(\frac{\sigma_{x_1} + \sigma_{x_2}}{2}\right). \end{aligned} \tag{2}$$

In (2), σ_{x_1} and σ_{x_2} are standard deviation of distribution of x_t in positive and negative directions, respectively, and m is median of distribution of x_t.

Considering (2) and (1), one-dimensional asymmetric gaussian distribution of x_t can be achieved as follows:

$$\begin{aligned} &f(x_t) \\ &= \begin{cases} \dfrac{1}{\sqrt{2\pi}((\sigma_{x_1} + \sigma_{x_2})/2)} \exp\left(-\dfrac{1}{2}\dfrac{(x_t - m)^2}{\sigma_{x_1}^2}\right) & x_t > m, \\ \dfrac{1}{\sqrt{2\pi}((\sigma_{x_1} + \sigma_{x_2})/2)} \exp\left(-\dfrac{1}{2}\dfrac{(x_t - m)^2}{\sigma_{x_2}^2}\right) & x_t < m. \end{cases} \end{aligned} \tag{3}$$

For $x_t > m$, $f(x_t)$ is same as typical Gaussian distribution with standard deviation σ_{x_1} and for $x_t < m$, it is the same as typical Gaussian distribution with standard deviation σ_{x_2}.

If $\sigma_{x_1} = \sigma_{x_2}$, (3) is standard Gaussian distribution and if $\sigma_{x_1} \neq \sigma_{x_2}$, (3) is asymmetrical Gaussian distribution. It means

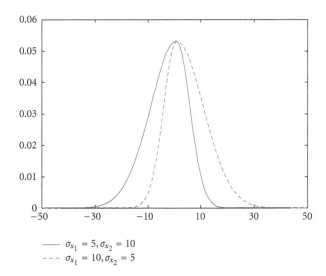

FIGURE 1: Distribution of $f(x_t)$ with zero mean and two variant variances.

that distribution is not symmetrical around median m, and dampings of distribution are different around of the median.

In Figure 1, distribution of $f(x_t)$ with zero median and two different standard deviations is shown.

It is assumed that Probability Distribution Function (PDF) of target in orthogonal to the direction of movement is zero mean gaussian with standard deviation as follows:

$$f(y_t) = \frac{1}{2\pi\sigma_y} \exp\left(-\frac{1}{2}\frac{(y_t)^2}{\sigma_y^2}\right). \tag{4}$$

In this paper, $z_t = [x_t\ y_t]^T$ is defined in centric coordinate system, in which x_t and y_t are measured values of target in centric coordinate system.

Probability distribution of z_t in centric coordinate system is illustrated as follows:

$$\begin{aligned} &f(x_t, y_t) \\ &= \begin{cases} \dfrac{1}{k} \exp\left(-\dfrac{1}{2}(z_t - m_z)\Sigma_1^{-1}(z_t - m_z)^T\right) & x_t > m, \\ \dfrac{1}{k} \exp\left(-\dfrac{1}{2}(z_t - m_z)\Sigma_2^{-1}(z_t - m_z)^T\right) & x_t < m, \end{cases} \end{aligned} \tag{5}$$

where

$$m_z = \begin{bmatrix} m & 0 \end{bmatrix}, \qquad \Sigma_1 = \begin{bmatrix} \sigma_{x_1}^2 & 0 \\ 0 & \sigma_y^2 \end{bmatrix}, \qquad \Sigma_2 = \begin{bmatrix} \sigma_{x_2}^2 & 0 \\ 0 & \sigma_y^2 \end{bmatrix}. \tag{6}$$

In (5), k is normalization factor and can be calculated as

$$
\begin{aligned}
k &= \int_{-\infty}^{m}\int_{-\infty}^{+\infty} \exp\left(-\frac{1}{2}\left(\frac{(x-m)^2}{\sigma_{x_2}^2}+\frac{y^2}{\sigma_y^2}\right)\right) dy\, dx \\
&\quad + \int_{m}^{+\infty}\int_{\infty}^{+\infty} \exp\left(-\frac{1}{2}\left(\frac{(x-m)^2}{\sigma_{x_1}^2}+\frac{y^2}{\sigma_y^2}\right)\right) dy\, dx \\
&= 2\pi\frac{\sigma_{x_1}\sigma_y}{2}+2\pi\frac{\sigma_{x_2}\sigma_y}{2} = 2\pi\sigma_y\left(\frac{\sigma_{x_1}+\sigma_{x_2}}{2}\right) \\
&= \pi\left|\Sigma_1^{1/2}+\Sigma_2^{1/2}\right|.
\end{aligned}
\tag{7}
$$

Considering (5) and (7), probability distribution of $f(x_t,y_t)$ in centric coordinate system can be achieved as follows:

$$
f(x_t,y_t)
$$
$$
=\begin{cases}
\dfrac{1}{2\pi\sigma_y((\sigma_{x_1}+\sigma_{x_2})/2)} \\
\quad \times \exp\left(-\dfrac{1}{2}(z_t-m_z)\Sigma_1^{-1}(z_t-m_z)^T\right) & x_t>m, \\[2ex]
\dfrac{1}{2\pi\sigma_y((\sigma_{x_1}+\sigma_{x_2})/2)} \\
\quad \times \exp\left(-\dfrac{1}{2}(z_t-m_z)\Sigma_2^{-1}(z_t-m_z)^T\right) & x_t<m.
\end{cases}
\tag{8}
$$

Probability distributions of $f(x_t,y_t)$ in (8) with surfaces of distribution are illustrated in Figure 2.

As it can be shown from Figures 2(a) and 2(b), with variation of ratio of σ_{x_1} and σ_{x_2}, it is easy to stretch distribution surface in movement direction or opposite of movement direction. Application of tuning of variances is that, for maneuvering targets that have positive or negative accelerations on direction of movement, it is possible to modify surface of distribution, optimally.

If maneuvering target has positive acceleration in direction of movement, it is better to select $\sigma_{x_1}>\sigma_{x_2}$ to stretch gate in positive direction of movement as Figure 2(a) and if maneuvering target has been negative acceleration in direction of movement, it is better to select $\sigma_{x_1}<\sigma_{x_2}$ to stretch gate in the negative direction of movement as Figure 2(b). Therefore, with appropriate choosing of σ_{x_1} and σ_{x_2}, it is possible to stretch the gate in direction that probability of target detection inside of the gate increases, whereas volume of gate remains constant.

3. Gate's Parameters Estimation

In this section, parameter estimation of target position distribution is considered. If process and measurement noise have Gaussian distribution, Kalman filter would be optimal recursive method to estimate parameters of distribution. Therefore, typical elliptical gate would be optimal tracking gate in such cases [14].

In this paper, maneuvering target with positive or negative acceleration in movement direction is considered.

Kalman filter as a standard recursively estimation method is used to recursively estimate of asymmetrical gate's parameters.

Let us assumed that parameters of asymmetrical gate on time $t-1$ are m_{t-1}, $\sigma_{x_1,t-1}$, $\sigma_{x_2,t-1}$, $\sigma_{y,t-1}$, θ_{t-1}, where m_{t-1} is center of gate, $\sigma_{x_1,t-1}$, $\sigma_{x_2,t-1}$ shows asymmetric stretching of gate in the direction of movement, $\sigma_{y,t-1}$ is the stretching parameter of gate in orthogonal to the movement direction and θ_{t-1} is rotation angle of centric coordinate system. The goal is to estimate parameters of gate at time t.

Using Kalman filter as a standard method in parameter estimation, median and covariance matrixes could be calculated as follows:

$$
\begin{aligned}
m_{t|t-1} &= Am_{t-1|t-1}, \\
\Sigma_{t|t-1} &= A\Sigma_{t-1|t-1}A^T + Q, \\
m_{t|t} &= m_{t|t-1} + K_t(z_t - Cm_{t|t-1}), \\
\Sigma_{t|t} &= \Sigma_{t|t-1} - K_tC\Sigma_{t|t-1}, \\
S_t &= C\Sigma_{t|t-1}C^T + R, \\
K_t &= \Sigma_{t|t-1}C^T S_t^{-1}.
\end{aligned}
\tag{9}
$$

Typical elliptical tracking gate at time t, could be formulated using median $m_{t|t}$ and innovation covariance S_t as follows:

$$
(z_t - m_{t|t})^T S_t^{-1}(z_t - m_{t|t}) \le \gamma,
\tag{10}
$$

where z is the validated measurement and γ is a parameter to adjust gate size.

Diagonal terms of innovation covariance S_t are diameters of elliptical gate which are standard deviations of gaussian distribution on centric coordinate system. Off-diagonal terms of S_t represent rotation angle of centric coordinate system.

Parameters of typical elliptical gate at time t are $\sigma_{x,t}$, $\sigma_{y,t}$ and θ_t.

In Figure 3, elliptical gate in x_1ox_1 is represented as $x^T\Sigma_2^{-1}x = 1$ and in X_1OX_1 is represented as $X^T\Sigma_1^{-1}X = 1$, where

$$
\Sigma_2 = \begin{bmatrix} \sigma_{x,t}^2 & 0 \\ 0 & \sigma_{y,t}^2 \end{bmatrix}, \quad \Sigma_1 = S_t,
$$
$$
X = \begin{bmatrix} X_1 & X_2 \end{bmatrix}^T, \quad x = \begin{bmatrix} x_1 & x_2 \end{bmatrix}^T.
\tag{11}
$$

Coordinate systems x_1ox_1 is transferred to the X_1OX_1 using simple transfer matrix T as follows:

$$
X = Tx \quad \text{where } T = \begin{bmatrix} \cos\theta & -\sin\theta \\ \sin\theta & \cos\theta \end{bmatrix}.
\tag{12}
$$

In the following, relation between parameters of Σ_2 and Σ_1 are shown:

$$
\begin{aligned}
x^T\Sigma_2^{-1}x &= X^T\Sigma_1^{-1}X, \\
\Sigma_2^{-1} &= T^T\Sigma_1^{-1}T.
\end{aligned}
\tag{13}
$$

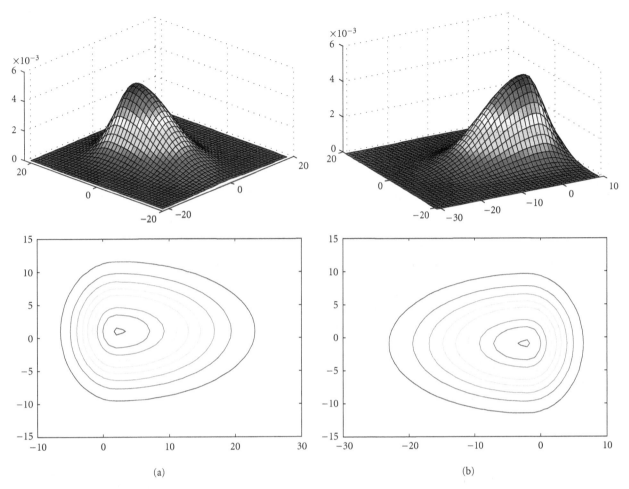

FIGURE 2: (a) Probability distribution of $f(x_t, y_t)$ for $m = 7$, $\sigma_y = 5$, $\sigma_{x_1} = 10$, $\sigma_{x_2} = 4$, (b) probability distribution of $f(x_t, y_t)$ for $m = 7$, $\sigma_y = 5$, $\sigma_{x_1} = 4$, $\sigma_{x_2} = 10$.

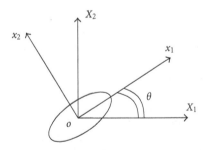

FIGURE 3: Elliptical gate in coordinate systems $x_1 o x_2$ and $X_1 O X_2$.

After some simplification, relations between parameters of elliptical gate and elements of innovation covariance could be achieved as follows:

$$\theta_t = \frac{1}{2} tg^{-1}\left(\frac{2S_{12,t}}{S_{11,t} - S_{22,t}}\right),$$

$$\sigma_{x,t}^2 = -S_{11,t}\cos^2\theta_{t-1} + S_{22,t}\sin^2\theta_{t-1},$$

$$\sigma_{y,t}^2 = S_{11,t}\sin^2\theta_{t-1} - S_{12,t}\sin^2\theta_{t-1} + S_{22,t}\cos^2\theta_{t-1},$$

(14)

where $S_{11,t}$, $S_{12,t}$, $S_{21,t}$, $S_{21,t}$ and $S_{22,t}$ are elements of matrix S_t.

In this paper, Klaman filter is used to estimate parameters of asymmetric gate. The median that is achieved from Kalman filter is set as median of asymmetric Gaussian distribution which is the center of asymmetrical gate m_t. Using (14), $S_{11,t}$, $S_{12,t}$, $S_{21,t}$, $S_{21,t}$, and $S_{22,t}$ are used to estimate θ_t, $\sigma_{x,t}$, and $\sigma_{y,t}$. It is assumed that $\sigma_{x_1,t} = \sigma_{x,t}$ as a standard deviation of asymmetrical gate on movement direction. To calculate parameter $\sigma_{x_2,t}$, estimated acceleration in movement direction, $\hat{a}_{x,t}$ is used which could be estimated from constant acceleration model and Kalman filter.

If $\hat{a}_{x,t} = 0$, probability of existence of target in both side of median in movement direction are equal. Therefore, $\sigma_{x_1,t}$ is set equal to $\sigma_{x_2,t}$ and asymmetrical gate is converted to elliptical gate.

If $\hat{a}_{x,t} > 0$, probability of target existence in movement direction is greater than negative side. It means that $\sigma_{x_1,t}$ should be greater than $\sigma_{x_2,t}$ which is resulted to following proposed equation:

$$\frac{\sigma_{x_1,t}}{\sigma_{x_2,t}} = 1 + \frac{1}{2}\hat{a}_{x,t}T^2,$$

(15)

where T is sampling time and $\hat{a}_{x,t}$ is estimation of acceleration in movement direction.

If $\hat{a}_{x,t} < 0$, probability of existence of target in negative side of movement direction is greater than positive sight. So $\sigma_{x_2,t}$ should be greater than $\sigma_{x_1,t}$ which is resulted to following proposed equation:

$$\frac{\sigma_{x_2,t}}{\sigma_{x_1,t}} = 1 - \frac{1}{2}\hat{a}_{x,t}T^2. \qquad (16)$$

In proposed estimation method, the ratio of standard deviations in direction of movement is proportional to sampling time and estimated acceleration in movement direction.

4. Analytical Comparison between Asymmetrical and Elliptical Gate

In this part, analytical comparison between asymmetrical gate and typical elliptical gate in tracking of targets with nonzero acceleration are studied. Volumes of gates are considered as a proper criterion in comparison. To compare volumes of gates, it is assumed that in-gate probabilities of distributions are equal for both gates.

In tracking with elliptical gate, probability of distribution in centric coordinate system is Gaussian as following:

$$f_1(z_t) = \frac{1}{2\pi\sigma_{x_0}\sigma_{y_0}}$$
$$\times \exp\left(-\frac{1}{2}(z_t - m_0)^T \begin{bmatrix} \sigma_{x_0} & 0 \\ 0 & \sigma_{y_0} \end{bmatrix}^{-1} (z_t - m_0)\right), \qquad (17)$$

where m_0 is median, σ_{x_0} is standard deviation of distribution on movement direction, and σ_{y_0} is standard deviation of distribution on orthogonal to movement direction.

In tracking with asymmetric gate, it is assumed that probability of target distribution in centric coordinate system is asymmetric gaussian as follows:

$$f_2(z_t)$$
$$= \frac{1}{2\pi\sigma_{y_1}((\sigma_{x_1} + \sigma_{x_2})/2)}$$
$$\times \exp\left(-\frac{1}{2}(z_t - m_1)^T \begin{bmatrix} \sigma_{x_i} & 0 \\ 0 & \sigma_{y_1} \end{bmatrix}^{-1} (z_t - m_1)\right) \quad i = 1, 2, \qquad (18)$$

where m_1 is median, σ_{x_1} and σ_{x_2} are standard deviations of distribution on movement direction, and σ_{y_1} is standard deviation of distribution on orthogonal to movement direction.

Because of the fact that probability distributions in (17) and (18) are represented in centric coordinate system, off-diagonal elements of covariance matrixes are zero.

To compare between asymmetric gate and elliptical gate, it is assumed that the target has positive acceleration in movement direction. Parameters of distributions (17) and

(18) could be estimated using Kalman filter and the proposed method in (15) and (16). Therefore, the relation between parameters of asymmetric gate and elliptical gate are achieved as follows:

$$\sigma_x \triangleq \sigma_{x_0} = \sigma_{x_1},$$
$$\sigma_y \triangleq \sigma_{y_0} = \sigma_{y_1},$$
$$m \triangleq m_0 = m_1, \qquad (19)$$
$$\sigma_{x_2} < \sigma_{x_1}.$$

In-gate symmetric and asymmetric probability of distribution could be calculated as follows, respectively [14],

$$P_{1G_t} = \iint_{G_t} f_1(z_t)dx\,dy$$
$$= \int_0^{d_1/2} \exp(-u)du = 1 - \exp\left(-\frac{d_1}{2}\right),$$
$$P_{2G_t} = \iint_{G_t} f_2(z_t)dx\,dy$$
$$= \int_0^{d_2/2} \exp(-u)du = 1 - \exp\left(-\frac{d_2}{2}\right). \qquad (20)$$

Symmetric gate volume V_{1G_t} and asymmetric gate volume V_{2G_t} are considered as follows:

$$V_{1G_t} = d_1\pi\sigma_{y_0}\sigma_{x_0},$$
$$V_{2G_t} = d_2\pi\sigma_{y_1}\left(\frac{\sigma_{x_1} + \sigma_{x_2}}{2}\right). \qquad (21)$$

It is assumed that, gate probabilities are equal in symmetric and asymmetric gate. Therefore, regarding (19), the following relation could be achieved:

$$\left.\begin{array}{l} \{P_{1G_t} = P_{2G_t} \implies d_1 = d_2\} \\ \sigma_{y_0} = \sigma_{y_1} \\ \left(\frac{\sigma_{x_1} + \sigma_{x_2}}{2}\right) < \sigma_{x_0} \end{array}\right\} \implies V_{2G_t} < V_{1G_t}. \qquad (22)$$

Using the above equation, we get that with equal in-gate probability for symmetric and asymmetric gates, volume of asymmetric gate would be smaller than volume of symmetric gate. It means that with equal probability for asymmetric and elliptical gate, computational complexity to find target inside asymmetrical gate would be less than computational complexity inside of elliptical gate. It is because of the fact that volume of asymmetrical gate is smaller than volume of elliptical gate with equal in-gate probability of distribution.

5. Optimal Size of Gate

Elliptical gates in [14] are represented as follows:

$$(z_t - m_z)^T S_t^{-1}(z_t - m_z) \leq d, \qquad (23)$$

where $z_t = [x_t\ y_t]$, m_z is center of gate, and S_t is innovation covariance matrix that has information about rotation direction of gate and ratio of diameters of gate. Asymmetrical gate that is proposed in this paper could be represented similar to (23) as

$$(z_t - m_z)^T S_t^{-1}(z_t - m_z) \leq d, \qquad (24)$$

where $z_t = [x_t \ y_t]$, $m_z = [m_t \ 0]$, and

$$S_t = \begin{bmatrix} \sigma_{x_i,t}^2 & 0 \\ 0 & \sigma_{y,t}^2 \end{bmatrix}_{i \in \{1,2\}}. \tag{25}$$

If $x_t > m_t$, we choose $i = 1$ and if $x_t < m_t$, we choose $i = 2$.

z_t would be inside the gate if two following constraints are satisfied.

(a) If $x_t > m_t$, then

$$(z_t - m_z)^T \begin{bmatrix} \sigma_{x_1,t}^2 & 0 \\ 0 & \sigma_{y,t}^2 \end{bmatrix}^{-1} (z_t - m_z) < d. \tag{26}$$

(b) If $x_t < m_t$, then

$$(z_t - m_z)^T \begin{bmatrix} \sigma_{x_2,t}^2 & 0 \\ 0 & \sigma_{y,t}^2 \end{bmatrix}^{-1} (z_t - m_z) < d. \tag{27}$$

Otherwise, z_t is out of the gate.

It is easy to see from (24) that shape of the gate could be determined by m_z, $\sigma_{x_2,t}^2$, $\sigma_{x_1,t}^2$, and $\sigma_{y,t}^2$, whereas the size of the gate could be smaller or larger using just d.

As the gate is made larger, more clutter or observation vectors other than the tracked target are included within it, so that tracking becomes more difficult. On the other hand, if the gate is made smaller, there is an increasing danger that the observation vector from the tracked target may no longer fall within the gate.

So, in this paper, we define a cost function to find optimum size of gate using the cost function for elliptical gates that is proposed in [14]. In this paper, using the method proposed in [14], optimum size of asymmetrical proposed gate is calculated.

Suppose that whole points inside of the gate are defined as follows:

$$G_t = \left\{ z_t \mid (z_t - m_z)^T S_t^{-1} (z_t - m_z) \leq d \right\}. \tag{28}$$

In-gate probability could be calculated by:

$$P_{G_t} = \iint_{G_t} f(x_t, y_t) \, dx \, dy, \tag{29}$$

where $f(x_t, y_t)$ is asymmetrical Gaussian distribution.

After some simplifications, in-gate probability simplifies as follows:

$$P_{G_t} = \int_0^{d/2} e^{-u} du. \tag{30}$$

From (30), it is visible that in-gate probability is independent from the shape of the gate which is defined using parameters m_z, $\sigma_{x_2,t}^2$, $\sigma_{x_1,t}^2$, and $\sigma_{y,t}^2$, and it is just function of the gate size d.

Volume of gate could be considered as

$$V_{G_t} = \iint_{G_t} dx \, dy. \tag{31}$$

After simplification, volume of gate reduced to

$$V_{G_t} = d\pi\sigma_{y,t-1}\left(\frac{\sigma_{x_1,t-1} + \sigma_{x_2,t-1}}{2}\right). \tag{32}$$

Assuming that probability of false alarm observation at time t is a constant value B_f^t, mean number of false observed signals inside of the gate are $B_f^t V_{G_t}$:

$$B_f^t V_{G_t} = B_f^t d\pi\sigma_{y,t-1}\left(\frac{\sigma_{x_1,t-1} + \sigma_{x_2,t-1}}{2}\right). \tag{33}$$

With the assumption that target observation probability is constant P_D, the probability that target is observed inside of the gate is $P_D P_{G_t}$. In other side, mean number of false signals inside of the gate is $B_f^t V_{G_t}$. The goal is to find optimum size of the gate so that $P_D P_{G_t}$ is maximum and $B_f^t V_{G_t}$ is minimum. With respect to the fact that $P_D P_{G_t}$ and $B_f^t V_{G_t}$ are function of d, so it is possible to define $h(d)$ in such a way that, with maximizing it, optimum value of d is calculated:

$$h(d) = P_D P_{G_t} - cB_f^t V_{G_t},$$
$$h(d) = P_D \int_0^{d/2} e^{-u} du - cB_f^t d\pi\sigma_{y,t-1}\left(\frac{\sigma_{x_1,t-1} + \sigma_{x_2,t-1}}{2}\right), \tag{34}$$

where c is a constant value:

$$\frac{\partial h(d)}{\partial d} = 0 \Longrightarrow d_{\text{opt}} = -2\ln c - 2\ln 2\pi - 2\ln B_f^t$$
$$- 2\ln\left(\sigma_{y,t-1}\left(\frac{\sigma_{x_1,t-1} + \sigma_{x_2,t-1}}{2}\right)\right)$$
$$+ 2\ln P_D. \tag{35}$$

Larger c increase emphasis on $B_f^t V_{G_t}$ and number of false observed signals inside of the gate decreases.

6. Simulation Result

To simulate the preferences of the new method, in first we generate samples of a track using model (36). In this model, let $r_x(t)$ be position, let $s_x(t)$ be velocity, let $a_x(t)$ be acceleration of the target in movement direction, let $r_y(t)$ be position, let $s_y(t)$ be velocity, and let $a_y(t)$ be acceleration of the target in orthogonal to movement direction at time t in centric coordinate system, where t stands for continues time index. Dynamics of the target is described by system model that could be written in stochastic differential equation:

$$\dot{X}(t) = AX(t) + Bn(t), \tag{36}$$

where $X(t)$ is state vector

$$X(t) = \begin{bmatrix} r_x(t) & s_x(t) & a_x(t) & r_y(t) & s_y(t) & a_y(t) \end{bmatrix}^T. \tag{37}$$

A is state transition matrix:

$$A = \begin{bmatrix} 0 & 1 & 0 & 0 & 0 & 0 \\ 0 & 0 & 1 & 0 & 0 & 0 \\ 0 & 0 & 0 & 0 & 0 & 0 \\ 0 & 0 & 0 & 0 & 1 & 0 \\ 0 & 0 & 0 & 0 & 0 & 1 \\ 0 & 0 & 0 & 0 & 0 & 0 \end{bmatrix}, \tag{38}$$

vector B is defined as

$$B = \begin{bmatrix} 0 & 0 & 1 & 0 & 0 & 0 \\ 0 & 0 & 0 & 0 & 0 & 1 \end{bmatrix}^T, \tag{39}$$

vector $n(t)$ is defined as

$$n(t) = \begin{bmatrix} n_1(t) & n_2(t) \end{bmatrix}^T, \tag{40}$$

where $n_1(t)$ is random noise with uniform distribution between zero and one and $n_2(t)$ is zero mean white gaussian noise.

By applying time discretization to (36) with sampling time T, we have a discrete time system model:

$$X_k = A_d X_{k-1} + B_d n_k. \tag{41}$$

State transition matrix A_d is

$$A_d = \begin{bmatrix} 1 & T & \dfrac{T^2}{2} & 0 & 0 & 0 \\ 0 & 1 & T & 0 & 0 & 0 \\ 0 & 0 & 1 & 0 & 0 & 0 \\ 0 & 0 & 0 & 1 & T & \dfrac{T^2}{2} \\ 0 & 0 & 0 & 0 & 1 & T \\ 0 & 0 & 0 & 0 & 0 & 1 \end{bmatrix}, \tag{42}$$

and vector B_d is

$$B_d = \begin{bmatrix} \dfrac{T^3}{3} & \dfrac{T^2}{2} & T & 0 & 0 & 0 \\ 0 & 0 & 0 & \dfrac{T^3}{3} & \dfrac{T^2}{2} & T \end{bmatrix}^T. \tag{43}$$

Measured position of the target in centric coordinate system is denoted by z_k and is assumed to be obtained by observation model:

$$z_k = C X_k + w_k, \tag{44}$$

where C is

$$C = \begin{bmatrix} 1 & 0 & 0 & 0 & 0 & 0 \\ 0 & 0 & 0 & 1 & 0 & 0 \end{bmatrix}, \tag{45}$$

and w_k is defined as

$$w_k = \begin{bmatrix} w_{1k} & w_{2k} \end{bmatrix}^T, \tag{46}$$

where w_{1k} is random noise with uniform distribution between zero and one and w_{2k} is zero mean white gaussian noise.

In Figure 4, target positions are shown that is generated using the above model. Monte Carlo simulation is used to approximate probability distribution of target position in next time step. Approximated probability of distribution is shown in Figure 4.

It is easy to understand from Figure 4 that probability distribution in next time could be illustrated using asymmetric distribution that formulated previously.

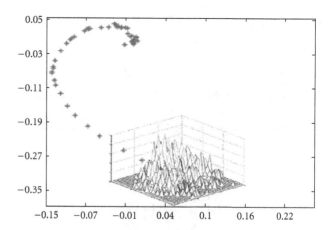

FIGURE 4: Target track and estimation of probability of distribution in next time step using Monte Carlo simulation.

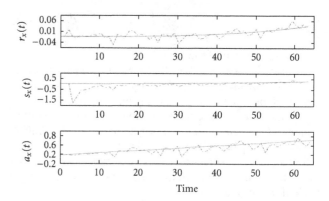

FIGURE 5: Actual (blue solid) and estimated (red dash) values of $r_x(t)$, $s_x(t)$, and $a_x(t)$ in centric coordinate system.

Kalman filter is used to estimate parameters of asymmetric gate that are considered in part 3. Actual and estimated values of $r_x(t)$, $s_x(t)$, and $a_x(t)$ in centric coordinate system are shown in Figure 5.

To show proficiency of the proposed asymmetrical gating method in comparison with previous gating methods such as circular gating, elliptical gating, and rectangular gating, similar simulation scenarios are studied for circular, elliptical, and rectangular gates. The volumes of gates in each simulation are equal and the location of the target in the next time step is important in the comparison between different gates. The number of times that the target falls in a gate in the next time step is a comparison index between gates. In Table 1, comparison results between circular gate, elliptical gate, rectangular gate, and proposed asymmetrical gate are shown for different gate volumes.

In Table 1, percent falls of the target inside each gate are shown for different volumes of gate. For example, for volume of gate 0.0025, percent fall of the target inside rectangular gate is 51%, inside circular gate is 65%, inside elliptical gate is 73% and inside asymmetrical gate is 92%.

For different volumes of gates, it could be seen from Table 1 that proposed asymmetrical gate has more in-gate probability than other gating methods and the number of

TABLE 1: Comparison results between circular gate, elliptical gate, rectangular gate and asymmetrical gate for different gate volumes.

Gate volume	Rectangular gate	Circular gate	Elliptical gate	Asymmetrical gate
0.0025	51%	65%	73%	92%
0.005	68%	78%	84%	96%
0.01	90%	98%	100%	100%

target falls inside of the asymmetrical gate in the next step is more than others. It is because of the asymmetrical gate ability to shape itself to have more percent falls of the target inside the gate. Although parameters of other gates can be updated in each step to have more percent falls inside the gates, the ability of shape changing in other gates is less than asymmetrical gate specially in maneuvering target tracking applications. Not that the percent falls of the target inside of the gates increases by increasing gate volume that could be seen easily from Table 1.

7. Conclusion and Future Remarks

In this paper, we introduced asymmetric gating technique for tracking maneuvering targets that have nonzero acceleration in movement direction. Asymmetric gate is defined as a cross-surface of asymmetric Gaussian distribution. Standard Kalman filter is used to estimate some parameters of asymmetrical gate. Standard deviation of asymmetrical distribution in opposite to the movement direction is estimated using a proposed method in which sampling time and estimated acceleration are used. Preference of asymmetrical gate to the elliptical gate is proved analytically subject to constant in-gate probability of distribution for both gates, in which volumes of gates are used as a comparison criterion. We derived an optimization method to finding optimum size of asymmetrical gate. Optimum size of asymmetrical gate is obtained as a function of some parameters such as probability of target observation and probability of false alarms that should be tune manually in each special applications.

As a future remarks, it could be assumed that probability of distribution in orthogonal to the movement direction in centric coordinate system is considered asymmetric. Also, estimation of gate parameters could be studied in typical coordinate system, after enough research, and proves on generalization of Kalman filter for linear systems with asymmetric gaussian probability of distributions for both process and measurement noise.

References

[1] C. B. Chang and J. A. Tabaczynski, "Application of state estimation to target tracking," *IEEE Transactions on Automatic Control*, vol. 29, no. 2, pp. 98–109, 1984.

[2] Y. Bar-Shalom, "Tracking methods in a multi target environment," *IEEE Transactions on Automatic Control*, vol. 23, no. 4, pp. 618–626, 1978.

[3] X. R. Li and V. P. Jilkov, "A survey of maneuvering target tracking—part II: ballistic target models," in *Signal and Data Processing of Small Targets*, vol. 4473 of *Proceedings of SPIE*, pp. 559–581, 2001.

[4] D. C. Woffinden and D. K. Geller, "Observability criteria for angles-only navigation," *IEEE Transactions on Aerospace and Electronic Systems*, vol. 45, no. 3, pp. 1194–1208, 2009.

[5] Y. Bar-Shalom and E. Tse, "Tracking in a cluttered environment with probabilistic data association," *Automatica*, vol. 11, no. 5, pp. 451–460, 1975.

[6] T. E. Fortmann, Y. Bar-Shalom, and M. Scheffe, "Multitarget tracking using joint probabilistic data association," in *Proceedings of IEEE Conference on Decision and Control*, pp. 807–812, December 1980.

[7] D. B. Reid, "An algorithm for tracking multiple targets," *IEEE Transactions on Automatic Control*, vol. 24, no. 6, pp. 843–854, 1979.

[8] Y. Kosuge, S. Tsujimichi, and Y. Tachibana, "Track-oriented multiple hypothesis multi target tracking algorithm," *IEICE Transactions*, pp. 677–685, 1996.

[9] Y. Kosuge, S. Tsujimichi, S. Mano, and S. Betsudan, "Suboptimal techniques for track-oriented multiple hypothesis tracking algorithm and JPPA algorithm for multi target tracking to be equivalent," *IEICE Transactions*, pp. 889–898, 1997.

[10] S. S. Blackman, "Multiple Target Tracking with Radar Applications," p. Artech House, 1986.

[11] Y. Bar-Shalom and T. E. Fortman, *Tracking and Data Association*, Academic Press, New York, NY, USA, 1988.

[12] Y. Oshman, "An information fusion approach to missile guidance," in *International Conference on Control, Automation and Systems (ICCAS '07)*, October 2007.

[13] E. M. Saad et al., "Filtered Gate Structure Applied to Joint Probabilistic Data Association Algorithm for Multi-Target Tracking in Dense Clutter Environment," *International Journal of Computer Science*, pp. 161–170, 2011.

[14] Y. Kosuge and T. Matsuzaki, "The gate size estimation method and the optimal gate shape for target tracking," *Electronics and Communications in Japan, Part III*, vol. 85, no. 5, pp. 10–22, 2002.

7

An Entropy-Based Multiobjective Evolutionary Algorithm with an Enhanced Elite Mechanism

Yufang Qin, Junzhong Ji, and Chunnian Liu

Beijing Municipal Key Laboratory of Multimedia and Intelligent Software Technology, College of Computer Science and Technology, Beijing University of Technology, Beijing 100124, China

Correspondence should be addressed to Junzhong Ji, jjz01@bjut.edu.cn

Academic Editor: Christian W. Dawson

Multiobjective optimization problem (MOP) is an important and challenging topic in the fields of industrial design and scientific research. Multi-objective evolutionary algorithm (MOEA) has proved to be one of the most efficient algorithms solving the multi-objective optimization. In this paper, we propose an entropy-based multi-objective evolutionary algorithm with an enhanced elite mechanism (E-MOEA), which improves the convergence and diversity of solution set in MOPs effectively. In this algorithm, an enhanced elite mechanism is applied to guide the direction of the evolution of the population. Specifically, it accelerates the population to approach the true Pareto front at the early stage of the evolution process. A strategy based on entropy is used to maintain the diversity of population when the population is near to the Pareto front. The proposed algorithm is executed on widely used test problems, and the simulated results show that the algorithm has better or comparative performances in convergence and diversity of solutions compared with two state-of-the-art evolutionary algorithms: NSGA-II, SPEA2 and the MOSADE.

1. Introduction

Optimization problems exist in all kinds of engineering and scientific areas. When there is more than one objective in an optimization problem, it is called a multiobjective optimization problem (MOP). Since these objectives are usually in conflict with each other, the goal of solving a MOP is to find a set of compromise solutions regarding all objectives rather than a best one as in single-objective optimization problems. The solutions of MOP, also called as the Pareto-optimal solutions, are optimal in the sense that there exist no other feasible solutions which would decrease some criteria without causing the increase of at least one other criterion. Evolutionary algorithm (EA) is an optimization algorithm based on the evolution of a population. As it can search for multiple solutions in parallel, it has gained great attention from researchers. In recent years, many excellent EAs [1–4] have been proposed to solve the MOPs efficiently and MOEA has been recognized as one of the best methods to solve the MOPs.

Generally, there are two performance measures in evaluating the Pareto-optimal solutions obtained by MOEA. One is the convergence measurement, which evaluates the adjacent degree between the Pareto solutions and the true optimal front. Another one is the diversity measurement, which evaluates the distribution of solutions in the objective space. In order to achieve good performance, many excellent strategies and methods have been presented in MOEA [1, 2, 5–9]. For the convergence, the elite mechanism has proved to be very helpful to accelerate the evolution of population [6]. The basic idea of the elite mechanism is that the information of good solutions, which have occurred in the progress of the evolution, is used to ensure the solution set converge to the optimal front as soon as possible. Its usual practice is that a certain number of best solutions are selected from the population as the parents to produce the good offspring [1]. However, in the early stage of the algorithm applying this strategy, because there are many dominated solutions existing in the population selected as the parents, the population cannot converge at a fast speed. In order to maintain the diversity of nondominated solutions, two main methods are applied. The first is using the grid to maintain the diversity [7]. It draws grids in the objective space and controls the number of solutions in a grid. Although this way can find the better solutions quickly, sometimes it cannot accurately reflect the global distribution of solutions because the grid position is fixed. The second one is the way based on the density [2, 8, 9]. Every solution obtains a value of the density and an outstanding density calculation can help to form a good distribution of solutions.

Since 1948, Shannon [10] introduced the information theoretic entropy to measure information content of a stochastic process, which led to the establishment of the field of information theory. Then, many different applications for entropy are given in various fields. In solving the multiobjective optimization problems, Farhang-Mehr and Azarm [11] and Gunawan et al. [12] have applied the entropy to maintain the diversity of the solution set well in multiobjective problems and multilevel multiobjective problems. Wang et al. proposed the MOSADE algorithm [13], which combines the self-adaptive differential evolution and the crowding entropy-based diversity measure to obtain the nondominated solution set. In this algorithm, every solution can calculate its crowding degree through the improved the information entropy formula according to solutions' distribution. In essence, this method is similar to the crowding distance in NSGA-II. Thus, for some three objective problems, this algorithm cannot obtain the very ideal solution set.

In this paper, we propose a new MOEA to solve the MOP more effectively, in which an enhanced elitism makes the nondominated solutions play the better guide role and an entropy-based strategy is applied to preserve the diversity of the population. We call it an entropy-based multiobjective evolution algorithm with an enhanced elitism, namely, E-MOEA in brief. Specifically, we employ the enhanced elitism in which only the nondominated solutions in the union population are selected as the parents to ensure that the solution set converges to the optimal front more quickly. With the algorithm going on, the number of the nondominated solutions in union population will increase gradually. In order to keep the size of the elitist population (the maximum number of the elitist population in our algorithm is set as N) and maintain the diversity of solutions, the strategy based on entropy is applied. In this strategy, a region is determined by taking a solution as its center and the most crowded regions with the most uneven distribution of solutions are found through applying the entropy; then, in these regions, the most crowded solutions are deleted one by one. Compared with the MOSADE, the enhanced elitism can make the solution set approach to the Pareto-optimal front more easily in our algorithm, and the surface of the Pareto solution set is more uniform through the combination of the region and entropy. Experimental results on the 2-objective problems and the 3-objective problems show that the novel algorithm has better performance in both convergence and diversity, compared with NSGA-II, SPEA2 and MOSADE.

2. Multiobjective Optimization Problems

In this paper, we consider the following continuous multiobjective optimization problem (continuous MOP):

$$\text{minimize } \vec{F} = \left(f_1(x), f_2(x), \ldots, f_m(x) \right)^T$$
$$\text{subject to } x \in X, \tag{1}$$

where $X \subset R^n$ is the decision space and $x = (x_1, \ldots, x_n)^T \in R^n$ is the decision variable vector. $F : X \rightarrow R^m$ consists of m real value objective functions $f_i(x)$ $(i = 1, 2, \ldots, m)$, and R^m is the objective space.

Let $a = (a_1, \ldots, a_m)^T$, $b = (b_1, \ldots, b_m)^T \in R^m$ be two vectors, and a is said to dominate b, denoted by $a \prec b$, if $a_i \leq b_i$ for all $i = 1, \ldots, m$, and $a \neq b$.

A point $x^* \subset X$ is called Pareto-optimal if there is no $x \subset X$ such that $F(x) \prec F(x^*)$. The set of all the Pareto-optimal vectors is called Pareto set, denoted by PS. The set of all the Pareto objective vector, PF = $\{y \subset R^m \mid y = F(x), x \subset \text{PS}\}$, is called the Pareto front [2, 9].

3. The Entropy-Based Multiobjective Evolutionary Algorithm with an Enhanced Elite Mechanism

In this section, we first present an enhanced elitist mechanism; then an entropy-based strategy is proposed to maintain the diversity of population. Finally, the entropy-based multiobjective evolutionary algorithm with the enhanced elitism is described.

3.1. The Enhanced Elitist Mechanism. Recent researches have proved that the elite mechanism is an excellent method to speed up the convergence of evolutionary algorithm. The population can produce a good offspring population through the elitism's guide role, which achieves the rapid evolution of the population. On the basis of this idea, different forms of the elite mechanism have been proposed in some EAs [1, 14]. Among them, the most popular and effective one is used in NSGA-II, which first combines parent and offspring population then chooses a certain number of solutions from the union population as the parent population of the next iteration according to the nondominated sort and crowd distance assignment. As mentioned above, in the early running of the algorithm, a part of the dominated solutions may be selected into the elitist population so that the offspring produced by them are not good enough. Thus, we make some improvements to enhance the guiding role of good solutions when producing good offspring and we call it the enhanced elite mechanism.

According to the elite mechanism, it is reasonable that the better the solutions chosen as the parents are, the better the offspring solutions which are produced by these parents are. Therefore, in order to enhance the guide of the elitism in our algorithm, we just only select all the nondomination solutions as the parents of the next iteration instead of a certain number of relatively good solutions, which may include dominated solutions because the number of nondominated solutions in the union population is less than N during the early running of the algorithm. This enhanced mechanism can avoid several complex operations, such as the hierarchical nondominated sort and the crowd distance computation. On the other hand, all offspring solutions are generated by the nondominated population, which makes use of the best solutions to improve the efficiency of the evolution of the population. When the

TABLE 1: Performance comparison of the three MOEAs on the test problems.

Test problems	MOEAs	GD		SP	
		Average	Std. dev	Average	Std. dev
ZDT1	E-MOEA	**0.000221511**	$4.88744e-05$	**0.00424942**	$4.3571e-04$
	NSGA-II	0.000682375	$1.39413e-04$	0.00837093	$1.20323e-03$
	SPEA2	0.000440864	$4.85921e-05$	0.00673195	$5.59690e-04$
ZDT2	E-MOEA	**0.000117987**	$4.14203e-05$	**0.00416924**	$3.63994e-04$
	NSGA-II	0.000512546	$1.338e-04$	0.00906621	$1.9978e-03$
	SPEA2	0.000358487	$6.39963E-05$	0.00426378	$6.47733E-04$
ZDT3	E-MOEA	**0.000181589**	$4.08439e-05$	**0.00463638**	$6.10117e-04$
	NSGA-II	0.000501522	$1.20519e-04$	0.00926551	$1.5051E-03$
	SPEA2	0.000467296	$1.90819E-04$	0.00674565	$2.00025E-03$
ZDT6	E-MOEA	**$3.4402e-05$**	$3.25e-06$	0.00295588	$2.87438e-04$
	NSGA-II	$3.62327e-05$	$3.28188E-06$	0.00696434	$7.99786E-04$
	SPEA2	$3.55231e-05$	$2.90700E-06$	**0.00264811**	$3.26533E-04$
DTLZ1	E-MOEA	**0.00331697**	$2.602846e-03$	**0.0126931**	$3.5927e-03$
	NSGA-II	0.0112144	$2.227298E-02$	0.0254555	$1.90124E-02$
	SPEA2	0.00731387	$2.51490E-02$	0.0134803	$2.77126E-02$
DTLZ2	E-MOEA	**0.000606691**	$2.04103e-05$	**0.0214341**	$1.4247e-03$
	NSGA-II	0.021829197	$2.56158e-03$	0.0281401	$2.09720e-03$
	SPEA2	0.0024392	$2.82469e-04$	0.0258512	$7.13532e-03$
DTLZ3	E-MOEA	**0.000927311**	$2.6767e-04$	**0.0211134**	$1.1026e-03$
	NSGA-II	—	—	—	—
	SPEA2	—	—	—	—

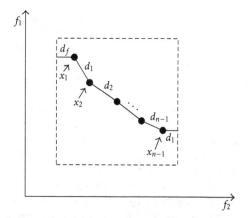

FIGURE 1: Computation entropy of a grid.

FIGURE 2: Selecting the worst solution in the grid.

number of the nondominated solutions exceeds N, we delete the solutions with the worst distribution one by one through the entropy-based strategy, which accurately considers the distribution information of all solutions to obtain the elitist population with better distribution.

3.2. The Entropy-Based Strategy for Maintaining Diversity. In the enhanced elitist mechanism, the number of the nondominated solutions in union population will gradually increase with the algorithm going on. For keeping the maximum size of the elitist population N and maintaining the diversity of the population, we proposed the entropy-based strategy by combining the regional information and

the knowledge about entropy. The strategy deletes the most crowded solutions one by one, and all the related values will be recalculated before deciding which solutions should be deleted from the population, which can reflect the distribution of solutions dynamically and accurately. It is obvious that the key operation of the strategy is how to select the most crowded solution in nondominated population. First we select the most crowded region with the most uneven distribution through applying the information entropy, and then the solution which seriously influences the distribution of the solution set in this region is picked and removed from the elitist population. The previous process is looped until the size of the nondominated population decreases to N to

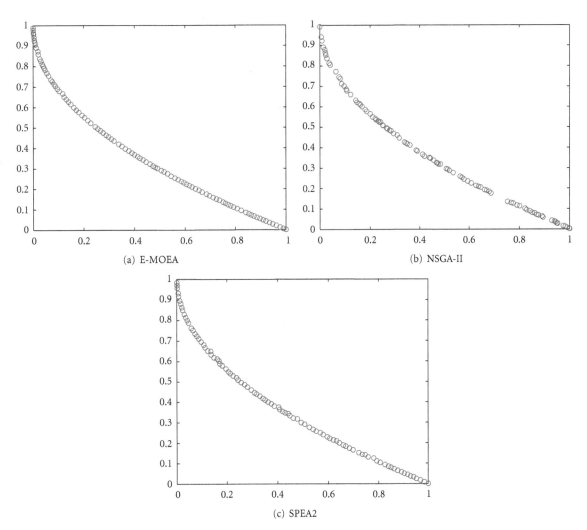

FIGURE 3: The final solutions obtained by three MOEAs on ZDT1.

form the elitist population. The strategy is described in detail as follows.

For ease of operations, we order the nondominated solutions by one objective, and then, the region taking each solution as the center is defined as $[f_i(x) - D, f_i(x) + D]$ ($i = 1, 2, \ldots, m$, $0 < D < L/2$), where $f_i(x)$ represents the ith objective value of a solution x, D is a parameter which controls the area of the region, and L is the length of numerical range for the objective. Obviously, for a 2-objective problem, the region is a square; for a 3-objective problem, the region is a cube. Because the areas of those regions for all solutions are the same, there is no doubt that the more the total number of solutions existing in a region is, the more crowded the region is. Thus, it is easy to find the most crowded region based on the number of solutions in a region. If there is only one region including the most solutions, the most crowded solution in this region will be deleted. However, in most case, there may be several regions which include the same and maximum number of solutions. The region with the most uneven distribution of solutions will be selected from these regions by applying the knowledge about entropy.

In light of the Shannon information theory [15], the entropy can be used to measure the uniformity of the probability distribution in a normalized system. Assume a stochastic process with n possible outcomes where the probability of the ith outcome is p_i. The probability distribution of this process denoted as a probability vector $\mathbf{P}$ can be shown as

$$\mathbf{P} = [p_1, p_2, \ldots, p_n]; \quad \sum_{i=1}^{n} p_i = 1, \quad p_i \geq 0. \quad (2)$$

This probability vector has an associated Shannon's entropy, H, of the form

$$H(\mathbf{P}) = -\sum_{i=1}^{n} p_i \ln(p_i), \quad (3)$$

where $p_i \ln(p_i)$ is assumed to be zero when $p_i = 0$. This function is at its maximum. $H_{\max} = \ln(n)$, when all probabilities have the same value, and it is at a minimum of zero when one component of the $\mathbf{P}$-vector is 1 and the rest of the entries in the $\mathbf{P}$-vector are zero. Inspired by this, we

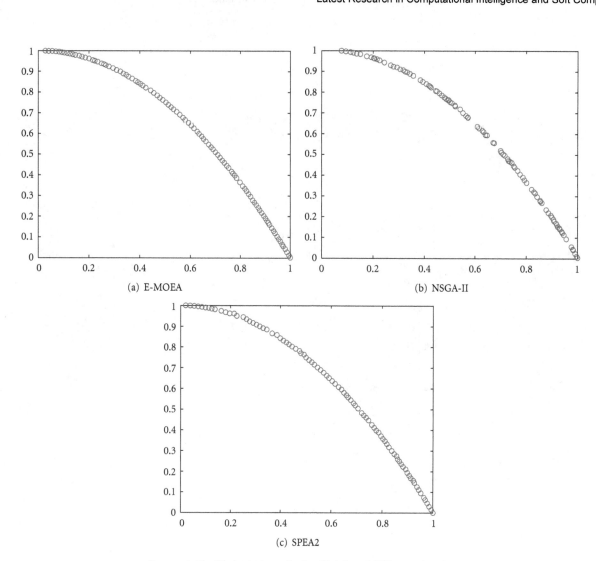

FIGURE 4: The final solutions obtained by three MOEAs on ZDT2.

compute the entropy of a region through taking the region as **P** and viewing every distance between two adjacent solutions as a p_i. If a region has a more uniform distribution where the distances between the adjacent solutions are roughly similar, its entropy will be bigger, and when a region has a more uneven distribution where the distances between the adjacent solutions vary greatly, its entropy will be smaller.

The schematic diagram for computing the entropy of a region is shown in Figure 1. There are n solutions $x_1, \ldots, x_n$ sorted by an objective in this region, $d_1, \ldots, d_{n-1}$ are the distances between two adjacent solutions, and d_l and d_f are, respectively, the edge distances from two extreme solutions x_1, x_n, to the corresponding boundaries of the region at the objective ordered. In order to obtain a normalized system and be more reasonable to employ the entropy formula, some transforms need to be performed. Let $d_0 = 2 * d_l$, $d_n = 2 * d_f$, then

$$p_i = \frac{d_i}{\sum_{i=0}^{n} d_i}. \tag{4}$$

In light of (3), the entropies of those regions with the most solutions are computed and the region whose entropy is the smallest is obtained. It implies that not only this region includes the most solutions, but also its distribution of solutions in this region is the most uneven. Next, we will choose the most crowded solution from this region to delete. Here, a simple and effective method is used. In the region, first the two solutions with the smallest adjacent distance are found, and then we compare distances between them and their other adjacent solutions. Finally, the solution with smaller distance will be deleted from the population. A simple example is shown in Figure 2. x_1 and x_2 are found having the smallest distance, and then we compare the distance d_2 between x_1 and x_3 with the distance d_4 between x_2 and x_4. Since $d_4 < d_2$, the solution x_2 will be deleted. The main difference between our method and the archive truncation method in SPEA2 is that all solutions in our algorithm have been sorted and we only perform some comparisons among the adjacent distances. This method not only can reduce the computation, but also can keep the even solution distribution reasonably.

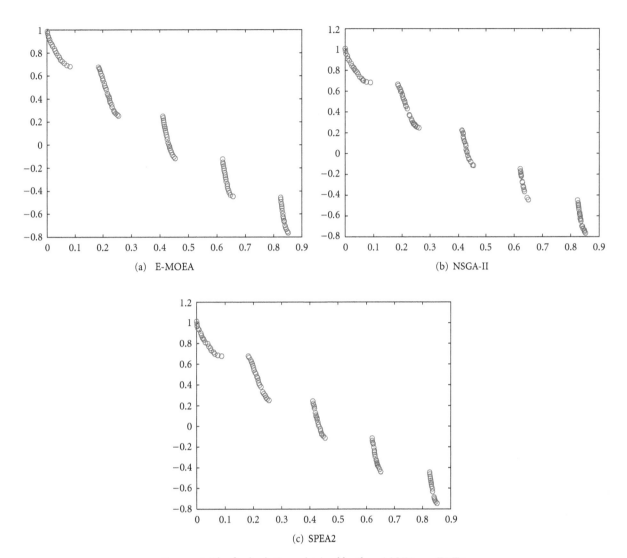

(a) E-MOEA

(b) NSGA-II

(c) SPEA2

FIGURE 5: The final solutions obtained by three MOEAs on ZDT3.

3.3. The Framework of E-MOEA. Combing the basic evolutionary algorithm and the tradition of the method producing offspring (crossover and mutation) in genetic algorithm, we proposed the entropy-based multiobjective evolutionary algorithm with an enhanced elite mechanism (E-MOEA). The main steps are shown in the following.

Parameters. We have the following: N (population size), T (maximum number of generation), P (the current population), Q (the elitist population), R (the offspring population).

Step 1. Generate an initial population P and set $t = 0$.

Step 2. Copy all the nondominated solutions in P to the population Q.

Step 3. If $|Q| > N$, reduce the size of Q by the entropy-based strategy one by one until $|Q| = N$.

Step 4. If $t = T$, then go to Step 7.

Step 5. Execute recombination and mutation operators to the Q to obtain the offspring population R.

Step 6. $P = Q + R$, $t = t + 1$, and go to Step 2,

Step 7. Output the current elitist population Q.

4. Experimental Design and Results

In this section, a large number of experiments are conducted to test the performance of E-MOEA on the biobjective and the 3-objective problems. Specifically, our algorithm is compared with other advanced MOEAs: NSGA-II and SPEA2 which have the different strategy of constructing the elitist population. And then, the comparisons of the proposed E-MOEA and the MOSADE are presented.

4.1. Test Instances and Performance Metrics. In our experiment, the biobjective problem is from ZDT series: ZDT1, ZDT2, ZDT3, and ZDT6. The 3-objective problems we

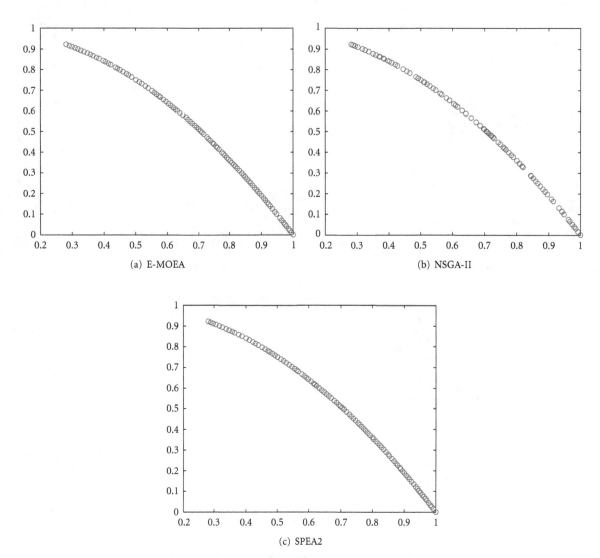

FIGURE 6: The final solutions obtained by three MOEAs on ZDT6.

selected is composed of the DTLZ family of scalable test problems [16].

There have been several metrics proposed for measuring the performance of the Pareto-optimal obtained by MOEAs. In our work, we choose the GD metric [17] and SP metric [18]. GD can measure the distance between the non-dominated solutions obtained and the real Pareto-optimal front

$$GD = \frac{\sqrt{\sum_{i=1}^{|Q|} e_i^2}}{|Q|}, \qquad (5)$$

where e_i represents the Euclidean distance between the solution $q_i \in Q$ and the nearest member of p^* (p^* is a solution set of uniform sampling from the true Pareto-optimal front). In our experiment, we use 10000 uniformly spaced Pareto-optimal solutions as the approximation of the true Pareto front.

The metric SP can be used to measure the diversity of obtained solutions. Here, $\bar{e}$ is the average value of all e_i, and m is the number of objectives:

$$SP = \sqrt{\frac{1}{|Q| - 1} \sum_{i=1}^{|Q|} \bar{e} - e_i^2},$$

$$e_i = \min_{q_j \in Q \wedge q_j \neq q_i} \sum_{k=1}^{m} \left| f_k(q_i) - f_k(q_j) \right|. \qquad (6)$$

The another indicator which is used usually to evaluate the diversity of the solution set is Δ [1]. However, this indicator works only for biobjective problems and cannot be used directly to evaluate for problems of more than two objectives. Based on the metric proposed in [19], the indicator is extended to fit problems of more than two objectives by computing the distance from a given point to its nearest neighbor. The indicator is modified as

$$\Delta = \frac{\sum_{k=1}^{m} d(E_i, \Omega) + \sum_{X \in \Omega} \left| d(X, \Omega) - \bar{d} \right|}{\sum_{k=1}^{m} d(E_i, \Omega) + (|\Omega| - m)\bar{d}}, \qquad (7)$$

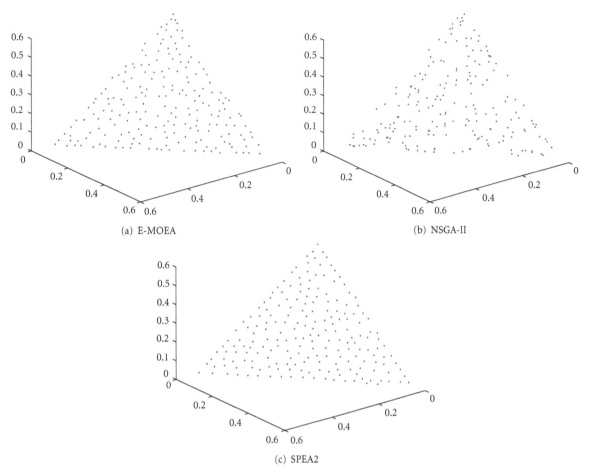

(a) E-MOEA

(b) NSGA-II

(c) SPEA2

FIGURE 7: The final solutions obtained by three MOEAs on DTLZ1.

where Ω is a set of solutions, $(E_i, \ldots, E_m)$ are m extreme solutions in the set of Pareto-optimal solutions, m is the number of objectives, and

$$d(X, \Omega) = \min_{Y \in \Omega, Y \neq X} \|F(X) - F(Y)\| ,$$

$$\overline{d} = \frac{1}{|\Omega|} \sum_{X \in \Omega} d(X, \Omega). \tag{8}$$

4.2. Comparison of E-MOEA and Other MOEAs. In this part, we will compare the E-MOEA proposed and two state-of-the-art algorithms, NSGA-II and SPEA2. All three algorithms are given real-valued decision variables. Simulated binary crossover (SBX) [20] and polynomial mutation (PM) [21] are applied with distribution indexes of $\eta_c = 2$ and $\eta_m = 10$, respectively. A crossover probability $p_c = 1$ and a mutation probability $p_m = 1/n$ (where n is the number of decision variables for test problems) are used. In E-MOEA, D should not be too big in order to decrease the computation of our algorithm; on the contrary, our experimental results also show that if D is set too small, the algorithm also do not get good result. So for 2-objective problems, we set $D = 0.04$, and for 3-objective problems, $D = 0.07$. In all three MOEAs, the size of the population is 100 and the maximum number of function evaluation is 25000 for 2-objective problems.

And for 3-objectives problems these two numbers are 200 and 80000, respectively.

Four biobjective problems, ZDT1–3 and ZDT6, and three 3-objective problems DTLZ1–3 are used. For each test problem, 30 times runs are executed. Convergence metric GD and diversity metric SP are employed to evaluate the performance. The results are given in Table 1, where Average and Sdt. dev, respectively, represent the mean and the standard deviation of indicators. In terms of the GD metric, we can clearly see that E-MOEA is nearer to the Pareto-optimal front than the others for all four 2-objective test problems. The reason for this is that the parent solutions are all made up of the nondominated solution in the current population in E-MOEA. Because of not using dominated solution, the population can approach the true Pareto-optimal front more quickly and efficiently. In light of the SP metric, for ZDT1, ZDT2, and ZDT3, E-MOEA is the best, SPEA2 is the second, and NSGA-II is the last. For ZDT6, SPEA2 is a little better than E-MOEA and they are much better than NSGA-II. The possible reason is that SPEA2 used the effective fitness assignment, however, which costs too much time. E-MOEA applies the strategy based on entropy to preserve the diversity of the population, which can evaluate the uniformity of distribution of solutions more scientifically so that the elitist population with excellent distribution is constructed.

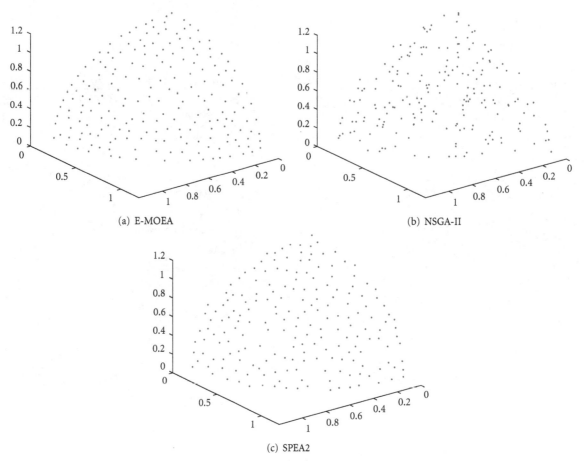

FIGURE 8: The final solutions obtained by three MOEAs on DTLZ2.

DTLZ serial test problems are proposed by Deb K, which can be set with the different number of objectives. In here, we choose the same settings as in [22]. For DTLZ1 and DTLZ2, all three algorithms can converge the Pareto-optimal front, but E-MOEA is the nearest to the true front, SPEA2 is the second, and NSGA-II is the last. For the diversity, E-MOEA and SPEA2 are much better than NSGA-II. Since DTLZ3 is the most difficult test problem, SPEA2 and NSGA-II cannot converge to the Pareto-optimal front. The reason is that both NSGA-II and SPEA2 always generate too much wild individuals in the obtained populations. Fortunately, E-MOEA can get solutions with good convergence and diversity for DTLZ3. Thus, Table 1 for DTLZ3 only gives the results obtained by E-MOEA, and "—" denotes that corresponding algorithms cannot obtain reasonable results.

Figures 3, 4, 5, and 6 show the final solutions obtained by three algorithms on four biobjective test problems. Obviously, we can see that solutions obtained by E-MOEA display the broadest and the most uniform distribution and are the nearer to the true Pareto-optimal front than the NSGA-II and SPEA2. Figures 7 and 8 clearly present the final solutions by three algorithms on DTLZ1 and DTLZ2. Figure 9 shows the final solutions by E-MOEA on DTLZ3.

4.3. Comparison of E-MOEA and MOSADE. Both of the E-MOEA and MOSADE make use of entropy to maintain the diversity of the solution sets. In E-MOEA, we select the region with the worst distribution to keep the distribution of solutions through applying the information entropy formula. In MOSADE, the improved information entropy formula is used to update the archive, which maintains the diversity of the solution set. For these two algorithms, further experiments are conducted to compare their performances. For E-MOEA, all parameters are the same as the parameters of E-MOEA as described in Section 4.2 except that the population size is 100 for all the test problems. For MOSADE, the population size and the external elitist archive size are 100, the lower and upper limits of mutant constant and crossover probability $F_l = 0.1$, $F_u = 0.9$, $CR_l = 0$, and $CR_u = 0.5$. The biobjective problems ZDT1–3 and ZDT6, the 3-objective problems DTLZ1–7 are considered. The GD and Δ are used as the evaluation indicators in this experiment, and results are presented in Table 2.

The results obtained from Table 2 show that these two algorithms have both the good convergence according to the GD; however, E-MOEA gets better values than MOSADE in all test problems except DTLZ7. This means the resulting Pareto fronts from E-MOEA are closer to the true optimal Pareto fronts. The solution set obtained by E-MOEA can converge more quickly to the optimal front, which may be due to the enhanced elitism applied in E-MOEA. As DTLZ7 has a wider range of the optimal solutions, the effect of

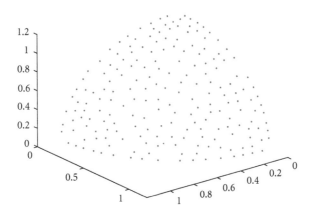

FIGURE 9: The final solutions obtained by E-MOEA on DTLZ3.

TABLE 2: Performance comparison of the E-MOEA and MOSADE on the test problems.

Test problems	GD		SP	
	E-MOEA	MOSADE	E-MOEA	MOSADE
ZDT1	**2.2151e− 4**	1.2485e − 3	0.19677	**0.13159**
	±4.88744e − 5	±9.7574e − 5	±1.7614e − 2	±5.6921e − 3
ZDT2	**1.1789e− 4**	9.8051e − 4	0.18056	**0.12099**
	±4.14203e − 5	±4.9107e − 5	±2.2941e − 2	±7.9444e − 3
ZDT3	**1.8158e− 4**	2.1620e − 3	0.49072	**0.43783**
	±4.08439e − 5	±1.9962e − 4	±1.5302e − 2	±8.0801e − 3
ZDT6	**3.4402e− 5**	2.5156e − 3	0.36294	**0.13319**
	±3.25e − 6	±1.0967e − 4	±1.5114e − 2	±9.8303e − 3
DTLZ1	**1.9635e− 3**	5.2512e − 3	**0.24111**	0.63755
	±1.0045e − 3	±1.5650e − 4	±1.1527e − 2	±3.0464e − 2
DTLZ2	**8.7374e− 4**	5.3344e − 3	**0.27939**	0.61323
	±5.6621e − 5	±1.7429e − 4	±1.1527e − 2	±3.6732e − 2
DTLZ3	**2.5954e− 3**	6.4632e − 3	**0.30944**	0.58601
	±3.0169e − 3	±3.3253e − 4	±0.10179	±2.9955e − 2
DTLZ4	**5.36887e− 4**	4.7736e − 3	**0.51411**	0.93230
	±2.0186e − 5	±2.7427e − 4	±0.1810e − 2	±1.0819e − 1
DTLZ5	**3.6979e− 4**	3.8930e − 3	0.42787	**0.35529**
	±1.0853e − 4	±2.0137e − 3	±1.5032e − 2	±2.2054e − 1
DTLZ6	**1.0800e − 5**	3.7701e − 3	0.43264	**0.30720**
	±9.9346e − 7	±3.1470e − 4	±1.35959	±4.7503e − 2
DTLZ7	4.7858e − 3	**2.3737e−3**	**0.59107**	0.85454
	±2.1121e − 3	±0.001303	±9.4664e − 2	±3.8634e − 2

convergence in E-MOEA is not better than the MOSADE which applied the differential evolution. For the indicator Δ, in the 2-objective problem, MOSADE has the more uniform distribution and in the 3-objective, E-MOEA has better results. The possible reason is that the crowding entropy diversity measure tactic in MOSADE is more effective to the test problems whose optimal front is an approximate curve. However, due to considering the spacial factor, the entropy-based strategy for maintaining diversity is more suitable to

solve the problem whose optimal front is a surface. Thus, E-MOEA has better diversity for DTLZ1–4 and DTLZ7.

5. Conclusion

In this paper, a novel entropy-based multiobjective evolutionary algorithm with an enhanced elite mechanism (E-MOEA) is proposed. The algorithm improves the elitism and presents a new strategy based on entropy to construct the elitist population. At first we only select the nondominated solutions in the population as the elitist solutions, and when the size of the nondominated solutions exceeds the size of population, we delete worse solutions one by one to preserve the diversity of the population through the entropy-based strategy. Experimental results on seven widely used popular test functions show that E-MOEA can obtain the solutions set with better or comparative convergence and diversity performances compared with NSGA-II, SPEA2, and MOSADE.

As eliminating one solution needs to recalculate the entropies of the crowded regions, the worst time complexity of the E-MOEA is $O(n^3)$, which is same with SPEA2. The future research will be how to reduce the computational expense while keeping good performance.

Acknowledgments

This work is supported by the NSFC major research program (60496322, 60496327), the Beijing Natural Science Foundation (4102010). The authors thank Professor Wu Lianghong very much for his guidance to the experiment of MOSADE.

References

[1] K. Deb, A. Pratap, S. Agarwal, and T. Meyarivan, "A fast and elitist multiobjective genetic algorithm: NSGA-II," *IEEE Transactions on Evolutionary Computation*, vol. 6, no. 2, pp. 182–197, 2002.

[2] E. Zitzler, M. Laumanns, and L. Thiele, "SPEA2: improving the strength pareto evolutionary algorithm for multiobjective optimization," in *Evolutionary Methods for Design, Optimisation and Control*, vol. 3242, pp. 95–100, CIMNE, Barcelona, Spain, 2002.

[3] Q. Zhang, A. Zhou, and Y. Jin, "RM-MEDA: a regularity model-based multiobjective estimation of distribution algorithm," *IEEE Transactions on Evolutionary Computation*, vol. 12, no. 1, pp. 41–63, 2008.

[4] B. Y. Qu and P. N. Suganthan, "Multi-objective evolutionary algorithms based on the summation of normalized objectives and diversified selection," *Information Sciences*, vol. 180, no. 17, pp. 317–318, 2010.

[5] J. Knowles and D. Corne, "The pareto archived evolution strategy: a new baseline algorithm for multiobjective optimization," in *Proceedings of the Congress on Evolutionary Computation*, pp. 98–105, IEEE Press, Piscataway, NJ, USA, September 1999.

[6] E. Zitzler, K. Deb, and L. Thiele, "Comparison of multiobjective evolutionary algorithms: empirical results," *Evolutionary Computation*, vol. 8, no. 2, pp. 173–195, 2000.

[7] K. Deb, M. Mohan, and S. Mishra, "Evaluating the epsilon-domination based multi-objective evolutionary algorithm for a quick computation of pareto-optimal solutions," *Evolutionary Computation*, vol. 13, no. 4, pp. 501–525, 2005.

[8] M. Li, J. Zheng, and G. Xiao, "An efficient multi-objective evolutionary algorithm based on minimum spanning tree," in *Proceedings of the IEEE Congress on Evolutionary Computation (CEC '08)*, pp. 617–624, IEEE Computer Society, Hong Kong, China, June 2008.

[9] T. Hanne, "A multiobjective evolutionary algorithm for approximating the efficient set," *European Journal of Operational Research*, vol. 176, no. 3, pp. 1723–1734, 2007.

[10] C. E. Shannon, "A mathematical theory of communication," *Bell System Technical Journal*, vol. 27, pp. 379–423 and 623–656, 1948.

[11] A. Farhang-Mehr and S. Azarm, "Diversity assessment of Pareto optimal solution sets: an entropy approach," in *Proceedings of the of the Congress on Evolutionary Computation*, pp. 723–728, 2002.

[12] S. Gunawan, A. Farhang-Mehr, and S. Azarm, *Multi-Level Multi-Objective Genetic Algorithm Using Entropy to Preserve Diversity*, Springer, Berlin, Germany, 2003.

[13] Y. N. Wang, L. H. Wu, and X. F. Yuan, "Multi-objective self-adaptive differential evolution with elitist archive and crowding entropy-based diversity measure," *Soft Computing*, vol. 14, no. 3, pp. 193–209, 2010.

[14] G. Rudolp, "Evolutionary search under paritialy ordered sets," Tech. Rep. CI-67-99, Department of Computer Science/LS11, University ofDortmund, Dortmund, Germany, 1999.

[15] C. E. Shannon, "A Mathematical theory of communication," *BellSystem Technical Journal*, vol. 27, pp. 379-423 and 623–656, 1948.

[16] K. Deb, L. Thiele, M. Laumanns et al., "Scalable test problems forevoltionary multi-objective optimization," Tech. Rep., ETH Zurich, Zurich, Switzerland, 2001.

[17] D. A. van Veldhuizen and G. B. Lamont, "Evolutionary computation and convergence to a pareto front," in *Proceedings of the Late Breaking Papers at the Genetic Programming Conference*, J. R. Koza, Ed., pp. 221–228, 1998.

[18] J. R. Schott, *Fault tolerant design using single and multicriteria genetic algorithm optimization [M.S. thesis]*, Department of Aeronautics and Astronautics, Massachusetts Institute of Technology, 1995.

[19] A. Zhou, Y. Jin, Q. Zhang, B. Sendhoff, and E. Tsang, "Combining model-based and genetics-based offspring generation for multi-objective optimization using a convergence criterion," in *Proceedings of the IEEE Congress on Evolutionary Computation (CEC '06)*, pp. 3234–3240, July 2006.

[20] D. Kalyanmoy and K. Amarendra, "Real-coded genetic algorithms with simulated binary crossover: studies on multimodal and multiobjective problems," *Complex Systems*, vol. 9, no. 6, pp. 431–454, 1995.

[21] K. Deb and M. A. Goyal, "Combined genetic adaptive search(GeneAs)for engineering design," *Computer Science and Informatics*, vol. 26, no. 4, pp. 30–45, 1996.

[22] K. Deb, L. Thiele, M. Laumanns, and E. Zitzler, "Scalable multi-objective optimization test problems," in *Proceedings of the IEEE Congress on Evolutionary Computation (CEC '02)*, D. B. Fogel, Ed., pp. 825–830, IEEE Service Center, Piscataway, NJ, USA, 2002.

8

A Hybrid Power Series Artificial Bee Colony Algorithm to Obtain a Solution for Buckling of Multiwall Carbon Nanotube Cantilevers Near Small Layers of Graphite Sheets

Aminreza Noghrehabadi,[1] Mohammad Ghalambaz,[1] Mehdi Ghalambaz,[2] and Afshin Ghanbarzadeh[1]

[1] *Department of Mechanical Engineering, Shahid Chamran University of Ahvaz, 6135743337 Ahvaz, Iran*
[2] *Engineering Part of Iman Madar Naslaha Co. (IMEN), Ahvaz, Iran*

Correspondence should be addressed to Aminreza Noghrehabadi, a.r.noghrehabadi@scu.ac.ir

Academic Editor: Erich Klement

A hybrid power series and artificial bee colony algorithm (PS-ABC) method is applied to solve a system of nonlinear differential equations arising from the distributed parameter model of multiwalled carbon nanotube (MWCNT) cantilevers in the vicinity of thin and thick graphite sheets subject to intermolecular forces. The intermolecular forces are modeled using van der Waals forces. A trial solution of the differential equation is defined as sum of two polynomial parts. The first part satisfies the boundary conditions and does contain two adjustable parameters. The second part is constructed as not to affect the boundary conditions, which involves adjustable parameters. The ABC method is applied to find adjustable parameters of trial solution (in first and second part). The obtained results are compared with numerical results as well as analytical solutions those reported in the literature. The results of the presented method represent a remarkable accuracy in comparison with numerical results. The minimum initial gap and the detachment length of the actuator that does not stick to the substrate due to the intermolecular forces, as important parameters in pull-in instability of MWCNT actuator, are evaluated by obtained power series.

1. Introduction

Multiwalled carbon nanotubes (MWCNTs) have attracted considerable attention among other nanomaterials because of the potential advantages on markedly improved stiffness, strength, and elimination of main failure mechanism [1]. These novel materials can usually be visualized as nanoscale concentric cylinders rolled up by graphene sheets. MWCNTs are produced by different techniques such as chemical vapor deposition, laser ablation, and arc discharge [1, 2]. The nanotubes can provide various ranges of conductive properties depending on their atomic and geometrical structure [3]. The unusual properties of MWCNTs have motivated worldwide engineers to explore their applications in different fields of science [4].

Experimental investigations show that the conductance of CNTs is strongly influenced by the occurrence of buckling [5]. The repeatable transformation between the buckled state and normal state of CNTs produces good potential applications to create devices such as nanotransistors [5], nano-valve, and so forth, [6]. With recent growth in nanotechnology, MWCNTs are increasingly used in developing atomic force microscope (AFM) probes [1, 3, 7, 8] and nanoelectromechanical system (NEMS) switches [9–11].

In the nanoscale, the surface forces play an important role in the design and operation of the MEMS and NEMS devices. The van der Waals force and Casimir force are two significant forces in the scale of nanometers [12]. These forces are basically electromagnetic in nature, and they are important when the separation space between objects is very small [12].

In general, there are two basic approaches to understand the behaviors of CNTs: one is atomistic molecular dynamics simulation and the second is continuum mechanics.

However, the molecular dynamic method is very time consuming and computationally expensive for a large-scale system.

In a recent work, Koochi et al. [13] applied a hybrid continuum model to investigate the molecular force-induced buckling of a freestanding MWCNT probes/actuators suspended over graphite sheets. They carried out a fourth order nonlinear ordinary differential equation for buckling of multiwalled carbon nanotube (MWCNT) probes/actuators. Koochi et al. [13] used Adomian decomposition method to obtain a solution for buckling and pull-in in stability of MWCNTs. Although, the results of Adomian decomposition method in comparison with numerical results are acceptable, but the results show that the accuracy of Adomian method near the pull-in instability conditions is decreased.

Many different methods have been developed to solve differential equations. However, the solution of nonlinear differential equations still is a challenge [14, 15]. Recently, artificial intelligence techniques are used to solve nonlinear differential equations and modeling engineering problems [16–21]. Lee and Kang [22] used parallel processor computers to obtain a trial solution for a first order differential equation. Meade and Fernandez [23] applied feed forward neural networks to solve linear and nonlinear ordinary differential equations. Lagaris et al. [15] introduced a new method to solve First order linear ordinary and partial differential equations using artificial neural networks. Malek and Beidokhti [24] applied a hybrid artificial neural network—Nelder-Mead optimization technique to solve high order linear differential equations. A hybrid artificial neural network-swarm intelligence method was used by Khan et al. [14] to solve a nonlinear differential equation.

The goal of an optimization problem can be stated as finding the combination of parameters (independent variables) which maximizes or minimizes the value of one or more dependent variables. The value or function to be optimized is called objective function.

Artificial bee colony (ABC) is one of the optimization algorithms, which is introduced by Karaboga in 2005 [25]. The motivation of this algorithm is the intelligent behavior of honey bees. ABC is a simple method with a few main common control parameters such as colony size and maximum cycle number.

Karaboga and Basturk [26] introduced artificial bee colony as an efficient algorithm for numerical function optimization. Karaboga and Akay [27] performed a comparative study on the ABC. They used ABC for optimizing a large set of numerical test functions. They compared the produced results of ABC algorithm with the results obtained by genetic algorithm, particle swarm optimization algorithm, differential evolution algorithm, and evolution strategies. They reported that the performance of the ABC is better than or similar to those of other population-based algorithms with the advantage of employing fewer control parameters.

In the present study, a combination of power series and artificial bee colony optimization algorithm is applied to obtain a power series solution for the nonlinear ordinary differential equations of MWCNT cantilevers. A remarkable accuracy for the presented method is achieved when the obtained results are compared with numerical results.

2. Mathematical Model

Figure 1 shows the schematic of a typical freestanding MWCNT near a surface consisted of N graphene layers, with interlayer distance $d = 3.35$ Å. Consider a MWCNT with the mean radius of R_W, the length of L, and multiwall nanotube layers of N_W. The gap between MWCNT and the surface is D.

2.1. Electrostatic Domain. Based on continuum mechanics, an MWCNT is modeled by concentric cylindrical tubes. E_{eff} is Young's modulus of MWCNT and the cross-sectional moment of inertia I is equal to $\pi(R_o^4 - R_i^4)/4$ [13]. By applying the Euler theory and neglecting the effect of large displacement (finite kinematics) for $L/D_e > 10$ [28], the governing equation of a cantilever MWCNT can be defined in the form of following boundary value differential equation [13]:

$$E_{eff}I\frac{d^4U}{dX^4} = q_{vdW}(D - U) \qquad (1a)$$

subject to geometrical and natural boundary conditions as

$$U(0) = \frac{dU}{dX}(0) = 0, \qquad \frac{d^2U}{dX^2}(L) = \frac{d^3U}{dX^3}(L) = 0, \qquad (1b)$$

where X is the position along MWCNT measured from the bended end, U is the deflection of MWCNT, and q_{vdw} denote the intermolecular force per unit length of MWCNT. The intermolecular force of q_{Wdv} base on double-volume integral of Lennard-Jones potential and some simplification can be represented as

$$q_{Wdv} = \frac{4C_6\sigma^2\pi^2NN_WR_W}{d(D - U + Nd/2)^4} \qquad (2)$$

for small number of graphene layers [13].

In the above equation, $C_6 = 15.2$ eV Å^6 is the attractive constants for the carbon-carbon interaction [29], and $\sigma \approx 38$ nm^{-2} is the graphene surface density [30]. By substituting (2) in (1a), (1b) and using the following substitutions

$$x = \frac{X}{L}, \qquad u = \frac{U}{D + Nd/2}, \qquad f_n = \frac{4C_6\sigma^2\pi^2NN_WR_WL^4}{E_{eff}I(D + Nd/2)^6}, \qquad (3)$$

the dimensionless form of (1a), (1b) can be obtained as follows:

$$\frac{d^4u}{dx^4} = \frac{f}{(1 - u(x))^5}$$

$$u(0) = u'(0) = 0, \qquad \text{at } x = 0,$$
$$u''(1) = u'''(1) = 0, \qquad \text{at } x = 1, \qquad (4)$$

where in all equations prime denotes differentiation with respect to x.

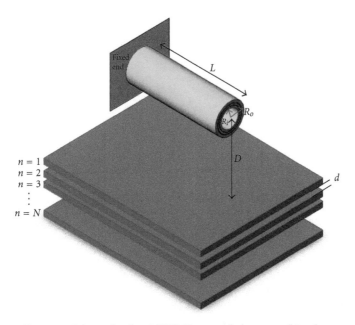

FIGURE 1: Schematic of an MWCNT suspended over graphite sheets.

3. Artificial Bee Colony Optimization Algorithm

The artificial bee colony (ABC) algorithm was proposed by Karaboga in 2005. This method is a gradient free optimization algorithm for real parameter optimization, which inspired from intelligent foraging behavior of a bee colony [25].

In a natural bee colony, some tasks are performed by specialized individuals. In the ABC algorithm, the colony of artificial bees contains three groups of bees as the employed bees, the onlookers, and the scouts [26]. The onlooker bee is a bee waiting for making decision to choose a nectar source. A bee which is going to the nectar source which it previously visited is an employed bee. A scout bee carries out a random search around the hive. In the ABC algorithm, first half of the colony consists of employed artificial bees and the second half constitutes the onlooker bees. In the method proposed by Karaboga, the number of employed bees is equal to the number of food sources around the hive. The employed bee whose food source is exhausted by the employed and onlooker bees becomes a scout bee. The main steps of the algorithm can be summarized as [26].

(i) Initializing the population which can be strategic or random.

(ii) Repeat procedure:

    (a) place the employed bees on the nectar sources in the memory;

    (b) place the onlooker bees on the nectar sources in the memory;

    (c) send the scouts to the search area for discovering new nectar sources.

(iii) Until requirements are met.

These specialized bees try to maximize the nectar amount stored in the hive by performing efficient division of labor and self-organization. The basic idea and details about ABC algorithm are explained in [25–27, 31]. In the ABC algorithm, proposed by Karaboga, the position of a nectar source represents a possible solution in the search space for the optimization problem, and the nectar amount of a food source represents the profitability (fitness) of the associated solution.

4. Solution Method

The governing equation of a nanotube cantilever was expressed by (1a), (1b). In order to solve (1a), (1b), assume a discretization of the domain D with m arbitrary points. Here, the problem can be written as the following set of equations:

$$\frac{d^4 u(x_i)}{dx^4} - \left(\frac{f}{(1 - u(x_i))^5} \right) = 0, \quad x_i \in D, i = 1, 2, \ldots, m \tag{5}$$

subject to given boundary conditions in (2).

Let us assume $y_T(x, \vec{v})$ as an approximate solution to (1a), (1b) in which $\vec{v}$ is a vector containing adjustable parameters. These parameters (i.e., the adjustable parameters) can be evaluated by minimizing the following sum of squared errors, subject to given boundary conditions in (2)

$$E(\vec{a}) = \sum_{i=1}^{m} \left(\frac{d^4 y_T(x_i, \vec{v})}{dx^4} - \frac{f}{(1 - y_T(x_i, \vec{v}))^5} \right)^2, \tag{6}$$

$$x_i \in [0 \quad 1].$$

In order to transform (5) to an unconstrained problem, $y_T(x, \vec{a})$ can be written as

$$Y_T(x, \vec{v}) = v_1 x^5 + v_2 x^4 - (10v_1 - 4v_2)x^3$$
$$+ (20v_1 + 6v_2)x^2 + x^2(x-1)^4 N(x, \vec{v}), \quad (7)$$

where v_1 and v_2 are adjustable parameters. $N(x, \vec{a})$ is a power series $(N(x, \vec{v}) = \sum_{i=0}^{n} v_{i+3} x^i)$ which involves adjustable parameters of v_3 to v_n. Here, (7) is in the form of a power series with adjustable coefficients, and it exactly satisfies the given boundary conditions of (1-b).

Now, an optimization technique can be applied in order to determine the optimal adjustable parameters of $y_T(x, \vec{v})$ (i.e., $\vec{v}$) to minimize $E(\vec{v})$ in (6). Here, the ABC algorithm is used to evaluate the adjustable vector parameter of v to minimize (6).

For different sizes of the series $(n = 5, 6, 7, \ldots, 10)$, the domain of solution is divided to 21 collocation points with equal spices of 0.05 $(x_i \in \{0, 0.05, 0.01 \ldots 1\})$. This configuration was applied for all solutions in the following text. The control parameters of ABC are essential for obtaining an accurate solution. Increase of colony size increases the calculation time, and decrease of colony size decreases the accuracy of solution and may lead to trap in the local optimums. Table 1 shows the best obtained combination of user-specified parameters of ABC method, which are used for this problem in the following text. This combination of parameters is obtained by trial and error.

In order to verify the convergence and accuracy of the present method, buckling of a typical nanotube-actuator with $f = 0.5$ is computed for different size of series using PS-ABC method. The obtained results are compared with the numerical data as well as Adomian decomposition results reported by Koochi et al. [13]. Numerical results are obtained using Maple commercial software, which uses a combination of trapezoid as base scheme and Richardson extrapolation as enhancement scheme [32, 33]. In the case of $f_n = 0.5$, the tip deflection was numerically obtained as $u_t = 0.08323$. The variation of the nanotube cantilever tip deflection (u_{tip}), using different selected terms of series is shown in Table 2. This table ensures the convergence and accuracy of the results. As seen, higher accuracy can be obtained by evaluating more terms of the solution $u(x)$. The relative error is computed from

$$\text{Error} = \left| \frac{u_{\text{Analytical}} - u_{\text{Numerical}}}{u_{\text{Numerical}}} \right|, \quad (8)$$

where $u_{\text{Analytical}}$ and $u_{\text{Numerical}}$ are the cantilever MWCNT tip deflection computed from analytical method and the tip deflection computed using numerical method, respectively. Here, error indicates the relative error.

The results of Table 2 show that the PS-ABC with series size of eight almost converged to the numerical result. Thus, the power series size of eight has been selected in the following text for convenience. Comparing this error with the same series size of Adomian method (i.e., eight terms and relative error of 0.12%) shows that the PS-ABC method could compute deflection of cantilever MWCNTs with more

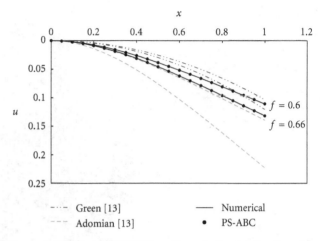

FIGURE 2: Buckling of MWCNT cantilever in the vicinity of graphite sheets for different values of f.

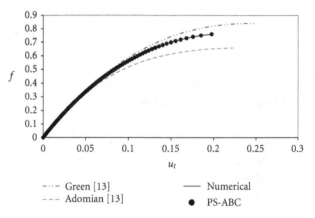

FIGURE 3: Comparison between the tip buckling of MWCNT cantilevers obtained by different methods.

accuracy than Adomian method. The obtained power series with eight term for $f = 0.5$ is as follows:

$$u(x) = 0.160624628\, x^2 - 0.097464959\, x^3 + 0.018038276\, x^4$$
$$+ 0.000022094\, x^5 + 0.003837749\, x^6$$
$$- 0.002404155\, x^7 + 0.000580025\, x^8. \quad (9)$$

5. Results and Discussion

Figure 2 shows the centerline deflection of nanotubes for selected values of parameter f.

This figure reveals that when the parameter of f is small, the buckling can be neglected, and by increase of f, the beam deflects into the substrate. As seen, the power series solution in comparison with the same size of Adomian series solution (i.e., [13]) is more powerful to simulate the deflection and instability of nanocantilever beams. Figure 3 shows the variation of tip deflection as a function of f. Figures 2 and 3 reveal that the Adomian method underestimated the bucking of nanotubes and Greens method overestimated it while the

A Hybrid Power Series Artificial Bee Colony Algorithm to Obtain a Solution for Buckling of Multiwall Carbon Nanotube
Cantilevers Near Small Layers of Graphite Sheets

73

TABLE 1: Control parameters of ABC algorithm.

Control parameter	Value
Type of initial population	Random
The number of colony size (employed bees + onlooker bees)	150 bees
The food source limit which will be abandoned if no improvement was observed	100 try
The maximum foraging try	450 try

TABLE 2: A comparison between the evaluated tip deflection of a typical MWCNT cantilever using different terms of PS-ABC method and Adomian decomposition method for $f = 0.5$.

Series size	Tip deflection adomian [13]	Error	Tip deflection PS-ABC	Error
5	0.06250	$2.491E - 01$	0.08278	$5.50E - 03$
6	0.09533	$1.453E - 01$	0.08319	$5.13E - 04$
7	0.07516	$9.700E - 02$	0.08324	$6.41E - 05$
8	0.09350	$1.233E - 01$	0.08323	0
9	0.07737	$7.046E - 02$	0.08323	0
10	0.08842	$6.228E - 02$	0.08323	0

presented method obtained buckling of nanotubes with very good accuracy in comparison with numerical results.

6. Conclusions

In this paper, an integration of power series and artificial bee colony optimization method has been utilized in order to obtain a solution for buckling of MWCNT cantilevers subject to small number of graphite layers. The governing differential equation is forth order and highly nonlinear due to the inherent of the van der Waals and electrostatic interactions. A trial solution which exactly satisfies the boundary conditions in the form of a power series with adjustable parameters was introduced. The artificial bee colony optimization algorithm was successfully applied to justify the adjustable parameters of the trial solution. The results of present method are compared with numerical results as well as Adomian decomposition method and Green's method reported in the literature. It is found that the accuracy of present method remarkably is better than the same size of Adomian power series. Therefore, the PS-ABC method can provide an accurate and stable solution for study of MWCNT cantilevers. The present method can be easily extended to solve other nonlinear boundary value differential equations. The future work can be focused on the comparison between the efficiently of the ABC method and other available optimization methods to tackle the present boundary value differential equation.

Acknowledgments

The authors are grateful to Shahid Chamran University of Ahvaz for its support through this paper.

References

[1] A. M. K. Esawi and M. M. Farag, "Carbon nanotube reinforced composites: potential and current challenges," *Materials and Design*, vol. 28, no. 9, pp. 2394–2401, 2007.

[2] S. J. Chowdhury and B. Howard, "Thermo-mechanical properties of graphite-epoxy composite," *International Review of Mechanical Engineering*, vol. 4, no. 6, pp. 785–790, 2010.

[3] C. Li, E. T. Thostenson, and T. W. Chou, "Sensors and actuators based on carbon nanotubes and their composites: a review," *Composites Science and Technology*, vol. 68, no. 6, pp. 1227–1249, 2008.

[4] M. S. Dresselhaus, G. Dresselhaus, and A. Jorio, "Unusual properties and structure of carbon nanotubes," *Annual Review of Materials Research*, vol. 34, pp. 247–278, 2004.

[5] H. W. C. Postma, T. Teepen, Z. Yao, M. Grifoni, and C. Dekker, "Carbon nanotube single-electron transistors at room temperature," *Science*, vol. 293, no. 5527, pp. 76–79, 2001.

[6] M. Grujicic, G. Cao, and W. N. Roy, "Computational analysis of the lattice contribution to thermal conductivity of single-walled carbon nanotubes," *Journal of Materials Science*, vol. 40, no. 8, pp. 1943–1952, 2005.

[7] S. Akita, "Nanotweezers consisting of carbon nanotubes operating in an atomic force microscope," *Applied Physics Letters*, vol. 79, pp. 1591–1593, 2001.

[8] Y. Cao, Y. Liang, S. Dong, and Y. Wang, "A multi-wall carbon nanotube (MWCNT) relocation technique for atomic force microscopy (AFM) samples," *Ultramicroscopy*, vol. 103, no. 2, pp. 103–108, 2005.

[9] M. Paradise and T. Goswami, "Carbon nanotubes—production and industrial applications," *Materials and Design*, vol. 28, no. 5, pp. 1477–1489, 2007.

[10] R. H. Baughman, C. Cui, A. A. Zakhidov et al., "Carbon nanotube actuators," *Science*, vol. 284, no. 5418, pp. 1340–1344, 1999.

[11] C. H. Ke, N. Pugno, B. Peng, and H. D. Espinosa, "Experiments and modeling of carbon nanotube-based NEMS devices," *Journal of the Mechanics and Physics of Solids*, vol. 53, no. 6, pp. 1314–1333, 2005.

[12] G. L. Klimchitskaya, E. V. Blagov, and V. M. Mostepanenko, "Van der Waals and Casimir interactions between atoms and carbon nanotubes," *Journal of Physics A*, vol. 41, no. 16, Article ID 164012, 2008.

[13] A. Koochi, A. S. Kazemi, A. Noghrehabadi, A. Yekrangi, and M. Abadyan, "New approach to model the buckling and stable

length of multi walled carbon nanotube probes near graphite sheets," *Materials and Design*, vol. 32, no. 5, pp. 2949–2955, 2011.

[14] J. A. Khan, R. M. A. Zahoor, and I. M. Qureshi, "Swarm Intelligence for the problems of non-linear ordinary differential equations and its application to well known Wessinger's equation," *European Journal of Scientific Research*, vol. 34, no. 4, pp. 514–525, 2009.

[15] I. E. Lagaris, A. Likas, and D. I. Fotiadis, "Artificial neural networks for solving ordinary and partial differential equations," *IEEE Transactions on Neural Networks*, vol. 9, no. 5, pp. 987–1000, 1998.

[16] M. Ghalambaz, A. R. Noghrehabadi, M. A. Behrang, E. Assareh, A. Ghanbarzadeh, and N. Hedayat, "A hybrid neural network and gravitational search algorithm (HNNGSA) method to solve well known Wessinger's equation," *Proceedings of World Academy of Science, Engineering and Technology*, vol. 73, pp. 803–807, 2011.

[17] A. Noghrehabadi, M. Ghalambaz, and M. Ghalambaz, "A hybrid power series—artificial bee colony to solve magnetohydrodynamic viscous flow over a nonlinear permeable shrinking sheet," *International Review on Modelling and Simulations*, vol. 4, no. 5, pp. 2696–2700, 2011.

[18] M. A. Behrang, M. Ghalambaz, E. Assareh, and A. R. Noghrehabadi, "A new solution for natural convection of darcian fluid about a vertical full cone embedded in porous media prescribed wall temperature by using a hybrid neural network-particle swarm optimization method," *World Academy of Science, Engineering and Technology*, vol. 73, pp. 1108–1113, 2011.

[19] E. Assareh, M. A. Behrang, M. Ghalambaz, A. R. Noghrehabadi, and A. Ghanbarzadeh, "*A New Approach to Solve Blasius Equation using Parameter Identification of Nonlinear Functions based on the Bees Algorithm (BA)*, vol. 73, World Academy of Science, Engineering and Technology, 2001.

[20] M. Ghalambaz, A. Noghrehabadi, and A. Vosoogh, "A hybrid Power series—Artificial Bee Colony algorithm to solve electrostatic pull-in instability and deflection of nano cantilever actuators considering Casimir Attractions," *International Review of Mechanical Engineering*, vol. 5, no. 4, 2011.

[21] A. Yekrangi, M. Ghalambaz, A. Noghrehabadi et al., "Approximate solution for a simple pendulum beyond the small angles regimes using hybrid artificial neural network and particle swarm optimization algorithm," *Procedia Engineering*, vol. 10, pp. 3742–3748, 2011.

[22] H. Lee and I. S. Kang, "Neural algorithm for solving differential equations," *Journal of Computational Physics*, vol. 91, no. 1, pp. 110–131, 1990.

[23] A. J. Meade Jr. and A. A. Fernandez, "The numerical solution of linear ordinary differential equations by feedforward neural networks," *Mathematical and Computer Modelling*, vol. 19, no. 12, pp. 1–25, 1994.

[24] A. Malek and R. S. Beidokhti, "Numerical solution for high order differential equations using a hybrid neural network—optimization method," *Applied Mathematics and Computation*, vol. 183, no. 1, pp. 260–271, 2006.

[25] D. Karaboga, "An idea based on honey bee swarm for numerical optimization," Tech. Rep. TR06, Erciyes University, Engineering Faculty, Computer Engineering Department, 2005.

[26] D. Karaboga and B. Basturk, "A powerful and efficient algorithm for numerical function optimization: Artificial Bee Colony (ABC) algorithm," *Journal of Global Optimization*, vol. 39, no. 3, pp. 459–471, 2007.

[27] D. Karaboga and B. Akay, "A comparative study of Artificial Bee Colony algorithm," *Applied Mathematics and Computation*, vol. 214, no. 1, pp. 108–132, 2009.

[28] W. H. Lin and Y. P. Zhao, "Casimir effect on the pull-in parameters of nanometer switches," *Microsystem Technologies*, vol. 11, no. 2-3, pp. 80–85, 2005.

[29] L. A. Girifalco, M. Hodak, and R. S. Lee, "Carbon nanotubes, buckyballs, ropes, and a universal graphitic potential," *Physical Review B*, vol. 62, no. 19, pp. 13104–13110, 2000.

[30] M. Dequesnes, S. V. Rotkin, and N. R. Aluru, "Calculation of pull-in voltages for carbon-nanotube-based nanoelectromechanical switches," *Nanotechnology*, vol. 13, no. 1, pp. 120–131, 2002.

[31] B. Akay and D. Karaboga, "A modified Artificial Bee Colony algorithm for real-parameter optimization," *Information Sciences*, vol. 192, pp. 120–142, 2012.

[32] U. Ascher, R. Mattheij, and R. Russell, *Numerical Solution of Boundary Value Problems for Ordinary Differential Equations*, vol. 13 of *SIAM Classics in Applied Mathematics*, 1995.

[33] U. Ascher and L. Petzold, *Computer Methods for Ordinary Differential Equations and Differential-Algebraic Equations*, SIAM, Philadelphia, Pa, USA, 1998.

9

A Novel Feature Extraction Method for Nonintrusive Appliance Load Monitoring

Khaled Chahine[1] and Khalil El Khamlichi Drissi[2]

[1] *Department of Electrical and Electronics Engineering, Lebanese International University, Mazraa, Beirut 146404, Lebanon*
[2] *Pascal Institute, UMR 6602, 24 Avenue des Landais, 63177 Aubière Cedex, France*

Correspondence should be addressed to Khaled Chahine; khaled.chahine@liu.edu.lb

Academic Editor: Baoding Liu

Improving energy efficiency by monitoring household electrical consumption is of significant importance with the climate change concerns of the present time. A solution for the electrical consumption management problem is the use of a nonintrusive appliance load monitoring (NIALM) system. This system captures the signals from the aggregate consumption, extracts the features from these signals and classifies the extracted features in order to identify the switched-on appliances. This paper focuses solely on feature extraction through applying the matrix pencil method, a well-known parametric estimation technique, to the drawn electric current. The result is a compact representation of the current signal in terms of complex numbers referred to as poles and residues. These complex numbers are shown to be characteristic of the considered load and can thus serve as features in any subsequent classification module. In the absence of noise, simulations indicate an almost perfect agreement between theoretical and estimated values of poles and residues. For real data, poles and residues are used to determine a feature vector consisting of the contribution of the fundamental, the third, and the fifth harmonic currents to the maximum of the total load current. The result is a three-dimensional feature space with reduced intercluster overlap.

1. Introduction

The reason behind the drive for the installation of smart meters in homes and businesses is that they facilitate for consumers to monitor their energy consumption, thereby making it easier for them to save energy, carbon emissions, and money. To help customers as well as utilities in the monitoring process, researchers have been studying load disaggregation schemes for more than two decades.

One method of load disaggregation is distributed direct sensing which requires a sensor at each device or appliance in order to measure consumption. The one-sensor-per-device requirement is both the blessing and the curse of this method, for it is highly accurate but expensive. To overcome the limitations associated with the direct sensing approach, researchers have explored methods to infer disaggregated energy usage via a single sensor. Pioneering work in this area is non intrusive appliance load monitoring (NIALM), first introduced by Hart in the late 1980s [1]. In contrast to the direct sensing methods, NIALM relies solely on single-point measurements of voltage and current on the power feed entering the household. NIALM consists of four steps: data acquisition, event detection, feature extraction, and event classification. The raw current and voltage waveforms are transformed into a feature vector, that is, a more compact and meaningful representation that may include real power, reactive power, current-voltage phase difference, and harmonics (e.g., [2]). These extracted features are monitored for changes, identified as events (e.g., an appliance turning "on" or "off"), and classified down to the appliance or device category level using a classification algorithm, which usually compares the features to a preexisting database of signatures. Several reviews of feature extraction methods for electric loads in residential and commercial buildings can be found in the literature [3, 4].

Based on the degree of nonintrusiveness, the literature draws a distinction between manual-setup NIALM (MS-NIALM) and automatic-setup NIALM (AS-NIALM) systems. While the former requires switching individual appliances on and off manually to learn their signatures, the latter sets itself up using prior information about potential appliances. AS-NIALM hence extracts the signatures and labels them without any sort of manual intervention which would greatly facilitate mass installation of smart meters. To the authors' knowledge, no AS-NIALM system has hitherto been implemented. It is hence the main goal of this work to pave the way for such a solution.

In this paper, the matrix pencil method, a well-known parametric estimation technique, is applied to the electric current drawn by some elementary linear and nonlinear electric loads driven by a sinusoidal voltage source as well as real loads. The result is a compact representation of the current in terms of complex numbers referred to as poles and residues [5, 6]. These complex numbers are shown to be characteristic of the considered load and thus can serve as features for the subsequent classification phase [7]. For both synthetic and real data, results indicate that poles and residues extracted by the MPM allow an almost perfect reconstruction of drawn electric currents. Results obtained from a database of a household indicate that the extracted features succeed in reducing the intercluster overlap of different appliances.

The objectives of this paper are summarized in the following two points:

(1) show that the reduced number of poles and residues estimated by MPM enable an accurate reconstruction of synthetic and real signals;

(2) show that the fundamental and higher harmonic currents determined from poles and residues yield a feature space with reduced intercluster overlap.

The rest of the paper is organized as follows. Section 2 presents the signal model and the principle of the MPM. Sections 3 and 4 show the validation on simulated and real data, respectively. Finally, Section 5 provides the summary and conclusion.

2. Feature Extraction

2.1. Signal Model. For a sinusoidal driving voltage of the form $v(t) = V\sqrt{2}\sin(\omega t)$, the drawn electric current can be modeled as a linear combination of d cisoids (complex-valued sinusoidal signals) weighted by complex residues according to the following signal model:

$$i(t) \approx \sum_{m=1}^{d} r_m \exp\left\{(\alpha_m + j2\pi f_m)t\right\} + b(t), \quad (1)$$

where r_m is the residue of the mth cisoid, α_m is its attenuation factor, f_m is its frequency, and $b(t)$ is additive white Gaussian noise. After sampling, the time variable, t, is replaced by $t_k = kt_s$, where $t_s = 6.25 \times 10^{-4}$ is the chosen sampling period. The discrete current signal becomes

$$i(k) \approx \sum_{m=1}^{d} r_m z_m^k + b(k) \quad k = 1, 2, \ldots, N, \quad (2)$$

where

$$z_m = \exp\left\{(\alpha_m + j2\pi f_m)t_s\right\} \quad m = 1, 2, \ldots, d \quad (3)$$

is the mth complex pole. Under matrix form, the signal model is expressed by

$$\mathbf{i} = \mathbf{Ar} + \mathbf{b} \quad (4)$$

with the following notational definitions:

$$\mathbf{i} = \begin{bmatrix} i(1) & i(2) & \ldots & i(N) \end{bmatrix}^T,$$

$$\mathbf{A} = \begin{bmatrix} \mathbf{a}_1 & \mathbf{a}_2 & \ldots & \mathbf{a}_d \end{bmatrix},$$

$$\mathbf{a}_m = \begin{bmatrix} z_m & z_m^2 & \ldots & z_m^N \end{bmatrix}^T, \quad (5)$$

$$\mathbf{r} = \begin{bmatrix} r_1 & r_2 & \ldots & r_d \end{bmatrix}^T,$$

$$\mathbf{b} = \begin{bmatrix} b(1) & b(2) & \ldots & b(N) \end{bmatrix}^T.$$

The superscript T denotes the transpose operator.

The feature extraction problem can now be stated as follows. Given the electric current data sequence $\{i(k)\}_{k=1}^{N}$, use a feature extraction method to extract the complex poles $\{z_m\}_{m=1}^{d}$ and residues $\{r_m\}_{m=1}^{d}$ of the load.

2.2. Matrix Pencil Method (MPM). This section briefly recalls the principle of MPM which is a linear prediction method tailored to the parameter estimation of the damped/undamped exponential model. Starting from the signal model given in (1), MPM chooses a free parameter, L, known as the pencil parameter such as $d \leq L \leq N - d$. The proper choice of L results in significant robustness against noise. The next step is to construct a Hankel data matrix:

$$\mathbf{H} = \begin{bmatrix} i(1) & i(2) & \cdots & i(L+1) \\ i(2) & i(3) & \cdots & i(L+2) \\ \vdots & \vdots & \ddots & \vdots \\ i(N-L) & i(N-L+1) & \cdots & i(N) \end{bmatrix}. \quad (6)$$

Two matrices are then obtained by removing the last and first columns of $\mathbf{H}$. In MATLAB notation, they are given as follows:

$$\overrightarrow{\mathbf{H}} = \mathbf{H}(:, 1:L),$$
$$\overleftarrow{\mathbf{H}} = \mathbf{H}(:, 2:L+1). \quad (7)$$

The matrix pencil for the two matrices $\overrightarrow{\mathbf{H}}$ and $\overleftarrow{\mathbf{H}}$ is defined as their linear combination $\overleftarrow{\mathbf{H}} - \lambda \overrightarrow{\mathbf{H}}$, with λ a scalar parameter. In the absence of noise and owing to the assumed signal model, it is easily verified that $\overrightarrow{\mathbf{H}}$ and $\overleftarrow{\mathbf{H}}$ admit the following Vandermonde decomposition:

$$\overrightarrow{\mathbf{H}} = \mathbf{Z}_1 \mathbf{R} \mathbf{Z}_2,$$
$$\overleftarrow{\mathbf{H}} = \mathbf{Z}_1 \mathbf{R} \mathbf{Z}_0 \mathbf{Z}_2, \quad (8)$$

where

$$\mathbf{Z}_1 = \begin{bmatrix} z_1 & z_2 & \cdots & z_d \\ z_1^2 & z_2^2 & \cdots & z_d^2 \\ \vdots & \vdots & \ddots & \vdots \\ z_1^{N-L} & z_2^{N-L} & \cdots & z_d^{N-L} \end{bmatrix},$$

$$\mathbf{Z}_2 = \begin{bmatrix} 1 & z_1 & \cdots & z_1^{L-1} \\ 1 & z_2 & \cdots & z_2^{L-1} \\ \vdots & \vdots & \ddots & \vdots \\ 1 & z_d & \cdots & z_d^{L-1} \end{bmatrix}, \qquad (9)$$

$$\mathbf{Z}_0 = \text{diag}\{z_1, z_2, \ldots, z_d\},$$

$$\mathbf{R} = \text{diag}\{r_1, r_2, \ldots, r_d\},$$

revealing the fundamental shift-invariance property in the column and row spaces. The matrix pencil can then be written as

$$\underleftarrow{\mathbf{H}} - \lambda \underrightarrow{\mathbf{H}} = \mathbf{Z}_1 \mathbf{R} \left[\mathbf{Z}_0 - \lambda \mathbf{I}\right] \mathbf{Z}_2, \qquad (10)$$

where $\mathbf{I}$ is the identity matrix. Hence, each value of $\lambda = z_m$ is a rank-reducing number of the pencil. The estimates of z_m are, therefore, the generalized eigenvalues (GEVs) of the matrix pair $[\underleftarrow{\mathbf{H}}, \underrightarrow{\mathbf{H}}]$.

Once the complex poles $\{z_m\}_{m=1}^d$ are determined, the complex residues can be estimated using a least squares fit having the following solution:

$$\mathbf{r} = \left(\mathbf{A}^H \mathbf{A}\right)^{-1} \mathbf{A}^H \mathbf{i}. \qquad (11)$$

For noisy data, total least squares matrix pencil method (TLSMPM) is usually preferred in which the singular value decomposition is used to prefilter the complex signals, and then conventional procedures follow. For more details, the reader can refer to [8].

3. Validation on Synthetic Data

3.1. Linear Loads. To validate MPM as a feature extraction method, we shall first compare its poles and residues with those obtained from the theoretical expressions of the following linear elementary loads: series RC, series RL, parallel RL, and series RLC. The RC and RL circuits lead to first order differential equations in time whereas the RLC circuit leads to a second-order differential equation. Using Euler's formula and rearranging allow rewriting the current expression obtained from the solution of the differential equation characterizing the load in the form of (1). The poles and residues of each elementary load can then be readily identified. Tables 1, 2, 3, and 4 give the residues, attenuation factors, and frequencies of the four studied elementary loads. As can be seen from these tables, first-order circuits (RL and RC) are characterized by two pure imaginary conjugate poles representing their forced response and one real pole representing their natural response, whereas the second-order circuit (RLC) has, besides the two pure imaginary conjugate poles of its forced

TABLE 1: The residues, attenuation factors, and frequencies of the series RC load.

m	r_m	α_m	f_m (Hz)
1	$\dfrac{V\sqrt{2}}{2jR}\cos(\phi)e^{-j\phi}$	0	+50
2	$-\dfrac{V\sqrt{2}}{2jR}\cos(\phi)e^{j\phi}$	0	−50
3	$-\dfrac{1}{R}\left(v_{C_0} - V\sqrt{2}\sin(\phi)\cos(\omega t_0 - \phi)\right)e^{t_0/\tau}$	$-\dfrac{1}{\tau}$	0

TABLE 2: The residues, attenuation factors, and frequencies of the series RL load.

m	r_m	α_m	f_m (Hz)
1	$\dfrac{V\sqrt{2}}{2jR}\cos(\phi)e^{-j\phi}$	0	+50
2	$-\dfrac{V\sqrt{2}}{2jR}\cos(\phi)e^{j\phi}$	0	−50
3	$i_{L_0} - \dfrac{V\sqrt{2}}{R}\cos(\phi)\sin(\omega t_0 - \phi)e^{t_0/\tau}$	$-\dfrac{1}{\tau}$	0

TABLE 3: The residues, attenuation factors, and frequencies of the parallel RL load.

m	r_m	α_m	f_m (Hz)
1	$\dfrac{V\sqrt{2}}{2jR\cos(\phi)}e^{-j\phi}$	0	+50
2	$-\dfrac{V\sqrt{2}}{2jR\cos(\phi)}e^{j\phi}$	0	−50
3	$i_{L_0} - \dfrac{V\sqrt{2}}{R\cos(\phi)}\sin(\omega t_0 - \phi)$	0	0

TABLE 4: The residues, attenuation factors, and frequencies of the series RLC load.

m	r_m	α_m	f_m (Hz)
1	$\dfrac{V\sqrt{2}}{2jR}\cos(\phi)e^{-j\phi}$	0	+50
2	$-\dfrac{V\sqrt{2}}{2jR}\cos(\phi)e^{j\phi}$	0	−50
3	$Ae^{-k_1\omega_0 t_0}$	$k_1\omega_0$	0
4	$Be^{-k_2\omega_0 t_0}$	$k_2\omega_0$	0

response, two conjugate complex poles related to its natural response. The expressions of the dependent parameters are given in the appendix.

3.2. Nonlinear Loads. A nonlinear load is one for which the relationship between the current through the load and the voltage across the load is a nonlinear function. A simple view of the nature of nonlinear loads can be presented using Ohm's Law, which states that the voltage is the product of the load resistance and the current ($V = RI$). For a linear load, the resistance (R) is a constant; for a nonlinear load, the resistance varies. When AC power is supplied to a nonlinear load,

TABLE 5: Current composition of a nonlinear load.

I_1	I_5	I_7	I_{11}	I_{13}
100%	18.9%	11%	5.9%	4.8%

the result is the creation of currents that do not oscillate at the supply frequency. These currents are called harmonics. Harmonics occur at multiples of the supply (fundamental) frequency. For instance, if the fundamental frequency is 50 Hz, the so-called second harmonic is 100 Hz, the third harmonic is 150 Hz, and so on. Any number of harmonics can be created by a particular piece of equipment depending on that equipment's electrical characteristics. Therefore, the current drawn by nonlinear loads can still be represented by (1) where harmonics appear in the form of pole-residue couples at frequency multiples of 50 Hz.

3.3. Results. Assuming zero initial conditions ($i_{L_0} = 0$ and/or $v_{C_0} = 0$), the following numerical values were used to determine the electric current data sequence from which MPM extracted poles and residues: $\{R = 100\,\Omega, C = 0.1\,\text{mF}\}$ for the series RC circuit, $\{R = 10\,\Omega, L = 100\,\text{mH}\}$ for both the series and parallel RL circuits, and $\{R = 1\,\Omega, L = 20\,\text{mH}, C = 60\,\text{mF}\}$ for the series RLC circuit. A duration of ten periods or 0.2 seconds was chosen for the current which at $t_s = 6.25 \times 10^{-4}$ is equivalent to 320 samples, and MPM was applied at each period. Figures 1, 2, 3, and 4 show the current obtained from the analytic expression of poles and residues in the tables above and its reconstruction obtained from the poles and residues extracted by MPM. An almost perfect agreement can be seen between the two curves indicating the accuracy of the characteristic complex numbers extracted by MPM. In addition, the figures show the forced and natural responses of each of the four elementary circuits.

To evaluate the performance of MPM on nonlinear loads, we considered the current shown in Table 5. It consists of a fundamental and four harmonics and hence can be represented by ten pairwise complex conjugate pole-residue couples. We then used MPM to extract these ten couples which served to reconstruct the current as shown in Figure 5. As can be seen, MPM is successful in estimating the pole-residue couples of the load.

4. Validation on Real Data

4.1. Reconstruction Results. In this section, the validation of MPM is carried out on currents of three representative loads: a television set, a vacuum cleaner, and an economy lamp. As for the case of synthetic data, MPM was applied at each period. Figures 6, 7, and 8 show the current drawn by the appliances and its reconstruction based on the pole-residue estimates of MPM. The close agreement shown in the figures indicate that the exponential model of (1) and its parameters estimated by the MPM accurately predict the response of the actual loads. It is worth mentioning that the number of pole-residue couples d increases with the nonlinearity of the load. For instance, the current of the vacuum cleaner could be accurately reconstructed from four pole-residue couples,

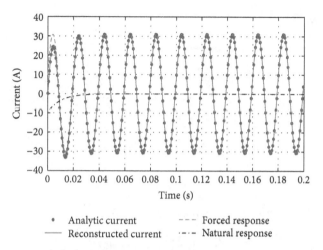

FIGURE 1: The analytic and reconstructed currents of the series RC circuit along with its forced and natural responses.

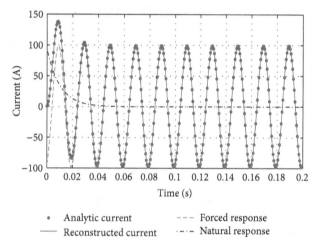

FIGURE 2: The analytic and reconstructed currents of the series RL circuit along with its forced and natural responses.

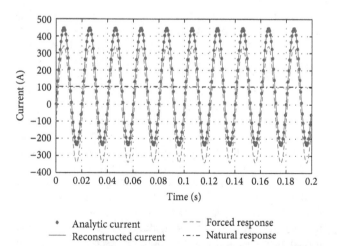

FIGURE 3: The analytic and reconstructed currents of the parallel RL circuit along with its forced and natural responses.

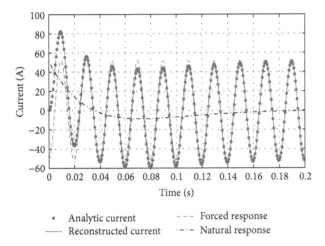

Analytic current   --- Forced response
Reconstructed current   -·- Natural response

FIGURE 4: The analytic and reconstructed currents of the series RLC circuit along with its forced and natural responses.

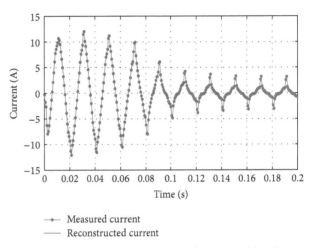

Measured current
Reconstructed current

FIGURE 6: The measured and reconstructed currents of the television set.

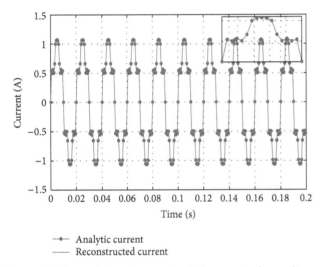

Analytic current
Reconstructed current

FIGURE 5: The analytic and reconstructed currents of a nonlinear load. The inset zooms in on a half period of the drawn current in order to show the accuracy of reconstruction.

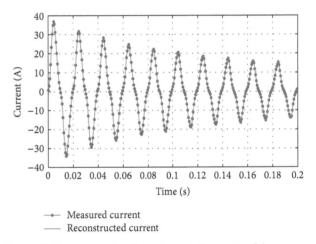

Measured current
Reconstructed current

FIGURE 7: The measured and reconstructed currents of the vacuum cleaner.

whereas that of the economy lamp needed up to twelve couples.

4.2. Feature Space. The feature space contains 900 signatures uniformly distributed among the following nine appliances: incandescent lamp, halogen lamp, economy lamp, water heater, electric convector, oven, two-burner hot plate, television set, and computer. As shown in Figure 9, each signature (represented by a point in the the three-dimensional feature space) is characterized by three pole-residue products corresponding to the maxima of the fundamental, third, and fifth harmonic currents. The restriction to three frequencies has the sole aim of representing the feature space graphically. From the feature space, ten clusters representing the nine appliances can be clearly distinguished. The additional cluster is due to the two-burner hot plate which is represented by two clusters, one for each burner. It can hence be concluded that

the studied appliances can be fairly distinguished using the fundamental and higher harmonics.

5. Conclusion

This paper presented a novel feature extraction method for non intrusive appliance load monitoring. First, the poles and residues estimated by the matrix pencil method were shown to enable accurate reconstruction of synthetic and real current signals. Second, these complex numbers were used to determine a three-dimensional feature space with reduced intercluster overlap. Future research will make use of the extracted features for the classification phase.

Appendix

The dependent parameters of first-order circuits are given in Table 6, where τ is the time constant and ϕ is the phase angle.

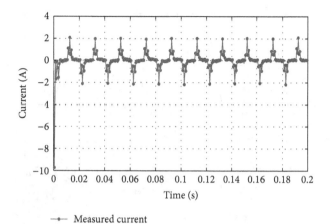

—•— Measured current
——— Reconstructed current

FIGURE 8: The measured and reconstructed currents of the economy lamp.

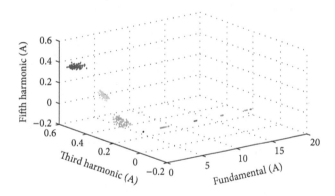

- Television
- Economy lamp
- Computer
- Incandescent lamp
- Halogen lamp

- Hotplate 1 burner
- Electric convector
- Oven
- Hotplate 2 burners
- Water heater

FIGURE 9: The feature space showing the disaggregated contribution of the fundamental and harmonic currents to the maximum of the total current for several appliances.

In addition to the phase angle ϕ, the dependent parameters of the series RLC circuit include the resonance angular frequency ω_0 and the damping factor ξ:

$$\phi = \arctan\left[\frac{1}{R}\left(L\omega - \frac{1}{C\omega}\right)\right] \text{ [rad]},$$

$$\omega_0 = \frac{1}{\sqrt{LC}} \text{ [rad/s]}, \qquad (A.1)$$

$$\xi = \frac{R}{2}\sqrt{\frac{C}{L}} \text{ [Np]}.$$

TABLE 6: Dependent parameters of first-order circuits.

Load	τ [s]	ϕ [rad]
Series RC	RC	$\arctan\left(\frac{-1}{RC\omega}\right)$
Series RL	$\frac{L}{R}$	$\arctan\left(\frac{L\omega}{R}\right)$
Parallel RL	—	$\arctan\left(\frac{R}{L\omega}\right)$

The roots of the characteristic equation of the second-order differential equation, k_1 and k_2, are expressed in terms of the the damping factor ξ as follows:

$$k_1 = -\xi - \sqrt{\xi^2 - 1},$$
$$k_2 = -\xi + \sqrt{\xi^2 - 1}. \qquad (A.2)$$

Finally, A and B, shown in Table 4, are expressed as follows:

$$A = \frac{k_1}{k_1 - k_2}\left(A_2 - k_2 A_1\right),$$

$$B = \frac{k_2}{k_2 - k_1}\left(A_2 - k_1 A_1\right), \qquad (A.3)$$

where

$$A_1 = v_{c0}\frac{C}{L} + \frac{V\sqrt{2}}{R}\cos\left(\phi\right)\cos\left(\omega t_0 - \phi\right)\frac{\omega_0}{\omega},$$

$$A_2 = i_{L0} - \frac{V\sqrt{2}}{R}\cos\left(\phi\right)\sin\left(\omega t_0 - \phi\right). \qquad (A.4)$$

Acknowledgment

This work was supported in part by Landis+Gyr.

References

[1] G. W. Hart, "Nonintrusive appliance load monitoring," *Proceedings of the IEEE*, vol. 80, no. 12, pp. 1870–1891, 1992.

[2] C. Laughman, K. Lee, R. Cox et al., "Power signature analysis," *IEEE Power and Energy Magazine*, vol. 1, no. 2, pp. 56–63, 2003.

[3] Y. Du, L. Du, B. Lu, R. Harley, and T. Habetler, "A review of identification and monitoring methods for electric loads in commercial and residential buildings," in *Proceedings of the 2nd IEEE Energy Conversion Congress and Exposition (ECCE '10)*, pp. 4527–4533, Atlanta, Ga, USA, September 2010.

[4] M. Zeifman and K. Roth, "Nonintrusive appliance load monitoring: review and outlook," *IEEE Transactions on Consumer Electronics*, vol. 57, no. 1, pp. 76–84, 2011.

[5] H. Najmeddine, K. E. K. Drissi, C. Pasquier et al., "Smart Metering by using matrix pencil," in *Proceedings of the 9th International Conference on Environment and Electrical Engineering (EEEIC '10)*, pp. 238–241, Prague, Czech Republic, May 2010.

[6] H. Najmeddine, K. El Khamlichi Drissi, A. Diop, and T. Jouannet, "Method and device for the non-intrusive determination of the electrical power consumed by an installation, by analysing load transients," French Patent, FR 0856717, October 2008.

[7] K. Chahine, K. El Khamlichi Drissi, C. Pasquier et al., "Electric load disaggregation in smart metering using a novel feature extraction method and supervised classification," *Energy Procedia*, vol. 6, pp. 627–632, 2011.

[8] Y. Hua and T. K. Sarkar, "Matrix pencil method for estimating parameters of exponentially damped/undamped sinusoids in noise," *IEEE Transactions on Acoustics, Speech, and Signal Processing*, vol. 38, no. 5, pp. 814–824, 1990.

10

Monthly Rainfall Estimation Using Data-Mining Process

Özlem Terzi

Faculty of Technical Education, Suleyman Demirel University, 32260 Isparta, Turkey

Correspondence should be addressed to Özlem Terzi, ozlemterzi@sdu.edu.tr

Academic Editor: Tzung P. Hong

It is important to accurately estimate rainfall for effective use of water resources and optimal planning of water structures. For this purpose, the models were developed to estimate rainfall in Isparta using the data-mining process. The different input combinations having 1-, 2-, 3- and 4-input parameters were tried using the rainfall values of Senirkent, Uluborlu, Eğirdir, and Yalvaç stations in Isparta. The most appropriate algorithm was determined as multilinear regression among the models developed with various data-mining algorithms. The input parameters of Multilinear Regression model were the monthly rainfall values of Senirkent, Uluborlu and Eğirdir stations. The relative error of this model was calculated as 0.7%. It was shown that the data mining process can be used in estimation of missing rainfall values.

1. Introduction

The meteorological events affect permanently human life. Considering the meteorological phenomena, which have no possibility of intervention, they cause the important results in human life, accurate estimation and analysis of these variables are also very important. Precipitation, which is generating flow, is an important parameter. The occurrence of extreme rainfall in a short time causes significant events that affect human life such as flood. However, in the event of insufficient rainfall in long period occurs drought. Thus, rainfall estimation is very important in terms of effects on human life, water resources, and water usage areas. However, rainfall affected by the geographical and regional variations and features is very difficult to estimate. Nowadays, there are many researches about artificial intelligence methods used in the estimation of rainfall [1–7]. Partal et al. [8] developed rainfall estimation models using artificial neural networks and wavelet transform methods. Bodri and Čermák [9] evaluated the applicability of neural networks for precipitation prediction. Chang et al. [10] applied a modified method, combining the inverse distance method and fuzzy theory, to precipitation interpolation. They used genetic algorithm to determine the parameters of fuzzy membership functions, which represent the relationship between the location without rainfall records and its surrounding rainfall gauges.

They worked to minimize the estimated error of precipitation with the optimization process.

One of the aims of storing this data in databases and receiving data from many sources is to convert raw data into information at present. This process is called as data-mining (DM) process of converting data into information. In recent years, the use of data-mining process in the field of hydrology is increasing. The studies have been performed using DM process in many areas [11–13]. Keskin et al. [14] developed integrated evaporation model using DM process for three lakes in Turkey. Terzi [15] developed the models to forecast flow of Kızılırmak River using rainfall and flow parameters with DM process. Terzi et al. [16] proposed various solar radiation models with DM process using air temperature, relative humidity, wind speed, and air pressure parameters and evaluated performance of the models. Teegavarapu [17] evaluated the use of association rule mining (ARM) in conjunction with a spatial interpolation technique to estimate of missing precipitation data and to overcome one of the major limitations of spatial interpolation techniques. Solomatine and Dulal [18] investigated the comparative performance of artificial neural networks (ANNs) and model trees (MTs) in rainfall—runoff transformation. They determined that both ANNs and MTs produce excellent results for 1-h ahead prediction, acceptable results for 3-h ahead prediction and conditionally acceptable result for 6-h

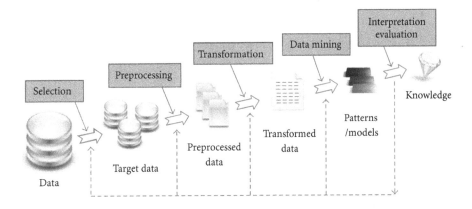

FIGURE 1: Knowledge discovery process.

ahead prediction. They obtained almost similar performance for 1-h ahead prediction of runoff, but the result of the ANN is slightly better than the MT for higher lead times from these techniques. Keskin et al. [19] applied data-mining process to river flow prediction. They determined that it was possible using data-mining process for river flow prediction. Teegavarapu and Chandramouli [6] developed a model that uses artificial neural network concepts and a stochastic interpolation technique. They tested the model for estimation of missing precipitation data.

The aim of the study is to evaluate the use of data-mining process to estimate rainfall of Isparta in Turkey. This study is performed using rainfall data of Senirkent, Uluborlu, Eğirdir, and Yalvaç stations in Isparta city.

2. Data-Mining Process

Knowledge discovery is a process that extracts implicit, potentially useful or previously unknown information from the data. The knowledge discovery process is described in Figure 1.

Let us examine the knowledge discovery process in the diagram in Figure 1 in details.

(i) Data coming from variety of sources is integrated into a single data store called target data.

(ii) Data then is preprocessed and transformed into standard format.

(iii) The data-mining algorithms process the data to the output in form of patterns or rules.

(iv) Then those patterns and rules are interpreted to new or useful knowledge or information.

The ultimate goal of knowledge discovery and data-mining process is to find the patterns that are hidden among the huge sets of data and interpret them to useful knowledge and information. As described in process diagram above, data-mining is a central part of knowledge discovery process.

The data-mining definition is defined as "the process of extracting previously unknown, comprehensible, and actionable information from large databases and using it to make crucial business decisions" [20]. This data-mining

definition has business flavor and for business environments. However, data-mining is a process that can be applied to any type of data ranging from weather forecasting, electric load prediction, product design, among others.

Data-mining also can be defined as the computer-aid process that digs and analyzes enormous sets of data and then extracting the knowledge or information out of it. By its simplest definition, data-mining automates the detections of relevant patterns in database [21].

The emergence of knowledge discovery in databases (KDD) as a new technology has been brought about with the fast development and broad application of information and database technologies. The process of KDD is defined as an iterative sequence of four steps: defining the problem, data preprocessing (data preparation), data-mining, and postdata-mining.

2.1. Defining the Problem. The goals of a knowledge discovery project must be identified. The goals must be verified as actionable. For example, if the goals are met, a business organization can then put the newly discovered knowledge to use. The data to be used must also be identified clearly.

2.2. Data Preprocessing. Data preparation comprises those techniques concerned with analyzing raw data so as to yield quality data, mainly including data collecting, data integration, data transformation, data cleaning, data reduction, and data discretization.

2.3. Data-Mining. Given the cleaned data, intelligent methods are applied in order to extract data patterns. Patterns of interest are searched for, including classification rules or trees, regression, clustering, sequence modeling, dependency, and so forth.

2.4. Postdata-Mining. Post data-mining consists of pattern evaluation, deploying the model, maintenance, and knowledge presentation.

The KDD process is iterative. For example, while cleaning and preparing data, it might be discovered that data from a certain source is unusable, or that data from a previously unidentified source is required to be merged with the other

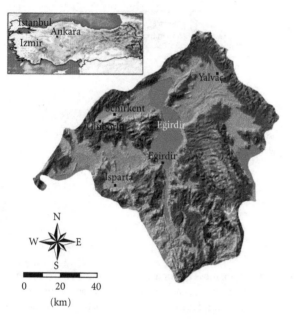

FIGURE 2: Locations of rain gauges in Isparta.

data under consideration. Often, the first time through, the data-mining step will reveal that additional data cleaning is required [22].

3. Study Region and Data

In this study, the data used to developed rainfall estimation models are the monthly rainfall data of Isparta, Senirkent, Uluborlu, Eğirdir, and Yalvaç stations. The Isparta city is located in the Lakes Region located in the north of the Mediterranean Region, and between $30°20'$ and $31°33'$ east longitudes and $37°18'$ and $38°30'$ north latitudes. The altitude of Isparta having a surface area of 8933 km^2 is the average of 1050 m. The average annual total rainfall of Isparta is 440.3 kg/m^2. The most of rainfall (72.69%) has occurred in winter and spring months. The summer and autumn months are quite dry (29.31% of total rainfall). While it is observed usually rain, occasional snow in winter in the region, it is observed in the form of rainstorm the in spring and summer months. The study region and the locations of rain gauges are shown in Figure 2.

The monthly rainfall data for 1964–2005 years used in this study were obtained from Turkish State Meteorological Service. The various rainfall estimation models were developed for Isparta using the rainfall values of Senirkent, Uluborlu, Eğirdir, and Yalvaç stations as input parameters. It was investigated whether or not there are any missing data. Then, the mean values were used for substitution of missing values. The training dataset consisted of the 1964–1996 years was used to develop the models. The trained models were used to run the testing dataset for 1997–2005 years.

4. Model Performance Criteria

In the model assessment stage, after it has built a set of models using different algorithms, these models were evaluated in terms of accuracy. There are a few popular criteria to evaluate the quality of a model. It was chosen coefficient of determination (R^2) and root mean-squared error (RMSE) which are the most well known and the commonly used performance criteria [23–25]. The R^2 is the proportion of variability in a dataset that is accounted for by the statistical model. The RMSE is valuable and because it indicates error in the units (or squared units) of the constituent of interest, which aids in analysis of the results. The coefficient of determination based on the rainfall estimation errors is calculated as

$$R^2 = 1 - \frac{\sum_{i=1}^{n} \left(P_{i(\text{rainfall})} - P_{i(\text{model})} \right)^2}{\sum_{i=1}^{n} \left(P_{i(\text{rainfall})} - P_{\text{mean}} \right)^2}, \quad (1)$$

where n is the number of observed data, $P_{i(\text{rainfall})}$ and $P_{i(\text{model})}$ are monthly rainfall measurement and the results of the developed model, respectively, and P_{mean} is mean rainfall measurements.

The root mean square error represents the error of model and defined as

$$\text{RMSE} = \sqrt{\frac{1}{n}\sum_{i=1}^{n} \left(P_{i(\text{rainfall})} - P_{i(\text{model})} \right)^2}, \quad (2)$$

where parameters have been defined above.

5. Rainfall Estimation Models

For rainfall estimation, Decision Table, KStar, Multilinear Regression, M5'Rules, Multilayer Perceptron, RBF Network, Random Subspace, and Simple Linear Regression algorithms were used in this study. The fifteen models were developed using different input combinations with the rainfall values of Senirkent, Uluborlu, Eğirdir and Yalvaç stations to estimate rainfall of Isparta station. These models including 1-input, 2-input, 3-input and 4-input parameters were given in Tables 1, 2, 3, and 4, respectively.

Firstly, the relationships between rainfall data of Isparta station and them of other stations (Senirkent, Uluborlu, Eğirdir, and Yalvaç) were investigated using statistical analyses. The effective variables on Isparta station were ranked in the order of Senirkent, Uluborlu, Eğirdir, and Yalvaç stations. The performance criteria of the models developed with 1-input parameters were given in Table 1 for testing set.

Examining the models given in Table 1, it was determined as the highest R^2 value was 0.745 and lowest RMSE value was 48.44 mm for models developed using Multilinear Regression (MLR), M5'Rules, and Simple Linear Regression algorithms with rainfall data of Senirkent station. These models have the same R^2 and RMSE values. The worst model with the highest RMSE (141.50) was developed with decision table. When the developed models by using MLR, M5'Rules, and Simple Linear Regression algorithms were analyzed, the input parameter of the best performing model was rainfall of Senirkent station. Later, the best models were generally ranked in Uluborlu, Eğirdir, and Yalvaç stations. In Table 2, it was given the R^2 and RMSE values of developed models with 2-input parameters.

TABLE 1: The performance criteria of the models having 1-input parameter.

Input parameters	Eğirdir		Senirkent		Uluborlu		Yalvaç	
Models	R^2	RMSE	R^2	RMSE	R^2	RMSE	R^2	RMSE
Decision Table	0.254	141.5	0.695	57.90	0.638	68.62	0.531	89.10
KStar	0.686	59.60	0.641	68.14	0.648	66.82	0.543	86.70
Multilinear Regression	0.671	62.49	0.745	48.44	0.717	53.63	0.616	72.84
M5'Rules	0.671	62.49	0.745	48.44	0.717	53.63	0.616	72.84
Multilayer Perceptron	0.711	54.89	0.649	66.58	0.653	65.81	0.578	80.06
RBF Network	0.533	88.67	0.641	68.13	0.672	62.28	0.495	95.81
Random Subspace	0.617	72.71	0.634	69.56	0.590	77.77	0.492	96.43
Simple Linear Regression	0.671	62.49	0.745	48.44	0.717	53.63	0.616	72.84

TABLE 2: The performance criteria of the models having 2-input parameters.

Input parameters	Eğirdir-Uluborlu		Eğirdir-Yalvaç		Eğirdir-Senirkent		Senirkent-Uluborlu		Senirkent-Yalvaç		Uluborlu-Yalvaç	
Models	R^2	RMSE	R^2	RMSE	R^2	RMSE	R^2	RMSE	R^2	RMSE	R^2	RMSE
Decision Table	0.638	68.62	0.254	141.52	0.695	57.90	0.695	57.90	0.695	57.90	0.638	68.62
KStar	0.765	44.52	0.732	50.83	0.751	47.21	0.727	51.81	0.668	62.93	0.684	60.07
Multilinear Regression	0.807	36.65	0.743	48.80	0.792	39.40	0.765	44.60	0.745	48.44	0.717	53.63
M5'Rules	0.807	36.65	0.743	48.80	0.792	39.40	0.765	44.60	0.745	48.44	0.717	53.63
Multilayer Perceptron	0.796	38.64	0.743	48.69	0.746	48.29	0.678	61.08	0.662	64.12	0.670	62.64
RBF Network	0.663	63.87	0.550	85.41	0.568	81.96	0.647	67.02	0.556	84.19	0.567	82.21
Random Subspace	0.782	41.45	0.620	72.05	0.725	52.27	0.695	57.93	0.610	74.12	0.638	68.65
Simple Linear Regression	0.717	53.63	0.671	62.49	0.745	48.44	0.745	48.44	0.745	48.44	0.717	53.63

TABLE 3: The performance criteria of the models having 3-input parameters.

Input parameters	Senirkent-Uluborlu-Eğirdir		Senirkent Uluborlu-Yalvaç		Senirkent-Yalvaç-Eğirdir		Uluborlu-Yalvaç-Eğirdir	
Models	R^2	RMSE	R^2	RMSE	R^2	RMSE	R^2	RMSE
Decision Table	0.695	57.90	0.695	57.90	0.695	57.90	0.638	68.62
KStar	0.771	43.54	0.693	58.20	0.745	48.33	0.771	43.43
Multilinear Regression	0.813	35.43	0.765	44.60	0.792	39.40	0.798	38.38
M5'Rules	0.808	36.43	0.765	44.60	0.792	39.40	0.711	54.89
Multilayer Perceptron	0.774	42.83	0.726	51.98	0.772	43.33	0.797	38.55
RBF Network	0.622	71.67	0.560	83.48	0.583	79.23	0.574	80.90
Random Subspace	0.760	45.62	0.680	60.83	0.714	54.31	0.757	46.12
Simple Linear Regression	0.745	48.44	0.745	48.44	0.745	48.44	0.717	53.63

TABLE 4: The performance criteria of the models having 4-input parameters.

Modeller	R^2	RMSE
Decision Table	0.695	57.90
KStar	0.761	45.33
Multilinear Regression	0.806	36.89
M5'Rules	0.766	44.35
Multilayer Perceptron	0.774	42.91
RBF Network	0.573	80.95
Random Subspace	0.757	46.17
Simple Linear Regression	0.745	48.44

As seen from Table 2, the highest R^2 (0.807) and lowest RMSE (36.65) values were obtained for MLR and M5'Rules models developed using rainfall values of Eğirdir and Uluborlu stations. Table 2 shows that increasing of number of the model input parameter improved the performance of the models. While R^2 value of the best model with one input parameter was 0.745, performance of the model with two input parameters is 0.807. The models having 3-input parameters are shown in Table 3.

It was shown that the R^2 values of the models having 3-input parameters (Senirkent—Uluborlu—Eğirdir) were 0.813 and 0.808 for MLR and M5'Rules models in Table 3, respectively. The MLR (Senirkent—Uluborlu—Eğirdir)

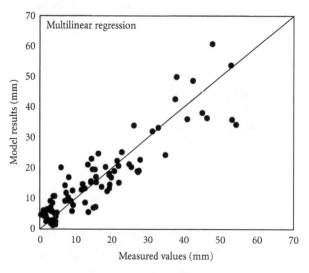

FIGURE 3: Comparison plot for MLR model.

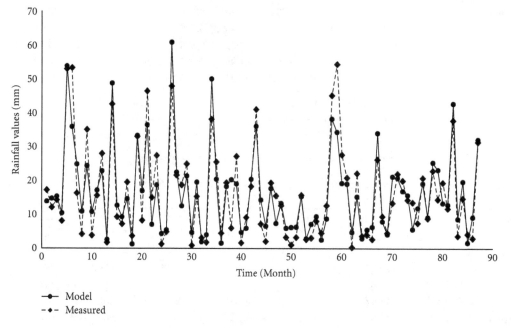

FIGURE 4: Time series for MLR model.

model showed the best performance. The models developed with Senirkent, Uluborlu, and Eğirdir stations ranked according to statistical analysis showed generally the better performance. The model with the worst performance was Radial Basis Function (RBF) network model. The models having 4-input parameters are shown in Table 4.

It was shown that the R^2 value of the model having three 4-input parameters were 0.806 for MLR model in Table 4. When Yalvaç station was added to the best 3-input model, the 4-input model performance had decreased slightly. The MLR and M5'Rules algorithms in all the DM algorithms gave generally the best results and had the almost same performance except the 4-input model. While the RBF network from artificial neural network algorithms

showed the worst performance in all DM models, MLR had relatively good results. Considering all the DM models, MLR model with 3-input parameters (R^2 = 0.813) showed the best performance. Examining RMSE values of the model, the model (Senirkent—Uluborlu—Eğirdir) had the lowest error. Thus, the monthly rainfall results of MLR model (Senirkent—Uluborlu—Eğirdir) are shown in Figures 3 and 4 as comparison plot and time series for testing data set. Figure 3 shows that the MLR model comparison plot was uniformly distributed around the 45° straight line implying that there were no bias effects. It was apparent a good relationship between estimated and measured rainfall values. The relative error between the measured values and the value of the developed MLR model was calculated as 0.7%.

It was shown that, for Isparta region, the developed MLR model gave the best results to estimate rainfall. They cannot be used to estimate rainfall of another region, because the MLR models were developed for Isparta region. For a different region, the models need to be reestablished or need to be calibrated according to data of a new region. In the future, when more data are obtained, the developed models need to be revised. The other methods can give better results than MLR when adding more data or developing model for different region.

6. Conclusions

The rainfall which is an important factor for the use of water resources is a difficult variable to estimate. In this study, data-mining process was used to estimate monthly rainfall values of Isparta. The monthly rainfall data of Senirkent, Uluborlu, Eğirdir, and Yalvaç stations were used to develop rainfall estimation models. When comparing the developed models to measured values, multilinear regression model from data-mining process gave more appropriate results than the developed models in this study. The input parameters of the best model were the rainfall values of Senirkent, Uluborlu, and Eğirdir stations. Consequently, it was shown that the data-mining process, producing a solution more quickly than traditional methods, can be used to complete the missing data in estimating rainfall.

References

[1] T. B. Trafalis, M. B. Richman, A. White, and B. Santosa, "Data mining techniques for improved WSR-88D rainfall estimation," *Computers and Industrial Engineering*, vol. 43, no. 4, pp. 775–786, 2002.

[2] K. C. Luk, J. E. Ball, and A. Sharma, "An application of artificial neural networks for rainfall forecasting," *Mathematical and Computer Modelling*, vol. 33, no. 6-7, pp. 683–693, 2001.

[3] M. Zhang, J. Fulcher, and R. A. Scofield, "Rainfall estimation using artificial neural network group," *Neurocomputing*, vol. 16, no. 2, pp. 97–115, 1997.

[4] T. Shoji and H. Kitaura, "Statistical and geostatistical analysis of rainfall in central Japan," *Computers and Geosciences*, vol. 32, no. 8, pp. 1007–1024, 2006.

[5] M. C. V. Ramírez, H. F. C. Velho, and N. J. Ferreira, "Artificial neural network technique for rainfall forecasting applied to the São Paulo region," *Journal of Hydrology*, vol. 301, no. 1–4, pp. 146–162, 2005.

[6] R. S. V. Teegavarapu and V. Chandramouli, "Improved weighting methods, deterministic and stochastic data-driven models for estimation of missing precipitation records," *Journal of Hydrology*, vol. 312, no. 1–4, pp. 191–206, 2005.

[7] Y.-M. Chiang, F. J. Chang, B. J. D. Jou, and P. F. Lin, "Dynamic ANN for precipitation estimation and forecasting from radar observations," *Journal of Hydrology*, vol. 334, no. 1-2, pp. 250–261, 2007.

[8] T. Partal, E. Kahya, and K. Cığızoğlu, "Estimation of precipitation data using artificial neural networks and wavelet transform," *ITU Journal*, vol. 7, no. 3, pp. 73–85, 2008 (Turkish).

[9] L. Bodri and V. Čermák, "Prediction of extreme precipitation using a neural network: application to summer flood occurrence in Moravia," *Advances in Engineering Software*, vol. 31, no. 5, pp. 311–321, 2000.

[10] C. L. Chang, S. L. Lo, and S. L. Yu, "Applying fuzzy theory and genetic algorithm to interpolate precipitation," *Journal of Hydrology*, vol. 314, no. 1–4, pp. 92–104, 2005.

[11] C. Damle and A. Yalcin, "Flood prediction using time series data mining," *Journal of Hydrology*, vol. 333, no. 2–4, pp. 305–316, 2007.

[12] K.-W. Chau and N. Muttil, "Data mining and multivariate statistical analysis for ecological system in coastal waters," *Journal of Hydroinformatics*, vol. 9, no. 4, pp. 305–317, 2007.

[13] E. P. Roz, *Water quality modeling and rainfall estimation: a data driven approach [M.S. thesis]*, University of Iowa, Iowa City, Iowa, USA, 2011.

[14] M. E. Keskin, Ö. Terzi, and E. U. Küçüksille, "Data mining process for integrated evaporation model," *Journal of Irrigation and Drainage Engineering*, vol. 135, no. 1, pp. 39–43, 2009.

[15] Ö. Terzi, "Monthly river flow forecasting by data mining process," in *Knowledge-Oriented Applications in Data Mining*, K. Funatsu, Ed., InTech, Rijeka, Croatia, 2011.

[16] Ö. Terzi, E. U. Küçüksille, G. Ergin, and A. İlker, "Estimation of solar radiation using data mining process," *SDU International Technologic Science*, vol. 3, no. 2, pp. 29–37, 2011 (Turkish).

[17] R. S. V. Teegavarapu, "Estimation of missing precipitation records integrating surface interpolation techniques and spatio-temporal association rules," *Journal of Hydroinformatics*, vol. 11, no. 2, pp. 133–146, 2009.

[18] D. P. Solomatine and K. N. Dulal, "Model trees as an alternative to neural networks in rainfall-runoff modelling," *Hydrological Sciences Journal*, vol. 48, no. 3, pp. 399–412, 2003.

[19] M. E. Keskin, D. Taylan, and E. U. Kucuksille, "Data mining process for modeling hydrological time series," *Hydrology Research*. In press.

[20] E. Simoudis, "Reality cheek for data mining," *IEEE Expert-Intelligent Systems and their Applications*, vol. 11, no. 5, pp. 26–33, 1996.

[21] http://www.dataminingtechniques.net/data-mining-tutorial/what-is-data-mining/.

[22] S. Zhang, C. Zhang, and Q. Yang, "Data preparation for data mining," *Applied Artificial Intelligence*, vol. 17, no. 5-6, pp. 375–381, 2003.

[23] D. N. Moriasi, J. G. Arnold, M. W. Van Liew, R. L. Bingner, R. D. Harmel, and T. L. Veith, "Model evaluation guidelines for systematic quantification of accuracy in watershed simulations," *Transactions of the ASABE*, vol. 50, no. 3, pp. 885–900, 2007.

[24] J. Piri, S. Amin, A. Moghaddamnia, A. Keshavarz, D. Han, and R. Remesan, "Daily pan evaporation modeling in a hot and dry climate," *Journal of Hydrologic Engineering*, vol. 14, no. 8, pp. 803–811, 2009.

[25] S. Lallahem and J. Mania, "A nonlinear rainfall-runoff model using neural network technique: example in fractured porous media," *Mathematical and Computer Modelling*, vol. 37, no. 9-10, pp. 1047–1061, 2003.

11

Qualitative Functional Decomposition Analysis of Evolved Neuromorphic Flight Controllers

Sanjay K. Boddhu and John C. Gallagher

Department of Computer Science and Engineering, Wright State University, Dayton, OH 45435, USA

Correspondence should be addressed to Sanjay K. Boddhu, sboddhu@cs.wright.edu

Academic Editor: P. Balasubramaniam

In the previous work, it was demonstrated that one can effectively employ CTRNN-EH (a neuromorphic variant of EH method) methodology to evolve neuromorphic flight controllers for a flapping wing robot. This paper describes a novel frequency grouping-based analysis technique, developed to qualitatively decompose the evolved controllers into explainable functional control blocks. A summary of the previous work related to evolving flight controllers for two categories of the controller types, called autonomous and nonautonomous controllers, is provided, and the applicability of the newly developed decomposition analysis for both controller categories is demonstrated. Further, the paper concludes with appropriate discussion of ongoing work and implications for possible future work related to employing the CTRNN-EH methodology and the decomposition analysis techniques presented in this paper.

1. Introduction

Most, if not all, existing bird-sized and insect-sized flapping-wing vehicles possess only a small number of actively controlled degrees of freedom. In these vehicles, the bulk of the wing motions are generated via a combination of actively driven linkages (motors and armatures, piezoelectric beams, etc.) and passively driven elements (wing flex or rotation via dynamic pressure loading, etc.) [1, 2]. The number of controlled degrees of freedom is often minimized to simplify control and to limit the number of bulky actuators carried on board. In theory, both bird-sized [1] and insect-sized [2] robots can sustain stable flight with controllers generating actuation signals for only few degrees of freedom. But it would require taking advantage of every possible degree of freedom available in the robot to achieve sophisticated maneuvers that are possible in their biological counterparts. Thus, there exists a possibility that applying a learning or adaptable controller techniques [1, 3–6] to the control of the insect-sized flapping wing vehicles, hereafter referred to as Microlevel Flapping Wing Robots (MFWRs), will likely to produce more biomimetic control and maneuver patterns that evade traditional controller design. One can imagine two basic approaches to the "adaptable controller" problem. First, one might attempt to hybridize an adaptive system to a traditional controller in the hope that the combined system could learn the specific needs of an individual vehicle by augmenting a base controller. Second, one might attempt to construct an adaptable controller that could learn acceptable control laws tabula rasa either all-at-once or via a staged approach. Even if tabula rasa methods could be made to work, one would incur a responsibility to explain the operation of controllers that, though functional, might operate in ways not conformant with existing explanatory paradigms. In previous work [4, 7–9], the authors were able to demonstrate controllers could be "learned from scratch" by verifying the idea within a framework of neuromorphic evolvable hardware. Further, this previous work also demonstrated the feasibility of neuromorphic adaptive hardware implementations that provide computational advantage over existing adaptive control techniques using similar neural substrates [10, 11]. The work mentioned in this paper focuses more intensely on that problem of explaining what those controllers do and how they do it. It will discuss subsequent work that was undertaken to analyze those evolved flight controllers with newly developed frequency-based and

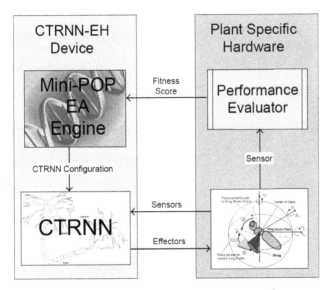

FIGURE 1: Schematic of CTRNN-EH Framework.

preexisting modularization decomposition methods. In this vein, the background knowledge necessary to understand the terminology, methods, and approaches employed as part of the above-mentioned CTRNN-EH framework are briefly explained in Section 2. Following is Section 3 describing the specific methods and models employed to successfully evolve CTRNN-EH flight controllers for a specific MFWR model. Section 4 describes the details of the proposed analysis methods and their applicability to the evolved flight controllers, followed by Section 5 with concluding remarks on the current work and ongoing future work.

2. Background and Previous Work

2.1. CTRNN-EH Framework. The CTRNN-EH framework introduced in the previous works [5, 12, 13] is summarized schematically in Figure 1. The CTRNN-EH framework is a neuromorphic variant of the standard Evolvable Hardware paradigm using Continuous Time Recurrent Neural Networks (CTRNNs) as the reconfigurable hardware substrate. CTRNNs are networks of Hopfield continuous model neurons [13] with unconstrained connection weight matrices. CTRNN neural activity and outputs are governed by an nth degree differential equation of the form:

$$\tau \frac{dy_i}{dt} = -y_i + \sum_{j-1}^{N} w_{ji} \sigma \left(y_j + \theta_j \right) + s_i I_i(t), \qquad (1)$$

where y_i is the state of neuron i, τ_i is time constant of neuron i, w_{ji} is the strength of the connection from the jth to ith the neuron, θ is a bias term, $\sigma(x) = 1/(1 + e^{-x})$ is the standard logistic activation function, and $I_i(t)$ represents a weighted sensory input with strength s_i. The set of parameters defining a neuron I (incoming weights, time constant, and bias) are called an individual *neuron configuration*, and a collection of these individual neuron configurations for a

given network is called a *network configuration* or *CTRNN configuration*. These CTRNNs have been proven to be universal approximators of any smooth dynamics [14]. The practical benefit of this is that in principle, any possible control law can be approximated arbitrarily well given enough CTRNN neurons. In practice, even small networks of CTRNN neurons are capable of producing complex dynamical behavior. Based on the Evolvable Hardware (EH), principle of evolving optimized and desired configurations in a reconfigurable substrate using evolutionary algorithm techniques. CTRNNs are evolved to produce, the right control signal, using the evolutionary algorithms. The training of the CTRNNs is finding the appropriate parameter settings, that is, configuring the neuron settings in the network. The evolutionary algorithms search the given possible settings of the neuron and find the optimal settings for the network as a whole, to produce the required control signals. The CTRNNs functioning with optimal settings produced by the EA is called as the evolved controller for the given control problem being dealt. Based on previous work, the Minipop algorithm [15] is chosen as the evolutionary algorithm for the CTRNN-EH framework. The Minipop algorithm is a light weight evolutionary algorithm driven by mutation and hypermutation [15], more details of the same can be found in [13, 15].

2.2. Previous Work. The above-mentioned CTRNN-EH framework has been successfully employed to control legged locomotion in both real and simulated hexapod walkers [3, 16] by author's colleagues. These efforts concentrated on solving a learning locomotion control problem for the hexapod robots with twelve degrees of freedom, from scratch, without any preknowledge of the robot's physical characteristics (like weight and any leg damages). Conceptually, each leg of the hexapod (with two degrees of freedom in its actuators) would require optimal oscillatory patterns in its two actuators, with appropriate phase relations to aid in generating forces to move the hexapod forward or backward directions. Moreover, any controller that claims to provide optimal locomotion controller for the hexapod has to take into consideration the required optimal oscillatory dynamics in each leg as well as the needed collaborative dynamics among all the six legs to generate optimal and energy-efficient motion in the hexapod [3]. This complex mix of local and distributed locomotion pattern generation problem was successfully addressed by the CTRNN-EH architecture mentioned in [6]. Moreover, the evolved oscillatory CTRNN-EH locomotion controllers in those experiments embedded a large amount of practical functionality in very small numbers of neurons. These evolved controllers were capable of optimally controlling variously weighted bodies with or without damaged legs. The controllers could do this without reevolution and could adapt their dynamics on the fly by entraining to external sensory input [6, 13]. Further the work conducted to understand these evolved CTRNN-EH controllers (for legged locomotion) has resulted in a set of dynamical module analysis concepts [5, 6, 16] that can be employed to predict and explain the behavior of these

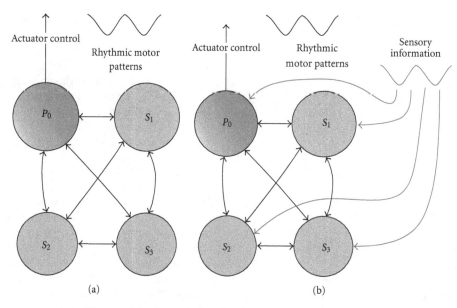

FIGURE 2: Illustrative representation of the assembly of neurons forming the autonomous neuromorphic (shown in (a)) and nonautonomous Neuromorphic (shown in (b)) controllers. "P" notation is used for primary neuron directly controlling the actuator of the robot under control and "S" is the secondary neuron, which aids in generating appropriate external dynamics required for the primary neuron. The numbering of the neurons in the network is arbitrarily chosen as appropriate.

evolved controllers, and controllers with similar nature, in terms of their functional sustainability and failure.

However, conceptually the flapping-wing flight problem shares the requirement of generating optimal oscillatory dynamics for desired flight behavior; with the hexapod walker problem, the former has inherent instability in its body dynamics, introduced by virtue of the medium of its flight (i.e., in three, dimensional space with constantly varying center of mass). This possible inherent instable body dynamics present in flapping-wing vehicles might make the CTRNN-EH based learning more challenging to be effective than when applied to the hexapod walkers, to generate optimal actuator dynamics. Further, the dynamical module analysis [6, 16] that was successful to understand the evolved locomotion controllers might not be applicable for the possible CTRNN-EH flight controllers. Nonetheless, the capabilities of CTRNN-EH controllers to produce smooth dynamics and provide provisions to adapt and modulate those produced dynamics observed in the previous work [5] sufficiently justifies the needed efforts presented in the authors published paper [4, 7–9] to evolve flapping flight controllers. Although providing the indetail description of varied possible modes of the CTRNN-EH controllers is beyond the scope of this paper, two basic modes are defined below, which are more pertinent to understand the experiments presented here in the paper.

Autonomous Controllers. These are neural network configurations that produce oscillatory signals without any external sensory inputs [3, 5]. As shown in the concept illustrative Figure 2(a), these configurations can generate autonomous and periodic dynamics in the neural network without any external triggers/sensor inputs; thus these would be referred

to as autonomous neuromorphic controllers in the later sections.

Nonautonomous Controllers. These are neural network configurations that can produce appropriate oscillatory patterns only when coupled to some other oscillatory system. They are more completely discussed in [8]. As shown in the concept illustrative Figure 2(b), these configurations can generate varied dynamics in the neural network only in sync with specific external triggers/sensor inputs provided to them, thus these would be referred as nonautonomous neuromorphic controllers in the later sections.

3. Evolved Flapping Wing Flight Controllers

This section describes authors's successful efforts aimed at evolving autonomous and non-autonomous CTRNN-EH controllers for a number of flapping-wing vehicle flight modes [4, 7, 9]. The section will begin with a brief description of the microlevel flapping winged robot (MFWR) model employed, followed by description of MFWR-specific CTRNN-EH control architecture and the evolution strategy applied at evolving different flight controllers.

3.1. Microlevel Flapping Winged Robot (MFWR). Micromechanical flying insect model was developed by MFI team at UC Berkeley [2] to facilitate the investigative study to build a real flapping wing robot with a 100 mg mass and a 25 mm wings span. Based on the available MFI literature on that robot's wing aerodynamics and body dynamics, we reconstructed a model with linear actuator dynamics called Microlevel Flapping Winged Robot (MFWR) [4]. Our model was verified in simulation and found to be a match for the

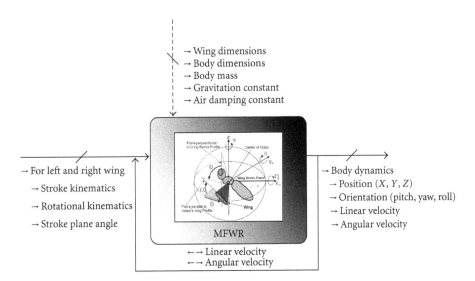

→ Wing dimensions
→ Body dimensions
→ Body mass
→ Gravitation constant
→ Air damping constant

→ For left and right wing
→ Stroke kinematics
→ Rotational kinematics
→ Stroke plane angle

MFWR

→ Body dynamics
→ Position (X, Y, Z)
→ Orientation (pitch, yaw, roll)
→ Linear velocity
→ Angular velocity

←→ Linear velocity
←→ Angular velocity

FIGURE 3: Schematic of the simulated Microlevel Flapping Winged Robot (MFWR).

Berkeley model in that we could reproduce their published flight envelopes and behaviors. The *Wing Aerodynamics* (WA) module of model is based on the mathematical model, developed from empirical study conducted on the Robofly [17]. The WA module generates the aerodynamic forces and torques for given wing kinematics. The *Body Dynamics Module* takes the aerodynamics forces and torques generated by the wing kinematics and integrates them along with the dynamical model of the MFI body, thus computing the body's position and the attitude as a function of time. The readers are directed to [18] for detail descriptions of these modules.

In brief, the implemented MFWR model takes wing (left and right) actuation parametric inputs like stroke and rotation trajectories and produces the position and attitude information of the MFWR in the world coordinate system as shown in Figure 3. Additionally, the model also takes the body linear velocity and angular velocity from the previous simulation step making it an internal feedback system. The MFWR model has been simulated with realistic and envisioned physical and environmental parameters like robot's mass of 100 mg, envisioned wing length of 25 mm, acceleration due to gravity value of 9.8 m/sec^2, air dampening coefficient of 62.3×10^{-6} N-sec/m, stroke angle range of -60 to $+60$, rotational angle range of -90 to $+90$, and with some constant parameters derived and mentioned in [2, 17]. Further, the differential equations characterizing the internal dynamics of the robot model have been computed using Runge-Kutta (RK4) numerical method.

3.2. Control Architecture and Evolutionary Algorithm Specifications. After some preliminary experimentation conducted with the MFWR model, the custom CTRNN-EH control architecture shown in Figure 4 was chosen to be less-redundant architecture and with enough flexibility to embed into its dynamics the optimal control laws required for different flight modes [4]. The actuation dynamics modeled

for each wing can presently control the stroke and rotational parameters of the wing, and the stroke plane of the wing is fixed at a constant angle. This distributed CTRNN architecture shown in Figure 4 has a central core network block that can produce signals, which are delivered to each wing trajectory actuation after being processed by a delay network block. Figure 4 shows the interfacing of the controller architecture with the MFI wing parameters. The delay networks are placed to produce asymmetric/symmetric actuations of left wing with respect to right wing or vice versa to produce net nonzero/zero torques and forces in Y-direction [2, 4]. For the set of experiments and results, being described in this paper, a fullyconnected eight neuron network is chosen for the central core network block and the evolutionary algorithm is employed to evolve the central core network and/or the delay duration in outer delay networks [4]. Further, the central core can accept sensory input, from the MFWR's status or external command, which is feed to each neuron in the core. The next subsection provides the details of the evolutionary algorithm employed in the present experiments.

As mentioned earlier, each individual CTRNN neuron is specified by one bias, one time constant, and eight weighted connections from all neurons in the network (seven connections to other neurons, one self-connection, and one sensor). Thus, the central core network, with eight-neurons, is fully specified by the numeric value settings of eighty-eight parameters, with eleven parameters for each neuron in a fully connected eight-neuron network. The aforementioned minipop EA is implemented with a population size of 4 and a mutation rate of 0.005. The genome length chosen was equal to total number of bits employed to encode a given CTRNN configuration. Each neuron parameter in the configuration is encoded in eight bits, which aggregates to a genome length of 704 bits to represent the central core network. The delay input interval duration for gate networks is encoded in an eight-bit string. Employing the aforementioned architecture and algorithm specifications

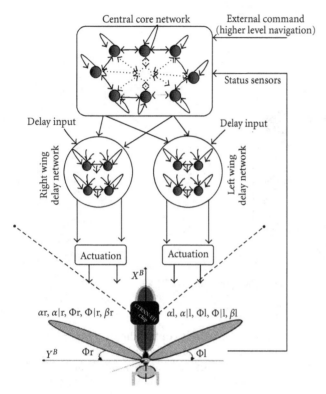

FIGURE 4: Interfacing CTRNN Architecture to MFWR Model to evolve and analyze flight controllers. In the figure, α (with range −90 to 90) indicates the instantaneous rotational angle of the wing, Φ (with range −60 to 60) indicates the instantaneous stroke angle of the wing, and β (with range −45 to 45) indicates the instantaneous stroke plane angle of the wing. The parameters with "|" indicate the rate of change for the parameter it is referring to and these parameters with "r" and "l" indicate the right (r) and left (l) wing parameters, respectively.

the next sections provide the details of the evolutionary runs and evaluation criterion applied to evolving autonomous and nonautonomous controllers.

3.3. Evolved Autonomous Flight Controllers.

Three kinds of autonomous flight controllers, namely, cruising, altitude gain, and steering, were successfully evolved using the aforementioned architecture and algorithm, but with type-specific fitness evaluation criterion. For example, an acceptable behavior of MFWR under an evolved cruise mode controller is to produce motion in a forward direction that is greater than the motion in altitude or sideward directions. Moreover, it should also maintain zero angular velocity along the three vehicle frame axes (zero pitch, roll, and yaw). The later criteria of the expected controller can be met by employing preevolved CTRNN-EH gate networks with symmetric delays. But the first and primary criteria of the controller should be evolved in central core, since this is the only module capable of generating any dynamics to drive the wings. Thus, an evaluation function to capture this established cruise criteria should observe the motion of the MFWR under the control of the potential controller

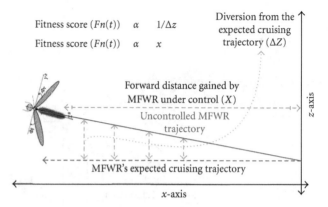

FIGURE 5: The figure shows the relation between the expected cruise behavior of MFWR and the fitness evaluation function employed to evolve the CTRNN-EH controllers to achieve the same behavior under control. An acceptable cruise controller has to propel the MFWR in forward direction and minimize the variation in the altitude. Thus, the fitness score employed to evolve the cruise controllers should reward any forward motion (in x-direction) and penalize any variations in altitude (in z-direction).

and reward the controller on generation of the forward motion and penalize it on generation of altitude variations. A pictorial representation of the expected autonomous cruise behavior and the established relation to its potential evaluation function is shown in Figure 5. Thus, the below evaluation function is designed with a minimizing fitness strategy [4], to capture the expected cruise behavior in MFWR:

$$\frac{\sum_{i=0}^{i=N} \left(|P_{zi}| - \left| P_{yi} \right| - P_{xi} \right)}{N}, \tag{2}$$

where P_{zi}, P_{xi}, and P_{yi} are the instantaneous positional data of MFWR moment in Z(altitude), X(forward), and Y(sideward) directions under the control of the wing kinematics generated by the controller and N is the total number of time steps present in each evaluation period.

It can be observed that the above evaluation function captures the expected forward motion by placing constraints on the controller to maximize P_{xi} term, because it is a negating summation variable in the above minimizing fitness strategy function. Further, the altitude sustainability constraint is enforced by $|P_{zi}|$ term, which captures the averaging absolute measure of the variation in the altitude across the evaluation time, and evolved cruising controller's fitness should minimize this factor so as to favor the overall fitness value contributed by the P_{xi} term. Thus, at least theoretically, the established fitness evaluation function for evolving cruising mode controllers rewards the forward motion of the MFWR and penalizes the variations in its altitude, when placed under the control. Figure 6 shows the behavior of the MFWR under an evolved cruise controller, which has successfully evolved to produce appropriate stroke and rotation kinematics in the wings of the MFWR. Based on the above-mentioned fitness evaluation strategy, that is, to capture the flight mode behavior in terms of the positional information of the MFWR over a specified period

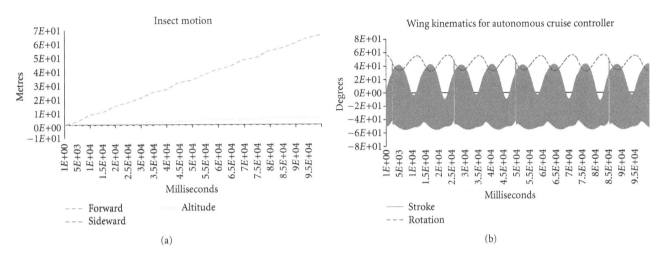

FIGURE 6: The motion of the MFWR in three dimensions (shown in (a)) controlled by a Cruise Mode Controller actuated wing kinematics (shown in (b)). Here the stroke kinematics has relatively higher beats rate than that of the rotation for the above controller shown in the figure, thus the oscillation cycles are cluttered, making it hard to visualize them with respect to the rotation kinematics.

of control, other two autonomous controllers, Altitude-gain and Steer, were also evolved successfully [8, 9]. Further details of the autonomous flight mode controller experiments can be found in [7–9].

3.4. Evolved Nonautonomous Flight Controllers. Two kinds of non-autonomous flight controllers were successfully evolved, namely, adaptive cruise mode controllers and polymorphic controllers [7, 8]. The adaptive cruise mode controllers were similar to their autonomous counterpart except that they were forced to sense the altitude of the MFWR and adapt accordingly during the evolution. The polymorphic controllers on the other hand were forced to change the behavior of the core central CTRNN module between autonomous altitude-gain controllers and autonomous cruise mode controllers, based on the external command. Both of these controllers employed the same fitness evaluation criterion, which was mentioned in the context of the autonomous controllers, on a varied range of the sensory inputs. An evolved nonautonomous cruise mode controller's effect on the wing kinematics of the MFWR is shown in Figure 7(a), along with the corresponding positional data of the MFWR and the sensory input. Also, one of the evolved CTRNN-EH polymorphic flight controller's effects on the wing kinematics is shown in Figure 7(b), along with the corresponding positional data of the MFWR robot and the external sensory input for invoking the desired modes.

4. Analysis of the Evolved Flight Controllers

The evolved CTRNN-EH flight controllers would be better accepted for practical deployment, at least for engineers, if their functionality can be explained using known general principles of engineering. As with all evolvable hardware-based methods, there exists a possibility that the acceptance of the evolved flight controllers, merely in terms of fitness score value (which is based on closely approximating the

acceptable overall body trajectory behavior), could have been exploited the possible underlying noise in the MFWR model to gain optimal controller status. Thus, the first possible analysis to accept the evolved flight controller is to diligently observe and validate the insect's temporal behavior when coupled with the evolved controller's dynamics and determine if they satisfy the known principal physical characteristics of the MFWR model flight behavior. Further, it would be of interest to explain the evolved controllers by possible decomposition of the CTRNN-EH layer in terms of logical control blocks. The next subsections deal with analyzing the evolved controllers with two deduced approaches mentioned below.

4.1. Acceptability Analysis. During the course of this work, it was deduced that the acceptability of the physical behavior of the MFWR flight, produced by the evolved flight controllers could be readily understood by qualitatively contrasting them, with the information discerned from the empirical study conducted on the MFI insect model [2, 18]. During the mentioned empirical study, it was demonstrated that an appropriately parameterized wing's rotational trajectory (the parameters being frequency, amplitude, and phase) can produce thrust in the wing motion plane that can counter air damping and drag on the insect's body, which in turn leads to proportional motion of the robot in forward direction. Additionally, it has been deduced that an appropriate and steady stroke trajectory envelope in the wing kinematics, at positive rotational position and rate of the wing (i.e., upstroke of the wing), can produce positive lift in MFI (which would counter the gravitational forces and leads to rise in the altitude), and the same stroke envelope at negative rotational position and rate would generate antilift (which leads to drop in the altitude). Thus, any designed or evolved controllers for MFWR model should at least qualitatively satisfy this empirically deduced criterion, established for the MFI insect model flight behavior.

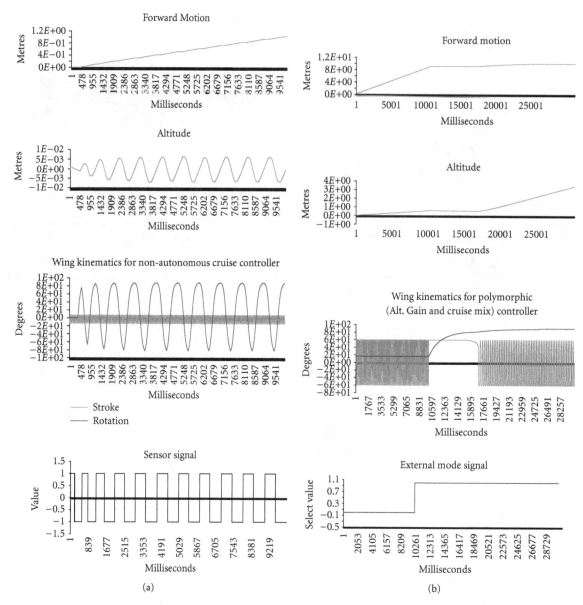

FIGURE 7: (a) shows the Wing Kinematics generated by the Central Core network of a Non-Autonomous Cruising Controller and the corresponding insect motion and sensory update (the stroke kinematics relatively has higher beats rate than that in rotation for the above controller). (b) shows the Wing Kinematics generated by the Central Core network of a Polymorphic flight Controller and the corresponding insect motion, when acted upon by external sensory inputs. One can see the initial cruising behavior is been switched to Alt. Gain behavior (with brief switching delay in wing kinematics).

It was demonstrated that the autonomous and nonautonomous controllers, evolved merely based on simple fitness evaluation functions, produced an acceptable physical behavior in the MFWR model in terms of overall body trajectory [8, 9]. Furthermore, when diligently observed, the wing trajectory (rotational and stroke) produced by the evolved flight controllers (for a given fitness criteria) seems to abide with the empirically established wing trajectory criterion (from MFI insect model flight behavior study). A detailed description of acceptability analysis is not in the scope of this paper and readers are directed to [8, 9] for more details on this analysis performed on individual flight mode controllers.

4.2. Qualitative Functional Decomposition Analysis. It would be of interest to interpret the evolved controllers by possible decomposition into easily explainable logical control blocks, and there exists a previous work [5, 16, 19] that relies on identifying the internal dynamics of the CTRNN-EH controller into Central Pattern Generators (CPGs) and Reflexive Pattern Generators (RPGs). To summarize succinctly, one can perceive the CPG patterned CTRNN controller as the collection of neuron modules that have been evolved appropriately at individual neuron level, to produce autonomous oscillatory dynamics, without any external oscillations or bias. The possibility of a two-neuron CTRNN-EH controller producing autonomous oscillatory dynamics has been demonstrated in [16, 19], and further the later work in the same realm [5, 6] provided a logical CPG template, in which neurons inhibit each other with a time delay, which further leads to continuously destabilizing each other to generate oscillatory dynamics. Further, an RPG patterned CTRNN-EH controllers can be perceived as the collection of neuron modules that have been evolved appropriately to produce oscillatory dynamics in presence of the external oscillations or bias.

The evolved autonomous altitude gain, cruising, and steering and controllers are suspected to fall under the CPG template and could be decomposed into a collection of explainable oscillatory and nonoscillatory neuron groups that produced desired control of the evolved flight behaviors.

On other hand, the nonautonomous cruising mode controllers and polymorphic mode controller (as a whole) are likely to fall under the RPG template and could be decomposed into a collection of sensor-dependent or -independent oscillatory neuron groups. Thus, it would be necessary to find and separate the possible independent and dependent oscillatory control modules in an evolved controller that could aid in characterizing a given controller using known CPG or RPG templates. Further this decomposition process could provide a qualitative view and human understandable structure of the lower-level coordination among these separated modules, which primarily govern the behavior of a given evolved controller. In this vein, a three-step frequency-based analysis procedure is proposed to qualitatively decompose the evolved controllers.

Dynamics-Deprived Neuron Elimination. To simplify the process of decomposing, the evolved controllers into a group of functional units, a step-by-step neuron elimination technique, shown in Figure 8, has been employed to possibly reduce the size of the existing 8-neuron CTRNN-EH controllers. As shown in Figure 8, one can assign a role to individual neurons in a given CTRNN-EH controller architecture, based on their functional value. The neurons that are connected directly to the effectors module of the MFWR can be designated as primary neurons, and others can be designated as secondary neurons. It is obvious that primary neurons cannot be dynamics-deprived neurons, but some of the secondary neurons that saturate to minimum or maximum of neuron output level during flight controller period qualify to be dynamics-deprived neurons. These detected dynamics-deprived neurons can be folded into the existing neurons by modifying the biases appropriately (i.e., "Bias-Forwarding"). Once the reduced architecture's dynamics qualitatively match the dynamics of the original complete network, the reduce network can be employed for further decomposition process.

Frequency-Based Grouping. Based on the previously mentioned general principle of acceptable controller dynamics, it was deduced that the steady oscillatory dynamics in the wing (stroke or rotation) dictate the flight behavior. Thus, based on this controller acceptability knowledge, it would be appropriate to group the neurons in the reduced network,

based on their individual time constants, into no more than two groups (one each for rotation and stroke). As shown in the Figure 9, the clustering criteria are based on the idea that the neurons with relatively lower time constants (i.e., higher frequency) are separated from the neurons with relatively higher time constants (i.e., lower frequency). As shown in Figure 9, the grouping of the neurons will simplify the decomposition process in the way that one can logically relate the individual wing kinematics (stroke or rotation) to the individual neuron groups (clustered) based on the qualitative difference in the frequency and phase of the wing kinematics.

Lesion Study. Once the frequency clustered neuron control modules are obtained for a given controller, it is necessary to understand the interactions of the individual neurons within those control modules and with the other existing control modules to qualitatively deduce the underlying governing principle of the controller functionality. Thus, in this lesion study, a general method of diligently observing the variations in the dynamics of an individual or group of neurons, while some of its connections are amputated from rest of the network, has been adopted. Though the number of lesion operations cannot be quantified and will vary depending on the complexity of the evolved controller, but as shown in Figure 10, the initial intuitive regions of the amputations across all the evolved controllers would be between the frequency clustered neuron groups to verify their interdependency followed by a series of further lesions, like intragroup lesion study, wherever deemed appropriate for the controller in the context. Employing the above-mentioned qualitative decomposition process; the best five of every evolved controller in each category have been analyzed as discussed below.

4.3. Analysis of Autonomous Controllers

4.3.1. Autonomous Cruise Mode Controllers. This section provides the detailed qualitative decomposition process for one of the best evolved autonomous cruise mode controllers, using the above-mentioned three general steps. For qualitative comparisons and to better understand the controller decomposition an unaltered original eight-neuron architecture of the controller to be analyzed is shown in Figure 11. The architecture has two primary neurons 0 and 1, which are directly connected to the stroke and rotation effectors of the MFWR and the neurons from 2 to 7 are the secondary neurons of the controller, whose role in governing the controller behavior would be determined as part of this decomposition process. The original outputs of each neuron in the controller's architecture, which are responsible for producing the desired cruising behavior in MFWR, are shown in Figure 12.

Moreover, the flight trajectory of the MFWR under the control of the original controller in the context is shown in Figure 13, which would be useful for qualitative comparisons that would be performed later when the original architecture of the controller has been simplified for analysis. As shown in Figure 12, it can be observed that the secondary neurons

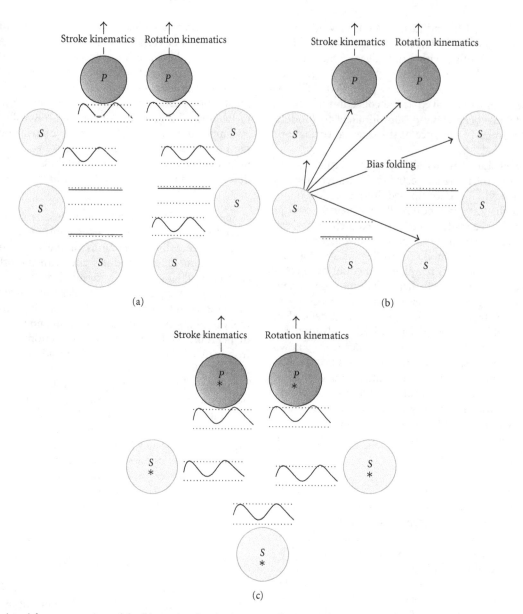

FIGURE 8: A pictorial representation of the "dynamics-deprived neuron elimination" process. The primary neurons are labeled as "P" and subsidiary neurons are labeled as "S". A three step process is adopted here, starting with eliminating the neurons with saturated dynamics in them as shown in (a), followed by folding the saturated output of the eliminated neurons as bias into the survival neurons as shown in (b). The final step shown in (c) is to verify the qualitative match of the dynamics produced by the bias modified (labeled with "*") individual neurons to their counterparts in the original architecture.

3, 5, and 6 seem to be saturated at constant output value during the flight control. Though it can be deduced, at least, from observations that these three neurons may not have contributed to the overall output dynamics produced by the controller, a detailed step-by-step process mentioned in the "Dynamics-deprived Neuron Elimination" procedure is necessary to rule out the possibility that these neurons might have played a critical role during the initialization of the controller by providing transient dynamics before saturating in the steady state. The obvious neurons that are contributing to the controller dynamics are 0, 1, 2, 4, and 7, but there exist distinct differences in the output

envelope and frequency characteristics of 0 and 1 neurons from 2, 4, and 7, which could be used for "frequency-based grouping" process later on the successful reduction of the architecture size, as shown in Figure 17. Since, the candidate dynamics-deprived neurons are determined by the neuron output state observations; the biases of the neurons 0, 1, 2, 4, and 7 are modified appropriately, as pictorially represented in Figure 8(b), by treating the individual input weight of the survival neuron from each eliminated neuron as an additional bias value to its output state. The resultant reduced neuron architecture of five neurons in it is pictorial represented in Figure 14. To further validate

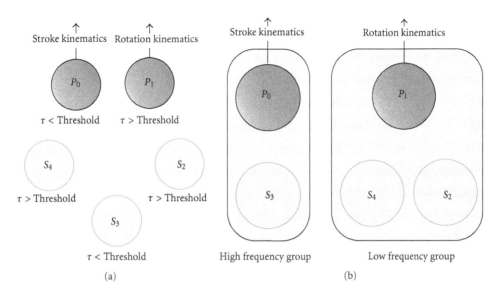

FIGURE 9: A pictorial representation of the "frequency-based grouping" process. The first step of the process, as shown in (a), is to determine a relative threshold time constant (Tau) for the reduced network, reduced by "dynamics-deprived neuron elimination" process, followed by grouping the neurons in the architecture based on the frequency of the output produced by individual neuron (i.e., the neurons with time constant less than the relative threshold are clustered into high frequency group, and neurons with time constants more than the relative threshold are clustered into low frequency group) as shown in (b).

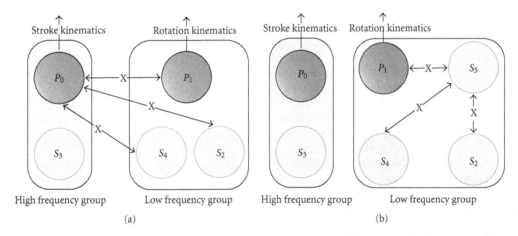

FIGURE 10: A pictorial representation of the "lesion study" process. The lesion study is based on the idea that it is possible to determine the underlying governing functional principle of the network with rigorously observing the behavior changes in the network for appropriate combinations of the amputations. Based on the complexity of the controller, the lesion study can be performed between neurons in distinct frequency groups, which is performing intergroup amputations, shown in (a), or between the neurons in the same frequency group, that is, intragroup amputations shown in (b).

that the dynamics-deprived neuron elimination process is applicable for this controller, two qualitative comparisons are necessary, primarily the architecturally reduced controller should at least qualitatively control the MFWR trajectory behavior that was intended by the original controller, and, moreover, the survival neuron output state envelopes during the flight control should match their output state envelopes from the original architecture.

The later condition eliminates the possibility that the reduced architecture could have changed dramatically and lost its internal dynamics, although it could have satisfied the primary condition to produce the desired cruise behavior in MFWR. Thus, the reduced five neuron controller is evaluated

against the MFWR, and the individual neuron output state envelope of the five-neurons is captured and shown in Figure 15, and accordingly the trajectory of MFWR under the control of the reduced controller is shown in Figure 16. It can be observed that there exists an acceptable qualitative match between the produced neuron outputs in the reduced five-neuron controller to its counterparts original eight neuron controller, including the in sync variations of the frequency and amplitude in the primary stroke neuron and the neuron 4 (of original architecture) to its new neuron position 3.

Moreover, the most convincing evidence that the reduced controller qualitatively controls the MFWR trajectory to

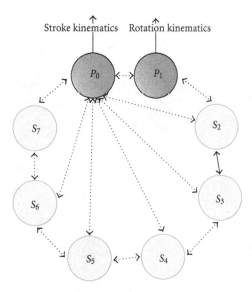

FIGURE 11: A pictorial representation of the fully connected eight neuron architecture of the autonomous cruise mode controller chosen for qualitative decomposition analysis. As mentioned earlier, the stroke and rotation neurons are marked "*P*" as primary and "*S*" as secondary for the other neurons and numbered accordingly from 0 to 7.

produce desired cruise behavior justifies that the dynamics-deprived neuron elimination process is applicable for this controller. Thus, moving forward with the reduced five-neuron architecture, applying frequency-based grouping would be uncomplicated, since it can be observed from the five neuron output envelopes that the primary stroke neuron and third secondary neuron seem to share a peculiar in sync frequency and amplitude variations, intuitively belonging to high frequency group. Moreover, the evolved time constant for both of these neurons is same and is 0.010000 units and on other hand, the neurons 1 and 4 along with the rotation primary neuron can be allocated to low frequency group with corresponding time constants 10.546157, 9.558393, and 20.176863, respectively. Thus, if a relative time constant threshold of 9 units is chosen, then there exist two distinct frequency-based groups as shown in Figure 18. After the grouping of the primary stroke neuron and third secondary neuron in a comparable frequency group, further interpretation on their interconnection weight revealed that there strongly inhibit each other, and further there exists a strong possibility that these two neurons can form a two-neuron (high frequency) oscillator with any other input dynamics from the low frequency group (consists of rotation primary neuron, fourth secondary neuron, and second secondary neuron). Thus, an intergroup lesion study, as shown in Figure 10(a), to amputate the neuron connections between the high frequency group neurons and the low frequency group neurons is performed. When this amputated network is evaluated, the above intuitive possibility of two-neuron oscillator formation in the high frequency group was validated along with a revelation of two-neuron oscillator formation in a low frequency group, as shown in Figure 18. It can observed that the primary stroke neuron and the third

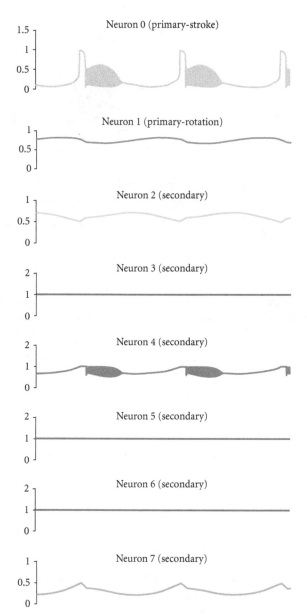

FIGURE 12: The above figure shows the neuron output state dynamics of each neuron in the fully connected original eight neuron controllers produced during the flight control of the MFWR to provide optimal cruise behavior.

secondary neurons oscillate at same frequency consistently, and their output amplitude is more than the lower frequency group consisting of primary rotation neuron and second secondary neuron along with a saturated fourth secondary neuron during the amputated evaluation. It is evident that the fourth secondary neuron's dynamics are not completely isolated from the high frequency stroke oscillator group (primary stroke neuron and third secondary neuron) since this fourth neuron has shown perfect oscillatory behavior when the reduced network was fully connected through this neuron. Moreover, when this amputated network controller is coupled to the MFWR, it has been observed that the controller was able to control the MFWR trajectory in an

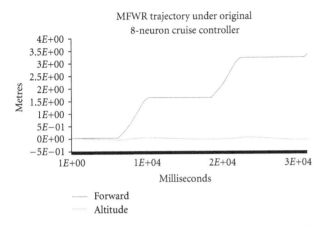

FIGURE 13: The MFWR trajectory produced by the original fully connected eight-neuron controller. It can be observed that the evolved controller was successful in producing forward motion in the MFWR without any overall gain in the altitude.

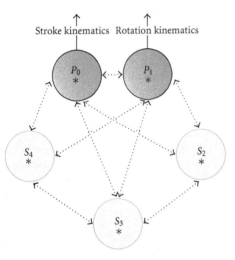

FIGURE 14: A pictorial representation of the reduced five-neuron architecture of the cruise controller referred in Figure 12. It should be noticed that the primary neurons and secondary neurons retain their position in the network, but neurons 4 and 7 from the original network are positioned in 3rd and 4th locations respectively. The "*" indicates that the neurons in this "dynamics-deprived neuron elimination" process-based architecture differ from the original neuron in the way that, their bias has been accounted for the eliminated neuron's saturated output effect on them. So, at least in steady state this reduced network should perform functionally equivalent to the original architecture.

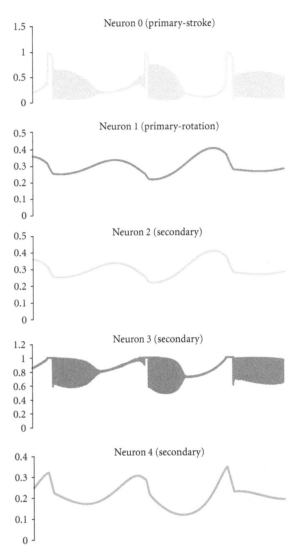

FIGURE 15: The above figure shows the neuron output state dynamics of each neuron in the reduced five-neuron architecture of the cruise controller architecture shown in Figure 12. It can be noticed that qualitatively the output dynamics of each neuron do not differ significantly from their original behavior shown in Figure 13.

acceptable cruise mode behavior template seen before in Figures 16 and 15, but gradually it drifted from the acceptable behavior and resulted in significant rise in MFWR's altitude, with a rise rate proportional to the MFWR forward motion rate, as shown in Figure 19. It would of interest to do a diligent comparison of the dynamics of the fully connected reduced five-neuron controller to that of the amputated controller shown in Figures 18 and 15 from behavior change perspective in each neuron output states during the flight evaluations. Though one might argue that quantitatively the

dynamics of neurons 0 to 3 (includes primary stroke and rotation neurons and two secondary neurons) are different in both the scenarios, for qualitative analysis purposes these neurons do project similar oscillatory dynamics, but the drastic difference of the dynamics is observed in the fourth secondary neuron, which seized to oscillate when amputated from the high frequency neuron group indicating a strong connection to the controller's performance degradation noticed in the Figure 24. When analyzing the neuron outputs of the fully connected controller, the dynamics of stroke neuron group (high frequency group) were altered periodically by a slow moving signal, with a period equivalent to the rotation neuron group (low frequency group). Moreover, it was already demonstrated that there exists the fourth secondary neuron in this low frequency group (rotation)

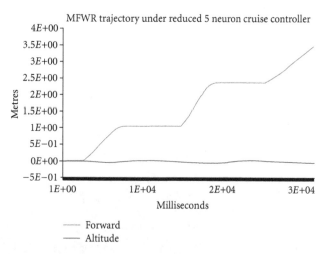

MFWR trajectory under reduced 5 neuron cruise controller

— Forward
— Altitude

FIGURE 16: The MFWR trajectory produced by the reduced five neuron controller. It can be observed that the architectural reduced controller was successful in producing qualitatively same cruise behavior possible by the fully connected eight neuron network. The MFWR trajectory produced by the eight-neuron network is shown in Figure 14.

that is susceptible and depends on the dynamics of the high frequency group (stroke), and though both groups were capable of producing independent oscillatory dynamics to control the MFWR trajectory, the control lasted for a short period of time in absence of the possible dynamics modification by the fourth secondary neuron. Further, an optimal control behavior was only possible with inclusion of this fourth secondary neuron, which now can be treated as a monitoring neuron, that was evolved appropriately to take the responsibility of performing complex dynamics computation across both the oscillator groups and provide the high frequency group with periodic signals to alter its amplitude and frequency to satisfy the cruise behavior in the MFWR. Additionally, it was mentioned earlier that the fourth neuron has an intermediate time constant value of 9.558, which makes it have enough temporal summation ability, the ability which could have possibly made it an observer (sink in the dynamics of the other neurons) of the other neurons and further have sufficient internal dynamics (sufficient firing rate to generate spikes) to modify their dynamics at slower but in a strong way thus modifying their frequency and amplitude periodically.

Based on the above analysis, it can be deduced that the evolved autonomous cruise mode controllers can be qualitatively explained as a composition of two steady and independent frequency oscillators, one governing the stroke kinematics of the wing with higher beat rate and another it is rotation with lower beat rate, in presence of a monitoring neuron which periodically tunes the amplitude and frequency of the stroke oscillator, which periodicity synchronized with the rotation oscillator. A pictorial representation of the above deduced compositional template is shown Figure 20. All of the 5 best evolved autonomous cruise mode controllers were reducible from an eight neuron to a five-neuron architecture using the "dynamics-deprived neuron elimination" process.

Further, four of them had distinct frequency features in their architecture that could be exploited by the "Frequency-based Grouping" process and were successfully reduced to two kinematics control modules. Only three of the best five controllers complied with the decomposed template discussed above, with steady independent oscillator blocks and a monitoring neuron, and others performed the same functionality with closely dependent oscillator blocks that were not complaint with frequency-based clustering criteria. Nonetheless, the rigorous intragroup lesion study on them exhibited the presence of monitor neuron, which aided in controlling the amplitude of the rotation dynamics for acceptable cruise behavior.

4.3.2. Autonomous Altitude Gain Mode and Steer Mode Controllers. The above decomposition analysis mentioned in the context of the cruise mode controllers is performed on the entire best five autonomous altitude gain mode and steer mode controllers. The individual controller architectures were reducible from an 8-neuron to 4-neuron architecture using "Dynamics-deprived Neuron Elimination" process in both categories. Only some of the best altitude gain controllers were complaint with clustering criteria and thus two functional templates were derived using the lesion study performed on the individual neurons in the reduced network. As shown in Figure 21(a), this derived functional template employed single oscillatory control group encompassing both the primary neurons in it, performing close-looped oscillations required for wing kinematics, with aid of two subsidiary neurons in the network resembling a typical CPG-like control module described earlier in the section. This decomposition template is applicable for the steer controller's entire central core and only for two of the altitude gain controllers. The other template, shown in Figure 21(b), had only the stroke primary neuron in an oscillatory control group with a saturated rotation kinematics in separate control module, which is applicable for only altitude gain controllers.

4.4. Analysis of Nonautonomous Controllers

4.4.1. Nonautonomous Cruise Mode Controllers. This section provides the detailed qualitative decomposition process for one of the best evolved non-autonomous cruise mode controllers. The applicability of the established three-step decomposition using Dynamics-Deprived Neuron Elimination, Frequency-based grouping, and Lesion Study methods will be presented and possible oscillatory level decomposition will be deduced. For qualitative comparisons and to better understand the controller decomposition, an unaltered original eight-neuron architecture of the controller to be analyzed is shown in Figure 22. The architecture has two primary neurons 0 and 1, which are directly connected to the stroke and rotation effectors of the MFWR and the neurons from 2 to 7 are the secondary neurons of the controller, whose role in governing the controller behavior would be determined as part of this decomposition process. Apart from the interconnections among the neurons, every

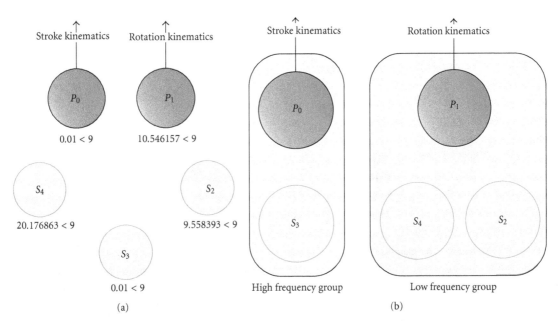

FIGURE 17: A pictorial representation of the "frequency-based grouping" process for the cruise mode controller shown in Figure 12. The first step of the process, as shown in (a), is to compare each neuron's time constant with determined relative threshold of 9.0 units, followed by grouping the neurons in the architecture based on the frequency of the output produced by individual neuron (i.e., the neurons with time constant less than the relative threshold are clustered into high frequency group and neurons with time constants more than the relative threshold are clustered into low frequency group) as shown in (b).

neuron is connected to an external altitude sensor, which is modeled to provide a relative altitude status of the MFWR from its initial altitude during the evaluation. The original outputs of each neuron in the controller's architecture, which are responsible for producing the desired cruising behavior in MFWR, along with the altitude sensor output, are shown in Figure 23. Moreover, the flight trajectory of the MFWR under the control of the original controller in the context is shown in Figure 24, which would be useful for qualitative comparisons that would be performed later when the original architecture of the controller has been simplified for analysis. As shown in the Figure 23, it can be observed that the secondary neurons 3 and 6 seem to be saturated at constant output value during the flight control. Though it can be deduced, at least, from observations that these three neurons, may not have contributed to the overall output dynamics produced by the controller, a detailed step-by-step process mentioned in the "dynamics-deprived neuron elimination" procedure is necessary to rule out the possibility that these neurons might have played a critical role during the initialization of the controller by providing transient dynamics before saturating in the steady state. The obvious neurons that are contributing to the controller dynamics are 0, 1, 2, 4, 5, and 7, but there exist distinct differences in the output envelope and frequency characteristics of 0, 2, 5, and 7 neurons from 1 and 4, which could be used for "frequency-based grouping" process later on the successful reduction of the architecture size. Moreover, as mentioned during the initial physical validation step of the evolution process, there exists an entrainment of the primary rotation neuron output state in amplitude and frequency with that of

the sensor status output characteristics. Since the candidate dynamics-deprived neurons are determined by the neuron output state observations, the biases of the neurons 0, 1, 2, 4, 5, and 7 are modified appropriately, by treating the individual input weight of the survival neuron from each eliminated neuron as an additional bias value to its output state. The resultant reduced neuron architecture of six neurons in it is pictorially represented in Figure 25. To further validate that the dynamics-deprived neuron elimination process is applicable for this controller, two qualitative comparisons are necessary; primarily the architecturally reduced controller should at least qualitatively control the MFWR trajectory behavior that was intended by the original controller, and, moreover, the survival neuron output state envelopes during the flight control should match their output state envelopes from the original architecture. As mentioned earlier, the later condition eliminates the possibility that the reduced architecture could have changed dramatically and lost its internal dynamics, although it could have satisfied the primary condition to produce the desired cruise behavior in MFWR.

Further, the interesting entrainment behavior between the sensor output and the rotation neuron output (and if possible the third (old designated position-fourth) secondary neuron output) should be maintained, at least qualitatively. Thus, the reduced six-neuron controller is evaluated against the MFWR, and the individual neuron output state envelope of the six neurons and the sensor status are captured and shown in Figure 26, and accordingly the trajectory of MFWR under the control of the reduced controller is shown in Figure 27. It can be observed that there exists an acceptable qualitative match between the produced neuron outputs in

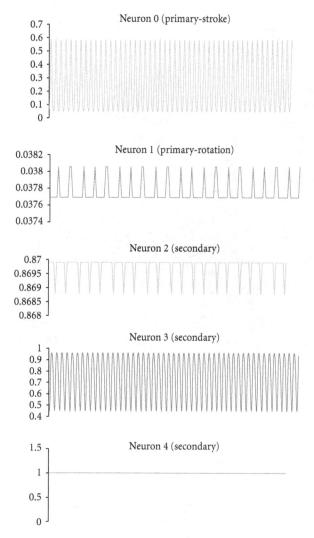

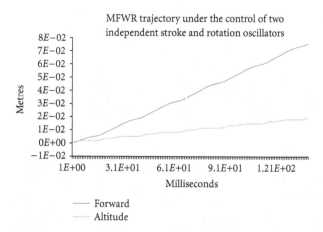

FIGURE 19: The trajectory of MFWR produced under the control of the amputated cruise controller. It can be noticed that the controller, with two independent oscillators for stroke, and rotation produces an acceptable cruise behavior during initial phases of the flight, but immediately loose its ability to control and reduce the altitude variations, in absence of the monitor neuron.

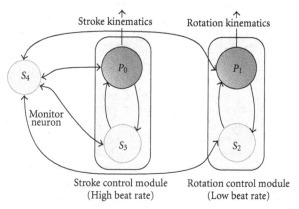

FIGURE 20: The Qualitative functional decomposition template derived for the autonomous cruise mode. Most of the autonomous cruise mode controllers can be decomposed into the above-shown template with a high frequency stroke control oscillator module and a low frequency rotation control oscillator along with an intermediate neuron called monitor neuron, which is responsible to coordinate and fine-tune the amplitude and frequency of the stroke oscillator with a period derived from the rotation oscillator. This functional template explains the general evolved behavior of the amplitude and frequency modulation of the stroke kinematics with rotation period for optimal cruise control of MFWR.

FIGURE 18: The output state dynamics of each neuron in the interfrequency group amputated network, amputated as part of the lesion study on the reduced five-neuron network. It can be observed that the primary stroke neuron and the third secondary neuron produced perfect in sync oscillations forming a two-neuron independent oscillator. On the other hand, the primary rotation neuron with second neuron formed a feeble two neuron oscillator. It should be noticed that the fourth neuron dynamics are saturated, in the amputated network, compared to its original oscillatory behavior seen in Figure 16 of the fully connected reduced controller.

the reduced six-neuron controller to its counterparts in the original eight-neuron controller, including the in entrainment behavior between the primary stroke neuron and the sensor status.

Thus, moving forward with the reduced six-neuron architecture, applying frequency-based grouping would be complicated, since it can observed from the six-neuron output envelopes that the primary stroke neuron, along with second, fourth, and fifth secondary neurons, seems to share the same frequency bandwidth, intuitively belonging to high frequency group.

Moreover, the evolved time constants for these neurons are in the range of 0.010000 to 0.05000 units. But, on the

other hand, the rotation primary neuron and the third secondary neuron can be allocated to low frequency group with corresponding time range of 10.034 to 16.532 units. Moreover, since the sensor module output can be treated as a pseudoneuron (with dynamics equivalent to the MFWR model and with interneuron connections to the primary neurons only), there exist two options to decompose the architecture further. The first approach is to group the sensor pseudoneuron into the low frequency group and perform the intergroup lesion study, which will provide the insight into the high frequency group oscillator's (if at all the group

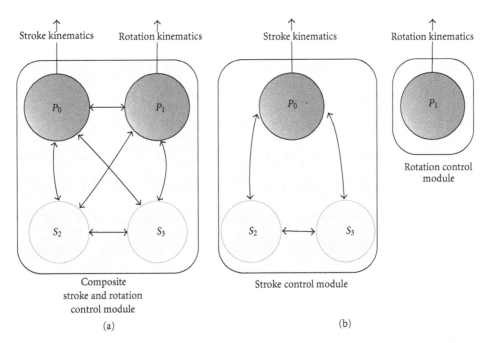

FIGURE 21: The qualitative functional decomposition derived for the evolved autonomous altitude gain controllers and steer controllers. Most of the steer controller's wing kinematics can be decomposed with a typical CPG-like functional template shown in (a) as a closely coupled stroke and rotation oscillators with steady beat rate and steady amplitude. Most of the altitude gain controllers can be decomposed with the functional template shown in (b), with a dedicated stroke oscillator along with a saturated rotation control module.

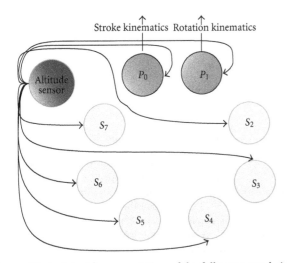

FIGURE 22: A pictorial representation of the fully connected eight-neuron architecture with a single altitude sensor, of the nonautonomous cruise mode controller chosen for qualitative decomposition analysis. Following the general neuron representation, the stroke and rotation neurons are marked with "P" as primary and "S" as secondary for the other neurons and numbered accordingly from 0 to 7.

exhibits independent oscillatory nature) dependency on the sensor state and further the same dependency can be derived by performing intragroup lesion study on the low frequency group by amputating the sensor pseudoneuron. The second approach is to group only the real neurons by completely ignoring the sensor signal (i.e., amputating the sensor

signal) into a high and low frequency groups and study their behavior independently, checking for independent oscillatory behavior, in the absence of the external sensor signal, followed by introducing the sensor signal to detect any significant behavior changes for deducing any possible independent control modules. Though both approaches would yield the same conclusions, the second approach is chosen since the sensor dynamics of the MFWR can be treated separately from the actual neuron dynamics, in two easy steps of complete sensor-independent neuron dynamics decomposition (frequency grouping and intragroup lesion study) followed by the sensor status injection into the possible neuron-level decomposed modules. Thus, moving forward, the six-neuron architecture is disconnected from the external sensor and a frequency-based grouping, with groups mentioned earlier is performed as shown in the pictorial representation Figure 28. Further, an intergroup lesion study is performed, as described earlier (shown in Figure 10(a)), and the outputs of the each neuron in the two groups are presented in Figure 29. It can be noticed that these two frequency groups have indeed self-sufficient dynamics in them to be independent oscillators, with two frequency groups, the high-frequency group and the low-frequency group as demosntrated in above analysis. Moreover, the outputs of each neuron in the high-frequency group match their original output envelope from the reduced six-neuron architecture suggesting that this group's internal dynamics is immune to the external sensor dynamics. But the same cannot be deduced for the low-frequency group, which has high time constants and have already shown its affinity to entrain with the sensor signal. Moreover, this intragroup amputated

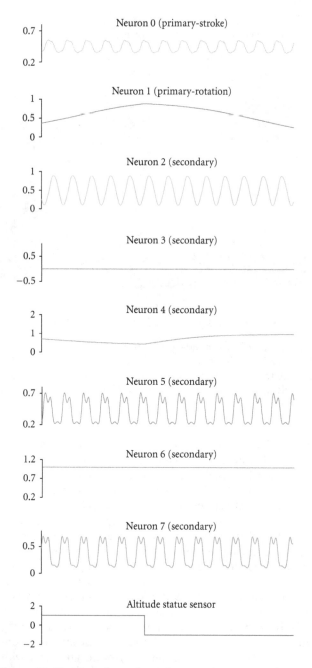

FIGURE 23: The above figure shows the neuron output state dynamics of each neuron in the fully connected original eight-neuron controller and the external altitude sensor, produced during the flight control of the MFWR to provide optimal cruise behavior. It can be observed that the output states of neurons 1 and 4 entrain with altitude sensor in phase and out of phase, respectively.

stroke and rotation neuron group independent oscillators have been partially successful in controlling the MFWR's expected cruise behavior as shown in Figure 30, in which it can be observed that the altitude of the MFWR is lost with the progression of the time, though the rate of the altitude drop is very much less than the rate of forward motion gain. The next step in this process to deduce any possible modular control structure is to inject the sensor signal dynamics

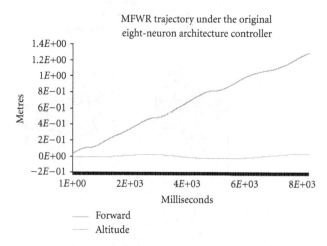

FIGURE 24: The MFWR trajectory produced by the original fully connected eight-neuron nonautonomous controller. It can be observed that the evolved controller was successful in producing forward motion in the MFWR without any overall gain in the altitude.

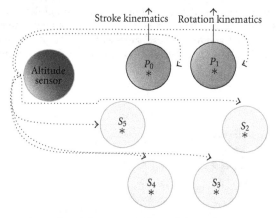

FIGURE 25: A pictorial representation of the reduced six-neuron architecture of the cruise controller referred in Figure 22. It should be noticed that the primary neurons and second secondary neuron retain their position in the network but the neurons 4, 5, and 7 from the original network are positioned in 3rd, 4th, and 5th locations respectively. The "*" indicates that the neurons in this "dynamics-deprived neuron elimination" process-based architecture differ from the original neuron in the way that, their bias has been accounted for the eliminated neuron's saturated output effect on them. So, at least in steady state, this reduced network should perform functionally equivalent to the original architecture.

into the established two frequency groups and check for the entrainment behavior and controller's expected cruise mode acceptability on MFWR. While performing the agreed final step in the decomposition process, it was deduced that injecting the sensor signal dynamics only into low-frequency group is sufficient to produce qualitatively acceptable cruise mode behavior in MFWR. Thus, a general qualitative functional decomposition template shown in Figure 31 is derived explaining the evolved non-autonomous cruise mode controllers, as a combination of two independent oscillators, of which the high-frequency oscillator controlled the stroke

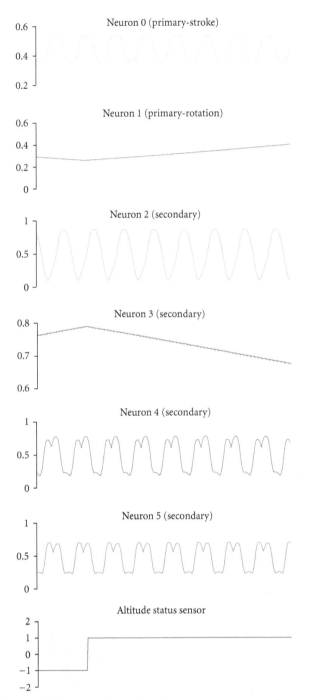

FIGURE 26: The above figure shows the neuron output state dynamics of each neuron in the reduced six neuron architecture of the cruise controller architecture shown in Figure 22. It can be noticed that the qualitative output dynamics of each neuron do not differ significantly from their original behavior shown in Figure 23. Moreover, It can be observed that the output states of neuron 1 and 3 entrain with altitude sensor in phase and out of phase, respectively.

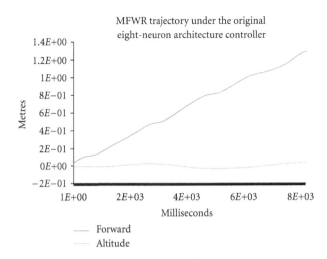

FIGURE 27: The MFWR trajectory produced by the reduced six-neuron controller. It can be observed that the architectural reduced controller was successful in producing qualitatively same cruise behavior possiblely by the fully connected eight-neuron network. The MFWR trajectory produced by the eight-neuron network is shown in Figure 24.

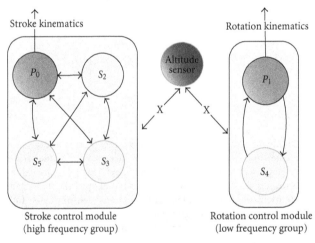

FIGURE 28: A pictorial representation of the "frequency-based grouping" process combined with intergroup lesion study in absence of the external sensor input for the nonautonomous cruise mode controller shown in Figure 22.

kinematics of the wing with steady amplitude and frequency and the low-frequency oscillator, which was evolved to monitor the altitude variations in the MFWR, through the available external sensor module, altered the rotation dynamics continuously to limit the variations in the altitude of the MFWR and simultaneously provided the forward

motion in it, by generating required lift and antilift with the behavior verified by the general principles of the empirical study (mentioned in the acceptability analysis). Three of the best five evolved controllers followed the deduced template, and the other two followed more closed template that is only different from the predominant one in that the stroke frequency group has a dependency on the external sensor status.

4.4.2. Nonautonomous Polymorphic Controllers. Since the polymorphic controllers embed in their architecture both the autonomous altitude gain and cruise mode controllers, which can be invoked as a separate controllers in isolation with a static external signal not a continuous dynamic signal, the qualitative functional decomposition templates

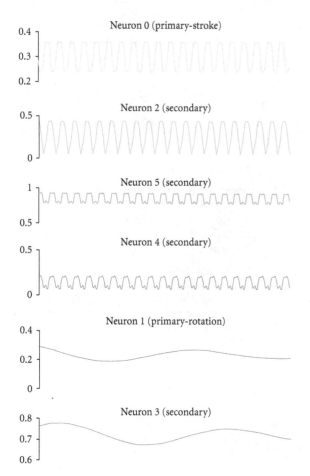

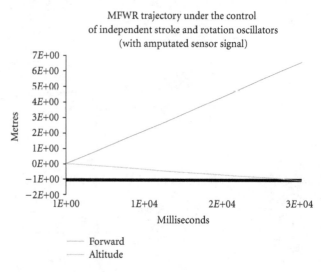

FIGURE 30: The MFWR trajectory produced by the controller during the lesion study performed with the techniques shown in Figure 28. It can be observed that the amputated two independent stroke and rotation oscillators, in absence of the external sensor, were partially successful in controlling the MFWR to have acceptable cruise behavior in it, suggesting the requirement of the external sensor ingestion to achieve the acceptable cruise control.

FIGURE 29: The above figure shows the neuron output state dynamics of each neuron in the low frequency group (1 and 3) and high frequency group (0, 2, 4, and 5) after intergroup amputation is performed and evaluated in absence of the external altitude sensor signal (represented in Figure 28). It can be noticed that each qualitative group is self-sufficient to generate internal dynamics to sustain steady oscillations independent of the external sensor signal. But, nonetheless low frequency group neurons seem to be susceptible to external sensor signal due to their high time constants.

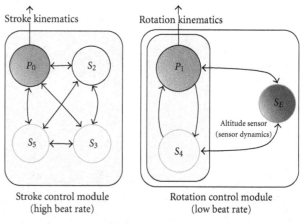

FIGURE 31: The Qualitative functional decomposition template derived for the non-autonomous cruise mode controllers. Most of the nonautonomous cruise mode controllers can be decomposed into the above-shown template, as a combination of two independent oscillator, of which the high-frequency oscillator, controlled the stroke kinematics of the wing with steady amplitude and frequency and the low-frequency oscillator which was evolved to monitor the altitude variations in the MFWR, through the available external sensor module, altered the rotation dynamics continuously to limit the variations in the altitude of the MFWR and simultaneously provided the forward motion in it, by generating required lift and anti-lift with the behavior verified by the general principles of the empirical study.

presented for the autonomous cruise and altitude gain controllers in the previous section would be applicable for decomposing the polymorphic controllers into two isolated general templates pictorial represented in Figure 21. To further validate the above presented templates, an evolved polymorphic controller's neuron outputs have been evaluated in isolation for cruise and altitude gain command (external sensor value of "0" and "1", resp.) and presented in Figure 32(a) and Figure 32(b), respectively. It can be observed from Figure 32(a) that there exist neurons 2, 3, 6, and 7 which meet dynamics-deprived criteria, and further when their saturated outputs are bias folded into neurons 0, 1, 4, and 5, the dynamics of the reduced four neuron network and its effect on MFWR behavior, namely, cruising behavior, matched the original eight-neuron network's generated behavior. Moreover, as anticipated, the reduced four-neuron network with same output dynamics frequency for

all the neurons falls under the composite stroke and rotation control module template presented in Figure 21(a).

Moving forward, it can be observed from Figure 32(b), that there exist neurons 1, 2, 3, 4, and 7, which meet dynamics deprived criteria, and further when their saturated outputs are bias folded into neurons 0, 5, and 6, the dynamics

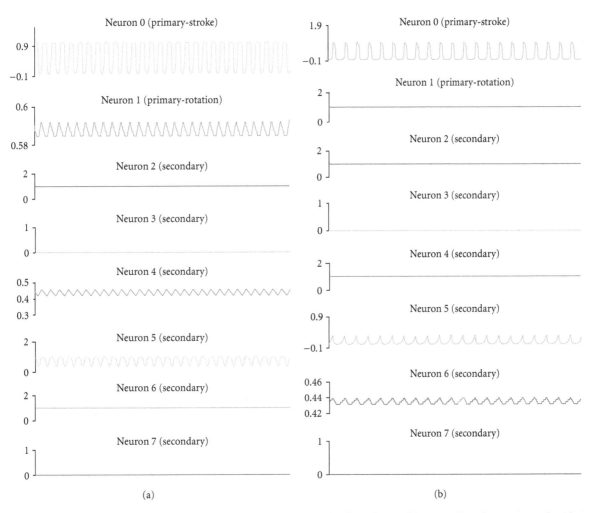

(a)   (b)

FIGURE 32: (a) shows the neuron output state dynamics of each neuron in the polymorphic controller when presented with a cruise command, whose the external sensor signal is "0." It can be seen that the neurons 0, 1, 4, and 5 form a composite module with same frequency and would not comply with established criteria for frequency-based grouping. But, the cruise mode controller has been verified to form a single frequency composite stroke and rotation control module as shown in Figure 21(a) and generating appropriate cruise behavior in the MFWR. (b) shows the neuron output state dynamics of each neuron in the polymorphic controller when presented with an altitude gain command whose external sensor signal is "1." It can be seen that the neurons 0, 5, and 6 forms same frequency group for stroke control and a constant rotation produced by saturated neuron 1. The altitude gain mode controller form a two separate independent stroke and rotation control blocks template as shown in Figure 21(b) and generates appropriate altitude gain behavior in the MFWR.

of the reduced four-neuron network and its effect on MFWR behavior, namely, altitude gain behavior, matched the original eight-neuron network's generated behavior. Moreover, as anticipated, the reduced four-neuron network with two independent stroke and rotation control module template presented in Figure 21(b). Thus, when presented with an appropriate external command (sensor) value, the static command would be folded into the exiting neurons in the polymorphic controller architecture, as an appropriately evolved external bias that is responsible to shift the dynamics of the rotation and stroke neurons between autonomous altitude gain and cruise mode controllers, generating appropriate wing kinematics in the MFWR as shown in Figure 7(b). Further, it can be observed by comparing the output neuron dynamics of the cruise mode (shown in Figure 32(a)) and the altitude gain mode (shown in Figure 32(b)) that the external sensor's dynamics modification process is evidently

observed when the dynamically active neuron 4 in cruise mode saturates in altitude gain mode, and vice versa for dynamics of output of the neuron 6.

5. Conclusion

In this paper, we have summarized author's prior efforts using the Neuromorphic Evolvable Hardware (CTRNN-EH) framework to successfully evolve locomotion and different flight mode controllers, with detailed emphasis on the flight mode controllers. Further, a new frequency-based analysis procedure has been introduced to analyze the different evolved flight mode controllers, besides providing a brief qualitative analysis suggesting the acceptability of the evolved controllers for the given flight mode in the context. Moreover, the proposed frequency-based analysis methodology has been successfully applied to the evolved autonomous and nonautonomous controllers, and it has been demonstrated that the methodology can be indeed used to decompose the evolved controllers into logically explainable control blocks for further control analysis. Finally, it can be perceived from the presented results and discussion that the proposed Neuromorphic Evolvable Hardware (CTRNN-EH) and frequency-based analysis methodologies can be employed to control problems that are similar to the flapping flight domain, using tabularasa approach. Though, it is not always an appropriate recommendation to employ a tabularasa approach to the control problems at hand; it can serve as an only approach where a suitably impressive closed-form traditional controller does not exist. Moreover, the above-proposed CTRNN-EH methodologies have also been successfully employed to design and evolve hybrid controllers, with evolvable module in the base traditional controller being evolved to supplement the control characteristics of the traditional controllers with rich dynamics of CTRNNs [20]. These CTRNN-EH-based hybrid controllers have been shown to increase the overall robustness and efficacy of the base traditional controllers to handle unforeseen changes in the assumed environment of the controller and the controlled vehicle [21].

References

[1] V. B. Floris and H. Lipson, "Evolving buildable flapping ornithopters," in *Proceedings of Genetic and Evolutionary Computation Conference (GECCO '05)*, 2005.

[2] L. Schenato, X. Deng, W. C. Wu, and S. Sastry, "Virtual Insect Flight Simulator (VIFS): a software testbed for insect flight," in *Proceedings of the IEEE International Conference on Robotics and Automation (ICRA '01)*, vol. 4, pp. 3885–3892, May 2001.

[3] J. C. Gallagher, "An evolvable hardware layer for global and local learning of motor control in a hexapod robot," *International Journal on Artificial Intelligence Tools*, vol. 14, no. 6, pp. 999–1017, 2005.

[4] S. K. Boddhu and J. C. Gallagher, "Evolved neuromorphic flight control for a flapping-wing mechanical insect model," in *Proceedings of the IEEE Congress on Evolutionary Computation (CEC '08)*, IEEE Press, Hong Kong, China, June 2008.

[5] H. J. Chiel, R. D. Beer, and J. C. Gallagher, "Evolution and analysis of model CPGs for walking: I. Dynamical modules," *Journal of Computational Neuroscience*, vol. 7, no. 2, pp. 99–118, 1999.

[6] J. C. Gallagher, "Evolution and analysis of non-autonomous neural networks for walking: reflexive pattern generators," in *Procdings of the Congress on Evolutionary Computation*, IEEE Press, Seoul, South Korea, May 2001.

[7] S. K. Boddhu and J. C. Gallagher, "Evolving non-autonomous neuromorphic flight control for a flapping-wing mechanical insect," in *Proceedings of the IEEE Workshop on Evolvable and Adaptive Hardware (WEAH '09)*, Nashville, Tenn, USA, April 2009.

[8] S. K. Boddhu and J. C. Gallagher, "Evolving neuromorphic flight control for a flapping-wing mechanical insect," *International Journal of Intelligent Computing and Cybernetics*, vol. 3, no. 1, pp. 94–116, 2010.

[9] S. K. Boddhu, *Evolution and analysis of neuromorphic flapping-wing flight controllers [Ph.D. thesis]*, Wright State University, 2010.

[10] D. Sbarbaro-Hofer, D. Neumerkel, and K. Hunt, "Neural control of a steel rolling mill," *IEEE Control Systems Magazine*, vol. 13, no. 3, pp. 69–75, 1993.

[11] C. M. Lin and C. F. Hsu, "Supervisory recurrent fuzzy neural network control of wing rock for slender delta wings," *IEEE Transactions on Fuzzy Systems*, vol. 12, no. 5, pp. 733–742, 2004.

[12] S. K. Boddhu, J. C. Gallagher, and S. A. Vigraham, "A commercial off-the-shelf implementation of an analog neural computer," *International Journal on Artificial Intelligence Tools*, vol. 17, no. 2, pp. 241–258, 2008.

[13] S. K. Boddhu, J. C. Gallagher, and S. Vigraham, "A reconfigurable analog neural network for evolvable hardware applications: Intrinsic evolution and extrinsic verification," in *Proceedings of the IEEE Congress on Evolutionary Computation (CEC '06)*, IEEE Press, Vancouver, Canada, July 2006.

[14] K. I. Funahashi and Y. Nakamura, "Approximation of dynamical systems by continuous time recurrent neural networks," *Neural Networks*, vol. 6, no. 6, pp. 801–806, 1993.

[15] G. R. Kramer and J. C. Gallagher, "An analysis of the search performance of a mini-population evolutionary algorithm for a robot-locomotion control problem," in *Proceedings of the IEEE Congress on Evolutionary Computation (IEEE '05)*, pp. 2768–2775, IEEE Press, September 2005.

[16] R. D. Beer, H. J. Chiel, and J. C. Gallagher, "Evolution and analysis of model CPGs for walking: II. General principles and individual variability," *Journal of Computational Neuroscience*, vol. 7, no. 2, pp. 119–147, 1999.

[17] M. H. Dickinson, F. O. Lehmann, and S. P. Sane, "Wing rotation and the aerodynamic basis of insect right," *Science*, vol. 284, no. 5422, pp. 1954–1960, 1999.

[18] L. Schenato, X. Deng, and S. Sastry, "Flight control system for a micromechanical flying insect: architecture and implementation," in *Proceedings of the IEEE International Conference on Robotics and Automation (ICRA '01)*, vol. 2, pp. 1641–1646, May 2001.

[19] R. D. Beer, "On the dynamics of small continuous time recurrent neural networks," in *Adaptive Behavior*, vol. 3, 4, pp. 469–509, The MIT Press, Boston, Mass, USA, 1995.

[20] J. C. Gallagher, B. David Doman, and W. Michael Oppenheimer, "The technology of the gaps: an evolvable hardware synthesized oscillator for the control of a flapping-wing micro air vehicle," *IEEE Transactions on Evolutionary Computation*. In press.

[21] J. C. Gallagher and M. Oppenheimer, "An improved evolvable oscillator for all flight mode control of an insect-scale flapping-wing micro air vehicle," in *Proceedings of the IEEE Congress on Evolutionary Computation (CEC '11)*, IEEE Press, 2011.

12

Power Load Event Detection and Classification Based on Edge Symbol Analysis and Support Vector Machine

Lei Jiang,[1] Jiaming Li,[2] Suhuai Luo,[1] Sam West,[3] and Glenn Platt[3]

[1] School of DCIT, University of Newcastle, Callaghan, NSW 2308, Australia
[2] ICT Centre, Commonwealth Scientific and Industrial Research Organization, Clayton South, VIC 3169, Australia
[3] Energy Technology Division, Commonwealth Scientific and Industrial Research Organization, Clayton South, VIC 3169, Australia

Correspondence should be addressed to Lei Jiang, lei.jiang@csiro.au

Academic Editor: F. Morabito

Energy signature analysis of power appliance is the core of nonintrusive load monitoring (NILM) where the detailed data of the appliances used in houses are obtained by analyzing changes in the voltage and current. This paper focuses on developing an automatic power load event detection and appliance classification based on machine learning. In power load event detection, the paper presents a new transient detection algorithm. By turn-on and turn-off transient waveforms analysis, it can accurately detect the edge point when a device is switched on or switched off. The proposed load classification technique can identify different power appliances with improved recognition accuracy and computational speed. The load classification method is composed of two processes including frequency feature analysis and support vector machine. The experimental results indicated that the incorporation of the new edge detection and turn-on and turn-off transient signature analysis into NILM revealed more information than traditional NILM methods. The load classification method has achieved more than ninety percent recognition rate.

1. Introduction

Nowadays, multifarious classification techniques are widely used in many signal-processing areas, such as face recognition, road traffic analyze, medical image, weather forecasting, and so forth [1, 2]. It has been considered whether this kind of techniques could serve the purposes of power load monitoring, which is a process for obtaining what appliances are used in the house as well as their individual energy consumption by analyzing changes in the voltage and current. In particular, information about the operating conditions of consumers (such as what appliances are operated and what state they are in) is useful for demand estimation and prediction. In addition, the operating conditions of electrical appliances in modern society clearly reflect consumers' lifestyles and behavior patterns [3]. Research is being performed on the use of such information for circuit diagnoses, safety confirmation systems for elderly persons living alone [4], demand management, and optimization [5–10], and for other uses [11].

There are mainly two classes of approaches in power monitoring algorithm, including intrusive appliance load monitoring (IALM) and nonintrusive appliance load monitoring (NIALM) [12]. In order to measure consumption, IALM distributes direct sensors at each device or appliance. Although conceptually straightforward and potentially highly accurate, direct sensing is often expensive due to time consuming installation and the requirement for one sensor for each device or appliance. In response to limitations with the direct sensing approach, researchers have explored methods to infer energy usage via a single sensor.

In contrast to the direct sensing methods, the standard NIALM configuration includes a sole sensor set to measure current and voltage, as well as a processing algorithm for determining the status of various devices [13]. It was firstly studied by Hart of MIT in the early 1990s with funding from the Electric Power Research Institute [12]. Since then, different strategies for NIALM have been developed. One of the important approaches on classification is to apply support vector machine (SVM) [14–18] in the nonintrusive appliance load monitoring. It is imperative for power system research field to evaluate the SVM on this task from a practical point of view. As the preprocess for finding out the features for SVM, transient detection also plays an important role in NIALM.

In order to decompose the total loads into their components, Bijker et al. employed different power level, or named step change for the purpose [19]. Chang et al. used DWT and a new method coreless HCT to detect the power events [20]. Nonetheless, they only supposed to detect the events of appliances with complicated features, such as motor, microwave oven, and thyristor rectifier. In 2002, Onoda et al. used the data proposed in [21] for the purpose of estimating the state of household electric appliances. They compared different types of SVMs obtained by choosing different kernels. They reported results of polynomial kernels, radial basis function kernels, and sigmoid kernels. All results for the three different kernels achieved almost same error rates. However, in the estimation of the state of household electric appliances, the results for the three different kernels achieved different error rates. They also compared different capacity of SVMs obtained by choosing different regularization constants and parameters of kernels experimentally. The results showed that the capacity control is as important as the choice of kernel functions. Kadouche and his colleagues later presented [22] their ongoing work on the house occupant prediction issue based on daily life habits in smart houses. Most of their works were based on supervised learning technical. They used SVM to build behavior classification model for learning the user's habits, analyzed the publicly available dataset from the Washington State University Smart Apartment Test-bed. Particularly, they evaluated the grooming, having breakfast, and bed to toilet activities [23]. Their experimental results showed that the user can be recognized with a high precision which means that each user has his own way to perform activities. As future work, the users' patterns which allow a person to be discriminated and recognized among a group, performing multiactivities in the same environment without using intrusive technologies were being studied.

Grinblat and his fellows presented a new method for generating adaptive classifiers and capable of learning concepts that change with time, which is the time-adaptive support vector machine (TA-SVM) [24]. The basic idea of TA-SVM is to use a sequence of classifiers, each one is appropriate for a small time window but, in contrast to other proposals, learning all the hyperplanes in a global way. Starting from the solution of independent SVMs, they showed that the addition of a new term in the cost function (which penalizes the diversity between consecutive classifiers) produces in fact a coupling of the sequence. Once coupled, the set of SVMs acts as a single adaptive classifier. They evaluated different aspects of the TA-SVM using artificial drifting problems. In particular, they showed that changing the number of classifiers and the coupling constant can effectively regularize the sequence of classifiers. They compared TA-SVM with other state-of-the-art methods in three different settings: estimation, prediction, and extrapolation, including problems with small datasets,

high-dimensional input spaces, and noise. TA-SVM showed in all cases to be equivalent to or better than the other methods. Even for the most unfavorable situation for TA-SVM, that is, the sudden changes of the dataset, their new method showed a very good performance. However, the limitation of this method may be reflected in the long drifting time and the requirement of additional hardware. A more recent research of Liang's group [25], combined various features including current waveform (CW), active/reactive power (PQ), harmonics (HAR), instantaneous admittance waveform (IAW), instantaneous power waveform (IPW), eigenvalues (EIG), and switching transient waveform (STW). The results of their research provided a higher degree of recognition precision, but the algorithm requires mountains of work on collecting and processing appliance signatures.

In this paper, the data collected in real world is used and clearly analyzed what are the important issues for applying SVM to power system research field. The remainder is organized as below. Section 2 gives the details of the new transient event detection process named ESA and the reasons why we choose SVM as our method and the main process of load classification. The details of data collecting and preprocessing along with the experiment results are shown in Section 3. Finally, conclusions are made in Section 4.

2. Power Load Events Detection and Classification

It is known that although NIALM based on different techniques, it has several common principles [26].

(i) Load features classification: specific appliance features, or signatures, need to be selected and mathematically characterized.

(ii) Mechanism: a hardware installation (sensor and data acquisition system) that can detect the selected features is required.

(iii) Decomposition: a mathematical algorithm detects the features in the overall signal and output.

Based on this theory, Figure 1 describes the process of this research. The mechanism collects the whole operation of a circuit, then, the appropriate algorithms draw out all the electrical events in the circumstance. After successfully seeking the point "load x switch on," it is feasible to classify load x, afterwards seek the point "load $x + 1$ switch on" excluding faked edges generated by previous loads. The same procedure subsequently goes for searching switch off events.

2.1. Power Load Events Detection Using Edge Symbol Analysis Method

2.1.1. Background. Methods of edge detection have been widely studied in many areas, primarily developed in the discrete cases and have been confined to slightly noisy signals. The regularization or smoothing and optimal approaches of Canny [27] have led to several efficient continuous operators for noisy and blurred signals. Other advanced methods that

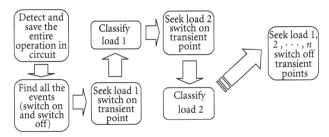

FIGURE 1: The load events detection procedure.

consider the Canny criterion have been developed to deal with noise, uneven illumination, and image contrast. In a marginal way, discrete approaches for regularization have been developed and have improved results by considering the discrete nature of the signals [28, 29].

Introducing nonlinearity into the global filtering process, as in noisy edge detection, is a marginal yet efficient method of obtaining good performance. Generally, nonlinear filtering is used in a preliminary regularization stage. Pitas and Venetsanopoulos proposed a class of nonlinear filters that reject additive and impulse noise, while preserving the edges [30]. More recently, Benazza-Benyahia et al. introduced a nonlinear filter bank leading to a multiresolution approximation of the signal in which discontinuities are well preserved [31]. A nonlinear filter for edge enhancement, using a morphological filter, has been proposed by Schulze [32]. The author showed that local variation analysis allows enhancing edges corrupted by multiplicative noise. Hwang and Haddad presented an integrated nonlinear edge-detection-based denoising scheme [33]. A thresholded derivative is computed from two half filters (median for impulse noise, mean for Gaussian noise, and min-max for uniform noise) and edge detection is used to select the second filtering stage, that is, mean for noise or median for edge points. In the scheme, edge detection could be considered as a by-product and the optimal performance is obtained only when the correct first filter is selected according to the noise statistic. Based on these theories, Laligant and his colleague propose to obtain both noise reduction and edge detection by a one-stage nonlinear derivative scheme [34]. The scheme, which consists of combining two polarized differences, yields significant improvements in signal-to-noise ratio without using regularization or increasing the computational requirements.

2.1.2. The Approach. It is known that three kinds of slopes can be found in all power waveforms, including positive, negative, and constant. So the edge symbol analysis method (ESA) can find the position of the edge point according to the sign of the signal area. In this way, the edge point will be located after the transition if the slope is positive. Otherwise, when it is negative, the edge point will be located before the slope. Here, for the sake of detecting these two kinds of edges, two detector filters L_+ and L_- have to be introduced. Since L is chosen as an antisymmetric linear filter, which gives the localization changes and this shifted

pixel localization depending on edge's orientation. These filters have the relationship described in (1).

$$L_-(S) = -L_+(S^{-1}). \tag{1}$$

With the simple threshold H, we use the combination of L_+ and L_- as below to detect edge points of the original input signal I.

$$O_+(S) = H[L_+(S)I(S)],$$
$$O_-(S) = -H[-L_-(S)I(S)]. \tag{2}$$

2.2. SVM-Based Power Load Classification. The proposed power classification method is composed of two major stages, including: first a frequency feature analysis is applied on current signal, and then a trained classifier based on SVM is applied to identify different appliances. The following sections give the details of the approach.

2.2.1. Current Feature Analysis. To save computational resources and improve performance, only current signals were used for frequency analysis with fewer sample points [35]. For example, according to previous experiments, the accuracy rate of the classification is almost the same or even higher when employing 500 frequency signal points as features instead of 2000 unprocessed current signal points.

After collecting the data of single device and extracting the current signals, a short-time fast Fourier transform (FFT) of the signal is performed as in (3). Where $\omega_N = e^{(2\pi i)/N}$ is an nth root of the unity.

$$X(k) = \sum_{j=1}^{N} x(j)\omega_N^{(j-1)(k-1)},$$
$$x(j) = \left(\frac{1}{N}\right)\sum_{k=1}^{N} X(k)\omega_N^{-(j-1)(k-1)}, \tag{3}$$

and an example is shown as Figure 2.

2.2.2. SVM-Based Classification. SVM, as one of the method of NIALM system, is relatively insensitive to the number of data points and the classification complexity does not depend on the dimensionality of the feature space [36]. Therefore, it can potentially learn a larger set of patterns and be able to scale better than some other methods. Once the data are classified into two classes, a suitable optimizing algorithm can be used if necessary for further feature identification, depending on the application.

Support vector machine is a training algorithm for learning classification and regression rules from data SVM was first introduced by Cortes and Vapnik [37] in the 1990s for classification and have recently become an area of intense research owing to developments in the techniques and theory coupled with extensions to regression and density estimation. It is based on the structural risk minimization principle which incorporates capacity control to prevent overfitting. It is a partial solution to the bias-variance trade-off dilemma [38]. It has been widely used in different areas.

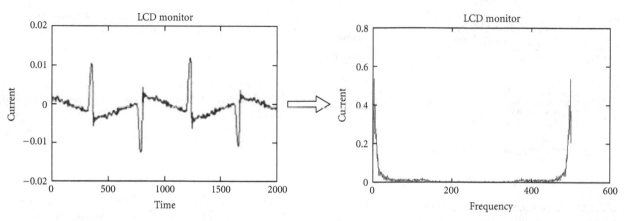

FIGURE 2: Load current signal of LCD monitor in time and frequency domains.

As a classifier, it gives a set of training examples, each marked as belonging to one of two categories. The SVM training algorithm builds a model that predicts whether a new example falls into one category or the other. Intuitively, an SVM model is a representation of the examples as points in space, mapped so that the examples of the separate categories are divided by a clear gap that is as wide as possible [39]. New examples are then mapped into that same space and predicted to belong to a category based on which side of the gap they fall on.

SVM delivers state-of-the-art performance in real-world applications such as text categorization, hand-written character recognition, biosequences analysis, image classification, and so forth. It is now established as one of the standard tools for machine learning and data mining. The SVM decision function is defined as (4)

$$f(y) = \sum_{i=1}^{N} \alpha_i K(x_i, y) + b.$$ (4)

Here, y is the unclassified tested vector, x_i is the support vectors and α_i is their weights, and b is a constant bias. $K(x, y)$ is the kernel function introduced into SVM to solve the nonlinear problems by performing implicit mapping into a high-dimensional feature space [40].

Consider the problem of separating the set of training vectors belonging to two separate classes [41].

$$D = \left\{ (x^1, y^1), \dots, (x^l, y^l) \right\}, \quad x \in R^n, \ y \in \{-1, 1\}$$ (5)

with a hyperplane,

$$\langle \omega, x \rangle + b = 0.$$ (6)

The kernel function chosen in our algorithm is Gaussian

$$k(x_i, x_j) = \exp\left(-\gamma \|x_i - x_j\|2\right), \quad \text{for } \gamma > 0,$$ (7)

where scalar γ is identical for all coordinates.

TABLE 1: Data collecting details.

Load	Description
Dremel	High speed electric motor (a Dremel is a handheld tool for grinding, engraving, etc.). Has built-in speed control which modifies the current sine wave in all except full speed settings.
Fan heater	Small fan heater with fan, medium heat, and high heat modes selected using a slide switch
Heat gun	2-fanspeed digital temperature controlled heat gun
Kettle	A normal kettle
Laptop charger	Dell laptop charger for a D630 laptop
LCD monitor	A Dell LCD monitor
Incandescent light	Incandescent light bulb in small desk lamp
Fluorescent light	Circular fluorescent tube light from soldering station magnifying light stand
Mini PC	Dream PC (labeled PGWY1)
PC	A normal personal computer
Pedestal fan	A cheap $15 3-speed plastic pedestal fan

3. Experiments

3.1. Data Collecting and Preprocessing. All the data are collected in Commonwealth Scientific and Industrial Research Organization (CSIRO) and a residential house in Newcastle, NSW, Australia. Collecting details are shown in Table 1.

Figure 3 shows the segmentation process in this experiment. Each signal of load has three phrases: on phrase, steady state, and off phrase.

3.2. Experiment Result and Discussion

3.2.1. Implementation of ESA. In Figure 4, the overlapped data of Kettle and Toaster are shown as an example. Figure 4(a) is the original overlapped data of kettle and oven. The red figures in Figure 4(b) are the output of edge detection and the original data. The on and off edges are represented in red color. To clearly observe the resultant edge

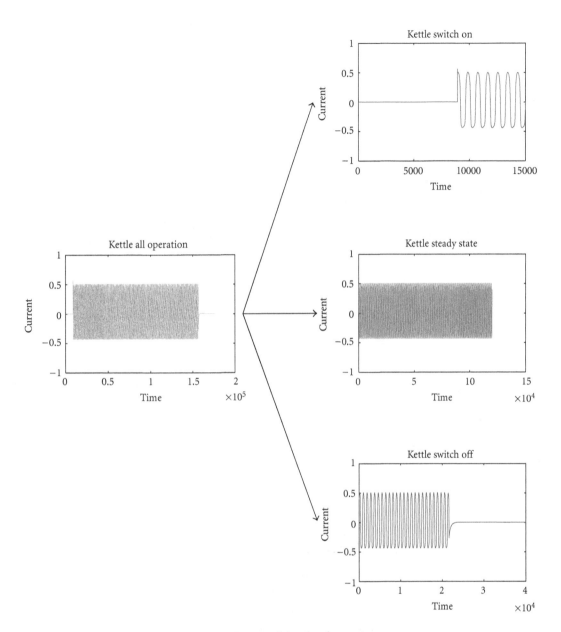

FIGURE 3: Process of signal segmentation.

points, the edge points in Figure 4(b) (i.e., the red curve) are redrawn in Figure 4(c).

The example of overlapping kettle with microwave oven (Figure 5(a)) and PC (Figure 5(b)) is shown in Figure 5. It can easily find the edges (as the yellow arrows shown in Figure 5) by repeating the process that mentioned above, and then relocate the transient points in the original data. When the transient features are recognized as "microwave oven on" or "PC on" by SVM, the algorithm ignores the next "Off" and "On" events because they are fake symbols. It is thus able to obtain the full process of the whole event.

Data of 2 loads combinations from four typical appliances are employed for testing in this experiment. The algorithm runs on 10 different data for each group. As for a single case, the performance time consumption is lower than 4 seconds. The result of this process is shown in Table 2.

Practically, all events are accurately detected by ESA except the Load2-On, whereas the accuracy is still higher than 80%.

3.2.2. Implementation of Load Classification. The recognition process on each phrase is running with Gaussian as the function kernel. Using the segmented steady-state power data for the test, some selected features are shown in Figures 6 and 7, where Figure 6 shows the training unprocessed current data in time domain, and Figure 7 shows the training current data in frequency domain. The algorithm runs 70 times on the data collected from the 11 different loads. As for a single case, the performance time consumption is lower than 2 seconds. The recognition results are shown in Table 3.

It can be seen that all the recognition accuracy rates are higher than 90%. It shows the ideal recognition performance

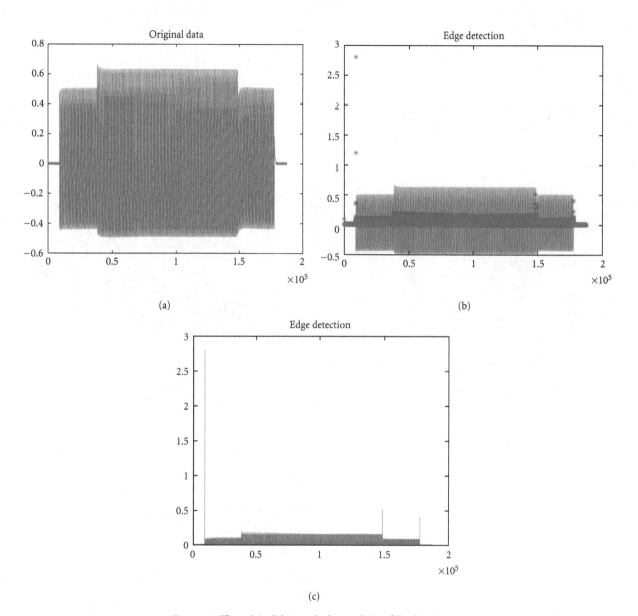

FIGURE 4: The original data and edge analysis of Kettle + Oven.

TABLE 2: Result of ESA on four typical loads.

Overlapped load appliances groups	Accuracy of recognizing transient events (switch on and switch off) %			
	Load 1 On	Load 2 On	Load 2 Off	Load 1 Off
Kettle + Oven	100	100	100	100
Oven + Kettle	100	100	100	100
Kettle + Microwave oven	100	80	100	100
Microwave oven + Kettle	100	90	100	100
Kettle + PC	100	100	100	100
PC + Kettle	100	90	100	100
Oven + Microwave oven	100	100	100	100
Microwave oven + Oven	100	80	100	100
Oven + PC	100	100	100	100
PC + Oven	100	80	100	100

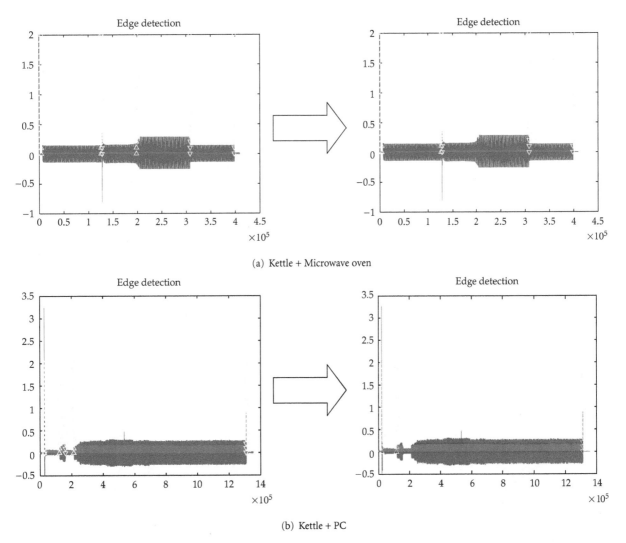

(a) Kettle + Microwave oven

(b) Kettle + PC

FIGURE 5: Examples of power signal edge analysis.

of our algorithm. Moreover, despite the training processes always take several minutes, it avoid a mess of pre-work on processing signatures. The testing processes are much quicker than previous methods because of employing comparatively a small quantity of points from load frequency features. However, we would like to indicate that the number of appliance is limited and no transient event is involved. The performance may come down when more devices and events are used in experiments.

4. Conclusion

This paper has proposed one approach of nonintrusive appliance load monitoring for electrical consumption managing. This approach can automatically detect the switch-on and switch-off events of domestic appliances and classify different appliances using load features and advanced algorithms, therefore, monitoring the house power consumption of individual devices. The new transient detection algorithm, in combination with turn-on and turn-off transient waveforms

TABLE 3: Results of 11 loads classification.

| Load appliance | Accuracy of features (500-currence) | |
	Unprocessed current data	Current harmonic data
Dremel	100%	100%
Fan heater	97%	100%
Heater gun	97%	100%
Kettle	90%	97%
Laptop	100%	100%
LCD	100%	100%
Incandescent light	97%	97%
Fluorescent light	100%	100%
Mini PC	100%	100%
PC	100%	100%
Pedestal fan	100%	100%

analysis, is developed to detect the mutative power events. The load classification technique, which employs support

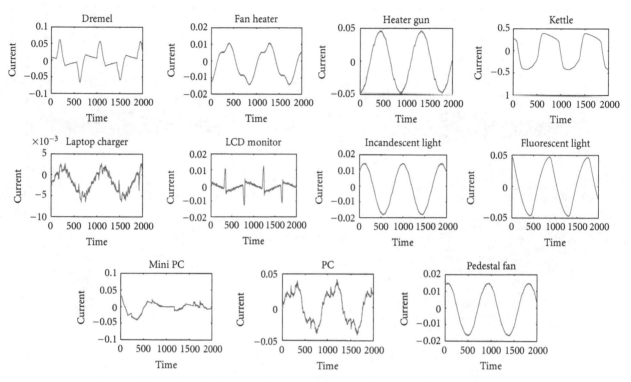

FIGURE 6: Examples of training set of unprocessed current data in time domain (steady state).

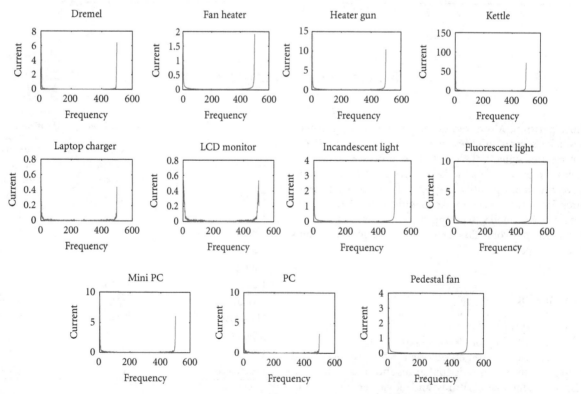

FIGURE 7: Examples of training set of current data in frequency domain (steady state).

vector machine to recognize different appliances, is capable of identifying kinds of power loads with improved recognition accuracy and computational speed of NILM results. A recognition rate of higher than 90% has been achieved in recognizing various electrical devices. Our experiments have shown that recognition approaches based on support vector machines will be a trend for the process of residential load monitoring.

References

[1] G. Guo, S. Li, and K. Chan, "Face recognition by support vector machines," in *Proceedings of the 4th IEEE International Conference on Automatic Face and Gesture Recognition*, pp. 196–201, 2000.

[2] S. Du and T. Wu, "Support Vector Machines for Regression," Acta Simulata Systematica Sinica, TP18, CNKI:SUN: XTFZ.0.2003-11-022, 2003.

[3] S. Inagaki, T. Egami, T. Suzuki, H. Nakamura, and K. Ito, "Noninstrusive appliance load monitoring based on integer programming," *Electrical Engineering in Japan*, vol. 174, no. 2, pp. 1386–1392, 2011.

[4] S. Aoki, M. Onishi, A. Kojima, and K. Fukunaga, "Detection of a solitude senior's irregular states based on learning and recognizing of behavioral patterns," *IEEJ*, vol. 125, pp. 259–265, 2005.

[5] C. Laughman, K. D. Lee, R. Cox et al., "Advanced nonintrusive monitoring of electric loads," *IEEE Power and Energy Magazine*, pp. 56–563, April 2003.

[6] J. Li, G. Poulton, and G. James, "Agent-based distributed energy management," in *Proceedings of the 20th Australian Joint Conference on Advances in Artificial Intelligence*, vol. 4830, pp. 569–578, December 2007.

[7] J. Li, G. Poulton, and G. James, "Coordination of distributed energy resource agents," *Applied Artificial Intelligence*, vol. 24, no. 5, pp. 351–380, 2010.

[8] Y. Guo, J. Li, and G. James, "Evolutionary optimisation of distributed energy resources," in *Proceedings of the 18th Australian Joint Conference on Advances in Artificial Intelligence*, vol. 3809, pp. 1086–1091, Sydney, Australia, December 2005.

[9] R. Li, J. Li, G. Poulton, and G. James, "Agent-based optimisation systems for electrical load management," in *Proceedings of the 1st International Workshop on Optimisation in Multi-Agent Systems*, pp. 60–69, Estoril, Portugal, May 2008.

[10] J. Li, G. James, and G. Poulton, "Set-points based optimal multi-agent coordination for controlling distributed energy loads," in *Proceedings of the 3rd IEEE International Conference on Self-Adaptive and Self-Organizing Systems (SASO '09)*, pp. 265–271, San Francisco, Calif, USA, September 2009.

[11] J. Li, G. Poulton, G. James, and Y. Guo, "Multiple energy resource agent coordination based on electricity price," *Journal of Distributed Energy Resources*, vol. 5, pp. 103–120, 2009.

[12] G. W. Hart, "Nonintrusive appliance load monitoring," *Proceedings of the IEEE*, vol. 80, no. 12, pp. 1870–1891, 1992.

[13] S. B. Leeb, S. R. Shaw, and J. L. Kirtley, "Transient event detection in spectral envelope estimates for nonintrusive load monitoring," *IEEE Transactions on Power Delivery*, vol. 10, no. 3, pp. 1200–1210, 1995.

[14] M. C. Ferris and T. S. Munson, "Interior point methods for massive support vector machines," Tech. Rep. 00-05, Computer Sciences Department, University of Wisconsin, Madison, Wis, USA, 2000.

[15] C. J. C. Burges, "A tutorial on support vector machines for pattern recognition," *Data Mining and Knowledge Discovery*, vol. 2, no. 2, pp. 121–167, 1998.

[16] J. J. Moré and G. Toraldo, "Algorithms for bound constrained quadratic programming problems," *Numerische Mathematik*, vol. 55, no. 4, pp. 377–400, 1989.

[17] O. L. Mangasarian and D. R. Musicant, "Active set support vector machine classification," in *Advances in Neural Information Processing Systems*, T. Leen, T. Dietterich, and V. Tresp, Eds., vol. 13, pp. 577–583, MIT Press, Cambridge, Mass, USA, 2001.

[18] J. Li, S. West, and G. Platt, "Power decomposition based on SVM regression," in *Proceedings of the 4th International Conference on Modelling, Identification and Control (ICMIC '12)*, pp. 1256–1261, Wuhan, China, June 2012.

[19] A. J. Bijker, X. Xia, and J. Zhang, "Active power residential non-intrusive appliance load monitoring system," in *IEEE AFRICON Conference*, pp. 1–6, September 2009.

[20] H.-H. Chang, K.-L. Chen, Y.-P. Tsai, and W.-J. Lee, "A new measurement method for power signatures of non-intrusive demand monitoring and load identification," in *Proceedings of the 46th IEEE Industry Applications Society Annual Meeting (IAS '11)*, pp. 1–7, Orlando, Fla, USA, 2011.

[21] T. Onoda, G. Murata, G. Rätsch, and K.-R. Müller, "Experimental analysis of Support Vector Machines with different kernels based on non-intrusive monitoring data," in *Proceedings of the International Joint Conference on Neural Networks (IJCNN '02)*, vol. 3, pp. 2186–2191, Honolulu, Hawaii, USA, 2002.

[22] R. Kadouche, B. Chikhaoui, and B. Abdulrazak, "User's behavior study for smart houses occupant prediction," *Annals of Telecommunications*, vol. 65, no. 9-10, pp. 539–543, 2010.

[23] S. R. Gunn, "Support vector machines for classification and regression," Faculty of Engineering, Science and Mathematics School of Electronics and Computer, University of Southampton, 1998.

[24] G. L. Grinblat, L. C. Uzal, H. A. Ceccatto, and P. M. Granitto, "Solving nonstationary classification problems with coupled support vector machines," *IEEE Transactions on Neural Networks*, vol. 22, no. 1, pp. 37–51, 2011.

[25] J. Liang, S. K. K. Ng, G. Kendall, and J. W. M. Cheng, "Load signature studypart I: basic concept, structure, and methodology," *IEEE Transactions on Power Delivery*, vol. 25, no. 2, pp. 551–560, 2010.

[26] M. Zeifman and K. Roth, "Nonintrusive appliance load monitoring: review and outlook," *IEEE Transactions on Consumer Electronics*, vol. 57, no. 1, pp. 76–84, 2011.

[27] J. Canny, "A computational approach to edge detection," *IEEE Transactions on Pattern Analysis and Machine Intelligence*, vol. 8, no. 6, pp. 679–698, 1986.

[28] D. Demigny and T. Kamlé, "A discrete expression of canny's criteria for step edge detector performances evaluation," *IEEE Transactions on Pattern Analysis and Machine Intelligence*, vol. 19, no. 11, pp. 1199–1211, 1997.

[29] F. Truchetet, F. Nicolier, and O. Laligant, "Subpixel edge detection for dimensional control by artificial vision," *Journal of Electronic Imaging*, vol. 10, no. 1, pp. 234–239, 2001.

[30] I. Pitas and A. Venetsanopoulos, "Nonlinear mean filters in image processing," *IEEE Transactions on Acoustics, Speech, and Signal Processing*, vol. 34, no. 3, pp. 573–584, 1986.

[31] A. Benazza-Benyahia, J. C. Pesquet, and H. Krim, "A nonlinear diffusion-based three-band filter bank," *IEEE Signal Processing Letters*, vol. 10, no. 12, pp. 360–363, 2003.

[32] M. A. Schulze, "An edge-enhancing nonlinear filter for reducing multiplicative noise," in *Nonlinear Image Processing VIII*,

E. R. Dougherty and J. Astola, Eds., vol. 3026 of *Proceedings of SPIE*, pp. 46–56, San Jose, Calif, USA, February 1997.

[33] H. Hwang and R. A. Haddad, "Multilevel nonlinear filters for edge detection and noise suppression," *IEEE Transactions on Signal Processing*, vol. 42, no. 2, pp. 249–258, 1994.

[34] O. Laligant and F. Truchetet, "A nonlinear derivative scheme applied to edge detection," *IEEE Transactions on Pattern Analysis and Machine Intelligence*, vol. 32, no. 2, pp. 242–257, 2010.

[35] L. Jiang, S. Luo, and J. Li, "An approach of household power appliance monitoring based on machine learning," in *Proceedings of the 5th International Conference on Intelligent Computation Technology and Automation (ICICTA '12)*, pp. 577–580, January 2012.

[36] T. Joachims, "Making large-scale SVM learning practical," LS8-Report, University of Dortmund, 1998.

[37] C. Cortes and V. Vapnik, "Support-vector networks," *Machine Learning*, vol. 20, no. 3, pp. 273–297, 1995.

[38] A. B. Ji, J. H. Pang, and H. J. Qiu, "Support vector machine for classification based on fuzzy training data," *Expert Systems with Applications*, vol. 37, no. 4, pp. 3495–3498, 2010.

[39] S. Luo, Q. Hu, X. He, J. Li, J. S. Jin, and M. Park, "Automatic liver parenchyma segmentation from abdominal CT images using support vector machines," in *Proceedings of the IEEE/CME International Conference on Complex Medical Engineering (ICME '09)*, p. 10071, Tempe, Ariz, USA, April 2009.

[40] L. Jiang, J. Li, S. Luo, and S. West, "Literature review of power disaggregation," in *Proceedings of the IEEE International Conference on Modelling Identification and Control*, pp. 38–42, 2011.

[41] R. Debnath and H. Takahashi, "Kernel selection for the support vector machine," *IEICE Transactions on Information and Systems*, vol. E87-D, no. 12, pp. 2903–2904, 2004.

13

The Aspects, the Origin, and the Merit of Aware Computing

Yasuji Sawada

Tohoku Institute of Technology, 35-1 Yagiyama-Kasumi, Taihaku, Sendai 982-8577, Japan

Correspondence should be addressed to Yasuji Sawada, sawada@tohtech.ac.jp

Academic Editor: Qiangfu Zhao

In this paper we tried to understand scientifically the awareness, a daily word. Some aspects of awareness, such as qualitative or quantitative, the targets of awareness, either the external world or the internal world, were discussed. Suggestion on the human awareness was described from the experimental results of visual hand tracking. The origin and the merit of awareness in the process of evolution of animals were discussed. Finally some characters of possible aware computers and aware robots were studied.

1. Introduction

For the scientists and the engineers to understand and to make use of the human ability, it is needed to translate into scientific terms, the words of human science expressing the human ability, which has been created in a long history. *awareness* is a word in human science. Now we are asking what it is explained in scientific terms.

Awareness in human science term naturally implies existence of a subject. There is no awareness in a system which has no subject. Subject implies existence of a central information processing system and an exterior self-expression device. There is no subject which has no mind and body. In the history of biological evolution, brain was originally created to produce information for body motion effective for survival against external change. A sensorial system was also created simultaneously to check the effectiveness of the motion.

In this paper, we survey how this word has been used in our daily life. We analyze them and try to extract essential factors and try to discuss them by scientific terms (Section 2). We also refer to the results of our recent experiments of visual tracking [1–4]. These experimental results suggested that two kinds of awareness exist in the human sensorial-motor system, which functions in the mutually exclusive manner (Section 3). Combination of the various aspects of the awareness, which we used in daily life and some experimental implication, has led us to believe that "usefulness" may be a keyword to understand the awareness and to apply the concept of awareness for the aware computers and aware robots. Thus, the paper is constructed in the following order:

(1) some aspects of awareness,

(2) experimental suggestions on the concept of awareness,

(3) usefulness of awareness,

(4) awareness of the internal world and mind,

(5) aware computer,

(6) an aware robot which behaves as if it had a free will.

2. Some Aspects of Awareness

In this section, we examine some sentences including awareness used in daily life and try to find some aspects among them.

2.1. Qualitative and Quantitative.

> "I am aware of following the preceding car within the distance of ten meters." (S1)

This sentence means existence of a subject, an action, and an evaluation. The evaluation is quantitative. We may call this awareness "quantitative awareness." On the other hand, human civilization has sorted the complex phenomena of the external world into a countable number of the concepts. Awareness is also used to identify the kind of the body action with one of the known concepts. For example,

> "I am aware of walking in spite of my original intention of running." (S2)

We might call this kind of awareness as "qualitative awareness." These examples show that for the awareness of any kind, body motion seems indispensable as an exterior self-expression device of self. We examine if this is true in the sections below.

2.2. External and Internal. Being aware of external phenomena is daily, as

> *"I am aware of snow falling outside the window."* (S3)

When we are aware of some phenomena which occurs with some distance from the observer's body, the target of awareness is external. However, it is important to realize the difference between (S3) and a sentence such as

> *"A camera is ready to take the record of falling snow outside."* (S4)

The difference is essential for understanding an aspect of awareness, which we discuss in Sections 2.4 and 4. Furthermore, it is also important to understand that the target of awareness is external even when the target of awareness is within our body.

> *"I am aware of my stomach aching."* (S5)

> *"I am aware of my skin hurting as the result of my falling down on the floor."* (S6)

One may think that the stomach is internal, whereas the skin is external. But there is no principal difference between the pain in the skin and the pain in the stomach, by assuming that all the body parts are external from the central information processor (CIP). As we mention later, even the memory system is external to the subject. In that sense, stomach is not internal. The stomach is painful because it was attacked by the external virus. Information of pain is sent to the CIP from a sensor system in a part of the body. This information was created to inform the damage of the parts of the body for survival. The information on the condition of the parts of the system is needed for the evaluation of the action. For survival purpose repair or replacement of the part may be important.

The targets of sensing a part of body (S5) and (S6) are considered also external.

2.3. Awareness of Thinking.

> *"I am aware of imagining the falling snow outside of the house."* (S7)

Thinking or imagining is definitely internal. But the time when he imagines the falling snow and the time when he is aware of imagining it is not simultaneous. Most of the time, he may be imagining the falling snow, and this fact is constantly memorized in the memory system. From time to time, the CIP is switched from the imagination to the memory system, and he became aware he had been imagining up to this moment. The switching is done so

smoothly and so quickly that he does not realize if the information is from past memory or real time. Although awareness is used in various ways, it can be unified by considering that the CIP is watching various parts of the external world including other body parts of the subject and even itself through the memory system.

2.4. Awareness and Experience. The awareness is identification of either observed phenomena or the image in the brain as one of the patterns experienced in the past. The awareness sometimes identifies information of the state of the local part of body, such as stomach, muscle, as one of the experienced patterns such as pain or itch. When we observe the dynamics of some object, we are aware what is going on. In contrast, a video-camera observes the same thing, but it is not aware what is going on. The difference clearly tells us that awareness is related to our knowledge.

When we say we are aware of something, the object of the awareness is either the phenomena in the external world, or the image of our internal world projected from the real world. In other words, we are never aware of the image which we never experienced. When the input signals into our brain are cutoff and when we are computing anticipatively what is going on in the external real world, the image is the imitation of the real world. Then, the brain commands the motor system to respond to the external world for adaptation or optimization.

2.5. Difference between the Awareness and Self-Monitoring. An important conceptual question arises: is the awareness different from self-monitoring? If a part failed and it was repaired automatically by a new part quickly enough to be in time for real-time processing, it is certainly a self-monitoring computer, but is it an aware computer?

Awareness is a kind of self-monitoring. But awareness is special in the sense that it monitors its own function by a CIP not by a distributed system. Any central monitor system observes the function of the total system by reducing information, either by identifying the pattern of function with one of the stored pattern, or by segmenting the total system into a relatively small number of groups and by identifying the type of mal-function with the stored pattern. The aware computer may say in the former case "I am aware that I am writing a paper." It may say in the latter case "I have a pain in my stomach." No CIP can be aware that the 31586th cell in my stomach has trouble in calcium channel.

3. Experimental Suggestions on the Concept of Awareness

Hand tracking is the experiments [1–4] in which a subject is asked to follow by a cursor as accurately as possible a target moving on a screen programmed by a computer. When the target is shown it is a visual tracking experiment, while it is an intermittently blind target tracking when the target is intermittently hidden. Among various facts found in the tracking experiment, two facts are relevant here. In the visible tracking experiments, the cursor is always in an error-corrective mode, and therefore is retarded with respect to the target. On the other hand, the cursor moves in an anticipatory mode and precedes the target in the blind tracking [2–4].

A question we ask here is whether visible tracking mode and blind tracking mode are both the aware computing? This question was a start which has lead me to a general question this present paper is studying. It should be most natural to say that a visual tracking is a typical aware computing, because it is an experiment in which a subject's brain computes a proper hand motion which should minimize the error he is aware of with respect to an external target. On the other hand, it should be discussed whether a blind tracking experiment is aware computing or not. From the discussion in Section 2 we can say that this mode is also aware computing. The brain computes the hand motion to follow the hidden target using the memory of target motion observed in the visible region.

Another experiment proved that the same acceleration occurs even in a fully visible target tracking, if the target motion is fast [1]. This result was explained that the information processing speed of the vision system is not fast enough to take in the positional information incessantly, and that the percept-motor system is controlled to partly use the predictive mode instead of error-corrective mode. In addition, it is shown that two modes do not operate simultaneously. They are mutually exclusive. Why it has to be mutually exclusive? Is it possible to make a system which is aware of the both? This question is probably related to the question why internal world exists first of all. It might be that the internal world is created to compensate information which is not always available by some reason, for example, when the external motion is too fast that the visual system cannot process the information of the instantaneous information which evolves too quickly, as shown experimentally [1]. If a computing system is fast enough by using a fast processor, there may be no need to have an internal world.

When the speed of the external world is not very fast, one may think it may be possible to use both external information and the internal information at the same time. But it is not the case, because it must creates its own consistent body motion. For this purpose, CPS must have one and only one awareness at a time. They are thus mutually exclusive.

4. Usefulness of Awareness

What is the merit of aware computing? The awareness has been developed in biological system for survival against both external enemies and internal troubles. A number of perceptive systems and predictive capabilities were developed to protect biological systems from the external enemies, and a variety of feelings and internal neural systems were developed for warning of the possible internal system troubles.

Are they necessary for the artificial computer systems, too? We shall discuss this problem in a later section.

The sentences from (S1) to (S7) except (S4) used in daily life shown in the previous section include awareness, but does not always seem to be related to evaluation of his action.

Present human society is deviating from the severe biological evolutional society. Each action of individual human is not necessarily related to the survival evaluation and therefore, awareness under these circumstances is not accompanied by evaluation. It is not important for survival whether he runs or walks in an ordinary life. But it is certainly important if he is trying to escape from a tsunami. An aware system has advantage for surviving, because it can sometimes predict the external world and can give a chance to move to avoid it.

Awareness is the real-time knowledge on the evaluation of the action with respect to the effectiveness for survival.

5. Awareness of the Internal World and Mind

The awareness of the internal world discussed so far is closely related to the mind, which is also a deep human language, not a scientific one. How close we are now to the concept of mind? We discussed awareness of thinking and awareness of the status of the body parts, pain of the stomach, pleasantness of the whole body, and so forth.

Perhaps only remaining part of mind is the problem of free will.

Proactive hand motion was observed in tracking experiments [1–3]. When they found that their hand moved proactively with respect to an object which they were supposed to follow as accurately as possible, many subjects reported that they felt as if they were intending to lead the object. This results pushed me to imagine a possible physical interpretation of the "inversion of causality," which is against principles of physics, but necessary for understanding the "free will" of human being.

The mechanism of proactive motion was clarified by a recent intermittently visible tracking experiments [2]. When the target is visible and moves slow enough, hand motion is error corrective and retarded with respect to the target motion (error-corrective mode). On the other hand, when the target is moving invisibly on an already known orbit, the hand motion was found to precede the target. It was measured that the hand motion is accelerated as soon as the target is hidden. It was understood that the hand is then controlled by a predictive mechanism (predictive mode).

As discussed in a previous section, the awareness of the internal world may be created to compensate a slow processing of the human perceptive information. The preceding research [2] showed that the internal clock moved faster than the evolution of the real physical world, and the proactiveness of the body motion caused by the faster internal clock helps to optimize the dynamic error [1]. Internal world is the predicted projection of the external world using the information obtained in the past. This evolution of the internal world referring to the external world is a part of the activity in the brain called mind. The other part of the mind is the awareness of the local part of the body such as pain, discussed in Section 2.2.

6. Aware Computer

Already, most of the present computer systems are equipped with aware functions to some extent. One of the external enemies is virus, and antivirus vaccination software was developed greatly. Some alarm softwares informing of possible local trouble have also been developed. Nevertheless, the security of the computers equipped with these functions are monitored and taken care by human being not by the computer itself. Computers may be considered to be exposed to a severe survival society, unlike humans whose awareness is not directly related to survival. But we realize that a computer itself is not exposed to the severe market competition in real time. It is the manager of the computer company who is aware of the competition. In this sense, the computer is not a self-closed machine. It is not automotile either, like a future aware robot. When a computer is installed in a future robot which may move independently of the human control, the security must be controlled by a CPS of the robot. For this purpose, the concept of the self-closed real time aware computing will be indispensable.

From the following examples that we notice, it requires evaluation of the function and choice for some unknown factors for a computer or for a robot to be aware. The computer watches its own performance, and if the CPS of the computer itself can modify the system, either hardwares or softwares to improve the function, it is an aware computer. In other words, there can be no aware computer if there is no evaluation and action by the computer itself.

6.1. Self-Improving Computer. Let us imagine an "aware computer" which is designed to compute various optimization problems, and it is equipped with an evaluation counter whose number changes by the performance of the computer for constantly changing request. It is designed to change the system somewhat randomly, when the index of the evaluation counter goes down, and when the number of the counter becomes below a critical number, the power line is cutoff. Among an ensemble of computers which has a software and a hardware different from each other, a small number of computers with good performance will survive. In this case, if the computer can search and change the software by itself, constantly monitoring the number of the counter, it will be one of the aware computers.

6.2. Self-Sequencing Computer. Let us imagine a computer which performs a sequence of many programs by choosing out of many other sequences. If it has a memory which records the process and speed of computing, and if the computer from time to time stops computing and checks the previous process of computing, using the memory system, and if it can change the sequence of the job to achieve a higher global performance, then this computer might be called one of the aware computers.

7. An Aware Robot Which Behaves as If It Had a Free Will

Awareness implies existence of a CPS which can identify macroscopically the type of the present function with one stored. When an aware computer fails to identify the state

of the machine, the computing system is not aware of what is going on.

It seems reasonable to define the aware computing as such having a CPS like ourselves. Some examples of sentiment we feel such as pleasantness, painfulness, happiness, and sadness are the awareness and identification of the present function of the system with one of the patterns we experienced in the past. When we say that the human being is an aware computer, how do we explain free will?

Even if we construct a very good aware robot which will monitor perfectly the macroscopic functions of the computer itself, it will not have free will. To implement free will, I propose here, based on the results of our experiments discussed in the Section 3, an aware robot with double time; one is the physical time and the other is a brain time. The robot is assumed to operate by the physical clock when the computer is functioning with external signal as a reference signal, and to operate with a brain clock which is a little faster than the physical clock when the computer is simulating the external world without the signals from the external world.

Such aware robot will find that his internal world is leading the real world when he compares both from time to time. He would feel that he is not following the change of the external world, but the world is following him. There are two conditions for this mechanism to work. One is that the dynamics of the world is simple enough that the computer can simulate it by learning. The second condition is that the brain clock moves faster than the physical clock when the external input is off. The experimental evidence [2–4] showed that this is really the case, when human is asked to track an object moving on a simple orbit.

8. Epilogue

Terms and concepts which the author discussed in the paper are

> awareness,
>
> external world,
>
> internal world,
>
> awareness of external world,
>
> awareness of internal world,
>
> mind,
>
> free will,
>
> self-closed system.

As the author mentioned in the Introduction, those words are terminologies in the human science domain, not in the natural science domain. The author tried in this paper to discuss them by the words of natural science, not to translate nor define them into natural science with the scientific precision, nor to create new terms which have strict definitions [5]. The terms in the human science have wide and various aspects because of the length of history it was used, compared to the terms used in the modern natural science. I believe it is more useful at present to discuss the aspects of the concept, not trying to define it in modern science terminology.

In the future, one will be able to make an aware robot which behaves as if it is implemented all the functions that a human has, and which stops functioning by cutting off the power when some number reaches to a critical value which is a measure of competition between the other robots. However, there remains a fundamental difference between the aware human and an aware robot. The former has a deep desire to keep living, while not for the latter.

Thus, we came finally to face a most fundamental question why we desire to live, and a question if we can implement the desire into an aware robot. At the present moment, we do not know why we desire to live. The only thing we know is these species which survived through a severe natural selection survived by obtaining the instinctive wish to live. It would be wonderful if we can understand this question either from genetic information or from brain structure. But, I am afraid that all these effort will fail.

Creators, by definition, whether it is a creator of a computer or the creator of animals design their products to survive as much as possible against their enemies. How have the creators of animals implemented the desire to live? I believe we can find some suggestions by translating this question into the scientific terms. To do so, we must look for the causal relation between the key word such as awareness, desire to live, natural selection, mind, and survival.

A following scenario seems most natural to the author.

(1) Animals have obtained awareness through the severe survival race through the evolution. Humans are most aware, hopefully.

(2) As a result, they obtained their internal world and mind.

(3) Then, they came to "think" that they have desire to live, because the mind they obtained was the kind which desire to live through the selection, although we do not know the physical mechanism of the desire yet.

(4) Important thing is to notice that it is not that we are aware because we have desire to live, but we desire to live because we are aware.

References

[1] F. Ishida and Y.E. Sawada, "Human hand moves proactively to the external stimulus; an evolutional strategy for minimizing transient error," *Physical Review Letters*, vol. 93, no. 16, Article ID 168105, 2004.

[2] Y. Hayashi, Y. Tamura, K. Sase, K. Sugawara, and Y. Sawada, "Intermittently-visual tracking experiments reveal the roles of error-correction and predictive mechanisms in the human visual-motor control system," *Transactions of The Society of Instrument and Control Engineers*, vol. 46, no. 7, pp. 391–400, 2010.

[3] Y. Hayashi, Y. Tamura, K. Sugawara, and Y. Sawada, "Why the hand motion proceeds the target in tracking experiment?" in *Proceedings of the 3rd International Symposium on Mobiligence*, vol. 34, 2009.

[4] Y. Hayashi and Y. Sawada, "A transition from an alternative error-correction mode to a synchronization mode in the mutual hand tracking and the mutual finger tapping," *Physical Review E*. Submitted.

[5] H. R. Maturana and F. J. Varela, *Autopoiesis and Cognition*, D. Reidel, Dordrecht, The Netherlands, 1980.

14

Nonnegative Matrix Factorizations Performing Object Detection and Localization

G. Casalino,[1] N. Del Buono,[2] and M. Minervini[3]

[1] *Dipartimento di Informatica, Università di Bari, Via E.Orabona 4, I-70125 Bari, Italy*
[2] *Dipartimento di Matematica, Università di Bari, Via E. Orabona 4, I-70125 Bari, Italy*
[3] *Computer Science and Engineering Ph.D Division, Institute for Advanced Studies Lucca (IMT),*
  Piazza S. Ponziano 6, 55100 Lucca, Italy

Correspondence should be addressed to N. Del Buono, delbuono@dm.uniba.it

Academic Editor: Cezary Z. Janikow

We study the problem of detecting and localizing objects in still, gray-scale images making use of the part-based representation provided by nonnegative matrix factorizations. Nonnegative matrix factorization represents an emerging example of subspace methods, which is able to extract interpretable parts from a set of template image objects and then to additively use them for describing individual objects. In this paper, we present a prototype system based on some nonnegative factorization algorithms, which differ in the additional properties added to the nonnegative representation of data, in order to investigate if any additional constraint produces better results in general object detection via nonnegative matrix factorizations.

1. Introduction

The notion of low dimensional approximation has played a fundamental role in effectively and efficiently processing and conceptualizing huge amount of data stored in large sparse matrices. Particularly, subspace techniques, such as Singular Value Decomposition [1], Principal Component Analysis (PCA) [2], and Independent Component Analysis [3], represent a class of linear algebra methods largely adopted to analyze high dimensional dataset in order to discover latent structures by projecting it onto a low dimensional space. Generally, a subspace method is characterized by learning a set of base vectors from a set of suitable data templates. This vector spans a subspace which is able to capture the essential structure of the input data. Once the subspace has been found (during the off-line learning phase), the detection of a new sample can be accomplished (in the so-called on-line detection phase) by projecting it on the subspace and finding the nearest neighbor of templates projected onto this subspace. These methods have found efficient applications in several areas of information retrieval, computer vision, and pattern recognition, especially in the fields of face identification [4, 5], recognition of digits and characters [6, 7], and molecular pattern discovery [8, 9].

However, pertinent information stored in many data matrices are often nonnegative (examples are pixels in images, the probability of a particular topic appearing in a linguistic document, the amount of pollutant emitted by a factory, and so on [10–15]). During the analysis process, taking into account this nonnegativity constraint could bring some benefits in terms of interpretability and visualization of large scale data, while maintaining the physical feasibility more closely. Nevertheless, classical subspace methods describe data as a combination of elementary features involving both additive and subtractive components; hence, they are not able to guarantee the conservation of nonnegativity.

The recent approach of low-rank nonnegative matrix factorization (NMF) becomes particularly attractive to obtain a reduced representation of data by using additive components only. This idea has been motivated in a couple of ways. Firstly in many applications (e.g., by the rules of physics) one knows that the quantities involved cannot be negative. Secondly, nonnegativity has been argued for based on the intuition that

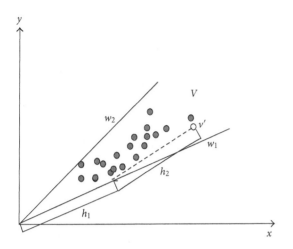

FIGURE 1: Nonnegative matrix factorization as conical coordinate transformation: illustration in two dimensional space.

parts are generally combined additively (and not subtracted) to form a whole; moreover, psychological and physiological principles assume that humans learn objects part-based. Hence, the nonnegativity constraints might be useful for learning part-based representations [16].

In this paper, we investigate the problem of performing "generic" object detection in images using the framework of NMF. By performing "generic" detection, we mean to detect, inside a given image, classes of objects, such as any car, any face, rather than finding a specific object (class instance), such a particular car, or a particular face.

Generally, object detection task is accomplished by comparing object similarities to a small number of reference features which can be expressed in holistic (global) or sparse (local) terms and then adopting a learning mechanism to identify regions in the feature space that correspond to the object class of interest. Among subspace techniques, PCA constitutes an example of approach which adopts global descriptors related to the variance of the image space (the so-called eigenfaces) to visually represent a set of given face images [17]. Other holistic approaches are based on global descriptors expressed by color, texture histogram, and global image transformations [18]. On the other hand, local features have been proved to be invariant regarding noise, occlusion or pose view and they are also supported by the theory of "recognition-by-components" introduced in [19]. The most adopted features of local type are Gabor features [20], wavelet features [21], and rectangular features [22]. Some approaches using part-based representation were proposed in [23, 24], but they present the drawback of requiring manually defined object parts and vocabulary of parts to represent object in the target class. More recently, automatic extraction of parts possessing high information contents in terms of local signal change has been illustrated in [25] together with a classifier based on a sparse representation of patches extracted around interesting points in the image.

The nonnegativity constraints of NMF make this subspace method a promising technique to automatically extract parts describing the structure of object classes. In fact, these localized parts can be added in a purely additive way (with varying combination coefficients) to describe individual objects and could be used as learning mechanism to extract interpretable parts from a set of template images. Moreover, making use of the concept of distance from the subspace spanned by the extracted parts, NMF, could be also adopted as learning method to detect when an object is present or not inside a given image.

An interesting example of part-based representation of the original data can be found in the context of image articulation libraries. Here, NMFs are able to extract realistic parts (limbs) from image depicting stick figures with four limbs with different articulations. However, it should be pointed out that the existence of such a part-based representation heavily depends on the objects itself [26].

The firstly proposed NMF algorithms (the multiplicative and additive updated rules presented in [11]) have been applied in the fields of face identification to decompose a face image into parts reminiscent of features such as lips, eyes, and nose. More recently, comparisons between other nonnegative part-based algorithms (such as nonnegative sparse coding and local NMF) have been presented in the context of facial features, learning, demonstrating a good performance in term of detection rate by using only a small number of bases components [27]. A preliminary comparison on three NMF algorithms (classical multiplicative NMF [11], local NMF [28], and discriminant NMF [29]) has been illustrated in [30] on the recognition of different object color images. Moreover, results on the influence of additional constraints on NMF, such as the sparseness proposed in [31], have been presented in [32] for various dimensions of subspaces generated for object recognition tasks (particularly, face recognition and handwritten digits identification).

Here, we investigate the problem of performing detection of single objects in images using different NMF algorithms, in order to inquire if the representation provided by the NMF framework can effectively produce added value in detecting and locating objects inside images. The problem to be explored here can be formalized as follows. Given a collection of template images representing objects of the same class, that is a group of objects which may differ slightly from each other visually but correspond to the same semantic concept, for example, cars, digits, and faces, we would like to understand if NMF is able to provide some kind of local feature representations which can be used to individuate objects in test images.

The rest of the paper is organized as follows. The next section describes the mathematical problem of computing nonnegative matrix factorization and reviews some of the algorithms proposed in the literature and adopted to learn such a matrix decomposition model. These algorithms will constitute the core of an object detection prototype system based on the learning via NMF, proposed in Section 3 together with a brief description of its off-line and on-line learning phases. Section 4 presents experimental results illustrating the properties of the adopted NMF learning algorithms and their performance in detecting objects in real images. Finally, Section 5 concludes with a summary and possible directions for future work.

FIGURE 2: Example of a sliding window moving across a test image.

FIGURE 3: Example of output provided by the prototype system during the on-line detection phase.

2. Mathematical Background and Algorithms

The problem of finding a nonnegative low dimensional approximation of a set of data templates stored in a large dimension data matrix $V \in \mathbb{R}_+^{n \times m}$ can be stated as follows.

Given an initial dataset expressed by a $n \times m$ matrix V, where each column is an n-dimensional nonnegative vector of the original database (m vectors), find an approximate decomposition of the data matrix into a basis matrix $W \in \mathbb{R}_+^{n \times r}$ and an encoding variable matrix $H \in \mathbb{R}_+^{r \times m}$, both having nonnegative elements, such that $V \approx WH$.

Generally the rank r of the matrices W and H is much lower than the rank of V (usually it is chosen so that $(n + m)r < nm$). Each column of the matrix W contains a base vector of the spanned (NMF) subspace, while each column of H represents the weights needed to approximate the corresponding column in V by means of the vectors in W.

The NMF is actually a conical coordinate transformation: Figure 1 provides a graphical interpretation in a two dimensional space. The two basis vectors w_1 and w_2 describe a cone which encloses the dataset V. Due to the nonnegative constraint, only points within this cone can be reconstructed through linear combination of these basis vectors:

$$v' = (w_1, w_2) \cdot (h_1, h_2)^\top. \qquad (1)$$

The factorization of $V \approx WH$ presents the disadvantages concerning the lack of uniqueness of its factors. For example, if an arbitrary invertible matrix $A \in \mathbb{R}^{r \times r}$ such that the two matrices $W' = WA$ and $H' = A^{-1}H$ are positive semidefinite can be found, then another factorization $V \approx W'H'$ exists. Such a transformation is always possible if A is an invertible nonnegative monomial matrix (a matrix is called monomial if there is exactly one element different from zero in each row

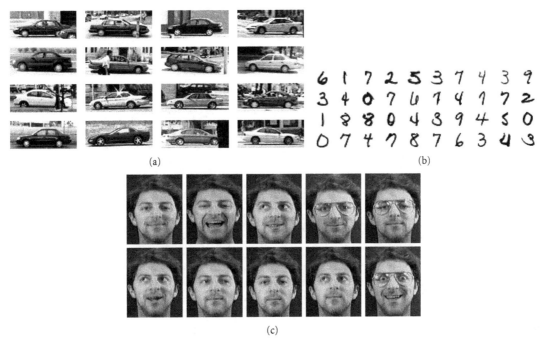

FIGURE 4: Examples of car images from (a) the CarData dataset, (b) USPS dataset, (c) ORL dataset.

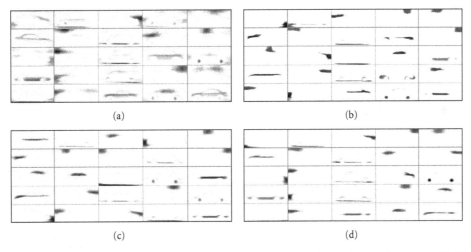

FIGURE 5: Illustration of the learnt bases (with $r = 20$) of the CarData dataset obtained via (a) NMF, (b) LNMF, (c)NMFsc, and (d) DLPP.

and column). However, if A is a nonnegative monomial matrix, in this case, the result of this transformation is simply a scaling and permutation of the original matrices [33].

An NMF of a given data matrix V can be obtained by finding a solution of a nonlinear optimization problem over a specified error function. Two simple error functions are often used to measure the distance between the original data V and its low dimensional approximation WH: the sum of squared errors (also known as the squared Euclidean distance), which leads to the minimization of the functional:

$$\|V - WH\|^2 \tag{2}$$

subject to the nonnegativity constraints over the elements W_{ij} and H_{ij}, and the generalized Kullback-Leibler divergence to the positive matrices:

$$\text{Div}(V \| WH) = \sum_{ij} \left(V_{ij} \log\left(\frac{V_{ij}}{(WH)_{ij}}\right) - V_{ij} + (WH)_{ij} \right), \tag{3}$$

subject to the nonnegativity of matrices W and H.

2.1. Classical Algorithm. The most popular approach to numerically solve the NMF optimization problem is the multiplicative update algorithm proposed in [11]. Particularly, it can be shown that the square Euclidean distance measure (2)

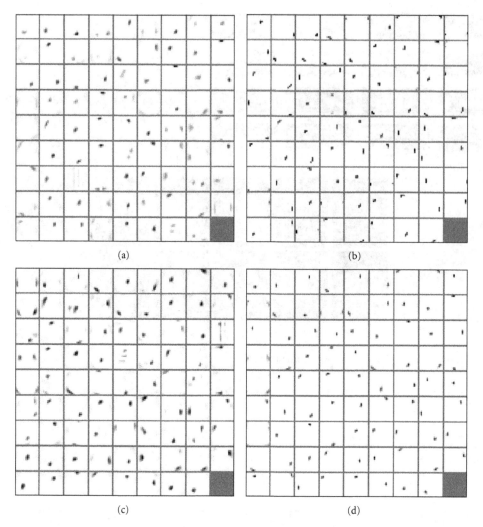

FIGURE 6: Illustration of the learnt bases (with $r = 80$) of the USPS dataset obtained via (a) NMF, (b) LNMF, (c) NMFsc, and (d) DLPP.

TABLE 1: Algorithm performances when applied to CarData, USPS, and ORL dataset, respectively. Reported values refer to the lowest and highest values of the factor rank r as previously described.

			CarData			
Rank		20			110	
Method	MSE	Time	orth(W)	MSE	Time	orth(W)
NMF	$2.441e^9$	275	$8.7411e^4$	$1.457e^9$	453	$4.4435e^5$
LNMF	$2.404e^{10}$	292	4.9734	$2.373e^{10}$	472	10.2373
NMFsc	$2.559e^9$	695	$6.7818e^9$	$1.422e^9$	1265	$1.5825e^9$
DLPP	$2.664e^9$	2271	1.5627	$1.657e^9$	2591	3.3221
			USPS			
Rank		80			220	
Method	MSE	Time	orth(W)	MSE	Time	orth(W)
NMF	$1.297e^4$	397	$2.8166e^4$	$3.031e^3$	847	$1.2142e^5$
LNMF	$1.331e^5$	374	6.6387	$1.609e^4$	1427	6.4695
NMFsc	$1.318e^4$	777	$5.2854e^4$	$5.568e^3$	1409	$2.7761e^4$
DLPP	$1.507e^4$	637	3.4077	$1.249e^3$	1144	3.2623
			ORL			
Rank		20			80	
Method	MSE	Time	orth(W)	MSE	Time	orth(W)
NMF	$1.027e^9$	496	$1.5701e^5$	$5.413e^8$	705	$6.0577e^5$
LNMF	$3.104e^{10}$	556	4.4656	$3.080e^{10}$	781	8.8920
NMFsc	$1.425e^9$	1362	$1.0762e^{10}$	$6.183e^8$	2164	$2.2674e^9$
DLPP	$1.323e^9$	14824	1.7690	$8.145e^8$	15278	3.4647

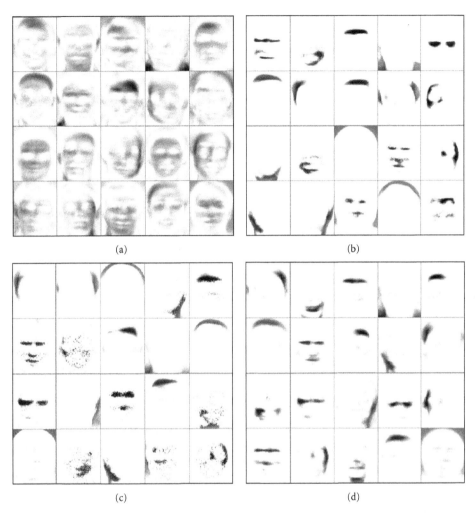

FIGURE 7: Illustration of the learnt bases (with $r = 20$) of the OPS dataset obtained via (a) NMF, (b) LNMF, (c)NMFsc, and (d) DLPP.

Initialize nonnegative matrices $W^{(0)}$ *and* $H^{(0)}$
While *Stopping criteria are not satisfied* **do**
$\quad W \leftarrow W \odot (VH^\top) \oslash (WHH^\top)$
$\quad H \leftarrow H \odot (W^\top V) \oslash (W^\top WH)$
end while
{$\odot$ and $\oslash$ denotes the Hadamard product, that is the element-wise matrix multiplication and the element-wise division, respectively}

ALGORITHM 1: The Lee and Seung multiplicative update rules (NMF).

Initialize nonnegative matrices $W^{(0)}$ *and* $H^{(0)}$
While *Stopping criteria are not satisfied* **do**
$\quad H \leftarrow H \odot (VH^\top) \oslash (WHH^\top)$
$\quad W \leftarrow W \odot ((VH^\top) \oslash (WW^\top VH^\top))^{\cdot (1/2)}$
end while
{$\odot$ and $\oslash$ denotes the Hadamard product and the element-wise division, respectively and $(\cdot)^{\cdot (1/2)}$ denotes the element-wise square root operation}

ALGORITHM 2: NMF with orthogonal constraint on W.

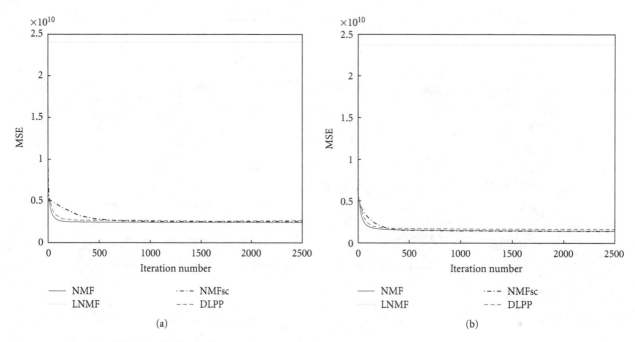

FIGURE 8: Behavior of the MSE during the learning iterations for the CarData dataset ((a) rank value $r = 20$, (b) rank value $r = 115$).

TABLE 2: Algorithm performances in terms of *recall* and *precision* when applied to CarData with factor ranks $r = 20$ and $r = 110$. Bold fonts indicate the highest values of precision and recall.

Method	TP	FP	Recall	Precision	F-measure
			$r = 20$		
NMF	103	67	0.52	0.61	0.56
LNMF	92	78	0.46	0.54	0.5
NMFsc	106	64	**0.53**	**0.62**	**0.57**
DLPP	37	133	0.19	0.22	0.2
			$r = 110$		
Method	TP	FP	Recall	Precision	F-measure
NMF	112	58	**0.56**	**0.66**	**0.61**
LNMF	86	85	0.43	0.5	0.46
NMFsc	110	60	0.55	0.65	0.59
DLPP	21	93	0.11	0.18	0.13

TABLE 3: Algorithm performances in terms of recall and precision when applied to Usps with factor ranks $r=80$ and $r=220$. Bold fonts indicate the highest values of precision and recall.

Method	TP	FP	Recall	Precision	F-measure
			$r = 80$		
NMF	2602	98	0.96	0.96	0.96
LNMF	2457	243	0.91	0.91	0.91
NMFsc	2615	85	**0.97**	**0.97**	**0.97**
DLPP	658	2042	0.24	0.24	0.24
			$r = 220$		
Method	TP	FP	Recall	Precision	F-measure
NMF	2602	98	**0.96**	**0.96**	**0.96**
LNMF	1708	1042	0.63	0.63	0.63
NMFsc	2603	97	**0.96**	**0.96**	**0.96**
DLPP	2195	505	0.81	0.81	0.81

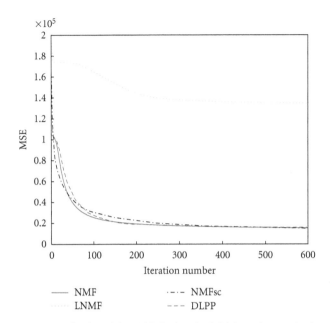

FIGURE 9: Behavior of the MSE during the initial 600 iterates in the learning phase on the USPS dataset.

TABLE 4: Algorithm performances in terms of recall and precision when applied to ORL with factor ranks $r = 20$ and $r = 80$.

			$r = 20$		
Method	TP	FP	Recall	Precision	F-measure
NMF	80	0	1	1	1
LNMF	80	0	1	1	1
NMFsc	80	0	1	1	1
DLPP	40	40	0.5	0.5	0.5
			$r = 80$		
Method	TP	FP	Recall	Precision	F-measure
NMF	80	0	1	1	1
LNMF	80	0	1	1	1
NMFsc	80	0	1	1	1
DLPP	41	39	0.51	0.51	0.51

is nonincreasing under the iterative updated rules described in Algorithm 1.

Lee and Seung update rules can be interpreted as a diagonally rescaled gradient descent method (i.e., a gradient descent method using a rather large learning rate). It has been proved that the above algorithm converges into a local minimum. Other techniques, such as alternating nonnegative least squares method or bound-constrained optimization algorithms, such as projected gradient method, have also been used when additional constraints are added to the nonnegativity of the matrices W or H [34–36].

2.2. NMF Algorithms with Orthogonal Constraints. Differently to other subspace methods, the learned basis vectors in NMF are not orthonormal to each other. Different modifications of the standard cost functions (2) and (3) have been proposed to include further constraints on the factors W and/or H, such as orthogonality or sparsity.

As concerning the possibility of making the bases or the encoding matrices closer to the Stiefel manifold (the Stiefel manifold is the set of all real $l \times k$ matrices with orthogonal columns $\{Q \in \mathbb{R}^{l \times k} \mid Q^\top Q = I_k\}$, being I_k the $k \times k$ identity matrix) (which means that vectors in W or H should be orthonormal to each other), two different update rules have been proposed in [37] to add orthogonality on W or H, respectively. Particularly, when one desires that matrix W is as close as possible to the identity matrix of conformal dimension (i.e., $W^\top W \approx I_r$), the multiplicative update rule (1) can be modified as described in Algorithm 2 (see [38] for details).

Different orthogonal NMF algorithms have been derived using directly the true gradient in Stiefel manifold [38, 39] and imposing the orthogonality between nonnegative basis vectors in learning the decomposition.

An interesting issue, strictly tied with the computation of the orthogonal NMF, when the adopted cost function is the generalized KL-divergence, is the connections with some probabilistic latent variable models. Particularly in [40], it has been pointed out that the objective function of a probabilistic latent semantic indexing model is the same of the objective function of NMF with an additional orthogonal constraint. Moreover, when the encoding matrix H is required to possess orthogonal columns, it can be proved that orthogonal NMFs are equivalent to the K-means clustering algorithm [40, 41].

2.3. NMF Algorithm with Localization Constraints. NMF algorithms optimizing a slight variation of the KL-divergence (3) can be adopted to yield a factorization which reveals local features in the data, as proposed in [28]. Particularly, local nonnegative matrix factorization uses the error function:

$$\sum_{ij} \left(V_{ij} \log \left(\frac{V_{ij}}{(WH)_{ij}} \right) - V_{ij} + (WH)_{ij} + \alpha U_{ij} \right) - \beta \sum_i Q_{ii}, \tag{4}$$

where $\alpha, \beta > 0$ are constants, and $U = W^\top W$ and $Q = HH^\top$. The function (4) is the KL-divergence (3) with three additional terms designed to enforce the locality of the basis features. Particularly, the modified objective function (4) attempts to minimize the number of basis components required to represent the dataset V and the redundancy between different bases, trying to make them as orthogonal as possible. Moreover, it maximizes the total activity on each component, that is, the total squared projection coefficients summed over all training data, so that only bases containing the most important information should be retained. The iterative update rules derived by the error function (4) are described in Algorithm 3.

It has been proved that the update rules in Algorithm 3 decrease monotonically the objective function (4) to a local minimum.

2.4. NMF Algorithm with Sparseness Constraints. NMF algorithms can be extended to include the option to control

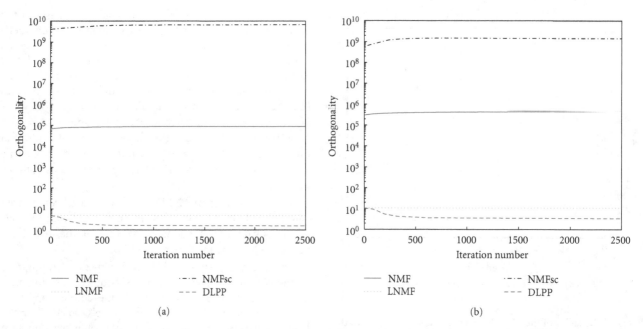

FIGURE 10: Behaviour of the orthogonality error for matrix W during the learning iterations on the CarData dataset: (a) rank value $r = 20$, (b) rank value $r = 115$.

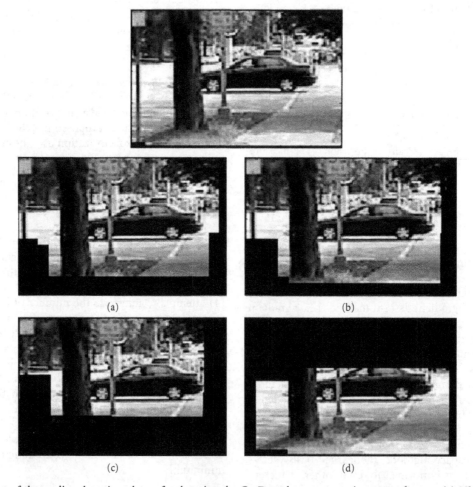

FIGURE 11: Output of the on-line detection phase after learning the CarData dataset: query image on the top, (a) NMF, (b) LNMF, (c) NMFsc, and (d) DLPP. The off-line phase has been performed with $r = 110$.

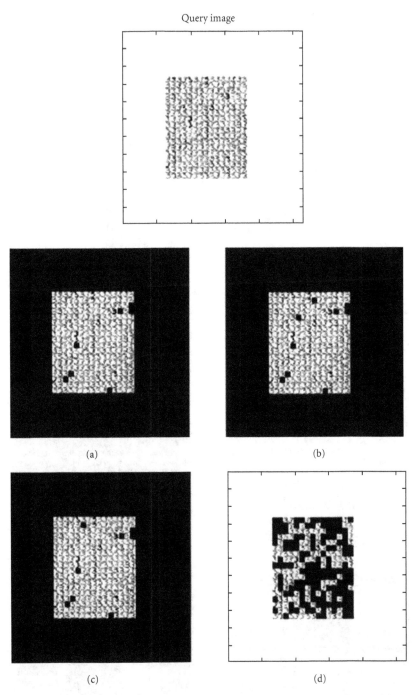

FIGURE 12: Output of the on-line detection phase after learning the USPS dataset: query image on the top, (a) NMF, (b) LNMF, (c) NMFsc, and (d) DLPP. The off-line phase has been performed with $r = 80$.

sparseness explicitly in order to discover parts-based representations that are qualitatively better than those given by standard NMF, as proposed in [31]. Particularly, to quantify the sparseness of a generic given vector $x \in \mathbb{R}^k$, the following relationship between the 1-norm and the Euclidean norm (in the original Hoyer's paper the terminology L_1-norm and L_2-norm is adopted) has been adopted:

$$\text{sparseness}(x) = \frac{\sqrt{k} - (\|x\|_1)/(\|x\|_2)}{\sqrt{k} - 1}. \qquad (5)$$

Function (5) assumes values in the interval $[0, 1]$, where 0 indicates the minimum degree of sparsity obtained when all the elements x_i possess the same absolute value, while 1 indicates the maximum degree of sparsity, which is reached when only one component of the vector x is different from zero. This measure can be adopted to impose a desired degree of sparseness on vectors in W and/or the encoding coefficient vectors in H, depending on the specific application the nonnegative decomposition is seeking for.

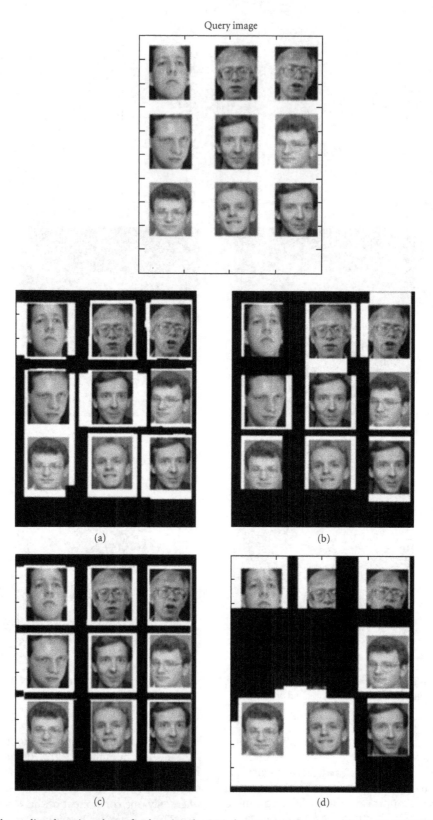

FIGURE 13: Output of the on-line detection phase after learning the ORL dataset: query image on the top, (a) NMF, (b) LNMF, (c) NMFsc, (d) and DLPP. The off-line phase has been performed with $r = 20$.

Initialize nonnegative matrices $W^{(0)}$ and $H^{(0)}$
While *Stopping criteria are not satisfied* **do**

$\quad H \leftarrow (H \odot (W^{\top}(V \oslash WH)))^{\cdot(1/2)}$

$\quad W \leftarrow W \odot ((V \oslash WH)H^{\top})$

$\quad W \leftarrow W \operatorname{diag}(\|W_{*1}\|_1, \|W_{*2}\|_1, \ldots, \|W_{*r}\|_1)^{-1}$

end while

$\{\odot$ and $\oslash$ denotes the Hadamard product and the element-wise division, respectively, $(\cdot)^{\cdot(1/2)}$ denotes the element-wise square root operation, $\operatorname{diag}(\|W_{*1}\|_1, \|W_{*2}\|_1, \ldots, \|W_{*r}\|_1)$ indicates the $r \times r$ diagonal matrix whose diagonal elements are the 1-norm of the column basis vectors in $W\}$

ALGORITHM 3: Local nonnegative matrix factorization update rules.

To compute NMF with sparseness constraints, a projected gradient descent algorithm has been developed. This algorithm essentially takes a step in the direction of the negative gradient of the cost function (2) and subsequently projects onto the constraint space, that is, the cone of nonnegative matrices with a prescribed degree of sparseness ensured imposing that sparseness $(W_i) = s_W$ and sparseness $(H_i) = s_H$, where W_i and H_i are the ith column of W and H, respectively, and s_W and s_H are the desired sparseness. The update rules used to compute W and H are described in Algorithm 4.

It should be observed that when the sparsity constraint is not required by W or H, the update rules are those provided by Algorithm 1 (the interested readers can be addressed to [31] for further details on this algorithm).

3. Object Detection System Based on NMF

In this section, we schematically present an object detection prototype system based on the learning via NMF. The working flow of the prototype system can be roughly divided in two main phases: the off-line learning phase and the on-line detection phase (mainly devoted to the object location activity).

The off-line learning phase consists in preparing the training image data and then learning a proper subspace representation of them. To be compliant to the format of the data matrix V (in order to obtain one of its nonnegative factorizations), each given $p \times q$ training image has to be converted into a pq-dimensional column vector (stacking the columns of the image matrix into a single vector) and then inserted as a column of the matrix V. It should be observed that this vector representation of an image data presents the drawback of losing the spatial relationship between neighborhood pixels inside the original image.

Once the image training matrix $V \in \mathbb{R}_+^{n \times m}$ is formed (now being $n = pq$), its NMF can be computed by applying one of the following algorithms:

(i) the Lee and Seung multiplicative update rule (indicated by NMF and described in Algorithm 1) [11],

(ii) NMF with orthogonal additional constraint on the basis matrix W (indicated by DLPP and described in Algorithm 2) [37],

(iii) local NMF (indicated by LNMF and described in Algorithm 3) [28],

(iv) NMF with sparseness additional constraint (indicated by NMFsc and described in Algorithm 4) [31].

Once the bases and the encoding matrices have been obtained using one of the previous algorithms, the on-line detection phase can be started. In particular, for each test sample image q, the distance from the subspace spanned by the learned basis matrix W is computed by means of the following formula:

$$\operatorname{dist}(W, q) = \|q - WW^{\top}q\|_2. \tag{6}$$

The value distance $\operatorname{dist}(W, q)$ is then compared with a fixed threshold ϑ, which is adopted to positively recognize the test image q as *known* object. Particularly, the decisional rule which can be easily derived is

"IF $\operatorname{dist}(W, q) \leq \vartheta$ THEN q is labelled as known object and the object is located inside". (7)

Since the dimensions of the test image are bigger than those of the training images, we adopt a common approach to detect rigid object such as faces or cars [42]. Particularly, a frame of the same dimensions of training images (i.e., a window-frame of $p \times q$ pixels) is slid across the test image in order to locate the subregions of the test image which contain *known* objects. To reduce computational costs, started from the left-up corner of the test image, the sliding frame is moved in steps of size 5 percent of the test image, first in the horizontal and in the vertical direction (as shown in Figure 2).

The detection threshold is relevant to label each query image as object belonging or not to the subspace representation of the training space. Lowering the threshold increases the correct detections, but also increases the false positives; raising the threshold would have the opposite effect. To overcome this weakness, a preliminary detection phase can

Input: *positive constants* : $\mu_W > 0$, $\mu_H > 0$
  Choose an appropriate Projection$(\cdot)$ to ensure the degree of sparseness
  Initialize nonnegative matrices $W^{(0)}$ $H^{(0)}$
  while *Stopping criteria are not satisfied* **do**
    $W_{ij} \leftarrow W_{ij} - \mu_W((WHH^\top)_{ij} - (XH^\top)_{ij})$
    $W \leftarrow Projection(W)$
    $H \leftarrow H_{ij} - \mu_H((W^\top WH)_{ij} - (W^\top X)_{ij})$
    $H \leftarrow Projection(H)$
  end while
  $\{\mu_W > 0$ and $\mu_H > 0$ are positive constants representing the step size
  of the algorithm and $Projection(\cdot)$ indicates the appropriate projection
  operator$\}$

ALGORITHM 4: NMF with space constraints.

be performed in order to determine a range $[d, D]$ used to fix a default threshold value as follows:

$$\vartheta_{\text{default}} = d + (D - d) * 0.1. \qquad (8)$$

The multiplicative factor 0.1 has been derived empirically. Although the simple mechanisms adopted to estimate the threshold value could cause the drawback, the proposed system identifies something also when it deals with images which do not contain any object of interest. Different estimation methods of the default threshold could be adopted to increase the detection rate; however, we delayed such aspect to a more detailed analysis to be tackled in a future work of ours. Figure 3 provides an example of the results obtained after the on-line detection phase: the picture on the left represents the test image, while the picture on the right represents a copy of the test image in which black pixels identify those pixels belonging to sliding windows which have not been identified as *known* objects.

4. Experimental Results

This section presents some experimental evaluation of the object detection/localization approach developed in the previous section. The prototype system is evaluated on single-scale images (i.e., images containing objects of the same dimension of the training data). After a brief description of the data sets adopted in the off-line training phase, some comparisons of the above-mentioned NMF algorithms are reported. Our primary concern is on the qualitative evaluation of the different algorithms in order to assess when additional constraints on basis matrix (such as sparseness and orthogonality) and/or different number of bases images (explicitly represented by the rank r) can produce better results in object detection.

All the numerical results have been obtained by Matlab 7.7 (R2008b) codes implemented on an Intel Core 2 Quad Q9400 processor, 2.66 GHz with 4 GB RAM. The execution time of each algorithm has been computed by the build in Matlab functions tic and toc.

In order to test the object detection prototype system based on the illustrated NMF algorithms, three image datasets have been adopted: CarData, USPS, and ORL.

The exploited datasets represent three different typologies of objects: cars, handwritten digits, and faces, respectively. Figure 4 illustrates some training images from the adopted datasets.

The CarData training set contains 550 gray scale training images of cars of size 100×40 pixels, while the test set is composed by 170 single-scale test images, containing 200 cars at roughly the same scale as in the training images. The USPS dataset contains normalized gray scale images of handwritten digits of size 16×16 pixels, divided into a training set of 7291 images and a test set of 2007 images including all digits from 0 to 9. A preprocessing of USPS has been applied to rescale pixel values from the range $[-1, 1]$ to the range $[0, 1]$. Figure 4 illustrates some training images from the adopted datasets. The ORL dataset contains gray scale images of faces of 40 distinct subjects. Each image is of size 92×112 pixels and has been taken against a dark homogeneous background with the subjects in an upright, frontal position, with slight leftright out-of-plane rotation. We use the first 8 images of each subject for the training set and the remaining 2 images for the test set.

4.1. Experimental Setup. The off-line learning phase has been run for different values of the rank r (representing the number of bases images) and with selected degree of sparsity imposed to NMFsc algorithm (particularly, the sparsity parameters in NMFsc have been fixed as $s_W = 0.5$ and $s_H = []$). As previously observed, we are interested in assessing the existence of any qualitative difference between the NMF learning algorithms in the context of generic object detection. In fact, the rank value r represents the dimensionality of the subspace spanned by the matrix W: an increase in its value can be interpreted as an information gain with respect to the original dataset. On the other hand, large values of r could introduce some redundancy in the basis representation of the dataset, nullifying the benefits provided by the part-based representation of the NMF. The algorithms have been trained on each dataset for various values of rank (CarData: $r = 20, 110$, USPS: $r = 80, 220$, ORL: $r = 20, 80$). We report the results related to the lowest and the highest rank values for each dataset. For the benefit of comparison, the same stopping criteria has been adopted for all NMF learning algorithms (i.e., the algorithms stop when the maximum number of iterations, set to 2500, is reached). Moreover, the results reported in the following sections represent the average values obtained over ten different random initializations of the nonnegative initial matrices $W^{(0)}$ and $H^{(0)}$. Note that, for each trial, the same initial matrices randomly generated (with proper dimensions with respect to the adopted dataset) have been used for all the algorithms.

The algorithms have been compared in terms of final approximation error, computed by $MSE(W, H) = \|V - WH\|_2$, execution time (indicating the number of seconds required by each algorithm to complete the learning phase) and degree of orthogonality of W, measured by $orth(W) = \|W^\top W - I\|_F$. This latter measure has been added for highlighting when additional constraints (in the specific case the orthogonality of the basis factor) provide better results in the detection phase.

4.2. Results of the Off-Line Learning Phase. This section reports the results obtained at the end of the off-line training phase for all the three chosen image datasets. Table 1 reports the MSE, the execution time, and the degree of orthogonality of W, when the algorithms are trained on the chosen datasets. For each dataset, the results obtained for the initial value and the final value of the rank are reported. These results are related to the lower and the higher subspace approximation of each dataset.

Figure 5 illustrates the part-based representation of Car-Data dataset learned by the adopted algorithms. For the benefit of appreciating some visual difference between the obtained bases, we plot the bases only for the smaller value $r = 20$. Analogously, Figures 6 and 7 report the bases representation of USPS (with rank value $r = 80$) and ORL dataset (with rank value $r = 20$), respectively. Algorithm NMF learns global representation of either set of face car and face image, while it provides local representation of handwritten digits. LNMF, DLPP, and NMFsc algorithms, instead, learn localized image parts some of which appear to roughly correspond to parts of faces, parts of cars, part of digit marks. Essentially, the NMF algorithms select a subset of the pixels which are simultaneously active across multiple images to be represented by a single bases vector.

As an example, Figure 8 illustrates the behavior of the MSE during the learning phase on the CarData dataset, with rank values $r = 20$ and $r = 115$, respectively. It should be observed that after some iterations all algorithms converge to similar values of the MSE. The LNMF algorithm presents a larger value of the MSE just because this algorithm is based on the KL-divergence cost function so it provides a rougher approximation of the dataset in term of MSE. To better appreciate the rate of convergence of all algorithms, Figure 9 reports the behavior of the MSE during the initial 600 iterates in the learning phase associated with the USPS dataset, with rank value $r = 80$. A behavior similar to that depicted in Figures 8 and 9 is shown for all the other datasets and for different values of the rank r.

As concerning the degree of orthogonality of the matrix W learned by each algorithm, Figure 10 reports the semilog plot of the orthogonality error for W during the learning iterations on the CarData dataset (with the rank values $r = 20$ and $r = 115$, resp.). It should be observed that both LNMF and DLPP produce a matrix W possessing a discrete degree of orthogonality. On the other hand, since NMF and NMFsc do not incorporate any additional constraint, they preserve or sometimes deteriorate the degree of orthogonality of the initial matrix W_0. Similar plots for the orthogonal error can be depicted for the matrices obtained using the USPS and ORL dataset, respectively.

4.3. Results of the On-Line Detection Phase. Once the bases and the encoding matrices have been obtained at the end of the learning phase, we are ready to enter the on-line detection and localization phase in order to assess a qualitative analysis of the considered algorithms (by means of the prototype system). To measure the performance of the NMF-based object detection/localization system, we are interested in knowing how many of the objects it detects and how often the detection it makes is false. Particularly, the two quantities of interest are the number of correct detections and the number of false detections: the former should be maximized while the latter quantity has to be minimized. As we have already observed in Section 3, the decisional rule (7), which allows to identify a test image as *known* object, is dependent on the detection threshold ϑ. Opportunely varying the threshold ϑ, a different tradeoff between correct and false detections can be reached. This tradeoff can be estimated considering the *recall* and the *precision*. The recall is the proportion of objects that are detected, the precision is the fraction of corrected detected objects among the total number of detection made by the system. Denoting by TP the number of true positive, TF the number of false positive, nP and nF the total number of positives and negatives in the dataset, respectively, the performance measures are *Recall* $= TP/nP$ and *Precision* $= TP/(TP + FP)$, and the number of false detections can be computed as $1 - Precision$. It should be pointed out that precision-recall is a more appropriate measure than the common ROC curve, since this metric is designed for binary classification tasks, not for detection tasks [25].

The evaluation results have been obtained by manually determining the location of the windows containing interesting objects. Tables 2, 3 and 4 report the performance results for Cardata, USPS, and ORL, respectively, when different values of the dimensionality r of the subspace dataset approximation are adopted. NMF algorithms evidence some differences in terms of recall and precision, particularly NMF anf NMFsc provide better results than LNMF and DLPP. The performance of the latter algorithms is also quite bad on the ORL face dataset, which represents one of the easiest database in terms of recognition.

Figure 11 reports the results obtained after the on-line phase on a car test example. The picture on the top illustrates the query image; the remaining pictures provide the positive pixels provided by (a) NMF, (b) LNMF, (c) NMFsc, and (d) DLPP, respectively (trained with $r = 110$).

Figure 12 illustrates the results obtained after the on-line phase on a handwritten digit test example. The picture on

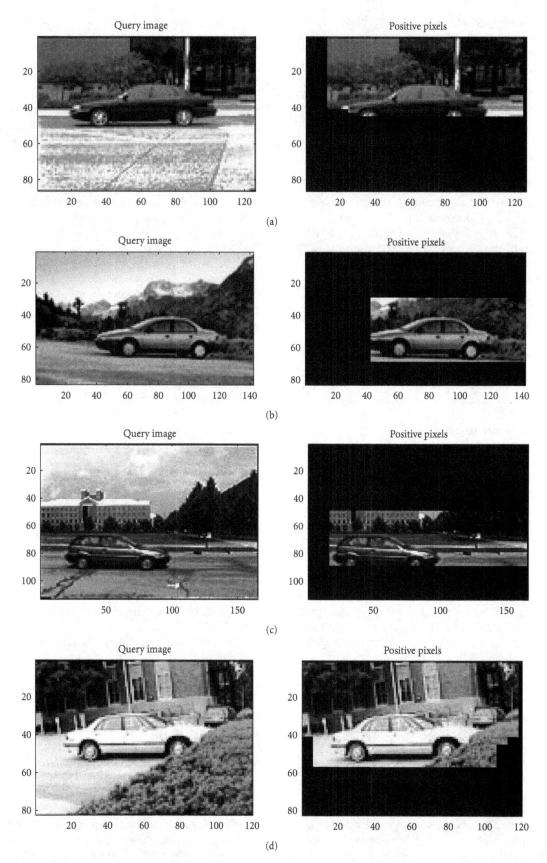

FIGURE 14: Output of the on-line detection phase after learning the CarData dataset: (a) NMF, (b) LNMF, (c) NMFsc, and (d) DLPP with $r = 110$ and $\vartheta = 2.6e^3$.

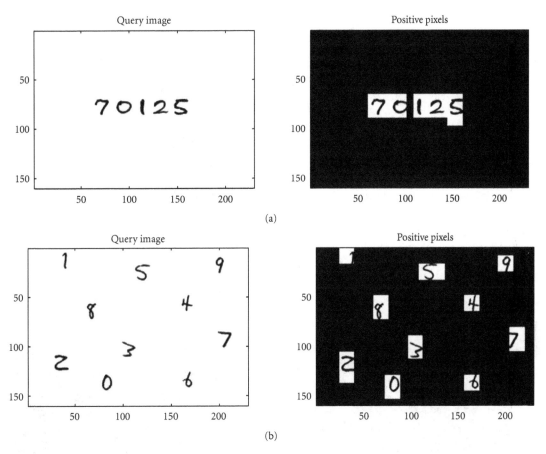

FIGURE 15: Output of the on-line detection phase after learning the USPS dataset: (a) NMF, (b) NMFsc with $r = 80$ and $\vartheta = 1.0e^8$.

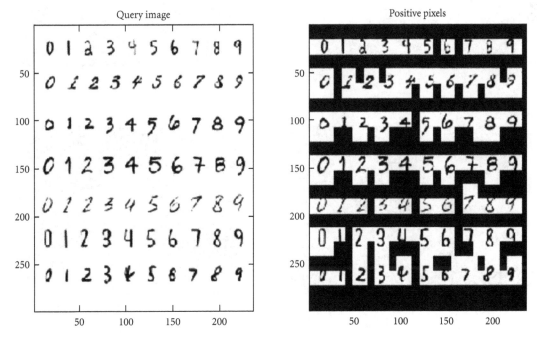

FIGURE 16: Output of the on-line detection phase on a white paper image presenting some handwritten digits. Test is made with NMFsc after learning the USPS dataset, with $r = 80$ and $\vartheta = 1.0e^8$.

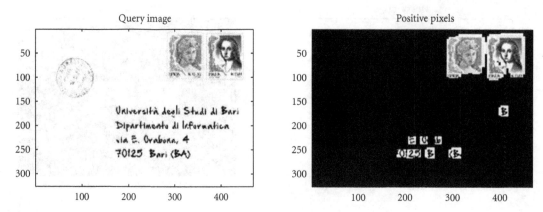

FIGURE 17: Output of the on-line detection phase on a letter envelope image presenting some handwritten digits. Test is made with LNMF after learning the USPS dataset, with $r = 80$ and $\vartheta = 2.3e^3$.

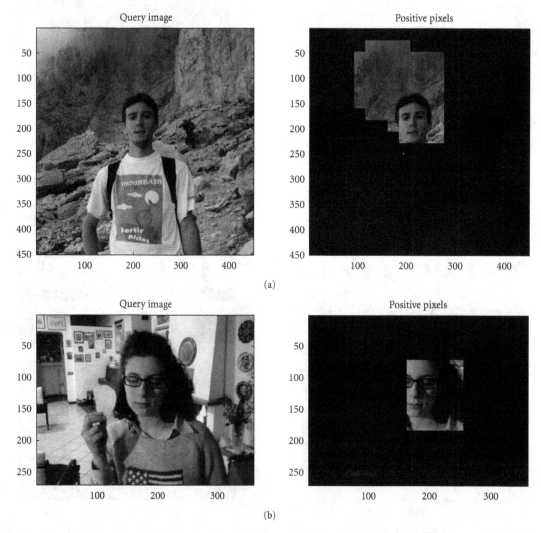

(a)

(b)

FIGURE 18: Output of the on-line detection phase after learning the ORL dataset. Test is made with NMFsc with $r = 20$ and $\vartheta = 2.4e^3$.

the top illustrates the query image, the remaining pictures provide the positive pixels provided by (a) NMF, (b) LNMF, (c) NMFsc, and (d) DLPP, respectively (trained with $r = 80$). As it can be noted the DLPP algorithm provides the worst result, since it locates all the background pixels around the digit images.

Figure 13 illustrates the results obtained after the on-line phase on a composited image with different ORL test images. Again, the picture on the top illustrates the query image, the remaining pictures provide the positive pixels provided by (a) NMF, (b) LNMF, (c) NMFsc, and (d) DLPP, respectively (trained with $r = 80$). Also in this case, the worst results are given by DLPP algorithm, which is not able to correctly locate all the ORL test images.

4.4. Qualitative Analysis in Natural Images. The following images illustrate the results obtained during the on-line detection phase for each considered algorithm with different query images. Particularly, Figure 14 provides an example of detection of a car inside some test images taken from the CarData test set.

Figure 15 illustrates the detection and location of some digit images inserted in a large scale image with white background while Figure 16 reports the detection/location results of some digit image written on a large white page. Figure 17 shows the detection of some handwritten digits presenting on an image of a real letter envelope. In the latter case, it could be observed that there are some false positive detections such as the two stamps and the letters in the address. This can be explained in the case of the stamps by considering their bigger dimension with respect to the sliding window and also the bases (see Figure 6) learnt by the algorithm, in the case of the letters by considering the inherent resemblance between some handwritten numbers and letters (such as "0" and "O," "B" and "8," "6" and "b").

Figure 18 gives evidence of the capability of NMF algorithms to recognize human face inside two real world pictures which portrait human figures with different backgrounds; as it can be observed the adopted algorithm is able to recognize the presence of a face different from the training faces learnt in the off-line training phase. This represents a confirmation that the part-based representation provided by NMF can effectively produce added value in detecting and locating objects inside images.

5. Conclusions and Future Work

To summarize, we have presented a prototype framework for learning how to detect and locate "generic" objects in images using the part-based representation provided by nonnegative matrix factorization of a set of template images. Comparisons between different NMF algorithms have been presented, evidencing that different additional constraints (such as sparseness) could be more suitable to identify localized parts describing some structures in object classes. Our experiments on the well-known databases demonstrated that the proposed NMF-based prototype system is able to extract such interpretable parts from a set of training images

in order to use them in localizing similar object in real world image.

Future work could be undertaken to allow the elaboration of object images with different scales, to improve final localization (using, for instance, a repeated part elimination algorithm), and to apply different criteria and/or measures to identify when a test image does or not belong to the subspace of known objects.

Acknowledgment

The authors would like to thank the anonymous referees for their suggestions and comments, which proved to be very useful for improving the paper.

References

[1] G. H. Golub and C. F. Van Loan, *Matrix Computations*, The Johns Hopkins University Press, 3rd edition, 2001.

[2] I. T. Jolliffe, *Principal Component Analysis*, Springer, 1986.

[3] A. Hyvarinen, "Independent component analysis," *Neural Computing Surveys*, vol. 2, 2001.

[4] D. Guillamet and J. Vitriá, "Non-negative matrix factorization for face recognition," *Lecture Notes in Computer Science*, vol. 2504, pp. 336–344, 2002.

[5] X. Sun, Q. Zhang, and Z. Wang, "Face recognition based on NMF and SVM," in *Proceedings of the 2nd International Symposium on Electronic Commerce and Security*, pp. 616–619, 2009.

[6] D. Guillamet and J. Vitrià, "Evaluation of distance metrics for recognition based on non-negative matrix factorization," *Pattern Recognition Letters*, vol. 24, no. 9-10, pp. 1599–1605, 2003.

[7] W. Liu and N. Zheng, "Non-negative matrix factorization based methods for object recognition," *Pattern Recognition Letters*, vol. 25, no. 8, pp. 893–897, 2004.

[8] Y. Gao and G. Church, "Improving molecular cancer class discovery through sparse non-negative matrix factorization," *Bioinformatics*, vol. 21, no. 21, pp. 3970–3975, 2005.

[9] H. Kim and H. Park, "Sparse non-negative matrix factorizations via alternating non-negativity-constrained least squares for microarray data analysis," *Bioinformatics*, vol. 23, no. 12, pp. 1495–1502, 2007.

[10] P. Paatero and U. Tapper, "Positive matrix factorization: a non-negative factor model with optimal utilization of error estimates of data values," *Environmetrics*, vol. 5, no. 2, pp. 111–126, 1994.

[11] D. D. Lee and S. H. Seung, "Algorithms for non-negative matrix factorization," in *Proceedings of the Advances in Neural Information Processing Systems Conference*, vol. 13, pp. 556–562, MIT Press, 2000.

[12] M. Novak and R. Mammone, "Use of nonnegative matrix factorization for language model adaptation in a lecture transcription task," in *Proceedings of the IEEE International Conference Acoustic, Speech and Signal Processing*, vol. 1, pp. 541–544, IEEE Computer Society, 2001.

[13] M. Chu and R. J. Plemmons, "Nonnegative matrix factorization and applications," *IMAGE, Bulletin of the International Linear Algebra Society*, vol. 34, pp. 2–7, 2005.

[14] V. P. Pauca, J. Piper, and R. J. Plemmons, "Nonnegative matrix factorization for spectral data analysis," *Linear Algebra and Its Applications*, vol. 416, no. 1, pp. 29–47, 2006.

[15] Chen D. and Plemmons R., "Nonnegativity constraints in numerical analysis," in *Proceedings of the Symposium on the Birth of Numerical Analysis*, pp. 541–544, World Scientific Press, 2008.

[16] D. D. Lee and H. S. Seung, "Learning the parts of objects by non-negative matrix factorization," *Nature*, vol. 401, no. 6755, pp. 788–791, 1999.

[17] M. A. Turk and A. P. Pentland, "Face recognition using eigenfaces," in *Proceedings of the IEEE Conference on Computer Vision and Pattern Recognition*, pp. 586–591, 1991.

[18] B. Schiele and J. L. Crowley, "Recognition without correspondence using multidimensional receptive field histograms," *International Journal of Computer Vision*, vol. 36, no. 1, pp. 31–50, 2000.

[19] I. Biederman, "Recognition-by-components: a theory of human image understanding," *Psychological Review*, vol. 94, no. 2, pp. 115–147, 1987.

[20] T. S. Lee, "Image representation using 2d gabor wavelets," *IEEE Transactions on Pattern Analysis and Machine Intelligence*, vol. 18, no. 10, pp. 959–971, 1996.

[21] R. N. Strickland and H. I. Hahn, "Wavelet transform methods for object detection and recovery," *IEEE Transactions on Image Processing*, vol. 6, no. 5, pp. 724–735, 1997.

[22] P. Viola and M. Jones, "Rapid object detection using a boosted cascade of simple features," in *Proceedings of the IEEE Computer Society Conference on Computer Vision and Pattern Recognition*, pp. I511–I518, December 2001.

[23] A. Mohan, C. Papageorgiou, and T. Poggio, "Example-based object detection in images by components," *IEEE Transactions on Pattern Analysis and Machine Intelligence*, vol. 23, no. 4, pp. 349–361, 2001.

[24] S. Ullman, M. Vidal-Naquet, and E. Sali, "Visual features of intermediate complexity and their use in classification," *Nature Neuroscience*, vol. 5, no. 7, pp. 682–687, 2002.

[25] S. Agarwal, A. Awan, and D. Roth, "Learning to detect objects in images via a sparse, part-based representation," *IEEE Transactions on Pattern Analysis and Machine Intelligence*, vol. 26, no. 11, pp. 1475–1490, 2004.

[26] D. Donoho and V. Stodden, "When does non-negative matrix factorization give a correct decomposition into parts?" in *Proceedings of the Neural Information Processing Systems*, vol. 16, pp. 1141–1149, 2003.

[27] B. J. Shastri and M. D. Levine, "Face recognition using localized features based on non-negative sparse coding," *Machine Vision and Applications*, vol. 18, no. 2, pp. 107–122, 2007.

[28] S. Z. Li, X. Hou, H. Zhang, and Q. S. Cheng, "Learning spatially localized, parts-based representation," in *Proceedings of the IEEE Computer Society Conference on Computer Vision and Pattern Recognition*, vol. 1, pp. 207–212, IEEE Computer Society, 2001.

[29] I. Buciu and I. Pitas, "A new sparse image representation algorithm applied to facial expression recognition," in *Proceedings of the 14th IEEE Signal Processing Society Workshop of the Machine Learning for Signal Processing*, pp. 539–548, October 2004.

[30] I. Buciu, "Learning sparse non-negative features for object recognition," in *Proceedings of the IEEE 3rd International Conference on Intelligent Computer Communication and Processing (ICCP '07)*, pp. 73–79, September 2007.

[31] P. O. Hoyer, "Non-negative matrix factorization with sparseness constraints," *Journal of Machine Learning Research*, vol. 5, pp. 1457–1469, 2004.

[32] D. Soukup and I. Bajla, "Robust object recognition under partial occlusions using NMF," *Computational Intelligence and Neuroscience*, vol. 2008, Article ID 857453, 14 pages, 2008.

[33] A. Berman and R. Plemmons, *Nonnegative Matrices in the Mathematical Sciences*, Academic Press, 1979.

[34] M. T. Chu, F. Diele, R. Plemmons, and S. Ragni, "Optimality, computation and interpretation of nonnegative matrix factorizations," Tech. Rep., NCSU, 2005.

[35] M. T. Chu and M. M. Lin, "Low-dimensional polytope approximation and its applications to nonnegative matrix factorization," *SIAM Journal on Scientific Computing*, vol. 30, no. 3, pp. 1131–1155, 2007.

[36] C.-J. Lin, "Projected gradient methods for nonnegative matrix factorization," *Neural Computation*, vol. 19, no. 10, pp. 2756–2779, 2007.

[37] C. Ding, T. Li, W. Peng, and H. Park, "Orthogonal nonnegative matrix tri-factorizations for clustering," in *Proceedings of the 12th ACM SIGKDD International Conference on Knowledge Discovery and Data Mining (KDD '06)*, pp. 126–135, August 2006.

[38] S. Choi, "Algorithms for orthogonal nonnegative matrix factorization," in *Proceedings of the International Joint Conference on Neural Networks (IJCNN '08)*, pp. 1828–1832, June 2008.

[39] N. Del Buono, "A penalty function for computing orthogonal non-negative matrix factorizations," in *Proceedings of the 9th International Conference on Intelligent Systems Design and Applications (ISDA '09)*, pp. 1001–1005, December 2009.

[40] C. Ding, T. Li, and W. Peng, "Nonnegative matrix factorization and probabilistic latent semantic indexing: equivalence, chi-square statistic, and a hybrid method," in *Proceedings of the 21st National Conference on Artificial Intelligence and the 18th Innovative Applications of Artificial Intelligence Conference (AAAI '06)*, pp. 342–347, July 2006.

[41] C. Ding, X. He, and H. D. Simon, "On the equivalence of nonnegative matrix factorization and spectral clustering," in *Proceedings of the SIAM Data Mining Conference*, pp. 606–610, 2005.

[42] K. Murphy, A. Torralba, D. Eaton, and W. Freeman, "Object detection and localization using local and global features," *Lecture Notes in Computer Science*, vol. 4170, pp. 394–412, 2006.

15

Discovery of Characteristic Patterns from Transactions with Their Classes

Shigeaki Sakurai[1, 2]

[1] *Business Intelligence Laboratory and Advanced IT Laboratory, Toshiba Solutions Corporation, Tokyo 183-8512, Japan*
[2] *Department of Computational Intelligence and Systems Science, Interdisciplinary Graduate School of Science and Engineering, Tokyo Institute of Technology, Kanagawa 226-8502, Japan*

Correspondence should be addressed to Shigeaki Sakurai, sakurai@hrt.dis.titech.ac.jp

Academic Editor: Tzung P. Hong

This paper deals with transactions with their classes. The classes represent the difference of conditions in the data collection. This paper redefines two kinds of supports: characteristic support and possible support. The former one is based on specific classes assigned to specific patterns. The latter one is based on the minimum class in the classes. This paper proposes a new method that efficiently discovers patterns whose characteristic supports are larger than or equal to the predefined minimum support by using their possible supports. Also, this paper verifies the effect of the method through numerical experiments based on the data registered in the UCI machine learning repository and the RFID (radio frequency identification) data collected from two apparel shops.

1. Introduction

Owing to the progress of computer environment and network environment, we can easily collect large amount of data and cheaply store it. We believe that the data includes useful knowledge which can help our decision making. Many researchers tackle on the discovery of the knowledge from the data since the mid-1990s. Various discovery tasks are studied in order to deal with various kinds of data.

The discovery task of frequent patterns composed of items from transactions is one of the tasks. Each transaction is composed of an item set. In the retail field, a receipt and a sales item correspond to a transaction and an item, respectively. In the initial researches, [1] proposes a method that efficiently generates candidate patterns and discovers frequent patterns by using the Apriori property. Here, the property shows that the frequencies of patterns monotonically decrease as items composing the patterns increase. Reference [2] proposes a bitmap index, [3] proposes a vertical ID list, and [4] proposes a frequent pattern tree (FP-tree) in order to speedily access the transactions and efficiently calculate the frequencies of the patterns. It is possible for these improvements to speedily discover the frequent patterns.

However, the discovered frequent patterns are not always the ones that are attractive for analysts. The discovery of patterns with different features is tried. For example, [5] tries to discover patterns whose orders based on the frequency are higher than the predefined order. Reference [6] does closed patterns representing many frequent patterns. Reference [7] does long patterns including many items. Reference [8] does patterns reflecting weights of items. Reference [9] does patterns reflecting hierarchical relationships among items. It is anticipated that more attractive patterns are discovered by these researches.

On the other hand, the discovery of patterns from different kinds of data is tried. For example, [10] tries to deal with tabular structured data. Here, each item is composed of an attribute and an attribute value. It proposes a method that efficiently discovers frequent patterns from the data by using relationships between attributes and attribute values. In the case of the data, missing values are often included. In order to deal with the values, [10–12] propose new evaluation criteria of the patterns.

The discovery task of patterns from transactions is expanding its research field more and more. This paper focuses on the difference of conditions in the data collection as one of expanding fields. This is because we would like to discover patterns which tend to be overlooked due to the difference. For example, we try to discover patterns of sales items from a chain of retail stores. If we collect the data from many stores, we cannot anticipate that each store sells the same items. Limited stores can sell specific items such as new items and regional items. It is difficult to discover patterns related to the items sold in the limited stores. This is because their sales volume tends to be much smaller than the one of items sold in all stores. Also, we cannot anticipate that each store sells the same items every day. It can sell seasoned items. Patterns related to the seasoned items tend to be overlooked. In addition, we cannot anticipate that each store sells items based on the same sales method. Customers may be able to buy items through the trial of items in a store. Patterns related to the trial tend to be buried in patterns unrelated to the one. We can easily find difference of conditions in the data collection. It is anticipated that more attractive patterns are discovered, if we reflect the difference in the discovery of patterns.

Thus, this paper regards the difference of conditions in the data collection as classes. It proposes a method that efficiently discovers patterns reflecting the classes. Also, this paper applies the method to the data registered in the UCI machine learning repository [13] and the RFID (radio frequency identification) data collected from apparel shops [14]. It compares patterns discovered by the proposed method with patterns discovered by an existing discovery method, verifies the validity of the patterns discovered by the proposed method, and shows the effect of the proposed method.

2. Discovery of Characteristic Patterns

2.1. Transactions with Their Classes. This paper regards an item set with a class as a transaction. That is, the transaction t is defined by Formula (1). In this formula, I is a set of all items, C is a set of all classes, and n is the number of items included in the transaction. C_{it_i} is a subset of C and is composed of classes where the item it_i can be included. This definition shows that the transaction does not have multiple same items. The constraint is introduced by the original discovery task [1] which does not deal with classes. It notes whether an item is sold or not. Also, this definition shows that each item is included in the class cl

$$t = (\text{cl} \mid it_1, it_2, \ldots, it_n), \quad it_i \in I, \ \text{cl} \in \bigcap_{\forall i} C_{it_i} \subseteq C, \tag{1}$$

$$\text{if } k \neq l, \text{ then } it_k \neq it_l.$$

Here, we note that the examples are composed of four classes: "spring", "summer", "autumn", and "winter", and three items: "apple", "watermelon", and "banana". Table 1 shows classes in which each item is sold. The set of classes corresponding to an item is called an item class hereafter. Tables 2 and 3 show legal examples and illegal ones, respectively.

In Table 2, t_1 is a transaction with its class, because "winter" is included in the item classes of "apple" and "banana". Also, t_2 is a transaction with its class, because "summer" is

TABLE 1: Item class.

Item	Class
apple	{autumn, winter}
watermelon	{spring, summer}
banana	{spring, summer, autumn, winter}

TABLE 2: Legal examples.

t_1 = (winter | apple, banana)
t_2 = (summer | watermelon, banana)

TABLE 3: Illegal examples.

t_3 = (autumn | apple, apple, banana)
t_4 = (spring | apple, watermelon)

included in the item classes of "watermelon" and "banana". In Table 3, t_3 is not a transaction with its class, because two "apple" are included in t_3. Also, t_4 is not a transaction with its class, because the item class of "apple" does not include "spring". Some readers may think that this restriction is too strict. However, it is not always strict. This is because we can add "spring" to the item class of "apple" if we need to regard t_4 as a transaction with its class. On the other hand, if a valid item class is assigned to each item, we can think of two possibilities. One is that the class in the transaction is wrong, and the other is that wrong items are included in the item set. We can think that some errors occur in the data collection.

2.2. Criteria. This section considers a method dealing with transactions with their classes. Also, it considers a method that discovers important patterns composed of items from the transactions. Here, we note that the numbers of the transactions with specific classes are not always equal to each other. That is, the number of transactions corresponding to a class can be large, and the one corresponding to another class can be small. Therefore, the numbers of items corresponding to the former class tend to be frequent, and patterns composed of the items tend to be frequent.

For example, transactions and item classes as shown in Table 4 are given. Also, they have three patterns composed of two items: (it_1, it_2), (it_1, it_3), and (it_2, it_3). Their frequencies are 4, 2, and 1, respectively. (it_1, it_2) is the most frequent pattern in the three patterns. Here, we note the ratio of the frequencies to the number of transactions where the patterns can be included. (it_1, it_2) can be included in all transactions $(t_1 \sim t_8)$. This is because both the item class of it_1 and the one of it_2 are $\{cl_1, cl_2\}$, and the class set corresponding to (it_1, it_2) is $\{cl_1, cl_2\}$. The ratio of (it_1, it_2) is 0.50(=4/8). On the other hand, (it_1, it_3) can be included in three transactions $(t_6 \sim t_8)$. This is because the item class of it_3 is $\{cl_2\}$. The ratio of (it_1, it_3) is 0.67(=2/3). Similarly, (it_2, it_3) can be included in three transactions $(t_6 \sim t_8)$. The ratio of (it_2, it_3) is 0.33(=1/3). Therefore, (it_1, it_3) is the pattern with the biggest ratio, and it is the most important pattern in the three patterns.

We anticipate that the important pattern based on the ratio is more valid than the frequent pattern because the

TABLE 4: An example of transactions and item classes (1).

(a) Transaction

$t_1 = (cl_1 \mid it_1)$
$t_2 = (cl_1 \mid it_1, it_2)$
$t_3 = (cl_1 \mid it_1, it_2)$
$t_4 = (cl_1 \mid it_1, it_2)$
$t_5 = (cl_1 \mid it_1, it_2)$
$t_6 = (cl_2 \mid it_1, it_3)$
$t_7 = (cl_2 \mid it_1, it_3)$
$t_8 = (cl_2 \mid it_2, it_3)$

(b) Item class

Item	Class
it_1	$\{cl_1, cl_2\}$
it_2	$\{cl_1, cl_2\}$
it_3	$\{cl_2\}$

TABLE 5: An example of transactions and item classes (2).

(a) Transaction

$t_1 = (cl_1 \mid it_1)$
$t_2 = (cl_3 \mid it_3)$
$t_3 = (cl_2 \mid it_2)$
$t_4 = (cl_2 \mid it_1, it_2)$
$t_5 = (cl_2 \mid it_1, it_2)$

(b) Item class

Item	Class
it_1	$\{cl_1, cl_2, cl_3\}$
it_2	$\{cl_2\}$
it_3	$\{cl_3\}$

latter one is often a well-known pattern and does not give a big impact to analysts. It is necessary to define a new criterion corresponding to the ratio. Formula (2) shows the definition. It is based on an idea similar to the support for missing values in tabular structured data [10, 11]. The criterion is called a characteristic support hereafter

$$\text{supp}_{\text{char}}(p) = \frac{N_p}{N_{C_p}}, \quad C_p = \bigcap_{it_i \in p} C_{it_i}. \tag{2}$$

In Formula (2), p is a pattern composed of items. N_p is the number of transactions including p. C_p is such a class set that all items composing p can be included. N_{C_p} is the number of transactions whose classes are included in C_p. C_p and N_{C_p} are called a pattern class and a total transaction number for C_p hereafter. We note that C_p can be ϕ. However, if $C_p = \phi$, N_p is 0. It is not necessary to calculate the characteristic support of p. Therefore, it is not necessary to care about the possibility $C_p = \phi$. Also, we note that the characteristic support is in $[0, 1]$. This is because N_p is smaller than or equal to N_{C_p}.

We can anticipate that if the discovery method extracts patterns whose characteristic supports are larger than or equal to a predefined threshold, the patterns can reflect the class distribution in transactions. However, the patterns may be accidentally extracted from a very small transaction subset. We cannot always believe that the patterns are characteristic. Thus, this paper introduces the other criterion assuring the minimum frequency of the pattern. The criterion is equal to the representativity introduced by [12].

This paper tries to discover patterns satisfying two conditions: the minimum support and the minimum frequency. That is, if the characteristic supports of the patterns are larger than or equal to the minimum support and their frequencies are larger than or equal to the minimum frequency, the patterns are extracted as characteristic patterns. In the case of transactions without their classes, these conditions are equal to each other. This is because if the support of a pattern p_1 is always larger than the one of the other pattern p_2 in the

latter case, the frequency of p_1 is larger than the one of p_2. It is sufficient for the transactions without their classes to evaluate one of the conditions.

Next, we note the property of characteristic supports and frequencies. If two patterns p_1 and p_2 satisfy the relationship $p_1 \subseteq p_2$, the frequency of p_1 is clearly larger than or equal to the one of p_2. The frequencies monotonically decrease as patterns grow. However, the monotonic property is not always satisfied in the case of the characteristic supports. For example, we note transactions and item classes as shown in Table 5.

Table 5 shows that the frequency of it_1 is 3 and the total transaction number for it_1 is 5. This is because it_1 is included in three item classes cl_1, cl_2, and cl_3. The characteristic support of it_1 is 0.60(=3/5). Also, Table 5 shows that the frequency of (it_1, it_2) is 2 and the total transaction number for (it_1, it_2) is 3. This is because a pattern class of (it_1, it_2) is $\{cl_2\}$. The characteristic support of (it_1, it_2) is 0.67(=2/3). This example shows that the monotonic property is not satisfied.

The monotonic property is very important for the discovery method of patterns in order to efficiently discover them. The method can avoid their redundant evaluation by using the property. Therefore, it is difficult for the characteristic support to efficiently discover patterns. Certainly, we can try to discover patterns based on the monotonic property of the frequency. However, the frequency is a limited criterion. The minimum frequency tends to be set as a small value. We cannot anticipate that sufficient efficiency is gained by the frequency.

Thus, this paper introduces another criterion. The criterion is based on an idea similar to the possible support proposed by [10]. The support reflects missing values in tabular structured data. This paper redefines the possible support in order to deal with transactions with their classes. Formula (3) shows the definition. In Formula (3), N_{cl_i} is the number of transactions assigned class cl_i. $\min_{cl_i \in C_p} \{N_{cl_i}\}$ is called the minimum transaction number for p hereafter

$$\text{supp}_{\text{pos}}(p) = \frac{N_p}{\min_{cl_i \in C_p} \{N_{cl_i}\}}. \tag{3}$$

The redefined possible support is larger than or equal to 0 and can be larger than or equal to 1. This is because N_p can be larger than $\min_{\mathrm{cl}_i \in C_p}\{N_{\mathrm{cl}_i}\}$. Also, the redefined possible support satisfies the monotonic property. The reason is shown in the following. Firstly, we note the numerator of the formula. The numerator is the frequency of a pattern and monotonically decreases. On the other hand, if two patterns p_1 and p_2 have the relationship $p_2 \supseteq p_1$, the relationship $C_{p_2} \subseteq C_{p_1}$ is clearly satisfied. Thus, $\min_{\mathrm{cl}_i \in C_{p_2}}\{N_{\mathrm{cl}_i}\} \geq \min_{\mathrm{cl}_i \in C_{p_1}}\{N_{\mathrm{cl}_i}\}$. That is, the denominator monotonically increases as the patterns grow. Therefore, the possible supports monotonically decrease as the patterns grow.

Next, we note the relationships between the characteristic support and the possible support. The formulae of these supports show that the numerators are equal to each other. Also, they show that the relationship $N_{C_p} \geq \min_{\mathrm{cl}_i \in C_p}\{N_{\mathrm{cl}_i}\}$ is satisfied in any patterns. Therefore, the relationship described in Formula (4) is always satisfied

$$\mathrm{supp}_{\mathrm{pos}}(p) \geq \mathrm{supp}_{\mathrm{char}}. \tag{4}$$

Formula (4) shows that the possible support of a pattern p_1 gives the upper bound to characteristic supports of any super patterns $(\supseteq p_1)$. Therefore, if the possible support of p_1 is smaller than the minimum support, the characteristic supports of the supper patterns are smaller than the minimum support. The supper patterns cannot be characteristic patterns. Thus, the discovery method keeps patterns whose possible supports are larger than or equal to the minimum support and whose frequencies are larger than or equal to the minimum frequency in order to grow them. The patterns are called possible patterns hereafter. Also, the discovery method extracts patterns whose characteristic supports are larger than or equal to the minimum support from the possible patterns. The discovery method based on the two-stepwise evaluation method can efficiently discover all characteristic patterns.

2.3. Discovery Method. This paper proposes a method that discovers all characteristic patterns from transactions with their classes. The method is based on the FP tree and the FP growth proposed by [4]. Here, the FP tree is the data structure storing transactions with tree format. The FP growth is a method discovering all frequent patterns by using the FP tree. The FP growth generates the FP trees from transaction subsets and generates new transaction subsets from generated FP trees. Two kinds of generation steps are recursively repeated. This paper proposes the refined FP tree and the refined FP growth in order to deal with transactions with classes.

The original FP tree is composed of nodes assigned an item name and its frequency, links tying to the nodes with the same item name, a header table storing item, and links tying to items in the table with nodes including the item names. In the FP tree, the root node is a special node and is assigned "null". The refined FP tree is basically equal to the original one. But, the refined one is assigned a pattern class and an identification flag to each item in the header table. Here, the flag shows whether the pattern corresponding to each item in the header table is included in a characteristic pattern. The refined FP tree is generated by an algorithm as

TABLE 6: A generation method of the refined FP tree.

(1) Search transaction and calculate frequencies of each item.

(2) **Calculate a product set between a pattern class C_{Its} of a conditioned item set Its and an item class C_{it_i} of each item it_i, and set the product set as a pattern class C_{p_i} of a pattern p_i (=Its $\cup$ it$_i$).**

(3) **Calculate the total number and the minimum number for p_i.**

(4) **Calculate a characteristic support and a possible support of p_i.**

(5) Repeat from step 2 to step 4 for any i.

(6) **Extract items whose patterns are possible patterns and generate a list Flist arranged the items in descending order, where the first key is the frequency, the second key is the characteristic support, and the third key is the possible support.**

(7) Regard Flist as a header table H in a refined FP tree T. **Also, tie C_{p_i} to it$_i$ in H. In addition, tie an identification flag fl$_i$ of p_i to it$_i$ in H. Here, if the pattern corresponding to it$_i$ is a characteristic pattern, the value of fl$_i$ is "C". Otherwise the value is "P". That is, "C" shows that the pattern is a characteristic pattern and "P" shows that the pattern is not a characteristic pattern and is a possible pattern.**

(8) Create a root node of T and assign the label "null" to it.

(9) Set the root node as a target node N.

(10) Pick up a transaction t_j. If the transaction cannot be picked up, then this algorithm stops.

(11) Pick up only items included in H from t_j, sort them in the order of items in H, and create a selected and sorted item set Its_{t_j}.

(12) Pick up an item it_{jk} from the top of Its_{t_j}. If the item cannot be picked up, then go to step 10.

(13) If an item name of it_{jk} is assigned to a child node of N, then the frequency of the node is counted up. Otherwise, a new node N' is created. N' is assigned the item name of it_{jk} and is set 1 to the frequency. Also, create a link between N and N', and register N' to it_{jk} in H. In addition, regard a selected child node or N' as a new target node N.

(14) Go to step 12.

shown in Table 6 from transactions with their classes, item classes, and a conditioned item set. In the first generation of the refined FP tree, the conditioned item set is ϕ. In the generation except the first one, it is at least possible patterns. In this algorithm, the minimum support ($\in (0,1]$) and the minimum frequency (≥ 1) are predefined. Table 6 describes the difference of the generation method for the original one with bold style.

In the following, we show an example which generates the refined FP tree from transactions and item classes as shown in Table 7.

In this case, the item set is ϕ. The minimum support is 0.5 and the minimum frequency is 1. The transactions of Table 7 show that frequencies of $\mathrm{it}_1 \sim \mathrm{it}_9$ are 6, 3, 3, 4, 3, 2, 1, 1, and 1, respectively. The item classes of Table 7 show that the total transaction numbers for it_1, it_2, it_4, it_5, and it_9 are 7, the ones for it_3 and it_8 are 3, and the ones for it_6 and it_7 are 4. Also, it shows that the minimum transaction

TABLE 7: An example of transactions and item classes (3).

(a) Transaction

$t_1 = (\text{cl}_1 \mid \text{it}_1, \text{it}_2, \text{it}_3, \text{it}_5)$
$t_2 = (\text{cl}_1 \mid \text{it}_1, \text{it}_3, \text{it}_4)$
$t_3 = (\text{cl}_1 \mid \text{it}_1, \text{it}_2, \text{it}_3, \text{it}_4, \text{it}_8)$
$t_4 = (\text{cl}_2 \mid \text{it}_1, \text{it}_2, \text{it}_4, \text{it}_7)$
$t_5 = (\text{cl}_2 \mid \text{it}_4, \text{it}_5, \text{it}_6)$
$t_6 = (\text{cl}_2 \mid \text{it}_1, \text{it}_5, \text{it}_6)$
$t_7 = (\text{cl}_2 \mid \text{it}_1, \text{it}_9)$

(b) Item class

Item	Class
it_1	$\{\text{cl}_1, \text{cl}_2\}$
it_2	$\{\text{cl}_1, \text{cl}_2\}$
it_3	$\{\text{cl}_1\}$
it_4	$\{\text{cl}_1, \text{cl}_2\}$
it_5	$\{\text{cl}_1, \text{cl}_2\}$
it_6	$\{\text{cl}_2\}$
it_7	$\{\text{cl}_2\}$
it_8	$\{\text{cl}_1\}$
it_9	$\{\text{cl}_1, \text{cl}_2\}$

TABLE 8: A selected and sorted transaction subset.

$t'_1 = (\text{it}_1, \text{it}_3, \text{it}_2, \text{it}_5)$
$t'_2 = (\text{it}_1, \text{it}_4, \text{it}_3)$
$t'_3 = (\text{it}_1, \text{it}_4, \text{it}_3, \text{it}_2)$
$t'_4 = (\text{it}_1, \text{it}_4, \text{it}_2)$
$t'_5 = (\text{it}_4, \text{it}_5, \text{it}_6)$
$t'_6 = (\text{it}_1, \text{it}_5, \text{it}_6)$
$t'_7 = (\text{it}_1)$

numbers for it_1, it_2, it_3, it_4, it_5, it_8, and it_9 are 3 and the ones for it_6 and it_7 are 4. Possible supports of $\text{it}_1 \sim \text{it}_9$ are 2.00(=6/3), 1.00(=3/3), 1.00(=3/3), 1.33(=4/3), 1.00(=3/3), 0.50(=2/4), 0.25(=1/4), 0.33(=1/3), and 0.33(=1/3), respectively. Therefore, the generation method can select it_1, it_2, it_3, it_4, it_5, and it_6 as possible items. The items are arranged in the descending order of frequencies, characteristic supports, and possible supports. The method generates the list Flist such as (it_1, it_4, it_3, it_2, it_5, it_6). But, indexes of the items are used as the fourth key, if three criteria are equal to each other.

Next, the method picks up possible items from the transactions and arranges the items in order of the Flist. It generates a selected and sorted transaction subset as shown in Table 8. The subset is used in order to generate the refined FP tree.

In the case that t'_1 is selected from the subset, the method generates a part of the refined FP-tree as shown in Figure 1(a). Also, in the case that t'_2 is selected from the subset, it generates a part of the refined FP tree as shown in Figure 1(b). That is, the method adds new nodes or updates the frequencies of the existing node in order from the root

node. Lastly, the refined FP tree as shown in Figure 2 is generated.

In the remaining part of this subsection, we explain the refined FP growth. The original FP growth detects a single prefix path. The path is a path linked from the root. Each node included in the path has only a child. If an FP tree has the single prefix path, the original FP growth divides the FP-tree into the single prefix path and the remaining part. The remaining part is added a new root node and a new FP tree is generated. The original FP growth separately discovers frequent patterns from the new FP-tree and from the single prefix path. Also, it combines the patterns based on the tree with the patterns based on the path. The combined patterns are frequent patterns. The original FP growth can discover all frequent patterns based on the combination.

On the other hand, in the case of the refined FP growth, we do not know whether characteristic supports increase as patterns grow. Even if characteristic patterns based on a single prefix path are given and characteristic patterns based on a new refined FP tree are given, their combinations are not always characteristic patterns. It is necessary to check whether the combinations are characteristic patterns by calculating their characteristic supports. The detection of the single prefix path does not give sufficient merits. Thus, the refined FP growth tries to discover characteristic patterns without detecting a single prefix path. In the following, we explain the FP growth without the detection.

The refined FP growth picks up an item it from the rear of Flist in the refined FP tree in order. It generates transactions conditioned by it. That is, the refined FP growth extracts nodes including it from the refined FP tree and extracts paths from upper nodes of the extracted nodes to the root node. A transaction is generated from each path and is assigned frequency which is equal to the frequency of the node including it. The refined FP growth generates a new refined FP tree from the conditioned transactions. it is added to the conditioned item set Its. Here, Its is assigned to the previous refined FP tree and is ϕ in the first process of the refined FP growth. The refined FP growth recursively repeats the generation of refined FP trees and conditioned transactions.

On the other hand, the refined FP growth needs pattern classes in order to calculate characteristic supports and possible supports. The pattern classes can be generated by referring to both items included in the patterns and their item classes. However, if the generation is always started from scratch, it is redundant. We can generate the pattern classes more efficiently by using a relationship among pattern classes. That is, if a pattern p' is generated by the combination of a pattern p and a new item it, a pattern class ($C_{p'}$) of p' is equal to the product set ($C_p \cap C_{it}$) based on both a pattern class (C_p) of p and an item class (C_{it}) of it. Therefore, the header table keeps pattern classes.

According to the above discussion, the refined FP growth is described as shown in Table 9. Table 9 describes the difference between the original FP growth and the refined one with bold style. The refined FP tree T and Its are input to the refined FP growth.

Lastly, a discovery method of characteristic patterns is described as shown in Table 10. The method appropriately

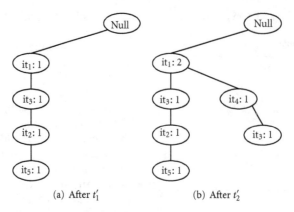

(a) After t'_1 (b) After t'_2

FIGURE 1: Refined FP tree (1).

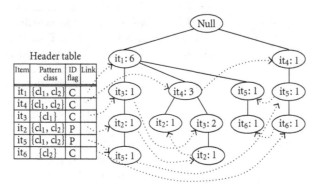

FIGURE 2: Refined FP tree (2).

TABLE 9: An algorithm of the refined FP growth algorithm.		TABLE 10: A discovery method of characteristic patterns.

TABLE 9: An algorithm of the refined FP growth algorithm.

(1) Extract an item it from the rear of Flist in a refined FP tree T. If the item is not extracted, this algorithm stops.

(2) Add it to an item set Its and **investigate an identification flag of it. If the flag shows a characteristic pattern, then output Its as a characteristic pattern.**

(3) Extract a node N whose item is equal to it from T. If the node is not extracted, then go to step 6.

(4) Extract a path from the upper node of N to the root. Generate an item set composed of item included in the extracted path and extract the frequency assigned to N. Regard the combination of the item set and the frequency as a transaction conditioned by it.

(5) Go to step 3.

(6) Apply a set Trans of the generated transactions to the algorithm shown in Table 6 and generate a new refined FP tree T'. If T' is not generated, then this algorithm stops. Otherwise, this algorithm recursively calls by giving T' and Its to it as arguments.

(7) Go to step 1.

TABLE 10: A discovery method of characteristic patterns.

(1) Search transactions and calculate the number of transactions for each class.

(2) Set ϕ to an item set Its and set all classes to its pattern class.

(3) Generate a refined FP tree T based on the algorithm shown in Table 6.

(4) If T is not generated, then this algorithm stops. Otherwise, it discovers characteristic patterns from T and Its based on the algorithm shown in Table 9.

3. Numerical Experiments

3.1. Data. This paper uses the UCI data sets registered in the UCI machine learning repository for numerical experiments. Also, it uses the RFID data sets collected from two apparel shops. In the case of the UCI data sets, three data sets "car", "hayes", and "nursery" are selected. This is because each data set is a data set for the classification task and is composed of discrete values. These data sets are tabular structured data. Each example in the data sets is composed of attribute values and a class and is regarded as a transaction. Then, the combination of an attribute and an attribute value is regarded as an item. A class of an example is regarded as a class of a transaction. The item classes are generated by checking the combinations of attribute values and classes. Table 11 shows features of transactions generated from the UCI data sets.

calls the algorithms as shown in Tables 6 and 9. It can generate all characteristic patterns from transactions with their classes, item classes, the minimum support, and the minimum frequency.

TABLE 11: UCI data sets.

Data set	Item	Transaction	Class
Car	21	1728	4
Hayes	15	160	3
Nursery	27	12960	5

TABLE 12: RFID data sets.

Shop	No fitting	Fitting
α shop	3695	1372
β shop	7612	1849

The RFID data sets are data sets collected in order to analyze a relationship between sales volume and actions of customers in the shops. RFID readers are set to fitting rooms, shelves, and cash registers, and RFID tags are assigned to sales items. We can grasp the actions of the customers by chasing the items to some extent. In this experiment, we regard the difference between fitting items and no fitting items as classes. This is because the fitting of items is one of the important customer actions but its frequency is not always high. Table 12 shows the distribution of classes in transactions. We can confirm that the number of fitting items is much smaller than the one of no fitting items.

3.2. Method. We compare the proposed method with the existing method [4], but the process of a single prefix path is not incorporated in it. The existing method is a discovery method of frequent patterns. It does not deal with classes. Also, it ignores classes assigned to transactions and item classes corresponding to each item. The proposed method aims at discovering at most hundreds of patterns. The minimum supports and the minimum frequencies are adjusted.

In the case of the UCI data sets, the proposed method discovers characteristic patterns by changing the minimum frequencies. The minimum support is fixed. Also, the proposed method outputs possible patterns in order to evaluate investigated patterns. On the other hand, the existing method discovers frequent patterns by changing the minimum frequencies. The minimum support is directly calculated by referring to the frequencies. The frequencies depend on both the minimum supports and the minimum frequencies of the proposed method. This experiment evaluates relationships between discovered patterns, minimum supports, and minimum frequencies.

In the case of the RFID data sets, this experiment focuses on the difference of characteristic patterns and frequent patterns. The proposed method and the existing method discover patterns by changing the minimum supports. The minimum frequency in the proposed method is fixed. This experiment evaluates the validity of the discovered patterns.

3.3. Experimental Results. Figures 3, 4, and 5 show experimental results in the case of the UCI data sets: "cars", "hayes", and "nursery", respectively. Graph (a) and Graph (b) show the difference of characteristic patterns and frequent patterns. Graph (a) shows the total number of patterns. In this

graph, we do not care about the number of items included in patterns. The number is called the length hereafter.

Graph (b) shows the difference of characteristic patterns and frequent patterns in the case of specific length. The lengths in the case of "cars," "hayes," and "nursery," are 2, 2, and 3, respectively. In each graph, "Class only" shows the number of patterns discovered only by the proposed method. "Class common" shows the numbers discovered by both the proposed method and the existing method. "No class only" shows the numbers discovered only by the existing method. But, in the case of the proposed method, the minimum support is fixed to 0.100. Also, the minimum frequencies in the case of "car" are 9, 18, 52, 87, and 173. The ones in the case of "hayes" are 1, 2, 5, 8, and 16. The ones in the case of "nursery" are 65, 130, 389, 649, and 1297. They correspond to the minimum supports of the existing method: 0.005, 0.010, 0.030, 0.050, and 0.100. In the case of the existing method, the minimum frequency for the data sets: "car", "hayes", and "nursery" are fixed and they are 173, 16, and 1297, respectively. They correspond to the minimum support 0.100.

Graph (c) shows the difference of possible patterns and frequent patterns. The thresholds in the proposed method are equal to the case of Graph (a) and Graph (b). The minimum supports in the existing method are changed according to the frequencies in the proposed method. In each graph, "Class" shows the total number of possible patterns and "No class" shows the total number of frequent patterns.

Graph (d) shows the calculation time of both the proposed method and the existing method. But, the calculation time of the existing method is estimated by modifying the program code of the proposed method. That is, the calculation of the characteristic support and the possible support, and the evaluation based on them are gotten rid of the program code. On the other hand, other additional processes are left because their calculation cost is comparatively small. The modified program code is used to the estimation of the calculation time for the existing method. In the experiment, the calculation time is measured by using the DOS command "time" with millisecond unit. The experiment uses the computer environment such as Windows 7 Home Premium Service Pack 1 and TOSHIBA dynabook Satellite PXW/59KW loading Intel Core(TM)2 Duo CPU T9600@2.80 GHz and 4.00 GB RAM memory. The program code is described by C language and is compiled by gcc command in MinGW-5.1.6.exe. In the case of the proposed method, the minimum support is fixed to 0.100 and the minimum frequencies are changed. The frequencies are used in the evaluation of the existing method.

In these graphs, horizontal axes are the minimum supports, and vertical axes except Graph (d) are the number of patterns. In Graph (d), vertical axes are the calculation time, and their calculation unit is millisecond.

Figure 6 shows experimental results in the case of the RFID data sets. In this experiment, the minimum frequency is 2 in the proposed method. The minimum supports are changed from 0.001 to 0.005 per 0.001 in the proposed method and the existing method. Graph (a) and Graph (b) show the total number of patterns in the case of α shop and β shop, respectively. In these graphs, "Class only",

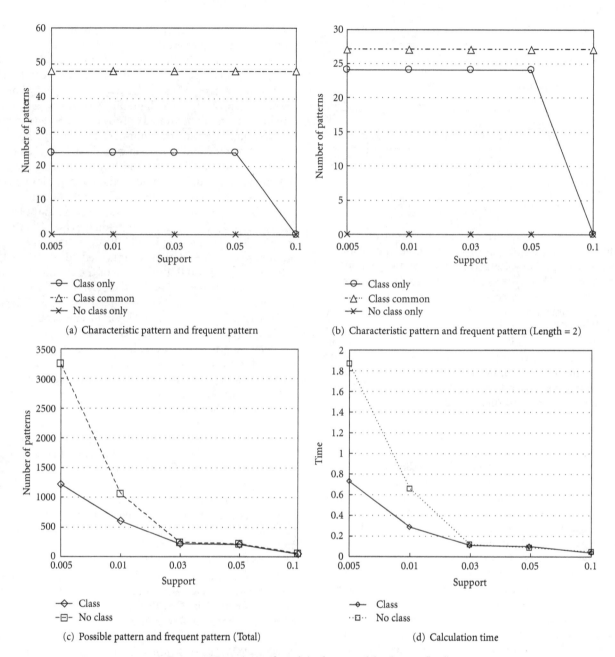

(a) Characteristic pattern and frequent pattern

(b) Characteristic pattern and frequent pattern (Length = 2)

(c) Possible pattern and frequent pattern (Total)

(d) Calculation time

FIGURE 3: Experimental result in the case of the data set "car".

"Class common", "No class", and the axes correspond to the ones in the case of the UCI data sets. On the other hand, Tables 13 and 14 show patterns discovered only by the proposed method from each shop. In these tables, the minimum support is 0.001, and the length is larger than or equal to 2.

3.4. Discussions. This section discusses the effect of the proposed method due to seven viewpoints: "difference of discovered patterns", "validity of discovered patterns", "frequency of items", "calculation time", "complexity of the refined FP tree", "pre-processing method", and "generality".

3.4.1. Difference of Discovered Patterns. Graph (a) and Graph (b) show that there are many patterns discovered only by the proposed method. Especially, when the minimum frequencies in the proposed method are small, the numbers of the patterns are big. We can anticipate that analysts are interested in the patterns because the ratios included in a specific class set are comparatively high. On the other hand, it is difficult for the existing method to discover the patterns. If the existing method tries to discover them, it is necessary to set smaller minimum frequencies. However, the smaller minimum frequencies tend to discover many frequent patterns. The existing method may overlook important patterns because the patterns are hidden in many frequent patterns.

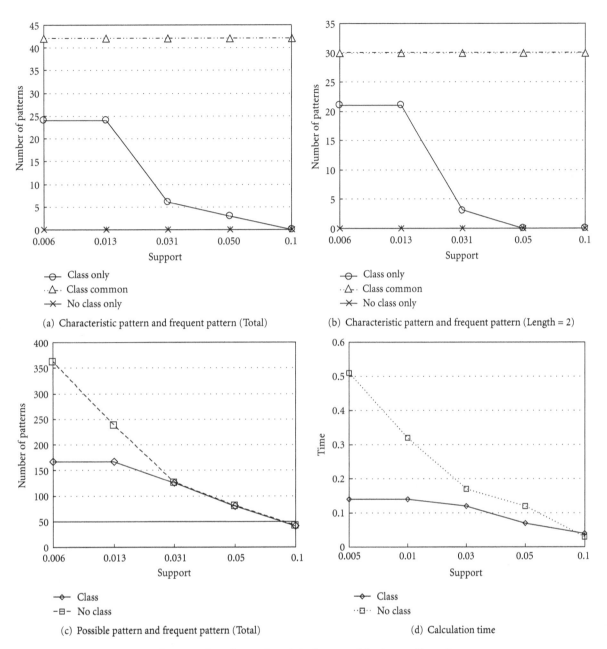

Figure 4: Experimental result in the case of the data set "hayes".

In order to avoid the overlook, we may be able to perform a two-stepwise method. The method combines the existing method with a postprocessing method. That is, the first step discovers frequent patterns by applying the existing method to its smaller minimum frequencies. The second step extracts characteristic patterns from the discovered patterns by evaluating their characteristic supports. However, Graph (c) shows that the number of possible patterns is smaller than the number of frequent patterns. The former numbers are 0.376 times, 0.461 times, and 0.404 times as small as the latter numbers in the case of "car", "hayes", and "nursery", respectively. The proposed method can discover all characteristic patterns by investigating possible patterns whose number is less than half as small as the numbers

based on the existing method. The proposed method is more efficient method with calculation cost.

3.4.2. Validity of Discovered Patterns. Tables 13 and 14 show that the proposed method discovers many patterns composed of a top wear and a bottom wear. If a customer is interested in only the top wear, the top wear is not usually fitted in a fitting room. However, if the customer is interested in the combination of the top wear and the bottom wear, the customer tends to fit the combination. The discovered patterns show the combination. On the other hand, the fitting is one of troublesome actions for the customer. The sales volume without the fitting is much larger than the one

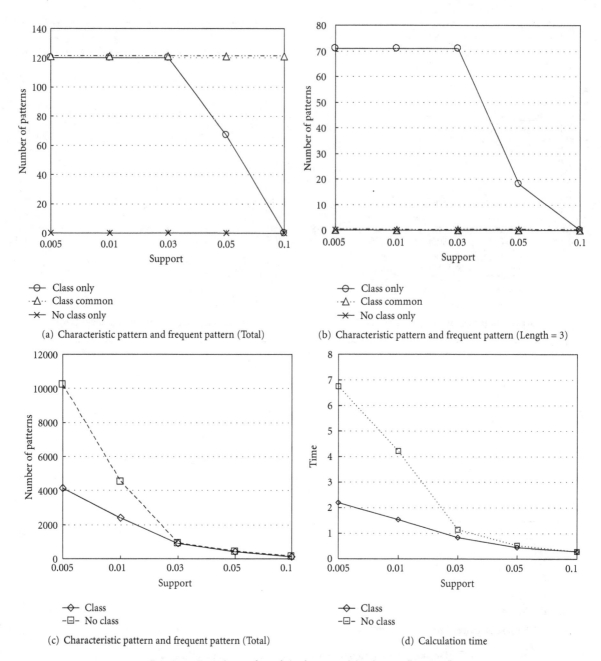

(a) Characteristic pattern and frequent pattern (Total)

(b) Characteristic pattern and frequent pattern (Length = 3)

(c) Characteristic pattern and frequent pattern (Total)

(d) Calculation time

FIGURE 5: Experimental result in the case of the data set "nursery".

with the fitting. It is difficult for the existing method to discover patterns related to the fitting. We can think that the proposed method discovers more valid patterns than the existing method does. In future work, we will try to show the patterns to retailers in the apparel shops and verify the validity of the patterns in detail.

3.4.3. Frequency of Items. In the case of "car" and "nursery", characteristic patterns whose length is 1 completely correspond to frequent patterns whose length is 1. Characteristic patterns whose length is more than equal to 2 include patterns which the existing method cannot discover. This is

because characteristic supports increase as the number of classes included in pattern classes decreases. The proposed method discovers the characteristic patterns related to the combination of specific classes. We think that the feature of the proposed method is experimentally confirmed.

3.4.4. Calculation Time. The results in Figures 3–5 show that the shapes of Graph (c) are similar to the ones of Graph (d). That is, the calculation time depends on the number of the patterns. It does not almost depend on the additional calculation cost related to the proposed method. The additional calculation cost of the proposed method is

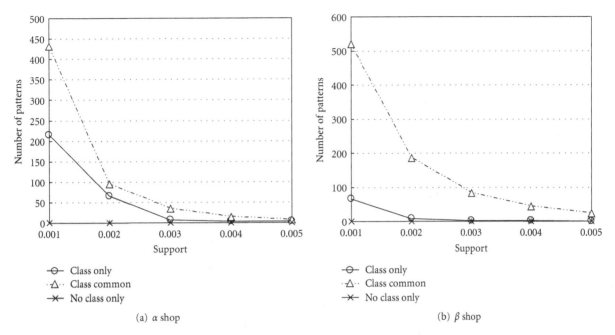

FIGURE 6: Experimental result in the case of the RFID data sets.

TABLE 13: Discovered patterns from α shop.

Pattern	Class
A-type jacket, A-type skirt	Fitting
X-type stole, Y-type gift box	No fitting
B-type one-piece wear, B-type jacket	Fitting
C-type jacket, D-type skirt	Fitting
C-type jacket, C-type skirt	Fitting
E-type jacket, E-type pants	Fitting
B-type jacket, B-type skirt	Fitting
F-type jacket, F-type skirt	Fitting
F-type jacket, G-type skirt	Fitting
F-type jacket, H-type blouse	Fitting
G-type skirt, H-type blouse	Fitting
F-type jacket, G-type skirt, H-type blouse	Fitting

TABLE 14: Discovered patterns from β shop.

Pattern	Class
I-type one-piece wear, H-type necklace	Fitting
C-type jacket, C-type pants	Fitting
K-type jacket, K-type skirt	Fitting

not so big. We can anticipate that the proposed method speedily discovers the patterns because it investigates small combinations of items.

3.4.5. Complexity of the Refined FP-Tree. The refined FP-tree has pattern classes and ID flags in the header table. It requires additional memory. However, the nodes composing the refined FP-tree occupy the greater part of memory. This

is because the number of transactions and the one of items are much larger than the number of classes. We think that the additional memory is not a big problem.

3.4.6. Preprocessing Method. Even if the existing method directly cannot deal with classes, a combination method of the existing method and a preprocessing method may be able to deal with them. That is, the preprocessing method can divide transactions into some transaction subsets by referring to the classes. The existing method can discover frequent patterns from divided transaction subsets. The combination method may be able to discover all characteristic patterns. However, if the number of classes is large, the combinations of classes exponentially increase. In addition, we do not usually have the knowledge for useful combinations of classes. It is necessary to discover patterns from various transaction subsets. The combination method requires large amount of calculation cost. On the other hand, the proposed method can discover characteristic patterns without requiring the additional knowledge. Therefore, the proposed method is more efficient than the combination method.

3.4.7. Generality. We can regard various conditions as classes. For example, in a retail field, the difference of sales period, shop, and salesperson is regarded as classes. Also, in a sensor network field, the difference of area, data collection interval, and data detection range is regarded as classes. Therefore, we think that the proposed method has high generality. The proposed method can analyze data with various viewpoints by using the classes.

According to the discussions, we believe that the proposed method can perform more efficient analysis for transactions.

4. Summary and Future Work

This paper proposed a method that discovers characteristic patterns from transactions with their classes. The method regards the difference of conditions in the data collection as classes. This paper redefined the possible support and the characteristic support in order to efficiently discover the patterns. Lastly, it verified the effect of the proposed method through numerical experiments based on three data sets registered in the UCI machine learning repository and two data sets collected by RFID readers and RFID tags set in apparel shops.

In future work, we try to improve the proposed method with a viewpoint of calculation speed. For example, we consider a method that calculates smaller possible supports in order to decrease the number of possible patterns. Concretely, we try to use relationships between the growth of patterns and their pattern classes. We believe that the relationships can estimate the possible supports as smaller values. Also, we try to reconsider the use of the single prefix path. In this paper, we ignore the path because characteristic patterns cannot be simply discovered from the combination of the single prefix path and the remaining FP tree. However, similar combinations may be useful for the speedy discovery. It is necessary to investigate the feature of the combinations in detail. In addition, we will consider to use the class information in nodes of a refined FP tree. The use may lead to the discovery of more valid patterns. On the other hand, it leads to a more complex FP tree with high calculation cost. It is important to clarify the relationships between the validity of patterns and the complexity of the FP tree. Lastly, we will try to apply the proposed method to many data sets in order to verify its effect in detail.

The discovery task from transactions without classes is expanding the research field more and more. The expansion may be useful for the discovery task from transactions with their classes. We try to incorporate the expansion in the proposed method.

References

[1] R. Agrawal and R. Srikant, "Fast algorithms for mining association rules in large databases," in *Proceedings of the 20th International Conferance on Very Large Data Bases*, pp. 487–499, Santiago, Chile, 1994.

[2] T. Morzy and M. Zakrzewicz, "Group Bitmap Index: a structure for association rules retrieval," in *Proceedings of the International Conference on Knowledge Discovery and Data Mining*, pp. 284–288, New York, NY, USA, 1998.

[3] M. J. Zaki, S. Parthasarathy, M. Ogihara, and W. Li, "New algorithms for fast discovery of association rules," in *Proceedings of the 3rd International Conference on Knowledge Discovery and Data Mining*, pp. 283–286, Newport Beach, Calif, USA, 1997.

[4] J. Han, J. Pei, and Y. Yin, "Mining frequent patterns without candidate generation," in *Proceedings of the ACM SIGMOD International Conference on Management of Data*, pp. 1–12, Dallas, Tex, USA, June 2000.

[5] Z. H. Deng and G. D. Fang, "Mining top-rank-K frequent patterns," in *Proceedings of the 6th International Conference on Machine Learning and Cybernetics (ICMLC '07)*, pp. 851–856, Hong Kong, August 2007.

[6] X. Yan, J. Han, and R. Afshar, "CloSpan: mining closed sequential patterns in large datasets," in *Proceedings of the SIAM International Conference on Data Mining*, pp. 166–177, San Fransisco, Calif, USA, 2003.

[7] R. J. Bayardo Jr., "Efficiently mining long patterns from databases," in *Proceedings of the ACM SIGMOD International Conference on Management of Data*, pp. 85–93, Seattle, Wash, USA, June 1998.

[8] C. H. Cai, A. W. C. Fu, C. H. Cheng, and W. W. Kwong, "Mining association rules with weighted items," in *Proceedings of the International Database Engineering and Applications Sympoium*, pp. 68–77, Cardiff, UK, 1998.

[9] M. Pater and D. E. Popescu, "Multi-level database mining using AFOPT data structure and adaptive support constrains," *International Journal of Computers, Communications & Control*, vol. 3, pp. 437–441, 2008.

[10] S. Sakurai and K. Mori, "Discovery of characteristic patterns from tabular structured data including missing values," *International Journal of Business Intelligence and Data Mining*, vol. 5, no. 3, pp. 213–230, 2010.

[11] A. Ragel and B. Crémilleux, "Treatment of missing values for association rules," in *Proceedings of the 2nd Pacific-Asia Conference on Research and Development in Knowledge Discovery and Data Mining*, pp. 258–270, Melbourne, Australia, 1998.

[12] T. Calders, B. Goethals, and M. Mampaey, "Mining itemsets in the presence of missing values," in *Proceedings of the ACM Symposium on Applied Computing*, pp. 404–408, Seoul, Korea, March 2007.

[13] University of California Irvine, UCI Machine Learning Repository, 2011, http://archive.ics.uci.edu/ml/.

[14] S. Sakurai, "Prediction of sales volume based on the RFID data collected from apparel shops," *International Journal of Space-Based and Situated Computing*, vol. 1, no. 2-3, pp. 174–182, 2011.

16

MIMO Lyapunov Theory-Based RBF Neural Classifier for Traffic Sign Recognition

King Hann Lim,[1] Kah Phooi Seng,[2] and Li-Minn Ang[3]

[1] *Electrical and Computer Department, School of Engineering and Science, Curtin University, Sarawak Malaysia, CDT 250, 98009 Miri Sarawak, Malaysia*
[2] *School of Computer Technology, Sunway University, No. 5, Jalan Universiti, Bandar Sunway, Selangor Darul Ehsan, 46150 Petaling, Malaysia*
[3] *Centre for Communications Engineering Research, Edith Cowan University, Joondalup, WA 6027, Australia*

Correspondence should be addressed to King Hann Lim, glkhann@curtin.edu.my

Academic Editor: Toly Chen

Lyapunov theory-based radial basis function neural network (RBFNN) is developed for traffic sign recognition in this paper to perform multiple inputs multiple outputs (MIMO) classification. Multidimensional input is inserted into RBF nodes and these nodes are linked with multiple weights. An iterative weight adaptation scheme is hence designed with regards to the Lyapunov stability theory to obtain a set of optimum weights. In the design, the Lyapunov function has to be well selected to construct an energy space with a single global minimum. Weight gain is formed later to obey the Lyapunov stability theory. Detail analysis and discussion on the proposed classifier's properties are included in the paper. The performance comparisons between the proposed classifier and some existing conventional techniques are evaluated using traffic sign patterns. Simulation results reveal that our proposed system achieved better performance with lower number of training iterations.

1. Introduction

Traffic sign recognition is important in autonomous vehicular technology for the sake of identifying a sign functionality through visual information capturing via sensors. The usage of neural networks has become increasingly popular in traffic sign recognition recently to classify various kinds of traffic signs into a specific category [1–3]. The reason of applying neural networks in traffic sign recognition is that, they can incorporate both statistical and structural information to achieve better performance than a simple minimum distance classifier [4]. The adaptive learning capability and processing parallelism for complex problems have led to the rapid advancement of neural networks. Among all neural networks, *radial basis function neural network* (RBFNN) has been applied in many engineering applications with the following significant properties: (i) universal approximators [5]; (ii) simple topological structure [6] which allows straightforward computation using a linearly weighted combination of single hidden-layer neurons. The learning characteristic of RBFNN is greatly related to the associative weights between hidden-output nodes. Therefore, an optimal algorithm is required to update the weights relative to an arbitrary training input.

Conventionally, the training process for RBFNN is mainly dependent on the optimization theory. The cost function of this network, for instance, the sum of squared errors or mean squared error between network's output and targeted input is firstly defined. It is followed by minimizing the cost function in weight parameter space to search for a set of optimal weights. These optimal weights which are acquired throughout network training process can be used to perform some unique tasks, such as pattern classification.

In order to obtain the optimum weights, a number of training algorithms have been developed for RBFNN. Due to the linear-weighted combiner, network's weights can be determined using *least mean square* (LMS) and *recursive least square* (RLS) algorithms. However, these algorithms suffer from several drawbacks and limitations. The LMS is highly dependent on the autocorrelation function associated with the input signals and slow convergence. RLS, on the other hand, provides faster convergence but they depend on the implicit or explicit computation using the inverse of input signal's autocorrelation matrix. Matrix inversion implies not only a higher computational cost and it also leads to network instability issue [7]. Other gradient search-based training algorithms also suffer so-called local minima problem, that is, the optimization search may trap at a local minimum of the cost function in the weight space if a set of initial values are arbitrarily chosen. For example, the cost function has a fixed structure in the weight space after the expression of the cost function is chosen. The parameter update law is only a means to search for the global minimum and independent of the cost function in the weight space.

To overcome the aforementioned problems, the optimization techniques using the Lyapunov stability theory has been proposed in [8] for adaptive filtering. This theory is further adopted to the design of RBFNN [9] which has been first proposed in realization of *finite-impulse response* (FIR) and *infinite-impulse response* (IIR) adaptive filters for signal noise filtering. The Lyapunov theory-based RBFNN has been increasingly popular in adaptive filter due to its stability guarantee by Lyapunov stability theory and an energy-space construction with a global minimum [9]. However, only single output is designed in the Lyapunov theory-based RBFNN and, hence, it is not suitable for classification problem. In the meantime, the Lyapunov stability theory is also applied to *multilayered neural network* (MLNN) [10] for solving *multiple inputs multiple outputs* (MIMOs) problems. With Taylor series expansion, all MLNN weights between input-output layers are rearranged into a linear configuration with an assumption made, that is, the input-output layer's weights adjustment is dependent on its corrective output error. Therefore, it leads to longer training time with a couple numbers of weight linkage and it prone to have more weights uncertainties. Nevertheless, the Lyapunov theory-based neural classifiers have offered the following advantages [9, 10]: (i) fast error convergence, (ii) guarantee of stability, (iii) insensitivity to initial condition, and (iv) construction of weight space with a global minimum if a proper Lyapunov function is selected.

In this paper, the notion of Lyapunov stability theory on RBFNN can be extended and modified to solve MIMO problems such as traffic sign recognition in order to obtain a fast and reliable classification system. To reveal the performance of proposed system, the application for traffic sign classification is used for further discussion and analysis. The performance of the proposed RBFNN will be compared with [10] and the differences for both methods will be stated in the later section. Experimental results show that the proposed method leads to faster error convergence rate and higher recognition rate as compared to the conventional techniques. This paper is organized as the following: Section 2 discusses about the fundamental theory of RBF neural classifier while Section 3 explains the theoretical design of the Lyapunov theory-based training algorithm. Section 4 describes an overview of traffic sign detection and recognition on Malaysia's traffic sign database. Some simulation results along with the application of traffic sign recognition are shown in Section 5 and it is finally followed by conclusion and future works.

2. Radial Basis Function Neural Network

A typical three-layer RBFNN [11] is illustrated in Figure 1 for pattern recognition. Such a network implements an input-output mapping: $\Re^n \rightarrow \Re^m$, where n depicts the number of inputs and m depicts the number of outputs. There are u hidden nodes connecting in between the input-output layer. Assuming the first layer of input vector, $\mathbf{X}^{(1)}$ is set to be $\mathbf{P} \in \Re^n$, where the input data is arranged into column vector as $\mathbf{P} = [p_1, p_2, \ldots, p_n]^T$. The RBF centers are denoted as $C_j \in \Re^n$ ($1 \leq j \leq u$). Each RBF unit is defined as:

$$X_j^{(2)}(P) = \exp\left(-\frac{\left\|X^{(1)} - C_j\right\|^2}{\sigma_j^2}\right), \qquad (1)$$

where $\| \cdot \|$ indicates the Euclidean norm on the input space while σ_j is the Gaussian width of the jth RBF unit. The vector generated after the RBF neurons is given as $\mathbf{X}$ below:

$$\begin{bmatrix} \psi\left(\|\mathbf{X}^{(1)} - C_1\|^2\right) \\ \psi\left(\|\mathbf{X}^{(1)} - C_2\|^2\right) \\ \vdots \\ \psi\left(\|\mathbf{X}^{(1)} - C_u\|^2\right) \end{bmatrix} = \begin{bmatrix} X_1^{(2)} \\ X_2^{(2)} \\ \vdots \\ X_u^{(2)} \end{bmatrix} = \mathbf{X}, \qquad (2)$$

where $\psi(\cdot)$ is the radial basis function. Consider the hidden nodes are linearly mapped to the output with the $u \times m$ weights matrix formed as below:

$$\begin{bmatrix} w_{1,1} & w_{2,1} & \cdots & w_{m,1} \\ w_{1,2} & w_{2,2} & \cdots & w_{m,2} \\ \vdots & & \ddots & \vdots \\ w_{1,u} & \cdots & \cdots & w_{m,u} \end{bmatrix} = \mathbf{W}, \qquad (3)$$

RBF network establishes a linear function mapping in the output layer. By multiplying (2) and (3), the weighted hidden values are summed to be the output matrix, $\mathbf{Y}$ is as follows:

$$\mathbf{Y} = \text{diag}\left(\mathbf{W}^T \mathbf{X}\right), \qquad (4)$$

where

$$\mathbf{Y} = \text{diag}(y_1, y_2, \ldots, y_m) = \begin{bmatrix} y_1 & \cdots & \cdots & 0 \\ 0 & y_2 & \cdots & 0 \\ \vdots & & \ddots & 0 \\ 0 & \cdots 0 & \cdots & y_m \end{bmatrix}, \qquad (5)$$

and $\text{diag}(a)$ is the $N \times N$ diagonal matrix whose entries are the N elements of the vector a.

Two important parameters are associated with each RBF unit. They are RBF center (C_j) and the Gaussian width (σ_j).

Every center should well represent the corresponding sub-class because the classification in RBFNN is mainly measured based on the distances between the input samples and the centers of each subclass. There are different strategies to select RBF centers [11]. These strategies can be classified into supervised [12, 13] and unsupervised algorithms [14–16]. Once centers are well selected, the network starts learning the training data with the weight updating scheme. The selection of center and radius is not the main concern in this paper. Therefore, k-mean cluster is applied to search for the RBF centers while p-nearest neighbor is used to measure the nearest radius for p consecutive centers in the network evaluations.

Learning algorithm plays an important role in updating the weight between hidden and output layer of RBFNN. Conventional RBF with LMS algorithm [17, 18] is trained using gradient descent method which finds the negative gradient on the error curve. It suffers from slow convergence and it is always trapped in the local minima instead of global minima. On the other hand, conventional RBF using RLS method [19] computes the inverse of autocorrelation matrix associated with the input data to update the system weights. However, the inversion of RLS algorithm gives instability of system convergence and increases computational cost.

3. Lyapunov Theory-Based RBFNN

The idea of Lyapunov theory-based RBF filter was initially developed in [9] for adaptive filtering. Lyapunov function of errors between targeted outputs and actual outputs are first defined. Network weights are then adjusted based on the Lyapunov stability theory, so that errors can asymptotically converge to zero. The selected Lyapunov function has a unique global minimum point in the state space. By properly choosing a weight update law in the Lyapunov sense, RBF outputs will be asymptotically converged to the target outputs. In this section, the design in [9] is adopted and modified to apply the Lyapunov theory-based RBF neural classifier for solving MIMO classification problem.

The input vector $\mathbf{P}$ is fed into RBF nodes and hence passed to the output layer by weighted sum with the formulas depicted in (1)–(4). For the given desired response $\hat{\mathbf{Y}}_k = \mathrm{diag}(d_1, d_2, \ldots, d_m) \in \Re^{m \times m}$ at discrete time k, the Lyapunov function is initially chosen as:

$$V_k = \|\mathbf{E}_k\|^2, \qquad (6)$$

and $\mathbf{E}_k$ is a posteriori error with $m \times m$ diagonal matrix defined as below:

$$\mathbf{E}_k = \hat{\mathbf{Y}}_k - \mathbf{Y}_k = \hat{\mathbf{Y}}_k - \mathrm{diag}(\mathbf{W}_k^T \mathbf{X}_k). \qquad (7)$$

For the given hidden layer input $\mathbf{X}_k$ and the desired output $\hat{\mathbf{Y}}_k$, the weight matrix $\mathbf{W}_k$ is updated as follows:

$$\mathbf{W}_k = \mathbf{W}_{k-1} + \mathbf{g}_k^T \boldsymbol{\alpha}_k. \qquad (8)$$

The adaptive gain is modified for MIMO such that $\Delta V < 0$:

$$\mathbf{g}_k = \left[\mathbf{I}_{m \times m} - \kappa \boldsymbol{\alpha}_k^{-1} \mathbf{E}_{k-1}\right] \times \mathbf{1}_{m \times 1} \times \frac{\mathbf{X}_k^T}{\|\mathbf{X}_k\|^2}, \qquad (9)$$

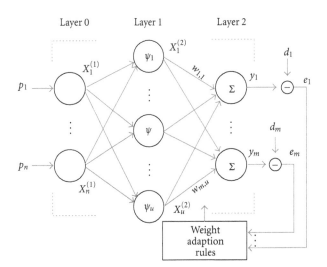

Layer 0   Layer 1   Layer 2

FIGURE 1: MIMO radial basis function network structure.

whereas $\mathbf{I}_{m \times m}$ is identity matrix, $\mathbf{1}_{m \times 1}$ is column vector of ones, κ is valid for the interval $[0, 1]$, and $\boldsymbol{\alpha}_k$ is the priori estimation error which is defined as:

$$\boldsymbol{\alpha}_k = \hat{\mathbf{Y}}_k - \mathrm{diag}(\mathbf{W}_{k-1}^T \mathbf{X}_k). \qquad (10)$$

Then the error $\|\mathbf{E}_k\|$ asymptotically converges to zero as the time k goes infinity.

The selection of Lyapunov function is important in constructing a new cost-function of the system. Regarding to the Lyapunov stability theory, V_k should be selected in the sense of Lyapunov that: $\Delta V_k = V_k - V_{k-1} < 0$. For mth output nodes RBFNN network, V_k is chosen to be (6) with the summation of squared errors. With the parameters predefined in expressions (7)–(10), it is proved in Appendix A that ΔV_k has a negative value and the Lyapunov stability theory is fulfilled. Only when the parameter update law is chosen in the Lyapunov sense, $V_k = \|\mathbf{E}_k\|^2$ is the Lyapunov function of RBFNN system, which has a unique global minimum.

As stated previously, the training error converges to zero asymptotically as time increases to infinity. For mth output nodes RBFNN, the classification error, $\|\mathbf{E}_k\|$ is proved to be asymptotically approaching zero when the training time increases with the gain given in (9). The proof of error convergence is given in Appendix B. The error is bounded to a single convergent value. It is noted that the error convergence rate is dependent on the positive constant κ. For the faster error converges, κ should be remained as a small value in the range of $0 \le \kappa < 1$.

To prevent the singularities, the expression (9) can be modified to:

$$\mathbf{g}_k = \left[\mathbf{I}_{m \times m} - \kappa \boldsymbol{\alpha}_k^{-1} \mathbf{E}_{k-1}\right] \times \mathbf{1}_{m \times 1} \times \frac{\mathbf{X}_k^T}{\beta_1 + \|\mathbf{X}_k\|^2}, \qquad (11)$$

where β_1 is a small positive integer.

TABLE 1: Malaysia traffic sign classification in shape and color.

Color	Shape				
	Diamond	Triangle downward	Square/rectangle	Circle	Octagon
Blue	—	—	Information	Obligation	—
Red		Yield sign	—	Prohibition	Stop sign
Yellow	Warning	—	Warning	—	—
Orange			Construction		
White	—	—	—	Speed limit	—

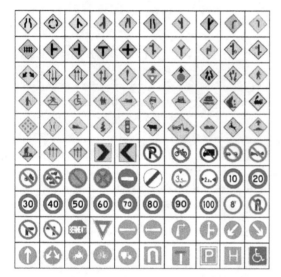

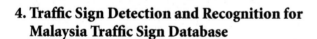

FIGURE 2: 100 classes of Malaysia traffic signs.

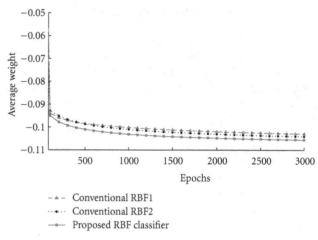

- - ▲ - Conventional RBF1
⋯ ▲ ⋯ Conventional RBF2
—■— Proposed RBF classifier

FIGURE 3: Weight convergence for different RBF classifiers.

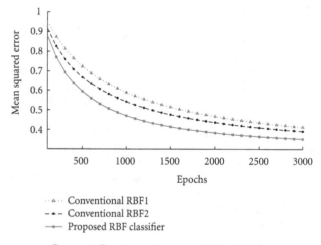

⋯ ▲ ⋯ Conventional RBF1
- - ◆ - Conventional RBF2
—■— Proposed RBF classifier

FIGURE 4: Error convergence on RBF networks.

4. Traffic Sign Detection and Recognition for Malaysia Traffic Sign Database

Traffic signs are important to alert driver of the current road situation. As demonstrated in Figure 2, 100 classes of traffic signs can often be found on Malaysia's roadside. The iconic traffic signs are acquired from the Malaysia's Highway Code Test booklet. They are designed in the standard geometrical shapes such as triangle, circle, octagon, rectangle, square, or diamond. The dominant colors that used for traffic signs are yellow, blue, red, orange, black, and white, which is greatly distinguishable from the natural scene. The message of warning, prohibition, guidance, construction and maintenance are represented by the specific color and shape as depicted in Table 1. They may contain a pictogram, a string of characters or both.

Traffic sign is detected based on color and shape information from a road scene. Possible sign is then extracted for further verification. Traffic sign can be verified by using its symmetrical property. Subsequently, the detected sign region is arranged into a column vector and this vector is inserted to the neural networks for classification. Some evaluations on traffic sign recognition using Malaysia's database with the proposed RBFNN and other neural classifiers will be discussed in the following section.

5. Experimental Results and Discussions

The Lyapunov theory-based RBFNN was developed in this paper to have multiple output classification and, therefore, traffic sign recognition was applied to be a MIMO problem throughout several experiments. In order to observe and evaluate the performance of proposed RBFNN, a basic structure of RBFNN was set up, where the output layer was assigned to classify 100 tasks. The task was to recognize any 100 signs randomly picked from Malaysia's database as displayed in the previous section. Each traffic sign subject

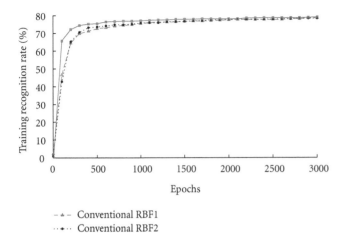

FIGURE 5: The training recognition rate in RBF networks versus epochs.

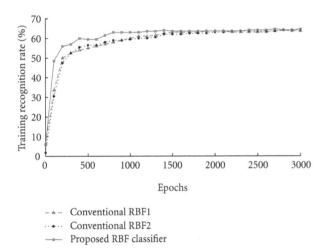

FIGURE 6: The testing recognition rate in RBF networks versus epochs.

contained five training images and two testing images respectively. All images were in the dimension of 32×32.

Three types of RBF classifiers with different learning schemes were used in the experiments, that is, (i) conventional RBF1 with LMS learning approach, (ii) conventional RBF2 with RLS technique, and (iii) Lyapunov theory-based RBF classifier. Network performance was compared in terms of weight and error convergence for these RBF systems. In addition, recognition rate was plotted along with the number of iterations for training and testing dataset. Lyapunov theory-based algorithm obtained a parameter, $\kappa = 0.1$, while LMS algorithm obtained a learning rate (η), whereas the range was varied from 0.1 to 1.0. Meanwhile, the forgetting factor (λ) of RLS algorithm was set to 0.1. During the experiments, the number of input neurons was set to be the image size and the number of output neurons was equal to the number of classes to be identified. The hidden layer of RBF nodes obtained the same size as the input layer. Two

initial conditions were set as (i) initial weights $\mathbf{W}_0$ were set to be some random small values and (ii) initial posterior error, $\mathbf{E}_0$ was set to be $0.01 \times \mathbf{I}_{m \times m}$, where $m = 100$. In the experiment, an epoch represented an efficient time used to train the entire set of input data. Hence, each epoch updated the weights once for the whole training dataset until the occurrence of weight convergence and this was referring to batch learning scheme.

Weight convergence was crucial in neural network learning characteristic. The weights for all RBF classifiers were converged at equilibrium with a random set of initial weights. Figure 3 showed a weight convergence plot, where x-axis denoted the number of epochs while y-axis denoted the average weight values connected from hidden layer to output layer of RBF network. At around 250 epochs, proposed RBF classifier started converging at -0.1. As time extended to infinity, only minor weight increment was added along with the continuous epoch. However, conventional RBF classifiers reached -0.1 equilibrium point at 1000 epochs, which took longer time than the Lyapunov theory-based RBF classifier. Therefore, the weight of proposed RBF classifier was converged faster than other conventional RBF classifiers.

As demonstrated in Figure 4, an error curve was plotted and it was exponentially decreased to the minimum. At 2000 epochs, the proposed RBF classifier reached 0.4 of mean squared error. For other conventional RBFNNs, they took longer period to achieve lower error rate as shown in Figure 4. Hence, the error convergence rate of proposed RBF training scheme was converged faster than other networks. However, the error value was not converged to zero yet due to some reasons, whereby this issue was caused by the redundancy information of input data. Moreover, similarity of subject pattern would confuse the classification of neural network as you could observe in Figure 2. The complexity of the input data would degrade recognition rate in classification. Hence, all neural classifiers' error was still remained at around 0.4, but the proposed neural classifier obtained lower error curve compared to the other networks. To reduce the classification error, some processing techniques could be applied to the input data before passing to the neural network for training process. In addition, traffic signs could first be classified into color and shape before they were recognized using neural network [4]. In this paper, the main concern was to focus on the property of RBF training schemes instead of traffic sign recognition, in which it was an application example for the proposed network discussion.

To investigate the performance of RBF classifiers, training and testing data were fed into system and an average recognition rate was calculated. Without any feature extraction method, the original images were tested with the RBF classifiers. The system performance was compared with conventional RBFNNs using different weight updating schemes. As demonstrated in Figure 5, the Lyapunov theory-based RBFNN obtained faster training speed which was within 500 epochs. Meanwhile, it achieved higher training recognition rate than other networks. Similar to Figure 6, the proposed RBF network obtained high recognition rate at 800 epochs while other training algorithms achieved maximum recognition rate at 1500 epochs. This implied that Lyapunov theory-based RBFNN could obtain high recognition rate in a smaller epoch's number. By comparing the network recognition rate, conventional RBF1 achieved 63.50%, while conventional RBF2 achieved 64% of recognition rate. However, the testing recognition rate of the proposed classifier was slightly increased with the rate of 64.50%. As it was reported in [12], high dimensional input data would cause low recognition rate of neural network because high dimensional input data and network complexity would need a large set training samples. Therefore, features extraction technique such as *Principle Component Analysis* (PCA) could be used to reduce the image dimension in order to further increase d the recognition rate.

Besides that, MLNN was also used to classify multidimensional patterns based on Lyapunov stability theory as it was developed in [10]. In order to test the performance between the Lyapunov theory-based RBFNN and MLNN, the number of hidden nodes was fixed to be 100 and the number of epochs was set to be 3000 for both networks. The constant parameter κ is set to be 0.1 for both the Lyapunov-theory based MLNN and RBFNN with similar training and testing images datasets as employed in the RBFNN experiments. An averaged recognition rate was recorded for the comparison.

As reported in Table 2, the Lyapunov theory-based RBFNN achieved better classification performance than [10]. Although both methods employ the Lyapunov stability theory as the basic design for training algorithm, there were some main differences between them. First, the structure for two networks was much distinguished from input to output layers. MLNN contained more weights linkage between input to hidden layer and hidden to output layer. Hence, the weights of MLNN were required to be linearized using Taylor series expansion before performing training process. With this MLNN configuration, it contributed to more uncertainties on the weight and error convergence compared to the linear topology of RBFNN. Second, the energy function of training error for MLNN was constructed for each output node where it contained tth number of output nodes. Unlike to [10], the energy function for the Lyapunov theory based RBFNN was designed for all output neurons in a matrix form and it provided a valid derivation in the appendices. Finally, the performance for the Lyapunov theory-based RBFNN achieved better training and testing recognition rate than [10] in the pattern recognition.

6. Conclusion

This paper has presented Lyapunov theory-based weights updating algorithm for RBFNN. The weight adaptation scheme is designed based on the Lyapunov stability theory and iteratively updated the RBFNN weight. The Lyapunov theory-based RBFNN is extended for traffic sign recognition as a MIMO problem. Simulation results have shown that our proposed system achieved faster training speed, as well as higher recognition rate. The recognition rate can be further improved by applying input dimensionality reduction to remove the information redundancy. The research on the optimization using Lyapunov stability theory is still at its

early stages, and many investigations of Lyapunov theory-based neural classifier will be conducted to improve the network efficiency and robustness. Future investigation on different Lyapunov functions and different weights updating laws is needed to further improve the performance.

Appendices

A. Proof of Lyapunov Stability Theory

The discrete form of ΔV_k is given as:

$$\begin{aligned}
\Delta V_k &= \|\mathbf{E}_k\|^2 - \|\mathbf{E}_{k-1}\|^2 \\
&= \left\| \hat{\mathbf{Y}}_k - \mathrm{diag}(\mathbf{W}_k^T \mathbf{X}_k) \right\|^2 - \|\mathbf{E}_{k-1}\|^2 \\
&= \left\| \boldsymbol{\alpha}_k - \boldsymbol{\alpha}_k^T \mathbf{g}_k \mathbf{X}_k \right\|^2 - \|\mathbf{E}_{k-1}\|^2 \\
&= \|\kappa \mathbf{E}_{k-1}\|^2 - \|\mathbf{E}_{k-1}\|^2 \\
&= \kappa^2 \|\mathbf{E}_{k-1}\|^2 - \|\mathbf{E}_{k-1}\|^2 \\
&= -(1 - \kappa^2)\|\mathbf{E}_{k-1}\|^2 < 0,
\end{aligned} \tag{A.1}$$

where $0 \le \kappa < 1$.

B. Proof of Error Convergence

$$\begin{aligned}
\mathbf{E}_k &= \hat{\mathbf{Y}}_k - \mathbf{Y}_k \\
&= \hat{\mathbf{Y}}_k - \mathrm{diag}\left(\mathbf{W}_k^T \mathbf{X}_k\right) \\
&= \hat{\mathbf{Y}}_k - \mathrm{diag}\left[\left(\mathbf{W}_{k-1}^T + \boldsymbol{\alpha}_k^T \mathbf{g}_k\right)\mathbf{X}_k \right] \\
&= \hat{\mathbf{Y}}_k - \mathrm{diag}\left(\mathbf{W}_{k-1}^T \mathbf{X}_k\right) - \mathrm{diag}\left(\boldsymbol{\alpha}_k^T \mathbf{g}_k \mathbf{X}_k\right) \\
&= \boldsymbol{\alpha}_k - \mathrm{diag}\Big\{ \boldsymbol{\alpha}_k^T \Big[\left(\mathbf{I}_{m \times m} - \kappa \boldsymbol{\alpha}_k^{-1} \mathbf{E}_{k-1}\right) \\
&\quad \times \mathbf{1}_{m \times 1} \times \frac{\mathbf{X}_k^T}{\|\mathbf{X}_k\|^2} \Big] \mathbf{X}_k \Big\}.
\end{aligned} \tag{B.1}$$

Since $\boldsymbol{\alpha}_k$ is a symmetric matrix, $\boldsymbol{\alpha}_k^T = \boldsymbol{\alpha}_k$,

$$\mathbf{E}_k = \boldsymbol{\alpha}_k - \mathrm{diag}[(\boldsymbol{\alpha}_k - \kappa \mathbf{E}_{k-1}) \times \mathbf{1}_{m \times 1}]. \tag{B.2}$$

Due to $(\boldsymbol{\alpha}_k - \kappa \mathbf{E}_{k-1}) \in \mathfrak{R}^{m \times m}$, $\mathrm{diag}(\cdot)$ and $\mathbf{1}_{m \times 1}$ can be canceled off from the equation:

$$\begin{aligned}
\mathbf{E}_k &= \boldsymbol{\alpha}_k - \boldsymbol{\alpha}_k + \kappa \mathbf{E}_{k-1} \\
&= \kappa \mathbf{E}_{k-1} \\
\therefore \|\mathbf{E}_1\|^2 &= \kappa \|\mathbf{E}_0\|^2 \\
\|\mathbf{E}_2\|^2 &= \kappa \|\mathbf{E}_1\|^2 = \kappa^2 \|\mathbf{E}_0\|^2 \\
&\vdots \\
\|\mathbf{E}_k\|^2 &= \lim_{k \to \infty} \kappa^k \|\mathbf{E}_0\|^2 \approx 0,
\end{aligned} \tag{B.3}$$

where $\|\mathbf{E}_0\|^2$ is an $m \times m$ diagonal matrix with small real integer and $0 \le \kappa < 1$.

TABLE 2: Performance comparison for the Lyapunov theory-based neural networks.

Method	Hidden nodes	Epochs	Training recognition (%)	Testing recognition (%)
Proposed RBF NN	100	3000	79.00	64.50
MLNN [10]	100	3000	62.80	56.00

References

[1] Y. Y. Nguwi and A. Z. Kouzani, "Detection and classification of road signs in natural environments," *Neural Computing and Applications*, vol. 17, no. 3, pp. 265–289, 2008.

[2] Y. Shao, Q. Chen, and H. Jiang, "RBF neural network based on particle swarm optimization," in *Proceedings of the 7th International Conference on Advances in Neural Networks (ISNN '10)*, L. Zhang et al., Ed., vol. 6063, pp. 169–176, Springer, Shanghai, China, 2010.

[3] G. A. P. Coronado, M. R. Muñoz, J. M. Armingol et al., "Road sign recognition for automatic inventory systems," in *Proceedings of the 18th International Conference on Systems, Signals, and Image Processing (IWSSIP '11)*, pp. 63–66, 2011.

[4] K. H. Lim, K. P. Seng, and L.-M. Ang, "Improved traffic sign recognition," in *Proceedings of the International Conference on Embedded Systems and Intelligent Technology (ICESIT '10)*, Chiang Mai, Thailand, 2010.

[5] J. Park and I. W. Sandberg, "Universal approximation using radial-basis-function networks," *Neural Computation*, vol. 3, no. 2, pp. 246–257, 1991.

[6] S. Lee and R. M. Kil, "A gaussian potential function network with hierarchically self-organizing learning," *Neural Networks*, vol. 4, no. 2, pp. 207–224, 1991.

[7] M. S. Mueller, "Least-squares algorithms for adaptive equalizers," *The Bell System Technical Journal*, vol. 60, no. 8, pp. 1905–1925, 1981.

[8] Z. H. Man et al., "Design of robust adaptive filters using Lyapunov stability theory," in *Proceedings of the IEEE Transactions on Circuits & Systems II: Express Briefs*, 2004.

[9] K. P. Seng, Z. Man, and H. R. Wu, "Lyapunov-theory-based radial basis function networks for adaptive filtering," *IEEE Transactions on Circuits and Systems I: Fundamental Theory and Applications*, vol. 49, no. 8, pp. 1215–1220, 2002.

[10] K. H. Lim, K. P. Seng, L. M. Ang, and S. W. Chin, "Lyapunov theory-based multilayered neural network," *IEEE Transactions on Circuits and Systems II: Express Briefs*, vol. 56, no. 4, pp. 305–309, 2009.

[11] S. Haykin, *Neural Networks: A Comprehensive Foundation*, Prentice Hall, 1994.

[12] M. J. Er, S. Wu, J. Lu, and H. L. Toh, "Face recognition with radial basis function (RBF) neural networks," *IEEE Transactions on Neural Networks*, vol. 13, no. 3, pp. 697–710, 2002.

[13] M. J. Er, W. Chen, and S. Wu, "High-speed face recognition based on discrete cosine transform and rbf neural networks," *IEEE Transactions on Neural Networks*, vol. 16, no. 3, pp. 679–691, 2005.

[14] J. A. Leonard and M. A. Kramer, "Radial basis function networks for classifying process faults," *IEEE Control Systems Magazine*, vol. 11, no. 3, pp. 31–38, 1991.

[15] M. John and J. D. Christian, "Fast learning in networks of locally-tuned processing units," *Neural Computation*, vol. 1, no. 2, pp. 281–294, 1989.

[16] F. Yang and M. Paindavoine, "Implementation of an rbf neural network on embedded systems: real-time face tracking and identity verification," *IEEE Transactions on Neural Networks*, vol. 14, no. 5, pp. 1162–1175, 2003.

[17] M. Kishan, *Elements of Artificial Neural Networks*, MIT Press, 1997.

[18] V. Espinosa-Duro, "Biometric identification system using a radial basis network," in *Proceedings of the 34th IEEE Annual International Carnahan Conference on Security Technology*, pp. 47–51, 2000.

[19] M. Birgmeier, "Fully kalman-trained radial basis function network for nonlinear speech modeling," in *Proceedings of the IEEE International Conference on Neural Networks*, pp. 259–264, December 1995.

17

Standard Precipitation Index Drought Forecasting Using Neural Networks, Wavelet Neural Networks, and Support Vector Regression

A. Belayneh and J. Adamowski

Department of Bioresource Engineering, Faculty of Agricultural and Environmental Sciences, McGill University, QC, Canada H9X 3V9

Correspondence should be addressed to J. Adamowski, jan.adamowski@mcgill.ca

Academic Editor: Quek Hiok Chai

Drought forecasts can be an effective tool for mitigating some of the more adverse consequences of drought. Data-driven models are suitable forecasting tools due to their rapid development times, as well as minimal information requirements compared to the information required for physically based models. This study compares the effectiveness of three data-driven models for forecasting drought conditions in the Awash River Basin of Ethiopia. The Standard Precipitation Index (SPI) is forecast and compared using artificial neural networks (ANNs), support vector regression (SVR), and wavelet neural networks (WN). SPI 3 and SPI 12 were the SPI values that were forecasted. These SPI values were forecast over lead times of 1 and 6 months. The performance of all the models was compared using RMSE, MAE, and R^2. The forecast results indicate that the coupled wavelet neural network (WN) models were the best models for forecasting SPI values over multiple lead times in the Awash River Basin in Ethiopia.

1. Introduction

Droughts, a natural occurrence in almost all climatic zones, are a result of the reduction, for an extended period of time, of precipitation from normal amounts. Extended periods of drought can lead to several adverse consequences, which include a disruption of the water supply, low agricultural yields, and reduced flows for ecosystems. Consequently, the ability to forecast and predict the characteristics of droughts, specifically their initiation, frequency, and severity, is important. Effective drought forecasts are an effective tool for water resource management as well as an effective tool for the agricultural industry.

Currently, drought monitoring in Ethiopia is conducted by the National Meteorological Services Agency (NMSA). The NMSA regularly produces a 10-day bulletin that gives an analysis of rainfall based on the long-term average or normal. This bulletin is then circulated to a wide range of users, ranging from local development agents to decision makers at a national level. In addition to rainfall analysis, the normalized vegetation index (NDVI) is provided, which is a satellite-based index widely used to monitor vegetation and drought conditions. The NMSA produces a regular 10-day bulletin regarding NDVI variation that compares the current vegetation condition with normal or conditions of the previous year [1]. However, the NDVI is sensitive to changes in vegetative land cover and may not be effective in areas where vegetation is minimal. In addition, the NMSA of Ethiopia produces medium and seasonal forecasts of precipitation using the aforementioned NDVI.

Unlike other natural hazards, droughts have a slow evolution time [2]. The consequences of droughts take a significant amount of time to come into effect with respect to their inception, and when they are perceived by ecosystems and hydrological systems. Due to this feature, effective mitigation of the most adverse drought impacts is possible, more than in the case of other extreme hydrological events such as floods, earthquakes, or hurricanes, provided

Standard Precipitation Index Drought Forecasting Using Neural Networks, Wavelet Neural Networks, and Support Vector Regression

163

a drought monitoring system, which is able to promptly warn of the onset of a drought and to follow its evolution in space and time, is in operation [3].

A common tool utilized to monitor current drought conditions is a drought index. Several drought indices can be used to forecast the possible evolution of an ongoing drought, in order to adopt appropriate mitigation measures and drought policies for water resources management [4]. This is because a drought index is expressed by a numeric number, which is believed to be far more functional than raw data during decision-making [2]. Several drought indices have been developed around the world in the past based on rainfall as the single variable, including the widely used Deciles [5], Standardized Precipitation Index (SPI) [6], and Effective Drought Index (EDI) [7]. There is also the well-known Palmer Drought Severity Index (PDSI) [8], which considers temperature along with rainfall. The SPI drought index was chosen to forecast drought in this study due to its simplicity, its ability to represent droughts on multiple time scales, and because it is a probabilistic drought index. In addition, the study by Ntale and Gan [9] determined that the SPI is the most appropriate index for monitoring the variability of droughts in East Africa because it is easily adapted to local climate, has modest data requirements, and can be computed at almost any time scale.

Forecasting any hydrologic phenomena can be done using either a physical, conceptual, or data-driven approach. The latter approach is widely used in hydrologic forecasting because data-driven models have low information requirements with respect to the number of variables required for inputs compared to physically based models. Data-driven models also have rapid development times. Unlike physical and conceptual models, data-driven models are not difficult to implement for the purposes of real-time forecasting. Artificial neural networks (ANNs) have been used in several studies as a drought-forecasting tool [10–16]. The most popular type of ANN used for the purposes of drought forecasting is the multilayer perceptron (MLP) that is usually optimized with a back propagation algorithm. However, ANNs are limited in their ability to deal with nonstationarities in the data, a weakness also shared by multiple linear regression (MLR) and autoregressive integrated moving average (ARIMA) models.

This limitation with nonstationary data has led to the recent formation of hybrid models, where data is preprocessed for nonstationary characteristics and then run through a forecasting method such as ANNs to cope with the nonlinearity. Wavelet analysis, an effective tool to deal with nonstationary data, has recently been applied in hydrological forecasting to examine the rainfall-runoff relationship in a Karstic watershed [17], to characterize daily streamflow [18, 19] and monthly reservoir inflow [20], to evaluate rainfall-runoff models [21], to forecast river flow [22–24], to forecast future precipitation values [25], and for the purposes of drought forecasting [26]. The study conducted by Kim and Valdes [26] is the only study that has explored the ability of a wavelet-neural network conjunction model (WN) to forecast a given drought index. However, no studies that assess the ability of WN models to forecast the SPI drought index in particular have been explored.

Support Vector Machines (SVMs) are a relatively new form of machine learning that was developed by Vapnik [27]. The term SVM is used to refer to both classification and regression methods as well as the terms Support Vector Classification (SVC) and Support Vector Regression (SVR), which refer to the problems of classification and regression, respectively [28]. There are several studies where SVRs were used in hydrological forecasting. Khan and Coulibaly [29] found that an SVR model was more effective at predicting 3–12 month lake water levels than ANN models. Rajasekaran et al. [30] used SVR successfully for storm surge predictions, and Kisi and Cimen [31, 32] used SVR to estimate daily evaporation and daily streamflow, respectively. Finally, SVR have been successfully used to predict hourly streamflow by Asefa et al. [33] and were shown to perform better than ANN and ARIMA models for monthly streamflow prediction by Wang et al. [34] and Maity et al. [35], respectively. Yuan and Tan [36] used SVRs as a screening tool to test for drought resistance of rice. However, to date SVRs have not been applied to forecast a given drought index.

This study compared the effectiveness of three data-driven models for forecasting drought conditions in the Awash River Basin of Ethiopia. The Standard Precipitation Index (SPI) was forecasted and compared using artificial neural networks (ANNs), support vector regression (SVR), and wavelet networks (WN). SPI 3 and SPI 12 were forecast over lead times of 1 and 6 months. The forecast lead times were chosen because a 1-month lead time is a typical short-term lead time and a 6-month lead time is representative of the bimodal rainfall pattern in the Awash River Basin. Forecast results of this study are useful for the agricultural water management sector and have the potential to be applied by water resources managers to effectively manage water resources in the region. In addition, accurate forecasts using these data-driven models can complement the forecasts already being used by the NMSA of Ethiopia.

2. Theoretical Development

In the following section, the computation of the SPI is briefly described. In addition to the description of the SPI, this section also describes the data-driven models that were used to forecast the SPI.

2.1. The Standard Precipitation Index (SPI). The Standard Precipitation Index (SPI) was developed by McKee et al. [6]. As mentioned in the previous section, one of the main advantages of the SPI is that it only requires precipitation data as an input, which makes it ideal for areas where data collection is not as extensive (such as in Ethiopia). The fact that the SPI is based solely on precipitation makes its evaluation relatively easy [37]. The SPI is a standardized index. Standardization of a drought index ensures independence from geographical position as the index in question is calculated with respect to the average precipitation in the same place [37].

TABLE 1: Drought classification based on SPI [6].

SPI values	Class
>2	Extremely wet
1.5–1.99	Very wet
1.0–1.49	Moderately wet
−0.99 to 0.99	Near normal
−1 to −1.49	Moderately dry
−1.5 to −1.99	Very dry
<−2	Extremely dry

The computation of the SPI drought index for any location is based on the long-term precipitation record (at least 30 years) cumulated over a selected time scale [38]. This long-term precipitation time series is then fitted to a gamma distribution, which is then transformed through an equal probability transformation into a normal distribution [38, 39]. Positive SPI values indicate wet conditions with greater than median precipitation, and negative SPI values indicate dry conditions with lower than median precipitation [38]. Table 1 below indicates SPI drought classes.

In most cases, the probability distribution that best models observational precipitation data is the Gamma distribution [37]. The density probability function for the Gamma distribution is given by the expression [37]:

$$g(x) = \frac{1}{\beta^\alpha \Gamma(\alpha)} x^{\alpha-1} e^{-x/\beta}, \quad \text{for } x > 0, \quad (1)$$

where $\alpha > 0$ is the shape parameter, $\beta > 0$ is the scale parameter, and $x > 0$ is the amount of precipitation. $\Gamma(\alpha)$ is the value taken by the standard mathematical function known as the Gamma function, which is defined by the integral [37]:

$$\Gamma(\alpha) = \int_0^\infty y^{\alpha-1} e^{-y} dy. \quad (2)$$

In general, the Gamma function is evaluated either numerically or using the values tabulated depending on the value taken by parameter α.

In order to model the data observed with a gamma distributed density function, it is necessary to estimate parameters α and β appropriately. Different methods have been suggested in the literature for the estimate of these two parameters. For example, the Thom [40] approximation is used for maximum probability in Edwards and McKee [41]:

$$\hat{\alpha} = \frac{1}{4A}\left(1 + \sqrt{1 + \frac{4A}{3}}\right), \quad (3)$$

$$\hat{\beta} = \frac{\bar{x}}{\hat{\alpha}},$$

where for n observations

$$A = \ln(\bar{x}) - \frac{\sum \ln(x)}{n}. \quad (4)$$

The estimate of the parameters can be further improved by using the interactive approach suggested in Wilks [42].

After estimating coefficients α and β the density of probability function $g(x)$ is integrated with respect to x and we obtain an expression for cumulative probability $G(x)$ that a certain amount of rain has been observed for a given month and for a specific time scale [37]:

$$G(x) = \int_0^x g(x)dx = \frac{1}{\hat{\beta}\Gamma(\hat{\alpha})} = \int_0^x x^{\hat{\alpha}-1} e^{-x/\beta} dx. \quad (5)$$

The Gamma function is not defined by $x = 0$, and since there may be no precipitation, the cumulative probability becomes [37]

$$H(x) = q + (1-q)G(x), \quad (6)$$

where q is the probability of no precipitation. $H(x)$ is the cumulative probability of precipitation observed. The cumulative probability is then transformed into a normal standardized distribution with null average and unit variance from which we obtain the SPI index.

The above approach, however, is neither practical nor numerically simple to use if there are many grid points of many stations on which to calculate the SPI index. In this case, an alternative method is described in Edwards and McKee [41] using the technique of approximate conversion developed in Abramowitz and Stegun [43] that converts the cumulative probability into a standard variable Z. The SPI index is then defined as

$$Z = \text{SPI}$$
$$= \begin{cases} -\left(t - \dfrac{c_0+c_1t+c_2t_2}{1+d_1t+d_2t_2+d_3t_3}\right), & \text{for } 0 < H(x) \le 0.5, \\ +\left(t - \dfrac{c_0+c_1t+c_2t^2}{1+d_1t+d_2t^2+d_3t^3}\right), & \text{for } 0.5 < H(x) < 1, \end{cases} \quad (7)$$

where

$$t = \begin{cases} \sqrt{\ln\left[\dfrac{1}{(H(x))^2}\right]}, & \text{for } 0 < H(x) \le 0.5, \\ \sqrt{\ln\left[\dfrac{1}{(1-H(x))^2}\right]}, & \text{for } 0.5 < H(x) < 1, \end{cases} \quad (8)$$

where x is precipitation, $H(x)$ is the cumulative probability of precipitation observed, and $c_0, c_1, c_2, d_0, d_1, d_2$ are constants with the following values:

$$c_0 = 2.515517, \quad c_1 = 0.802853, \quad c_2 = 0.010328,$$
$$d_0 = 1.432788, \quad d_1 = 0.189269, \quad d_2 = 0.001308. \quad (9)$$

2.2. *Artificial Neural Networks (ANNs).* Artificial neural networks (ANNs) are flexible computing frameworks that resemble the structure of a nerve system. ANNs have been used to model a broad range of hydrologic time series over the past two decades. The main advantage of using ANNs is that there is no need to define the physical processes between the inputs

Standard Precipitation Index Drought Forecasting Using Neural Networks, Wavelet Neural Networks, and Support Vector Regression

165

and outputs [11]. This feature makes ANNs suitable for the purposes of drought forecasting, where all the variables that may cause a drought are not fully understood.

In this paper, the multilayer perceptron (MLP) feed-forward network was used to forecast the SPI time series. Figure 1 is an illustration of a typical feed-forward neural network. ANN models in this study were trained with the Levenberg Marquardt (LM) back propagation algorithm. MLPs have been used extensively in hydrologic forecasting studies [10, 12, 23, 26, 44, 45] due to their simplicity. In terms of their architecture, MLPs consist of an input layer, one or more hidden layers, and an output layer. The hidden layer contains the neuron-like processing elements that connect the input and output layers and is given by [26]

$$y_k'(t_s) = f_0 \left[\sum_{j=1}^m w_{kj}.f_n \left(\sum_{i=1}^n w_{ji} x_i(t_s) + \left(w_{j0}\right) \right) + w_{k0} \right],$$
(10)

where n is the number of input variables; m is the number of hidden neurons; $x_i(t)$ = the ith input variable at time step t_s; w_{ji} = weight that connects the ith neuron in the input layer and the jth neuron in the hidden layer; w_{j0} = bias for the jth hidden neuron; f_n = activation function of the hidden neuron; w_{kj} = weight that connects the jth neuron in the hidden layer and kth neuron in the output layer; w_{k0} = bias for the kth output neuron; f_0 = activation function for the output neuron; $y_k'(t_s)$ is the forecasted kth output at time step t_s [26].

2.3. Support Vector Regression. Support vector machines (SVM) were developed by Vapnik [27] as a tool for classification and regression. SVMs embody the structural risk minimization principle, while neural networks embody the empirical risk minimization principle. In contrast to ANNs that seek to minimize training error, SVMs attempt to minimize the generalization error. SVMs have two components: support vector classification (SVC) and support vector regression (SVR). Since the main objective of this study is to forecast the SPI, the SVR was used.

Support vector regression (SVR) is used to describe regression with SVMs [27]. In regression estimation with SVR, the purpose is to estimate a functional dependency $f(\vec{x})$ between a set of sampled points $X = \{\vec{x}_1, \vec{x}_2, \ldots, \vec{x}_l\}$ taken from R^n and target values $Y = \{y_1, y_2, \ldots, y_l\}$ with $y_i \in R$ (the input and target vectors (x_i's and y_i's) refer to the monthly records of the SPI index). Assuming that these samples have been generated independently from an unknown probability distribution function $P(\vec{x}, y)$ and a class of functions [27]:

$$F = \left\{ f \mid f(\vec{x}) = \left(\vec{W}, \vec{x}\right) + B : \vec{W} \in R^n, R^n \longrightarrow R \right\}, \quad (11)$$

where $\vec{W}$ and B are coefficients that have to be estimated from the input data. The main objective is to find a function $f(\vec{x}) \in F$ that minimizes a risk functional [46]:

$$R[f(\vec{x})] = \int l(y - f(\vec{x}), \vec{x}) dP(\vec{x}, y), \quad (12)$$

where l is a loss function used to measure the deviation between the target, y, and estimate $f(\vec{x})$, values. As the probability distribution function $P(\vec{x}, y)$ is unknown, one cannot minimize the risk functional directly, but can only compute the empirical risk function as [46]

$$R_{emp}[f(\vec{x})] = \frac{1}{N} \sum_{i=1}^N l(y_1 - f(\vec{x}_i)), \quad (13)$$

where N is the number of samples. This traditional empirical risk minimization is not advisable without any means of structural control or regularization. To avoid this issue a regularized risk function with the smallest steepness among the functions that minimize the empirical risk function can be used as [46]

$$R_{reg}[f(\vec{x})] = R_{emp}[f(\vec{x})] + \gamma \|\vec{W}\|^2, \quad (14)$$

where γ is a constant ($\gamma \geq 0$). This additional term reduces the model space and thereby controls the complexity of the solution resulting in the following form of this expression [46, 47]:

$$R_{reg}[f(\vec{x})] = C_c \sum_{x_i \in X} l_\varepsilon(y_1 - f(\vec{x}_i)) + \frac{1}{2}\|\vec{W}\|^2, \quad (15)$$

where C_c is a positive constant that has to be selected beforehand. The constant C_c that influences a trade-off between or an approximation error and the regression (weight) vector $\|\vec{W}\|$ is a design parameter. The loss function in this expression, which is called an ε-insensitive loss function (l_ε), has the advantage that it will not need all the input data for describing the regression vector $\|\vec{W}\|$ and can be written as [46]

$$l_\varepsilon(y_1 - f(\vec{x}_i)) = \begin{cases} 0, & \text{for } |y_1 - f(\vec{x}_i)| < \varepsilon \\ y_1 - f(\vec{x}_i), & \text{otherwise.} \end{cases} \quad (16)$$

This function behaves as a biased estimator when it is combined with the regularization term $(\gamma\|\vec{W}\|^2)$. The loss is equal to 0 if the difference between the predicted and observed value is less than ε. The nonlinear regression function is described by the following expression [27, 46, 48]:

$$f(x) = \sum_{i=1}^N (\alpha_i^* - \alpha_i) K(x, x_i) + B, \quad (17)$$

where $\alpha_i, \alpha_1^* \geq 0$ are the Lagrange multipliers, B is a bias term, and $K(x, x_i)$ is the Kernel function which is based upon Reproducing Kernel Hilbert Spaces [32]. The Kernel function enables operations to be performed in the input space as opposed to the potentially high-dimensional feature space. Several types of functions are treated by SVR such as polynomial functions, Gaussian radial basis functions, exponential radial basis functions, multilayer perception functions, and functions with splines and so forth [32].

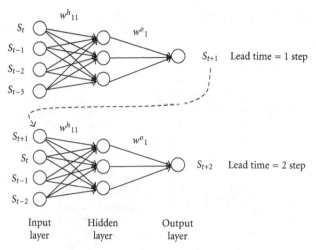

FIGURE 1: Typical Feed-forward Neural Network.

2.4. *Wavelet Transforms.* Wavelet transforms are mathematical functions that can be used for the analysis of time-series that contain nonstationarities. Wavelet transforms allow for the use of long time intervals for low frequency information and shorter intervals for high frequency information. They are capable of revealing aspects of data like trends, breakdown points, and discontinuities that other signal analysis techniques might miss [26]. Another advantage of wavelet analysis is the flexible choice of the mother wavelet according to the characteristics of the investigated time series [45].

An important step in the use of wavelet transforms is the choice of a mother wavelet (ψ). The continuous wavelet transform (CWT) is defined as the sum over all time of the signal multiplied by scale and shifted versions of the wavelet function ψ [26]:

$$W(\tau, s) = \frac{1}{\sqrt{|s|}} \int_{-\infty}^{\infty} x(t)\psi^*\left(\frac{t-\tau}{s}\right) dt, \qquad (18)$$

where s is the scale parameter; τ is the translation and $*$ corresponds to the complex conjugate [26]. The CWT produces a continuum of all scales as the output. Each scale corresponds to the width of the wavelet; hence, a larger-scale means that more of a time series is used in the calculation of the coefficient than in smaller scales. The CWT is useful for processing different images and signals; however, it is not often used for forecasting because its computation is complex and time consuming. As an alternative, in forecasting applications, the discrete wavelet transform (DWT) is used, due to its simplicity and shorter computation time. DWT scales and positions are usually based on powers of two (dyadic scales and positions). This is achieved by modifying the wavelet representation to [49]

$$\psi_{j,m}(m) = \frac{1}{\sqrt{\left|s_0^j\right|}} \sum_k \psi\left(\frac{k - m\tau_0 s_0^j}{s_0^j}\right) x(k), \qquad (19)$$

where j and m are integers that control the scale and translation, respectively, while $s_0 > 1$ is a fixed dilation step and

τ_0 is a translation factor that depends on the aforementioned dilation step. The effect of discretizing the wavelet is that the time-space scale is now sampled at discrete levels. The DWT operates two sets of functions: high-pass and low-pass filters. The original time series is passed through high-pass and low-pass filters, and detailed coefficients and approximation series are obtained.

One of the inherent challenges of using the DWT for forecasting applications is that if we change values at the beginning of our time series, all of the wavelet coefficients will subsequently change. To overcome this problem, a redundant algorithm, known as the à trous algorithm can be used, given by [50]

$$C_{i+1}(k) = \sum_{l=-\infty}^{+\infty} h(l) c_i \left(k + 2^i l\right), \qquad (20)$$

where h is the low pass filter and the finest scale is the original time series. To extract the details, $w_i(k)$, that were eliminated in (21), the smoothed version of the signal is subtracted from the coarser signal that preceded it, given by [51]

$$w_i(k) = c_{i-1}(k) - c_i(k), \qquad (21)$$

where $c_i(k)$ is the approximation of the signal and $c_{i-1}(k)$ is the coarser signal. Each application of (20) and (21) creates a smoother approximation and extracts a higher level of detail. Finally, the nonsymmetric Haar wavelet can be used as the low pass filter to prevent any future information from being used during the decomposition [52].

3. The Awash River Basin

This study forecasted the SPI in the Awash River Basin of Ethiopia. The mean annual rainfall of the basin varies from about 1,600 mm in the highlands north east of Addis Ababa, to 160 mm in the northern point of the basin [53]. The total amount of rainfall also varies greatly from year to year, resulting in severe droughts in some years and flooding in

Standard Precipitation Index Drought Forecasting Using Neural Networks, Wavelet Neural Networks, and Support Vector Regression

167

others. The total annual surface runoff in the Awash Basin amounts to some $4,900 \times 10^6$ m^3 [54].

The Awash River Basin (Figure 2) was separated into three smaller basins for the purpose of this study on the basis of various factors such as location, altitude, climate, topography, and agricultural development. A study conducted by Edossa et al. [54] separated the Awash Basin in a similar fashion. The subbasins were called the Upper, Middle, and Lower Awash Basins, respectively. The reasoning behind the use of these three subbasins was to ensure the methods used in this study were effective in forecasting short-term drought in different conditions. The characteristics of each sub-basin are briefly described in the following sections.

3.1. Upper Awash Basin. The Upper Awash Basin has a temperate climate with annual mean temperatures ranging between 15–22°C and an annual precipitation of between 500–2000 mm [54]. Rainfall distribution in the Upper Awash Basin is unimodal. Seven rainfall gauges located in the Upper Awash River Basin were chosen for this study (Table 2). These stations were chosen because their precipitation records from 1970–2005 were either complete or relatively complete. Any station, which had over 10% of their records missing was not selected.

3.2. Middle Awash Basin. The Middle Awash Basin is in the semiarid climatic zone with a long hot summer and a short mild winter. Annual rainfall varies between 200–1500 mm [54]. The rainfall distribution is bimodal in this subbasin. Minor rains normally occur in March and April and major rains from July to August. Eight rainfall gauges located in the Middle Awash Basin were selected using the same criteria as in the Upper Awash Basin and are shown in Table 2.

3.3. Lower Awash Basin. The Lower Awash River Basin has a hot, semi-arid climate. The annual mean temperature of the region ranges between 22 and 32°C with average annual precipitation between 500 and 700 mm [54]. Five rainfall gauges were selected form the Lower Awash Basin using the same criteria used in the two other sub-basins and are shown in Table 2.

4. Methodology

The methodology section of this paper describes how the SPI was calculated and then forecast over two separate lead times using ANN, WN, and SVR models.

4.1. SPI Calculation. In order to calculate the SPI, a probability density function that adequately describes the precipitation data must be determined. The gamma distribution function was selected to fit the raw rainfall data from each station in this study. The SPI is a z-score and represents an event departure from the mean, expressed in standard deviation units. The SPI is a normalized index in time and space. SPI values can be categorized according to classes. In this study, the near normal class is established from the aggregation of two classes: $-1 < SPI < 0$ (mild drought)

and $0 \leq SPI \leq 1$ (slightly wet). The departure from the mean is a probability indication of the severity of the wetness or drought that can be used for risk assessment. The time series of the SPI can be used for drought monitoring by setting application-specific thresholds of the SPI for defining drought beginning and ending times. Accumulated values of the SPI can be used to analyze drought severity. In this study, the SPI_SL_6 program developed by the National Drought Mitigation Centre, University of Nebraska-Lincoln, was used to compute time series of drought indices (SPI) for each station in the basin and for each month of the year at different time scales.

In each sub-basin, for each station, SPI 3 and SPI 12 were computed. These SPI values were subsequently forecast over lead times of 1 and 6 months. A 3-month SPI compares the precipitation for that period with the same 3-month period over the historical record. For example, a 3-month SPI at the end of September compares the precipitation total for the July–September period with all the past totals for that same period. A 3-month SPI indicates short and medium term trends in precipitation and is still considered to be more sensitive to conditions at this scale than the Palmer Index. A 3-month SPI can be very effective in showing seasonal trends in precipitation and is a good indicator of agricultural drought. SPI 12 reflects long-term precipitation patterns. SPI 12 is a comparison of the precipitation for 12 consecutive months with the same 12 consecutive months during all the previous years of available data and is a good indicator of long-term drought conditions. Because these time scales are the cumulative result of shorter periods that may be above or below normal, the longer SPIs tend toward zero unless a specific trend is taking place. Forecast lead times of 1 and 6 months were chosen because 1 month is the shortest possible monthly lead time and 6 months is representative of the bimodal rainfall pattern in parts of the Awash River Basin discussed in Section 3.2.

4.2. Wavelet Decomposition. In the proposed WN model, the SPI data for each of the rainfall stations was decomposed into subseries of approximations and details (DWs). The process consists of a number of successive filtering steps. The original SPI time series is first decomposed into an approximation and accompanying detail signal. The decomposition process is then iterated, with successive approximation signals being decomposed in turn. As a result the original SPI time series is broken down into many lower resolution components.

When conducting wavelet analysis, the number of decomposition levels that is appropriate for the data must be chosen. A commonly used method to determine the number of decomposition levels is based on the signal length [55] and is given by $L = \text{int}[\log(N)]$, where L is the level of decomposition and N is the length of the signal. The training set in this study comprised between 1290 and 3017 samples (samples varied depending on the number of inputs for each rainfall station). Thus, the decomposition level was selected as $L = 3$.

As discussed in Section 2.4, the "a trous" wavelet algorithm with a low pass Haar filter was used to create four

TABLE 2: Descriptive statistics for the Awash River Basin.

Basin	Station	Mean annual precipitation (mm)	Max annual (1970–2005) precipitation (mm)	Standard deviation (mm)
Upper Awash Basin	Bantu Liben	91	647	111
	Tullo Bullo	94	575	114
	Ginchi	97	376	90
	Sebeta	111	1566	172
	Ejersalele	67	355	75
	Ziquala	100	583	110
	Debre Zeit	73	382	81
Middle Awash Basin	Koka	97	376	90
	Modjo	76	542	92
	Nazereth	73	470	85
	Wolenchiti	76	836	95
	Gelemsso	77	448	75
	Hirna	78	459	86
	Dire Dawa	51	267	54
	Meisso	61	361	61
Lower Awash Basin	Dubti	15	192	23
	Eliwuha	44	374	57
	Mersa	87	449	89
	Mille	26	268	40
	Bati	73	357	80

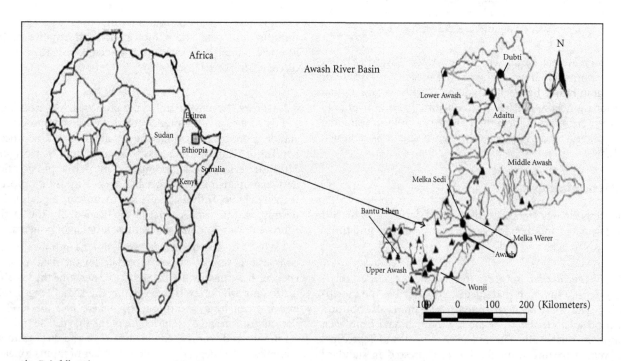

▲ Rainfall stations   ∧ Tributaries
● Stream gage stations   ∧ Awash River
▨ Lakes

FIGURE 2: Awash River Basin (Source: [54]).

Standard Precipitation Index Drought Forecasting Using Neural Networks,Wavelet Neural Networks, and Support Vector Regression

169

sets of wavelet subseries. These four sub-series included a low frequency component (the approximation) used to uncover the trend of each signal and a set of three high frequency components (the details) used to uncover the periodicity of the signal. All decomposed sub-series were added together to generate one time series and used as an input to the ANN models. Using the sum of all the sub-series as an input in this study provided more accurate results than using certain sub-series or sub-series that exhibited the highest correlations with the original time series.

4.3. ANN Models. All the ANN models were created with the MATLAB (R.2010a) ANN toolbox. The hyperbolic tangent sigmoid transfer function was the activation function for the hidden layer, while the activation function for the output layer was a linear function. All the ANN models in this study were trained using the LM back propagation algorithm. The LM back propagation algorithm was chosen because of its efficiency and reduced computational time in training models [45].

In this study, there were between 4–8 input neurons for each ANN model. The optimal number of input neurons for each station was selected using a trial and error procedure. The data-driven models were recursive models, where a model is forecast one lead time ahead, and the subsequent forecasts include the output from the previous forecast as an input. Hence, a forecast of 6 months lead time will have the outputs from forecasts of lead times of 1–5 months. Recursive models were used because it was determined that it would be simpler to use an ANN with one output neuron. Mishra and Desai [10] compared recursive ANN models and ANN models with more than one output neuron (direct ANN models) and found the results to be comparable for forecasting the SPI. The inputs and outputs were normalized between 0 and 1. A study by Wanas et al. [56] empirically determined that the best performance of a neural network occurs when the number of hidden nodes is equal to $\log(T)$, where T is the number of training samples. Another study conducted by Mishra and Desai [10] determined that the optimal number of hidden neurons is $2n + 1$, where n is the number of input layers. In this study the optimal number of hidden neurons was determined to be between $\log(T)$ and $(2n + 1)$. For example, if using the method proposed by Wanas et al. [56] gave a result of 4 hidden neurons and using the method proposed by Mishra and Desai [10] gave 6 hidden neurons, the optimal number of hidden neurons was between 4 and 6, thereafter the optimal number was determined using trial and error. These two methods helped establish an upper and lower bound for the number of hidden neurons.

For all the ANN models the cross validation technique [57] was used to partition the data sets; 80% of the data was used to train the models, while the remaining 20% of the data was used to test and validate the models, with 10% used for testing and 10% used for validation. The training set was used to compute the error gradient and to update the network weights and biases. The error from the validation set was used to monitor the training process. If

the network overfits the data, the error in the validation set will begin to rise. When the validation error increases for a specified number of iterations, the training is stopped, and the weights and biases at the minimum of the validation error are returned. The testing data set is an independent data set and is used to verify the performance of the model.

4.4. WN Models. The WN models were trained in the same way as the ANN models, with the exception that the inputs were made up from the wavelet decomposed subseries. In this study, the significant wavelets (approximation and detail series) were summed together once the insignificant coefficients were excluded, similar to what was done by Partal [58] and Kisi and Cimen [32]. In this study, the summed sub-series provided better results than using the individual wavelet coefficients as inputs.

For WN models, an input layer with 4–8 neurons, a single hidden layer composed of 4–6 neurons, and one output layer consisting of one neuron were developed. The number of neurons was determined in the same way as for the traditional ANN models. All the ANN models that had wavelet decomposed subseries as their inputs were also partitioned in a similar manner to the traditional ANN models.

4.5. SVR Models. All SVR models were developed using the OnlineSVR software created by Parrella [59]. OnlineSVR is a technique used to build support vector machines for regression. The OnlineSVR software partitions the data into only two sets: a training set and a testing set. The SVR models were partitioned in a similar manner to the ANN and WN models.

All SVR models used the nonlinear radial basis function (RBF) kernel. As a result, each SVR model consisted of three parameters that were selected: gamma (γ), cost (C), and epsilon (ε). The γ parameter is a constant that reduces the model space and controls the complexity of the solution, C is a positive constant that is a capacity control parameter, and ε is the loss function that describes the regression vector without all the input data [32]. These three parameters were selected based on a trial and error procedure. The combination of parameters that produced the lowest RMSE values for the training data sets was selected.

4.6. Performance Measures. The performance of the forecasts resulting from the data-driven models was evaluated by the following measures of goodness of fit:

The coefficient of determination $(R^2) = \dfrac{\sum_{i=1}^{N}\left(\hat{y}_i - \overline{y}_i\right)}{\sum_{i=1}^{N}\left(y_i - \overline{y}_i\right)^2},$

$$\overline{y}_i = \frac{1}{N}\sum_{i=1}^{N} y_i,$$

(22)

where $\overline{y}_i$ is the mean value taken over N, y_i is the observed value, $\hat{y}_i$ is the forecasted value, and N is the number of data points. The coefficient of determination measures the degree of association among the observed and predicted values. The higher the value of R^2 (with 1 being the highest possible value), the better the performance of the model

$$\text{The Root Mean Squared Error (RMSE)} = \sqrt{\frac{\text{SSE}}{N}}, \quad (23)$$

where SSE is the sum of squared errors and N is the number of data points used. SSE is given by

$$\text{SSE} = \sum_{i=1}^{N} (y_i - \widehat{y}_i)^2 \quad (24)$$

with the variables already having been defined. The RMSE evaluates the variance of errors independently of the sample size

$$\text{The Mean Absolute Error (MAE)} = \sum_{i=1}^{N} \frac{|y_i - \widehat{y}_i|}{N}. \quad (25)$$

The MAE is used to measure how close forecasted values are to the observed values. It is the average of the absolute errors.

5. Results and Discussion

For each subbasin of the Awash River Basin, the station that showed the best performance results for each data driven model are presented below. In this study, SPI 3 and SPI 12 were forecast over lead times of 1 and 6 months to determine the effectiveness of the data-driven models over short- and long-term lead times.

As shown in Table 3(a), the best data-driven model in the Upper Awash Basin for forecasts of SPI 3 and 12 is the WN model. All the models exhibited better results for forecasts of a 1-month lead time (L1) compared to forecasts of 6-months lead time (L6). Forecasts of SPI 12, for all the data-driven models, had better performance results than forecasts of SPI 3 in terms of R^2, RMSE, and MAE, regardless of forecast lead time. The best 1-month lead time WN forecast of SPI 12 had results of 0.9534, 0.0600, and 0.0536 in terms of R^2, RMSE, and MAE, respectively. The second best results were from ANN models with results of 0.9451, 0.0610, and 0.0603 in terms of R^2, RMSE and MAE, respectively. Figures 3 and 4 show the ANN and WN 1-month forecast results for SPI 12 at the Ejersalele station.

The performance of both these models is quite similar, as indicated by Figures 3 and 4. Both models adequately represent the periods of abundant and acute precipitation as indicated by the peaks and valleys in the figures.

Similar to the results for the Upper Awash Basin, the best forecast results in the Middle Awash Basin were from WN models. The WN models had the best results for both SPI 3 and SPI 12, for forecast lead times of 1 and 6 months, respectively (Table 3(b)). The forecast results of all the data-driven models deteriorated when the forecast lead time was increased from 1 to 6 months.

Figure 5 illustrates the relationship between the observed SPI 12 and the predicted SPI 12 from the ANN model at

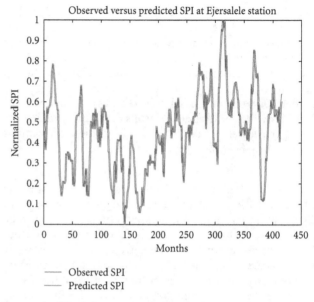

FIGURE 3: SPI 12 forecast results for the best ANN model at the Ejersalele station (1-month lead time).

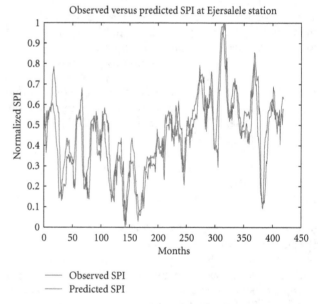

FIGURE 4: SPI 12 forecast results for the best WA-ANN model at the Ejersalele station (1-month lead time).

the Nazereth station. The ANN model underestimates the severity of the drought period at 112 months. In contrast, the WN model for SPI 12 at the Nazereth station displays improved results with respect to the drought period at 112 months (Figure 6).

In the Lower Awash Basin, the forecast results exhibited the same trend shown in the Upper and Middle sub-basins. The WN models had the best results for both SPI 3 and SPI 12, for forecast lead times of 1 and 6 months, respectively. Figures 7 and 8 illustrate the best SPI 12 forecasts at the Dubti station where both ANN and WN models predict

Standard Precipitation Index Drought Forecasting Using Neural Networks, Wavelet Neural Networks, and Support Vector Regression

171

TABLE 3: (a) Performance results for the Ejersalele station, Upper Awash Basin, (b) Performance results of Nazereth Station, Middle Awash Basin, (c) Performance results of Dubti Station, Lower Awash Basin.

(a)

Model-Lead time	SPI 3			SPI 12		
	R^2	RMSE	MAE	R^2	RMSE	MAE
ANN-L1	0.7694	0.1574	0.1433	0.9451	0.0610	0.0603
ANN-L6	0.6232	0.1744	0.1567	0.8614	0.1011	0.0885
WN-L1	0.8829	0.0700	0.0352	0.9534	0.0600	0.0536
WN-L6	0.6433	0.1070	0.0356	0.8731	0.0790	0.0662
SVR-L1	0.7219	0.1046	0.0915	0.7611	0.1312	0.1129
SVR-L6	0.6647	0.1118	0.1042	0.6941	0.1341	0.1247

(b)

Model-Lead time	SPI 3			SPI 12		
	R^2	RMSE	MAE	R^2	RMSE	MAE
ANN-L1	0.7319	0.1170	0.1016	0.9158	0.1003	0.0911
ANN-L6	0.6546	0.1240	0.1142	0.7542	0.1104	0.0919
WN-L1	0.9483	0.0510	0.0441	0.9167	0.0753	0.0629
WN-L6	0.8641	0.0727	0.0512	0.8012	0.1072	0.0802
SVR-L1	0.7114	0.1216	0.1114	0.7713	0.1147	0.1130
SVR-L6	0.6540	0.1320	0.1217	0.7326	0.1244	0.1215

(c)

Model-Lead time	SPI 3			SPI 12		
	R^2	RMSE	MAE	R^2	RMSE	MAE
ANN-L1	0.7368	0.1175	0.1095	0.9188	0.0710	0.0648
ANN-L6	0.6806	0.1302	0.1147	0.7135	0.0938	0.0836
WN-L1	0.9018	0.0652	0.0581	0.9473	0.0648	0.0560
WN-L6	0.8119	0.0706	0.0642	0.8641	0.0846	0.0747
SVR-L1	0.6990	0.1146	0.1022	0.7041	0.1102	0.1009
SVR-L6	0.6331	0.1309	0.1242	0.6705	0.1107	0.1025

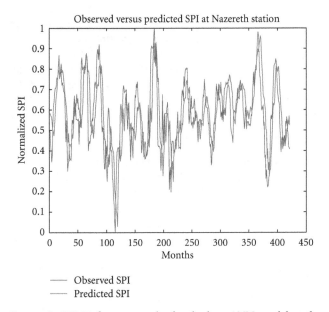

FIGURE 5: SPI 12 forecast results for the best ANN model at the Nazereth station (1 month lead time).

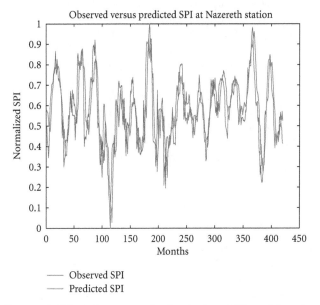

FIGURE 6: SPI 12 forecast results for the best WN model at the Nazereth station (1-month lead time).

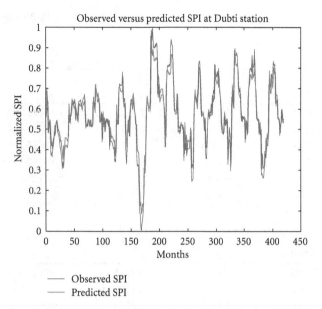

FIGURE 7: SPI 12 forecast results for the best ANN model at the Dubti station (1-month lead time).

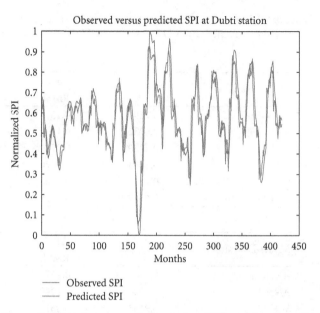

FIGURE 8: SPI 12 forecast results for the best WN model at the Dubti station (1-month lead time).

the periods of abundant and acute precipitation quite well. When the forecast lead time was increased, the performance of all the models deteriorated, especially with respect to R^2. Data-driven models in the Upper and Lower Awash basins exhibited their best results for forecasts of SPI 12, indicating that data-driven models are more effective in predicting long-term drought conditions in those two basins, while in the Middle Awash Basin most models also exhibited their best results for forecasts of SPI 12 except WN models, which exhibited their best results for forecasts of SPI 3. This trend could be due to the fact that long-term SPI, which is a cumulative of short-term time scales, tend toward zero unless a specific trend is taking place. The exception regarding the WN models in the Middle Awash Basin may be due to the fact that the precipitation record at this station is relatively stable, meaning there are not many changes from one month to the next and the SPI 3 is not sensitive to those changes.

Overall, all three data-driven models forecast SPI 3 and SPI 12 well for forecast lead times of 1 and 6 months. The results indicate that ANN models are more effective than SVR models at forecasting in this study. The use of wavelet analysis improved the forecast results of ANN models, specifically in predicting extreme events as shown in Figure 6. Indeed, using a measure for peak relative error as shown by

$$Z = 100 \left| \frac{q_s(\text{peak}) - q_o(\text{peak})}{q_o} \right|, \quad (26)$$

it was determined that the relative error of the ANN model, 95%, was reduced to 88% when a WN model was used.

The fact that wavelet analysis is an effective tool at revealing local discontinuities helps explain why it was more effective in predicting the extreme events in the Middle Awash Basin. Wavelet analysis may help de-noise the original

SPI time series compared to a traditional ANN model. The forecast of this de-noised signal may further explain the fact that extreme events are forecast better using wavelet analysis.

An increase in forecast lead time results in a deterioration of performance in all the models. However, this deterioration does not result in poor models, indicating the stability of these data-driven models in predicting the SPI. The results in terms of RMSE and MAE do not deteriorate drastically with an increase of lead time. For example, for the Dubti station, the RMSE and MAE of SVR models deteriorate by 0.05 and 0.26%, respectively.

There is variability with regards to the best forecasts of both SPI 3 and SPI 12 amongst the three subbasins. For example, the best forecast of SPI 3 at a 1-month lead time occurred in the Middle Awash Basin (WN model), while the best forecast of SPI 12 at a 1-month lead time occurred in the Upper Awash Basin (WN model). While each subbasin has a different climatology, there does not seem to be a clear trend linking climatology with forecast accuracy. It seems that the reason behind the best models for each data-driven method being in various subbasins is linked with the characteristics of the individual station and not the characteristics of the subbasin as a whole.

In addition, the forecast results for SPI 12 are better than the forecast results for SPI 3 in almost all cases. For SPI 3 and other short-term SPI, each new month has a large impact on the period sum of precipitation [6]. As a result, the SPI 3 is sensitive to any change in precipitation from one month to another. In the case of SPI 12, each individual month has less impact on the total and the index is not as sensitive to changes in precipitation from one month to the next. The fact that SPI 3 is more sensitive to changes in precipitation results in less accurate forecast results than SPI 12. However, the effects of wavelet analysis are more significant for SPI 3 than for SPI 12, especially for forecast lead times of 6

Standard Precipitation Index Drought Forecasting Using Neural Networks, Wavelet Neural Networks, and Support Vector Regression

173

months. As stated previously, the ANN forecasts of SPI 12 are not as sensitive to changes in precipitation and thus good results are obtained. The ability of wavelet analysis to improve these results exists as shown but is not as high as the improvement seen in SPI 3 forecasts because ANN forecasts of SPI 3 suffer due to the sensitivity of SPI 3 to slight changes in precipitation over the long-term record.

All three subbasins had a different climatology. The forecast results have all shown that WN models are the most effective at forecasting the SPI in all the sub-basins in terms of R^2, RMSE and MAE. Whether this is the case in all climatic zones needs to be explored in future studies.

6. Conclusion

This study tried to determine the most effective data-driven model for forecasts of the SPI drought index in the Awash River Basin of Ethiopia. WN models were shown to be the most effective model for forecasts of SPI 3 and 12 in all three subbasins. WN models showed greater correlation between observed and predicted SPI compared to simple ANNs and SVR models. WN models also consistently showed lower values of RMSE and MAE compared to the other data driven models explored in this study. All the data-driven models showed increased forecast results for SPI 12 compared to SPI 3. Forecast results deteriorated as the forecast lead time increased for all the models. Of the two machine learning techniques, ANNs are more effective in forecasting the SPI compared to SVR models. This trend occurs in all three subbasins and should be studied in other regions to determine if ANNs are more effective tools for drought forecasting compared to SVR models. It is thought that WN models provide more accurate results because preprocessing the original SPI time series with wavelet decompositions "denoises" the data. Future studies should attempt to explore WSVR models, ensemble WN and WSVR models, and explore SPI forecasts using these new methods in other regions with different characteristics. Future studies should also attempt to quantify time shift error as it is a part of forecasting problems with regression models.

Acknowledgments

An NSERC Discovery Grant and a FQRNT New Researcher Grant held by Jan Adamowski were used to fund this research.

References

[1] E. Mersha and V. K. Boken, "Agricultural drought in Ethiopia," in *Monitoring and Predicting Agricultural Drought: A Global Study*, V. K. Boken, A. P. Cracknell, and R. L. Heathcote, Eds., Oxford University Press, 2005.

[2] A. K. Mishra and V. P. Singh, "A review of drought concepts," *Journal of Hydrology*, vol. 391, no. 1-2, pp. 202–216, 2010.

[3] T. Ross and N. Lott, "A climatology of 1980–2003 extreme weather and climate events," National Climatic Data Center Technical Report No. 2003-01. NOAA/ NESDIS, National Climatic Data Center, Asheville, NC, USA.

[4] A. Cancelliere, G. di Mauro, B. Bonaccorso, and G. Rossi, "Stochastic forecasting of drought indices," in *Methods and Tools For Drought Analysis and Management*, G. Rossi, T. Vega, and B. Bonaccorso, Eds., Springer, 2007.

[5] W. J. Gibbs and J. V. Maher, *Rainfall Deciles as Drought Indicators*, vol. 48 of *Bulletin (Commonwealth Bureau of Meteorology, Australia)*, Bureau of Meteorology, Melbourne, Australia, 1967.

[6] T. B. McKee, N. J. Doesken, and J. Kleist, "The relationship of drought frequency and duration to time scales," in *Proceedings of the 8th Conference on Applied Climatology*, American Meteorological Society, Anaheim, Calif, USA, 1993.

[7] H. R. Byun and D. A. Wilhite, "Objective quantification of drought severity and duration," *Journal of Climate*, vol. 12, no. 9, pp. 2747–2756, 1999.

[8] W. Palmer, "Meteorological drought," Tech. Rep. 45, U.S. Weather Bureau, Washington, DC, USA, 1965.

[9] H. K. Ntale and T. Y. Gan, "Drought indices and their application to East Africa," *International Journal of Climatology*, vol. 23, no. 11, pp. 1335–1357, 2003.

[10] A. K. Mishra and V. R. Desai, "Drought forecasting using feed-forward recursive neural network," *Ecological Modelling*, vol. 198, no. 1-2, pp. 127–138, 2006.

[11] S. Morid, V. Smakhtin, and K. Bagherzadeh, "Drought forecasting using artificial neural networks and time series of drought indices," *International Journal of Climatology*, vol. 27, no. 15, pp. 2103–2111, 2007.

[12] U. G. Bacanli, M. Firat, and F. Dikbas, "Adaptive Neuro-Fuzzy inference system for drought forecasting," *Stochastic Environmental Research and Risk Assessment*, vol. 23, no. 8, pp. 1143–1154, 2009.

[13] A. P. Barros and G. J. Bowden, "Toward long-lead operational forecasts of drought: an experimental study in the Murray-Darling River Basin," *Journal of Hydrology*, vol. 357, no. 3-4, pp. 349–367, 2008.

[14] P. Cutore, G. Di Mauro, and A. Cancelliere, "Forecasting palmer index using neural networks and climatic indexes," *Journal of Hydrologic Engineering*, vol. 14, no. 6, pp. 588–595, 2009.

[15] M. Karamouz, K. Rasouli, and S. Nazif, "Development of a hybrid Index for drought prediction: case study," *Journal of Hydrologic Engineering*, vol. 14, no. 6, pp. 617–627, 2009.

[16] A. F. Marj and A. M. J. Meijerink, "Agricultural drought forecasting using satellite images, climate indices and artificial neural network," *International Journal of Remote Sensing*, vol. 32, no. 24, pp. 9707–9719, 2011.

[17] D. Labat, R. Ababou, and A. Mangin, "Wavelet analysis in karstic hydrology. 2nd part: rainfall-runoff cross-wavelet analysis," *Comptes Rendus de l'Academie de Sciences*, vol. 329, no. 12, pp. 881–887, 1999.

[18] P. Saco and P. Kumar, "Coherent modes in multiscale variability of streamflow over the United States," *Water Resources Research*, vol. 36, no. 4, pp. 1049–1067, 2000.

[19] L. C. Smith, D. L. Turcotte, and B. L. Isacks, "Stream flow characterization and feature detection using a discrete wavelet transform," *Hydrological Processes*, vol. 12, no. 2, pp. 233–249, 1998.

[20] P. Coulibaly, F. Anctil, and B. Bobée, "Daily reservoir inflow forecasting using artificial neural networks with stopped training approach," *Journal of Hydrology*, vol. 230, no. 3-4, pp. 244–257, 2000.

[21] S. N. Lane, "Assessment of rainfall-runoff models based upon wavelet analysis," *Hydrological Processes*, vol. 21, no. 5, pp. 586–607, 2007.

[22] J. F. Adamowski, "Development of a short-term river flood forecasting method for snowmelt driven floods based on wavelet and cross-wavelet analysis," *Journal of Hydrology*, vol. 353, no. 3-4, pp. 247–266, 2008.

[23] J. Adamowski and K. Sun, "Development of a coupled wavelet transform and neural network method for flow forecasting of non-perennial rivers in semi-arid watersheds," *Journal of Hydrology*, vol. 390, no. 1-2, pp. 85–91, 2010.

[24] M. Özger, A. K. Mishra, and V. P. Singh, "Long lead time drought forecasting using a wavelet and fuzzy logic combination model: a case study in Texas," *Journal of Hydrometeorology*, vol. 13, no. 1, pp. 284–297, 2012.

[25] T. Partal and Ö. Kişi, "Wavelet and neuro-fuzzy conjunction model for precipitation forecasting," *Journal of Hydrology*, vol. 342, no. 1-2, pp. 199–212, 2007.

[26] T. W. Kim and J. B. Valdes, "Nonlinear model for drought forecasting based on a conjunction of wavelet transforms and neural networks," *Journal of Hydrologic Engineering*, vol. 8, no. 6, pp. 319–328, 2003.

[27] V. Vapnik, *The Nature of Statistical Learning Theory*, Springer, New York, NY, USA, 1995.

[28] J. B. Gao, S. R. Gunn, C. J. Harris, and M. Brown, "A probabilistic framework for SVM regression and error bar estimation," *Machine Learning*, vol. 46, no. 1–3, pp. 71–89, 2002.

[29] M. S. Khan and P. Coulibaly, "Application of support vector machine in lake water level prediction," *Journal of Hydrologic Engineering*, vol. 11, no. 3, pp. 199–205, 2006.

[30] S. Rajasekaran, S. Gayathri, and T.-L. Lee, "Support vector regression methodology for storm surge predictions," *Journal of Ocean Engineering*, vol. 35, no. 16, pp. 1578–1587, 2008.

[31] O. Kisi and M. Cimen, "Evapotranspiration modelling using support vector machines," *Hydrological Sciences Journal*, vol. 54, no. 5, pp. 918–928, 2009.

[32] O. Kisi and M. Cimen, "A wavelet-support vector machine conjunction model for monthly streamflow forecasting," *Journal of Hydrology*, vol. 399, no. 1-2, pp. 132–140, 2011.

[33] T. Asefa, M. Kemblowski, M. McKee, and A. Khalil, "Multitime scale stream flow predictions: the support vector machines approach," *Journal of Hydrology*, vol. 318, no. 1–4, pp. 7–16, 2006.

[34] W. C. Wang, K. W. Chau, C. T. Cheng, and L. Qiu, "A comparison of performance of several artificial intelligence methods for forecasting monthly discharge time series," *Journal of Hydrology*, vol. 374, no. 3-4, pp. 294–306, 2009.

[35] R. Maity, P. P. Bhagwat, and A. Bhatnagar, "Potential of support vector regression for prediction of monthly streamflow using endogenous property," *Hydrological Processes*, vol. 24, no. 7, pp. 917–923, 2010.

[36] Z. M. Yuan and X. S. Tan, "Nonlinear screening indicators of drought resistance at seedling stage of rice based on support vector machine," *Acta Agronomica Sinica*, vol. 36, no. 7, pp. 1176–1182, 2010.

[37] C. Cacciamani, A. Morgillo, S. Marchesi, and V. Pavan, "Monitoring and forecasting drought on a regional scale: emilia-romagna region," *Water Science and Technology Library*, vol. 62, part 1, pp. 29–48, 2007.

[38] I. Bordi and A. Sutera, "Drought monitoring and forecasting at large-scale," in *Methods and Tools For Drought Analysis and Management*, G. Rossi, T. Vega, and B. Bonaccorso, Eds., pp. 3–27, Springer, New York, NY, USA, 2007.

[39] N. B. Guttman, "Accepting the standardized precipitation index: a calculation algorithm," *Journal of the American Water Resources Association*, vol. 35, no. 2, pp. 311–322, 1999.

[40] H. C. S. Thom, "A note on gamma distribution," *Monthly Weather Review*, vol. 86, pp. 117–122, 1958.

[41] D. C. Edwards and T. B. McKee, "Characteristics of 20th century drought in the United States at multiple scales," Atmospheric Science Paper 634, 1997.

[42] D. S. Wilks, *Statistical Methods in the Atmospheric Sciences an Introduction*, Academic Press, San Diego, Calif, USA, 1995.

[43] M. Abramowitz and A. Stegun, Eds., *Handbook of Mathematical Formulas, Graphs, and Mathematical Tables*, Dover Publications, New York, NY, USA, 1965.

[44] S. Morid, V. Smakhtin, and M. Moghaddasi, "Comparison of seven meteorological indices for drought monitoring in Iran," *International Journal of Climatology*, vol. 26, no. 7, pp. 971–985, 2006.

[45] J. Adamowski and H. F. Chan, "A wavelet neural network conjunction model for groundwater level forecasting," *Journal of Hydrology*, vol. 407, no. 1–4, pp. 28–40, 2011.

[46] M. Çimen, "Estimation of daily suspended sediments using support vector machines," *Hydrological Sciences Journal*, vol. 53, no. 3, pp. 656–666, 2008.

[47] A. J. Smola, *Regression Estimation with Support Vector Learning Machines [M.S. thesis]*, Technische Universitat Munchen, Munich, Germany, 1996.

[48] S. Gunn, "Support vector machines for classification and regression," ISIS Technical Report, Department of Electronics and Computer Science, University of Southampton, 1998.

[49] B. Cannas, A. Fanni, G. Sias, S. Tronci, and M. K. Zedda, "River flow forecasting using neural networks and wavelet analysis," in *Proceedings of the European Geosciences Union*, 2006.

[50] S. G. Mallat, *A Wavelet Tour of Signal Processing*, Academic Press, San Diego, Calif, USA, 1998.

[51] F. Murtagh, J. L. Starck, and O. Renuad, "On neuro-wavelet modeling," *Decision Support Systems*, vol. 37, no. 4, pp. 475–484, 2004.

[52] O. Renaud, J. Starck, and F. Murtagh, *Wavelet-Based Forecasting of Short and Long Memory Time Series*, Department of Economics, University of Geneve, 2002.

[53] C. E. Desalegn, M. S. Babel, A. Das Gupta, B. A. Seleshi, and D. Merrey, "Farmers' perception of water management under drought conditions in the upper Awash Basin, Ethiopia," *International Journal of Water Resources Development*, vol. 22, no. 4, pp. 589–602, 2006.

[54] D. C. Edossa, M. S. Babel, and A. D. Gupta, "Drought analysis in the Awash River Basin, Ethiopia," *Water Resources Management*, vol. 24, no. 7, pp. 1441–1460, 2010.

[55] M. K. Tiwari and C. Chatterjee, "Development of an accurate and reliable hourly flood forecasting model using wavelet-bootstrap-ANN (WBANN) hybrid approach," *Journal of Hydrology*, vol. 394, no. 3-4, pp. 458–470, 2010.

[56] N. Wanas, G. Auda, M. S. Kamel, and F. Karray, "On the optimal number of hidden nodes in a neural network," in *Proceedings of the 11th IEEE Canadian Conference on Electrical and Computer Engineering (CCECE '98)*, pp. 918–921, May 1998.

[57] J. C. Principe, N. R. Euliano, and W. Curt Lefebvre, *Neural and Adaptive Systems*, John Wiley & Sons, 2000.

[58] T. Partal, "Modelling evapotranspiration using discrete wavelet transform and neural networks," *Hydrological Processes*, vol. 23, no. 25, pp. 3545–3555, 2009.

[59] F. Parrella, *Online support vector regression [M.S. thesis]*, University of Genoa, 2007.

18

On the Variability of Neural Network Classification Measures in the Protein Secondary Structure Prediction Problem

Eric Sakk and Ayanna Alexander

Department of Computer Science, Morgan State University, Baltimore, MD 21251, USA

Correspondence should be addressed to Eric Sakk; eric.sakk@morgan.edu

Academic Editor: Cheng-Jian Lin

We revisit the protein secondary structure prediction problem using linear and backpropagation neural network architectures commonly applied in the literature. In this context, neural network mappings are constructed between protein training set sequences and their assigned structure classes in order to analyze the class membership of test data and associated measures of significance. We present numerical results demonstrating that classifier performance measures can vary significantly depending upon the classifier architecture and the structure class encoding technique. Furthermore, an analytic formulation is introduced in order to substantiate the observed numerical data. Finally, we analyze and discuss the ability of the neural network to accurately model fundamental attributes of protein secondary structure.

1. Introduction

The protein secondary structure prediction problem can be phrased as a supervised pattern recognition problem [1–5] for which training data is readily available from reliable databases such as the Protein Data Bank (PDB) or CB513 [6]. Based upon training examples, subsequences derived from primary sequences are encoded based upon a discrete set of classes. For instance, three class encodings are commonly applied in the literature in order to numerically represent the secondary structure set (alpha helix (H), beta sheet (E), coil (C)) [7–11]. By applying a pattern recognition approach, subsequences of unknown classification can then be tested to determine the structure class to which they belong. Phrased in this way, backpropagation neural networks [7, 12–14], and variations on the neural network theme [8, 10, 11, 15–18] have been applied to the secondary structure prediction problem with varied success. Furthermore, many tools currently applying hybrid methodologies such as PredictProtein [19, 20], JPRED [8, 17, 21], SCRATCH [22, 23] and PSIPRED [24, 25] rely on the neural network paradigm as part of their prediction scheme.

One of the main reasons for applying the neural network approach in the first place is that they tend be good universal approximators [26–30] and, theoretically, have the potential to create secondary structure models. In other words, after a given network architecture has been chosen and presented with a robust set of examples, the optimal parameters associated with the trained network, in principle, define an explicit function that can map a given protein sequence to its associated secondary structure. If the structure predicted by the network function is generally correct and consistent for an arbitrary input sequence not contained in the training set, one must be left to conclude that the neural network has accurately modeled some fundamental set of attributes that define the properties of protein secondary structure. Under these circumstances, one should then be able to extract information from the trained neural network model parameters; thus, leading to a solution to the secondary structure prediction problem as well as a parametric understanding of the underlying basis for secondary structure.

The purpose of this work is to revisit the application of neural networks to the protein secondary structure prediction problem. In this setting, we consider the commonly encountered case where three structure classes (alpha helix (H), beta sheet (E), and coil (C)) are used to classify a given protein subsequence. Given the same set of input training sequences, we demonstrate that, for the backpropagation neural network architecture, classification results and associated confidence measures can vary when two equally valid encoding schemes are employed to numerically represent the three structure classes (i.e., the "target encoding scheme"). Such a result goes against the intuition that the physical nature of the secondary structure property should be independent of the target encoding scheme chosen.

The contribution of this work is not to demonstrate improvements over existing techniques. The hybrid techniques outlined above have been demonstrated to outperform neural networks when used alone. Instead, we focus our attention on the ability of the neural network model-based approach to accurately characterize fundamental attributes of protein secondary structure given that certain models presented within this work are demonstrated to yield variable results. Specifically, in this work, we present

(1) numerical results demonstrating how secondary structure classification results can vary as function of classifier architecture and parameter choices;

(2) an analytic formulation in order to explain under what circumstances classification variability can arise;

(3) an outline of specific challenges associated with the neural network model-based approach outlined above.

The conclusions reported here are relevant because they bring into discussion a body of literature that has purported to offer a viable path to the solution of the secondary structure prediction problem. Section 3 describes the methods applied in this work examine the total number that retained their classification using. In particular, this section provides details concerning the encoding of the protein sequence data (Section 3.1), the encoding of the structure classes (Section 3.2) as well as the neural network architectures (Sections 3.3-3.4), and the classifier performance measures (Section 3.5) applied in this work. Section 4 then presents results from numerical secondary structure classification experiments. Section 5 presents an analytic formulation for the linear network and the backpropagation network described in Section 3 in order to explain the numerical results given in Section 4.

2. Notation for the Supervised Classification Problem

In the supervised classification problem [1, 2], it is assumed that a training set consists of N training pairs:

$$\{(X_1, Y_1), (X_2, Y_2), \ldots, (X_N, Y_N)\}, \tag{1}$$

where $X_i \in R^n$ are n-dimensional input column vectors and $Y_i \in R^p$ are p-dimensional output column vectors. The goal of the supervised classifier approach is to ensure that the desired response to a given input vector X_i of dimension n from the training set is the p-dimensional output vector Y_i. Furthermore, when the training data can be partitioned into

M distinct classes, a set $\mathscr{E} \equiv \{e_1, \ldots, e_j, \ldots, e_M\}$ of target p-dimensional column vectors $e_j \in R^p$ are chosen to encode (i.e., mathematically represent) each class for $j = 1, \ldots, M$. Under these circumstances, each output training vector Y_i is derived from the set $\mathscr{E}$. Based upon this discussion, we summarize the use of following symbols:

(i) n is the dimension of a classifier input vector;

(ii) p is the dimension of a classifier output vector;

(iii) M is the number of discrete classes for the classification problem;

(iv) N is the number of training pairs for the supervised classification problem.

3. Methods

In order to apply the neural network paradigm, two numerical issues must be addressed. First, since the input data comes in the form of an amino acid sequence, Section 3.1 discusses a simple encoding scheme for converting the amino acid alphabet into a usable numerical form. Second, for this work, our secondary structure target alphabet consists of elements from the set $\{E, H, C\}$ = {Beta Sheet, AlphaHelix, Coil}. Hence, an encoding scheme must also be chosen for representing the neural network classifier output. Section 3.2 discusses two approaches to encoding the output in fine detail because it is critical to the main point of this paper. Specifically, we choose two different target vector encoding schemes that can be related by a simple mathematical relationship. Such an approach will allow us to compare classifier performance measures based upon the *target* vector encoding; in addition, it will facilitate the analytic formulation presented in Section 5. Finally, Sections 3.3–3.5 review the neural network architectures and the specific classifier performance measures employed in this work. Section 6 then concludes with some final observations regarding the neural network model-based approach to the protein secondary structure prediction problem.

3.1. Encoding of Protein Sequence Input Data. For the numerical experiments, the training set was constructed using one hundred protein sequences randomly chosen from the CB513 database [6] available through the JPRED secondary structure prediction engine [21]. Furthermore, we employ a moving window of length 17 to each protein sequence where, in order to avoid protein terminal effects, the first and last 50 amino acids are omitted from the analysis. The secondary structure classification of the central residue is then assigned to each window of 17 amino acids. For the one hundred sequences analyzed, a total of 12000 windows of length 17 were extracted. The window size value of 17 was chosen based upon the assumption that the eight closest neighboring residues will have the greatest influence on the secondary structure conformation of the central residue. This assumption is consistent with similar approaches reported in the literature [7, 12–14].

To encode the input amino acid sequences of length 17, we employ sparse orthogonal encoding [31] which maps symbols from a given sequence alphabet onto a set of orthogonal vectors. Specifically, for an alphabet containing K symbols, a unique K-dimensional unit vector is assigned to each symbol; furthermore, the kth unit vector is one at the kth position and is zero at all other positions. Hence, if all training sequences and unknown test sequences are of uniform length L, an encoded input vector will be of dimension n where $n = LK$. In our case, $K = 20$ and $L = 17$; hence, the dimension of any given input vector is $n = 340$.

The above input vector encoding technique is commonly applied in the bioinformatics and secondary structure prediction literature [7, 15]. While many different and superior approaches to this phase of the machine learning problem have been suggested [3–5], we have chosen orthogonal encoding because of its simplicity and the fact that the results of this work do not depend upon the input encoding scheme. Instead, our work specifically focuses on potential neural network classifier variabilities induced by choice of the target vector encoding scheme.

3.2. Target Vector Encoding.

Analytically characterizing the invariance of classifier performance measures clearly involves first establishing a relationship between different sets of target vectors $\mathscr{E}$ and $\widetilde{\mathscr{E}}$. As a means of making the invariance formulation presented in this paper more tractable, we assume that two alternative sets of target vectors can be related via an affine transformation involving a translation, T, a rigid rotation, R, where R is an orthogonal matrix and a scale factor, a,

$$\widetilde{\Gamma} \equiv aR\left(\Gamma - T\right), \qquad (2)$$

where

$$\Gamma \equiv [e_1 \ e_2 \ \dots \ e_M], \qquad \widetilde{\Gamma} \equiv [\widetilde{e}_1 \ \widetilde{e}_2 \ \dots \ \widetilde{e}_M],$$
$$T \equiv [t_1 \ t_2 \ \dots \ t_M] \qquad (3)$$

is a matrix of translation column vectors applied to each target vector. Many target vector choices regularly applied in the literature can be related via the transformation in (2). For instance, two equally valid and commonly applied encoding schemes for the three class problem are orthogonal encoding [31] where

$$H \longrightarrow \begin{bmatrix} 1 \\ 0 \\ 0 \end{bmatrix}, \quad E \longrightarrow \begin{bmatrix} 0 \\ 1 \\ 0 \end{bmatrix}, \quad C \longrightarrow \begin{bmatrix} 0 \\ 0 \\ 1 \end{bmatrix}, \qquad (4)$$

and

$$H \longrightarrow \begin{bmatrix} -\dfrac{1}{2} \\ \dfrac{\sqrt{3}}{2} \\ 0 \end{bmatrix}, \quad E \longrightarrow \begin{bmatrix} -\dfrac{1}{2} \\ -\dfrac{\sqrt{3}}{2} \\ 0 \end{bmatrix}, \quad C \longrightarrow \begin{bmatrix} 1 \\ 0 \\ 0 \end{bmatrix} \qquad (5)$$

where class encodings are chosen on the vertices of a triangle in a two-dimensional plane [14]. It turns out that (4) and (5) can be phrased in terms of (2) [32]; hence, the numerical

results presented in this work will apply this set of encodings. More precisely, the secondary structure classification associated with a given input vector is encoded using (4) and (5) (hence, $p = 3$). The set of target vectors $\mathscr{E}$ is derived from (4) and the set of target vectors $\widetilde{\mathscr{E}}$ is derived from (5). Both the linear and the backpropagation networks are tested first by training using $\mathscr{E}$ and then comparing classifier performance with their counterparts trained using $\widetilde{\mathscr{E}}$. In all numerical experiments, MATLAB has been used for simulating and testing these networks.

3.3. The Linear Network.

When the supervised classifier model in (1) assumes an affine relationship between the input and output data sets (as in the case of multiple linear regression), matrices of the form

$$X \equiv [X_1 \ \dots \ X_N], \qquad (6)$$

$$Y \equiv [Y_1 \ \dots \ Y_N] \qquad (7)$$

are generally introduced. Specifically, the linear network seeks to determine a $p \times n$ matrix β of coefficients and a constant p-dimensional column vector c such that the ith output vector Y_i in the training set can be approximated by

$$\beta X_i + c. \qquad (8)$$

Given this model, we can form a weight matrix of unknown coefficients

$$W \equiv [\beta \ c] \qquad (9)$$

that, ideally, will map each input training vector into the corresponding output training vector. If the bottom row of the input data matrix X is appended with a row of ones leading to the $(n + 1) \times N$ matrix

$$A \equiv \begin{bmatrix} X_1 \ \dots \ X_N \\ 1 \ \dots \ 1 \end{bmatrix}, \qquad (10)$$

in matrix form, the goal is then to find a $p \times n + 1$ weight matrix W that minimizes the sum squared-error

$$E^{\text{linear}} \equiv \sum_{i=1}^{N} (WA_i - Y_i)^T (WA_i - Y_i) \qquad (11)$$

over the set of data pairs

$$A_i \equiv \begin{bmatrix} X_i \\ 1 \end{bmatrix} \qquad (12)$$

by satisfying the first derivative condition $\partial E^{\text{linear}}/\partial W = 0$. The least squares solution to this problem is found via the pseudoinverse $A^{\dagger}$ [33] where

$$W = YA^{\dagger}. \qquad (13)$$

Once the optimal set of weights has been computed, the network response to an unknown $n \times 1$ input vector x can be determined by defining the $(n + 1) \times 1$ vector

$$z \equiv [x \ 1]^T \qquad (14)$$

and calculating

$$f(z) = Wz, \qquad (15)$$

where $f(z)$ is a $p \times 1$ column vector.

3.4. The Backpropagation Network. Given an input vector $x \in R^n$, the model $f : R^n \to R^p$ for a backpropagation neural network with a single hidden layer consisting of m nodes is described as

$$f(x) = \begin{bmatrix} f_1(x) \\ f_2(x) \\ \vdots \\ f_p(x) \end{bmatrix} = \alpha\sigma(Wx - \tau), \qquad (16)$$

where $\alpha \in R^{p \times m}$, $W \in R^{m \times n}$, and $\tau \in R^m$ define the set of network weights $\mathcal{W} = \{W, \tau, \alpha\}$ and $\sigma : R^m \to R^p$ is a "sigmoidal" function that is bounded and monotonically increasing. To perform supervised training, in a manner similar to the linear network, $\mathcal{W}$ is determined by minimizing the objective function:

$$E^{bp} = \sum_{i=1}^{N}(f(X_i) - Y_i)^T (f(X_i) - Y_i) \qquad (17)$$

given the training data defined in (1). Since $f(X_i)$ is no longer linear, numerical techniques such as the gradient descent algorithm and variations thereof are relied upon to compute the set $\mathcal{W}$ that satisfies the first derivative condition $\partial E^{bp}/\partial \mathcal{W} = 0$.

Consider the following definitions:

$$\delta F_k \equiv f(X_k) - Y_k = \begin{bmatrix} f_1(X_k) - (Y_k)_1 \\ f_2(X_k) - (Y_k)_2 \\ f_p(X_k) - (Y_k)_p \end{bmatrix},$$

$$S_k \equiv \begin{bmatrix} \sigma\left(\sum_{j=1}^{n} W_{1j}(X_k)_j - \tau_1\right) \\ \sigma\left(\sum_{j=1}^{n} W_{2j}(X_k)_j - \tau_2\right) \\ \vdots \\ \sigma\left(\sum_{j=1}^{n} W_{mj}(X_k)_j - \tau_m\right) \end{bmatrix},$$

$$S_k' \equiv \begin{bmatrix} \sigma'\left(\sum_{j=1}^{n} W_{1j}(X_k)_j - \tau_1\right) \\ \sigma'\left(\sum_{j=1}^{n} W_{2j}(X_k)_j - \tau_2\right) \\ \vdots \\ \sigma'\left(\sum_{j=1}^{n} W_{mj}(X_k)_j - \tau_m\right) \end{bmatrix}, \qquad (18)$$

where $\sigma'(z) = d\sigma/dz$. The first derivative conditions for the network weights prescribed by (16) and (17) can then be written in matrix form as follows:

$$\frac{\partial E^{bp}}{\partial \alpha} = \sum_{k=1}^{N} \delta F_k S_k^T = 0, \qquad (19)$$

(where "T" denotes the matrix transpose),

$$\frac{\partial E^{bp}}{\partial \tau} = -\sum_{k=1}^{N} \text{diag}(S_k') \alpha^T \delta F_k^T = 0,$$

$$\frac{\partial E^{bp}}{\partial W} = \sum_{k=1}^{N} \text{diag}(S_k') \alpha^T \delta F_k^T X_k^T = 0, \qquad (20)$$

where $\text{diag}(S_k')$ is a square diagonal matrix such that the diagonal entries consist of components from the vector S_k'.

3.5. Classification Measures. After a given classifier is trained, when presented with an input vector $x \in R^n$ of unknown classification, it will respond with an output $f(x) \in R^p$. The associated class membership $C(x)$ is then often determined by applying a minimum distance criterion:

$$C(x) \equiv \arg\min_i d(f(x), e_i), \qquad (21)$$

where the target vector e_i that is closest to $f(x)$ implies the class. Furthermore, when characterizing the performance of a pattern classifier, one often presents a set S of test vectors and analyzes the associated output. In addition to determining the class membership, it is also possible to *rank* the distance between a specific target vector and the classifier response to S. In this case a similar distance criterion can be applied in order to rank an input vector $x \in S$ with respect to class $J \in \{1, \ldots, M\}$,

$$\rho_J(x) = d(f(x), e_J). \qquad (22)$$

For the purposes of this work, (15) facilitates the determination of the class membership and ranking with respect to class J for the linear network. Similarly, assuming a set of weights $\mathcal{W} = \{W, \tau, \alpha\}$ for a trained backpropagation network, (21) and (22) would be applied using (16).

It is well established that, in the case of a normally distributed data, the classification measures presented above minimize the probability of a classification error and are directly related to the statistical significance of a classification decision [1]. Given the neural network as the supervised classification technique and two distinct choices for the set of target vectors $\mathcal{E}$ and $\widetilde{\mathcal{E}}$, we demonstrate, in certain instances, that the classification and ranking results do not remain *invariant* such that $\widetilde{C}(x) \neq C(x)$ and $\widetilde{\rho}_J(x) \neq \rho_J(x)$ for any input vector x.

4. Noninvariance of Secondary Structure Predictions

In this section, we numerically demonstrate that, when different target vector encodings are applied, neural network classifier measures outlined above, in certain cases, are observed to vary widely. For each neural network architecture under consideration, an analytic formulation is then presented in Section 5 in order to explain the observed numerical data.

As mentioned in Section 3.2, numerical experiments are performed first by training using $\mathcal{E}$ and then comparing

Table 1: Ranking results for the linear network where i represents the test vector index and $\rho_1(x)$ and $\tilde{\rho}_1(x)$ represent the distance with respect to the helix class vectors e_1 and $\tilde{e}_1$. Out of 1800 vectors tested, vectors referred to in this table were ranked from 1 to 20.

$i_\mathscr{E}$	$\rho_1(x)$	$i_{\widetilde{\mathscr{E}}}$	$\tilde{\rho}_1(x)$
1205	0.0780	1205	0.1170
42	0.0867	42	0.1300
1031	0.0976	1031	0.1464
1773	0.1113	1773	0.1670
598	0.1238	598	0.1857
1761	0.1267	1761	0.1900
862	0.1354	862	0.2031
1073	0.1409	1073	0.2114
277	0.1459	277	0.2188
115	0.1540	115	0.2309
1505	0.1821	1505	0.2731
392	0.1839	392	0.2759
1421	0.1904	1421	0.2856
147	0.2001	147	0.3001
990	0.2044	990	0.3066
1457	0.2127	1457	0.3191
1288	0.2150	1288	0.3225
352	0.2160	352	0.3239
1232	0.2198	1232	0.3297
280	0.2311	280	0.3466

Table 2: Class membership results for the linear network. For each class, the total number of vectors classified using $\mathscr{E}$ is analyzed to examine the total number that retained their classification using $\widetilde{\mathscr{E}}$.

Class	$\mathscr{E}$	$\widetilde{\mathscr{E}}$	% change
H	202	202	0
E	621	621	0
C	977	977	0

that the class membership of a substantial number of test vectors changed when an alternative set of target vectors was employed. The data also indicates that the greatest change in class membership took place for alpha helical sequences; thus implying that there is substantial disagreement over the modeling of this secondary structure element by the backpropagation network due to a simple transformation of the target vectors.

5. Analysis

The results in Section 4 clearly show that while the pattern recognition results for the linear network remain invariant under a change in target vectors, those for the backpropagation network do not. In this section, we present analytic results in order to clearly explain and understand why these two techniques lead to different conclusions.

5.1. Invariance Formulation. Let us begin by considering two definitions.

Definition 1. Given two sets of target vectors $\mathscr{E}$ and $\widetilde{\mathscr{E}}$, the class membership is invariant under a transformation of the target vectors if, for any input vector x,

$$d\left(\tilde{f}(x), \tilde{e}_i\right) > d\left(\tilde{f}(x), \tilde{e}_j\right) \Longrightarrow d\left(f(x), e_i\right) > d\left(f(x), e_j\right), \tag{23}$$

where $\tilde{f}(x)$ is the output of the classifier with target vectors $\{\tilde{e}_j\}_{j=1}^M$.

Definition 2. Given two sets of target vectors $\mathscr{E}$ and $\widetilde{\mathscr{E}}$, the ranking with respect to a specific class J is invariant under a transformation of the target vectors if, for any input vectors x_1 and x_2,

$$d\left(\tilde{f}(x_1), \tilde{e}_J\right) > d\left(\tilde{f}(x_2), \tilde{e}_J\right) \Longrightarrow d\left(f(x_1), e_J\right) > d\left(f(x_2), e_J\right). \tag{24}$$

Based upon these definitions, the following has been established [32].

Proposition 3. Given two sets of target vectors $\mathscr{E}$ and $\widetilde{\mathscr{E}}$, if the ranking is invariant, then the class membership of an arbitrary input vector x will remain invariant.

In the analysis presented, the strategy for characterizing neural network performance depends upon the data from the previous section. For the linear network, since both ranking

classifier performance with their counterparts trained using $\widetilde{\mathscr{E}}$. Multiple cross-validation trials are required in order to prevent potential dependency of the evaluated accuracy on the particular training or test sets chosen [7, 15]. In this work, we apply a hold-n-out strategy similar to that of [14] using 85% of the 12000 encoded sequences as training data (i.e., $N = 10200$) and 15% as test data to validate the classification results. Recognition rates for both the linear and backpropagation rates using either set of target vector encodings were approximately 65% which is typical of this genre of classifiers that have applied similar encoding methodologies [7, 12–14]. Although these aggregate values remain consistent, using (21) and (22) we now present data demonstrating that, while class membership and ranking remain invariant for the linear network, these measures of performance vary considerably for the backpropagation network which was trained with, $m = 17$, seventeen hidden nodes and a mean squared training error less than 0.2. Ranking results from a representative test for the linear and backpropagation networks are presented for the top 20 ranked vectors in Tables 1 and 3. Class membership data are presented in Tables 2 and 4. Observe that, for the linear network, indices for the top 20 ranked vectors remain invariant indicating ranking invariance; in addition, no change in class membership is observed. On the other hand, Tables 3 and 4 clearly indicate a lack of consistency when considering the ranking and class membership of test vectors. A particularly troubling observation is that very few vectors ranked in the top 20 with respect to e_1 were ranked in the top 20 with respect to $\tilde{e}_1$. Furthermore, Table 4 indicates

TABLE 3: Ranking results for the backpropagation network where i represents the test vector index and $\rho_1(x)$ and $\tilde{\rho}_1(x)$ represent the distance with respect to the helix class vectors e_1 and $\tilde{e}_1$. Out of 1800 vectors tested, vectors referred to in this table were ranked from 1 to 20.

$i_{\mathscr{E}}$	$\rho_1(x)$	$i_{\widetilde{\mathscr{E}}}$	$\tilde{\rho}_1(x)$
817	0.0107	926	0.0101
887	0.0231	1604	0.0130
264	0.0405	887	0.0209
1183	0.0711	1145	0.0214
684	0.0727	461	0.0232
623	0.0874	583	0.0329
911	0.0891	1086	0.0339
1382	0.0917	1382	0.0478
1610	0.0939	413	0.0489
551	0.1060	225	0.0608
1042	0.1150	438	0.0609
924	0.1322	911	0.0613
727	0.1339	207	0.0774
438	0.1356	559	0.0885
577	0.1363	481	0.0945
896	0.1500	1548	0.0947
175	0.1513	962	0.0968
1138	0.1549	85	0.1012
583	0.1581	195	0.1111
559	0.1655	9	0.1167

TABLE 4: Class membership results for the backpropagation network. For each class, the total number of vectors classified using $\mathscr{E}$ is analyzed to examine the total number that retained their classification using $\widetilde{\mathscr{E}}$.

Class	$\mathscr{E}$	$\widetilde{\mathscr{E}}$	% change
H	225	142	36.9
E	581	476	18.1
C	994	878	11.7

and classification were observed to remain invariant, it is more sensible to characterize the invariance of this network using Definition 2. Then, based upon Proposition 3, class membership invariance naturally follows. On the other hand, to explain the noninvariance of both class membership and ranking observed in the backpropagation network, the analysis is facilitated by considering Definition 1. The noninvariance of ranking then naturally follows from Proposition 3.

5.1.1. Invariance Analysis for the Linear Network. When the target vectors are subjected to the transformation defined in (2), the network output can be expressed as

$$\tilde{f}(z) = \widetilde{W}z = \widetilde{Y}A^{\dagger}z = aR\left(Y - T'\right)A^{\dagger}z, \quad (25)$$

where T' is derived from T such that the translation vector t_i associated with $e_i \in \mathscr{E}$ is appropriately aligned with the correct target vector in matrix Y. In other words, when the output data matrix in (7) is of the form

$$Y = \begin{bmatrix} e_{i_1} & e_{i_2} & \cdots & e_{i_N} \end{bmatrix} \quad (26)$$

then

$$T' = \begin{bmatrix} t_{i_1} & t_{i_2} & \cdots & t_{i_N} \end{bmatrix}, \quad (27)$$

where $i_j \in \{1,\ldots,M\}$ for $j = 1,\ldots,N$. Given this network, the following result is applicable [32].

Proposition 4. *If*

(i) *the number of training observations N exceeds the vector dimension n;*

(ii) *the rows of the matrix A are linearly independent;*

(iii) *$\mathscr{E}$ and $\widetilde{\mathscr{E}}$ are related according to (2);*

(iv) *for some $t \in R^p$, $t_i = t$ for all $i = 1,\ldots,M$ in (2);*

then the ranking and, hence, the class membership for the linear network will remain invariant.

In other words, if the columns of the matrix T' in (25) are all equal, then using (15) and (25) will result in, (23) being satisfied. The above result is applicable to the presented numerical data with $n = 340$ and $N = 10200$; hence, ranking and class membership invariances are corroborated by the data in Tables 1 and 2.

5.1.2. Invariance Analysis for the Backpropagation Network. In this section, we seek to characterize the noninvariance observed in class membership using the backpropagation network. If the class membership varies due to a change in target vectors, then this variation should be quantifiable by characterizing the boundary separating two respective classes. The decision boundary between class i and class j is defined by points x such that

$$\left\| f(x) - e_i \right\|^2 = \left\| f(x) - e_j \right\|^2, \quad (28)$$

where $i,j \in \{1,\ldots,M\}$, $i \neq j$ and $f(x)$ is the classifier output. Under these circumstances, if an ℓ_2 norm is applied in (21),

$$\left(f(x) - e_i\right)^T \left(f(x) - e_i\right) = \left(f(x) - e_j\right)^T \left(f(x) - e_j\right). \quad (29)$$

The solution set to this equation consists of all x such that $f(x)$ is equidistant from e_i and e_j where, for the purposes of this section, $f(x)$ is defined by (16). Expanding terms on both sides of this equation leads to the condition

$$\left(e_i - e_j\right)^T f(x) = -\frac{1}{2}\left(e_j^T e_j - e_i^T e_i\right). \quad (30)$$

If the class membership of a representative vector is to remain invariant under a change of target vectors, this same set of points must also satisfy

$$\left(\tilde{e}_i - \tilde{e}_j\right)^T \tilde{f}(x) = -\frac{1}{2}\left(\tilde{e}_j^T \tilde{e}_j - \tilde{e}_i^T \tilde{e}_i\right). \quad (31)$$

Assuming that two networks have been trained using two different sets of target vectors $\mathcal{E}$ and $\widetilde{\mathcal{E}}$, the set of weights $\{W, \tau, \alpha\}$ and $\{\widetilde{W}, \widetilde{\tau}, \widetilde{\alpha}\}$ determines the network output in (16). Without loss of generality, we consider the case where all target vectors are normalized to a value of one such that $\|e_i\|^2 = 1$ and $\|\widetilde{e}_i\|^2 = 1$ for $i = 1, \ldots, M$. In this case, the conditions in (30) and (31) become

$$\left(e_i - e_j\right)^T \alpha \sigma \left(Wx - \tau\right) = 0, \tag{32}$$

$$\left(\widetilde{e}_i - \widetilde{e}_j\right)^T \widetilde{\alpha} \sigma \left(\widetilde{W}x - \widetilde{\tau}\right) = 0. \tag{33}$$

We first consider a special case where the target vectors are related according to $\widetilde{\Gamma} = aR\Gamma$ with $T = 0$ in (2). Under these circumstances, if the choice

$$\mathcal{W} \equiv \left\{\widetilde{W}, \widetilde{\tau}, \widetilde{\alpha}\right\} = \{W, \tau, aR\alpha\} \tag{34}$$

is made, it should be clear that, since $R^T = R^{-1}$ and $\widetilde{Y}_i = aRY_i$,

$$\begin{aligned}
\widetilde{E}^{bp} &= \sum_{i=1}^{N} \left(\widetilde{f}\left(X_i\right) - \widetilde{Y}_i\right)^T \left(\widetilde{f}\left(X_i\right) - \widetilde{Y}_i\right) \\
&= a^2 \sum_{i=1}^{N} \left(Rf\left(X_i\right) - RY_i\right)^T \left(Rf\left(X_i\right) - RY_i\right) \\
&= a^2 \sum_{i=1}^{N} \left(f\left(X_i\right) - Y_i\right)^T R^T R \left(f\left(X_i\right) - Y_i\right) \\
&= a^2 E^{bp}
\end{aligned} \tag{35}$$

is minimized by the condition $\partial E^{bp}/\partial \mathcal{W} = 0$. Another way to see this is to observe that (19), (20) remain invariant for this choice of target vectors and network weights. Hence, we have the following.

Proposition 5. *For a specific choice of a and R, if $T = 0$ in (2) and*

$$\widetilde{\mathcal{W}} = \left\{\widetilde{W}, \widetilde{\tau}, \widetilde{\alpha}\right\} = \{W, \tau, aR\alpha\}, \tag{36}$$

then the class membership for the backpropagation network will remain invariant.

Proof. Simply consider (32) and (33) and choose any $\overline{x}$ satisfying

$$\left(e_i - e_j\right)^T \alpha \sigma \left(W\overline{x} - \tau\right) = 0. \tag{37}$$

It then immediately follows that

$$\begin{aligned}
&\left(\widetilde{e}_i - \widetilde{e}_j\right)^T \widetilde{\alpha} \sigma \left(\widetilde{W}\overline{x} - \widetilde{\tau}\right) \\
&= \left(e_i - e_j\right)^T R^T R\alpha \sigma \left(W\overline{x} - \tau\right) \\
&= a^2 \left(e_i - e_j\right)^T \alpha \sigma \left(W\overline{x} - \tau\right) \\
&= 0.
\end{aligned} \tag{38}$$

Therefore, if $\overline{x}$ satisfies (32), then it also satisfies (33) and, hence, is a point on the decision boundary for both networks. $\square$

Intuitively, a scaled, rigid rotation of the target vectors should not affect the decision boundary. However, when the more general transformation of (2) is applied with $T \neq 0$, we now demonstrate that, due to the nonlinearity of σ in (16), no simple relationship exists such that (32) and (33) can simultaneously be satisfied by the same set of points. We first investigate the possibility of establishing an analytic relationship between the set of weights $\{\widetilde{W}, \widetilde{\tau}, \widetilde{\alpha}\}$ and $\{W, \tau, \alpha\}$ for both networks. In other words, we seek, ideally invertible, functions $G_\alpha, G_\tau,$ and G_W.

$$\begin{aligned}
\widetilde{\alpha} &= G_\alpha \left(W, \tau, \alpha\right), \\
\widetilde{\tau} &= G_\tau \left(W, \tau, \alpha\right), \\
\widetilde{W} &= G_W \left(W, \tau, \alpha\right)
\end{aligned} \tag{39}$$

such that the set $\mathcal{W}$ can be transformed into $\widetilde{\mathcal{W}}$. If this can be done, then an analytic procedure similar to that presented in the proof of Proposition 5 can be established in order to relate (32) to (33) for the general case. Since (19), (20) define the set $\mathcal{W}$, it is reasonable to rephrase these equations in terms of the objective function $\widetilde{E}^{bp}$:

$$\frac{\partial \widetilde{E}^{bp}}{\partial \widetilde{\alpha}} = \sum_{k=1}^{N} \left(\widetilde{f}\left(X_k\right) - \widetilde{Y}_k\right) \widetilde{S}_k^T = 0,$$

$$\frac{\partial \widetilde{E}^{bp}}{\partial \widetilde{\tau}} = -\sum_{k=1}^{N} \text{diag}\left(\widetilde{S}_k'\right) \widetilde{\alpha}^T \left(\widetilde{f}\left(X_k\right) - \widetilde{Y}_k\right)^T = 0, \tag{40}$$

$$\frac{\partial \widetilde{E}^{bp}}{\partial \widetilde{W}} = \sum_{k=1}^{N} \text{diag}\left(\widetilde{S}_k'\right) \widetilde{\alpha}^T \left(\widetilde{f}\left(X_k\right) - \widetilde{Y}_k\right)^T X_k^T = 0,$$

where $\widetilde{f}(X_k) = \widetilde{\alpha}\sigma(\widetilde{W}X_k - \widetilde{\tau})$ and $\widetilde{Y}_k = aR(Y_k - t')$ such that $t\prime$ is the translation vector associated with the target vector referred to by Y_k. From these equations, it should be clear that no simple analytic relationship exists that will transform $\widetilde{\mathcal{W}}$ into $\mathcal{W}$. A numerical algorithm such as gradient descent will, assuming a local minimum actually exists, arrive at some solution for both $\widetilde{\mathcal{W}}$ and $\mathcal{W}$. We must therefore be content with the assumed existence of some set of functions defined by (39). Again, let us consider any point $\overline{x}$ on the decision boundary such that

$$\left(e_i - e_j\right)^T \alpha \sigma \left(W\overline{x} - \tau\right) = 0. \tag{41}$$

Such a point must also simultaneously satisfy

$$\begin{aligned}
&\left(\widetilde{e}_i - \widetilde{e}_j\right)^T \widetilde{\alpha} \sigma \left(\widetilde{W}\overline{x} - \widetilde{\tau}\right) \\
&= \left(\left(aRe_i - t_i\right) - \left(aRe_j - t_j\right)\right)^T G_\alpha \left(W, \tau, \alpha\right)
\end{aligned}$$

$$\times \sigma \left(G_W\left(W, \tau, \alpha\right)\overline{x} - G_\tau\left(W, \tau, \alpha\right)\right)$$

$$= a\left(\left(e_i - e_j\right) - \left(t_i - t_j\right)\right)^T R^T G_\alpha\left(W, \tau, \alpha\right)$$

$$\times \sigma \left(G_W\left(W, \tau, \alpha\right)\overline{x} - G_\tau\left(W, \tau, \alpha\right)\right)$$

$$= 0.$$

$$(42)$$

At first glance, a choice such as $G_\alpha(W, \tau, \alpha) = aR\alpha$ and $t_i = t_j$ for $i, j = 1, \ldots, M$ (as in Proposition 4) appears to bring us close to a solution. However, the term involving $\sigma(G_W(W, \tau, \alpha)\overline{x} - G_\tau(W, \tau, \alpha))$ is problematic. Although a choice such as $G_W(W, \tau, \alpha) = W$ and $G_\tau(W, \tau, \alpha) = \tau$ would yield the solution to (42), it should be clear that these values would not satisfy (40).

Another way to analyze this problem is to first set $t_i = t_j$ for $i, j = 1, \ldots, M$. Then, for any $\overline{x}$ on the decision boundary, from (41) and (42), equate the terms

$$\alpha\sigma\left(W\overline{x} - \tau\right) = kR^T G_\alpha\left(W, \tau, \alpha\right)$$
$$\times \sigma \left(G_W\left(W, \tau, \alpha\right)\overline{x} - G_\tau\left(W, \tau, \alpha\right)\right),$$

$$(43)$$

where k is some constant and G_α, G_τ, and G_W satisfy (40). Given an arbitrary training set defined by (1), it is highly unlikely that this constraint can be satisfied. One remote scenario might be that the terms $G_W(W, \tau, \alpha)\overline{x} - G_\tau(W, \tau, \alpha)$ and $W\overline{x} - \tau$ are always small. In this case, given a sigmoidal function $\sigma(z)$ that is linear near $z = 0$, a linearized version of (43) could be solved using techniques described in [32]. However, this again is an unlikely set of events given an arbitrary training set. Therefore, given the transformation of (2), we are left to conclude that class membership invariance and, hence, ranking invariance are, in general, not achievable using the backpropagation neural network.

5.2. Discussion. Intuitively, given a reasonable target encoding scheme, one would desire that properties related to protein secondary structure would be independent of the target vectors chosen. However, we have presented numerical data and a theoretical foundation demonstrating that secondary structure classification and confidence measures can vary depending on the type of neural network architecture and target vector encoding scheme employed. Specifically, linear network classification has been demonstrated to remain invariant under a change in the target structure encoding scheme while the backpropagation network has not. As N increases, for the methodology applied in this work, recognition rates remain consistent with those reported in the literature; however, we have observed that adding more training data does not improve the invariance of classification measures for the backpropagation network. This conclusion is corroborated by the analytic formulation presented above.

6. Conclusions

As pointed out in the introduction, one major purpose of the neural network is to create a stable and reliable model that maps input training data to an output classification with the hope of extracting informative parameters. When methods similar to those in the literature are applied [7, 12–14], we have demonstrated that classifier performance measures can vary considerably. Under these circumstances, parameters derived from a trained network for analytically describing protein secondary structure may not comprise a reliable set for the model-based approach. Furthermore, classifier variability would imply that a stable parametric model has not been derived. It is in some sense paradoxical that the neural network has been applied for structure classification and, yet, associated parameters have not been applied for describing protein secondary structure. The neural network approach to deriving a solution to the protein secondary structure prediction problem therefore requires deeper exploration.

Acknowledgments

This publication was made possible by Grant Number G12RR017581 from the National Center for Research Resources (NCRR), a component of the National Institutes of Health (NIH). The authors would also like to thank the reviewers for their helpful comments.

References

[1] C. M. Bishop, *Pattern Recognition and Machine Learning*, Springer, 2007.

[2] M. T. Hagan, H. B. Demuth, and M. H. Beale, *Neural Network Design*, PWS Publishing, 1996.

[3] M. N. Nguyen and J. C. Rajapakse, "Multi-class support vector machines for protein secondary structure prediction," *Genome Informatics*, vol. 14, pp. 218–227, 2003.

[4] H. J. Hu, Y. Pan, R. Harrison, and P. C. Tai, "Improved protein secondary structure prediction using support vector machine with a new encoding scheme and an advanced tertiary classifier," *IEEE Transactions on Nanobioscience*, vol. 3, no. 4, pp. 265–271, 2004.

[5] W. Zhong, G. Altun, X. Tian, R. Harrison, P. C. Tai, and Y. Pan, "Parallel protein secondary structure prediction schemes using Pthread and OpenMP over hyper-threading technology," *Journal of Supercomputing*, vol. 41, no. 1, pp. 1–16, 2007.

[6] J. A. Cuff and G. J. Barton, "Application of enhanced multiple sequence alignment profiles to improve protein secondary structure prediction," *Proteins*, vol. 40, pp. 502–511, 2000.

[7] J. M. Chandonia and M. Karplus, "Neural networks for secondary structure and structural class predictions," *Protein Science*, vol. 4, no. 2, pp. 275–285, 1995.

[8] J. A. Cuff and G. J. Barton, "Evaluation and improvement of multiple sequence methods for protein secondary structure prediction," *Proteins*, vol. 34, pp. 508–519, 1999.

[9] G. E. Crooks and S. E. Brenner, "Protein secondary structure: entropy, correlations and prediction," *Bioinformatics*, vol. 20, no. 10, pp. 1603–1611, 2004.

[10] L. H. Wang, J. Liu, and H. B. Zhou, "A comparison of two machine learning methods for protein secondary structure prediction," in *Proceedings of 2004 International Conference on Machine Learning and Cybernetics*, pp. 2730–2735, chn, August 2004.

[11] G. Z. Zhang, D. S. Huang, Y. P. Zhu, and Y. X. Li, "Improving protein secondary structure prediction by using the residue conformational classes," *Pattern Recognition Letters*, vol. 26, no. 15, pp. 2346–2352, 2005.

[12] N. Qian and T. J. Sejnowski, "Predicting the secondary structure of globular proteins using neural network models," *Journal of Molecular Biology*, vol. 202, no. 4, pp. 865–884, 1988.

[13] L. Howard Holley and M. Karplus, "Protein secondary structure prediction with a neural network," *Proceedings of the National Academy of Sciences of the United States of America*, vol. 86, no. 1, pp. 152–156, 1989.

[14] J. M. Chandonia and M. Karplus, "The importance of larger data sets for protein secondary structure prediction with neural networks," *Protein Science*, vol. 5, no. 4, pp. 768–774, 1996.

[15] B. Rost and C. Sander, "Improved prediction of protein secondary structure by use of sequence profiles and neural networks," *Proceedings of the National Academy of Sciences of the United States of America*, vol. 90, no. 16, pp. 7558–7562, 1993.

[16] B. Rost and C. Sander, "Prediction of protein secondary structure at better than 70% accuracy," *Journal of Molecular Biology*, vol. 232, no. 2, pp. 584–599, 1993.

[17] J. A. Cuff, M. E. Clamp, A. S. Siddiqui, M. Finlay, and G. J. Barton, "JPred: a consensus secondary structure prediction server," *Bioinformatics*, vol. 14, no. 10, pp. 892–893, 1998.

[18] S. Hua and Z. Sun, "A novel method of protein secondary structure prediction with high segment overlap measure: support vector machine approach," *Journal of Molecular Biology*, vol. 308, no. 2, pp. 397–407, 2001.

[19] B. Rost, "PHD: predicting one-dimensional protein structure by profile-based neural networks," *Methods in Enzymology*, vol. 266, pp. 525–539, 1996.

[20] B. Rost, G. Yachdav, and J. Liu, "The PredictProtein server," *Nucleic Acids Research*, vol. 32, pp. W321–W326, 2004.

[21] C. Cole, J. D. Barber, and G. J. Barton, "The Jpred 3 secondary structure prediction server," *Nucleic Acids Research*, vol. 36, pp. W197–W201, 2008.

[22] G. Pollastri, D. Przybylski, B. Rost, and P. Baldi, "Improving the prediction of protein secondary structure in three and eight classes using recurrent neural networks and profiles," *Proteins*, vol. 47, no. 2, pp. 228–235, 2002.

[23] J. Cheng, A. Z. Randall, M. J. Sweredoski, and P. Baldi, "SCRATCH: a protein structure and structural feature prediction server," *Nucleic Acids Research*, vol. 33, no. 2, pp. W72–W76, 2005.

[24] D. T. Jones, "Protein secondary structure prediction based on position-specific scoring matrices," *Journal of Molecular Biology*, vol. 292, no. 2, pp. 195–202, 1999.

[25] K. Bryson, L. J. McGuffin, R. L. Marsden, J. J. Ward, J. S. Sodhi, and D. T. Jones, "Protein structure prediction servers at University College London," *Nucleic Acids Research*, vol. 33, no. 2, pp. W36–W38, 2005.

[26] G. Cybenko, "Approximation by superpositions of a sigmoidal function," *Mathematics of Control, Signals, and Systems*, vol. 2, no. 4, pp. 303–314, 1989.

[27] J. Moody and C. J. Darken, "Fast learning in networks of locally tuned processing units," *Neural Computation*, vol. 1, pp. 281–294, 1989.

[28] T. Poggio and F. Girosi, "Networks for approximation and learning," *Proceedings of the IEEE*, vol. 78, no. 9, pp. 1481–1497, 1990.

[29] D. F. Specht, "Probabilistic neural networks," *Neural Networks*, vol. 3, no. 1, pp. 109–118, 1990.

[30] P. András, "Orthogonal RBF neural network approximation," *Neural Processing Letters*, vol. 9, no. 2, pp. 141–151, 1999.

[31] P. Baldi and S. Brunak, *Bioinformatics: The Machine Learning Approach*, MIT Press, 1998.

[32] E. Sakk, D. J. Schneider, C. R. Myers, and S. W. Cartinhour, "On the selection of target vectors for a class of supervised pattern recognizers," *IEEE Transactions on Neural Networks*, vol. 20, no. 5, pp. 745–757, 2009.

[33] G. H. Golub and C. F. Van Loan, *Matrix Computations*, Johns Hopkins University Press, 1989.

19

Modelling of Water Quality: An Application to a Water Treatment Process

Petri Juntunen,[1] **Mika Liukkonen,**[1] **Marja Pelo,**[2] **Markku J. Lehtola,**[1] **and Yrjö Hiltunen**[1]

[1] *Department of Environmental Science, University of Eastern Finland, P.O. Box 1627, 70211 Kuopio, Finland*
[2] *Finnsugar Ltd., Sokeritehtaantie 20, 02460 Kantvik, Finland*

Correspondence should be addressed to Petri Juntunen, petri.juntunen@uef.fi

Academic Editor: Cheng-Jian Lin

The modelling of water treatment processes is challenging because of its complexity, nonlinearity, and numerous contributory variables, but it is of particular importance since water of low quality causes health-related and economic problems which have a considerable impact on people's daily lives. Linear and nonlinear modelling methods are used here to model residual aluminium and turbidity in treated water, using both laboratory and process data as input variables. The approach includes variable selection to find the most important factors affecting the quality parameters. Correlations of ~0.7–0.9 between the modelled and real values for the target parameters were ultimately achieved. This data analysis procedure seems to provide an efficient means of modelling the water treatment process and defining its most essential variables.

1. Introduction

Water quality is becoming an ever more important issue, as water of low quality causes many significant problems. In particular, there is a wide range of microbial and chemical constituents of drinking water that can cause either acute or chronic detrimental health effects, and the detection of these constituents in treated water is often time-consuming, complex, and expensive [1]. On the other hand, water of bad quality can also be harmful from an economic perspective, as resources have to be directed towards improving the water supply system every time a problem occurs. For these reasons, there is growing pressure to improve water treatment and water quality management in order to ensure safe drinking water at reasonable costs. Systematic assessments of raw water, treatment processes, and operational monitoring issues are needed to meet these challenges.

There are many parameters which can be used to measure the quality of water, of which turbidity is a common one, the purpose being to measure impurities in the water. In a physical sense, turbidity is a reduction in the clarity of water due to the presence of suspended or colloidal particles, and it is commonly used as an indicator of the general condition of drinking water [1]. Furthermore, turbidity has been used for many decades as an indicator of the efficiency of drinking water coagulation and filtration processes, so that it is an important operational parameter for this reason, too. High turbidity values refer to poor disinfection and possibly to fouling problems in the distribution network, so that turbidity should be minimized [2]. However, turbidity is a quite sensible and faulty measurement, and many variables and phenomena are influencing it. This makes turbidity challenging for modeling purposes [1, 2].

Another important quality parameter for treated water is residual aluminium, especially when aluminium flocculants are used in the treatment process [2]. Residual aluminium causes turbidity in water networks, resulting in acceptability problems for consumers [1]. Usually the phenomenon can be seen when residual aluminium exceeds 0.1–0.2 mg/L, which are the usual guideline levels for residual aluminium [1]. In addition, metals such as aluminium have been implicated in the pathogenesis of Alzheimer's disease [3]. Some epidemiological studies show that there can be a correlation between neural disorders and Al concentrations of 0.1 mg/L in the drinking water [3].

Many chemical and physical features of raw water affect the water treatment process. Many organic and inorganic compounds in suspended, colloid, or solved form influence the flocculation process. Organic compounds, which are usually measured by a $KMnO_4$ test, play an essential role in the process. Furthermore, many inorganic compounds such as the silicate or the pH of raw water also affect the process. As an example of physical parameters, the water temperature has a remarkable influence on the flocculation in water treatment processes [4–6]. Naturally process conditions also have a great effect. The dose of the flocculation chemical is naturally the key parameter, as is the adjusted pH value. Further, hydraulic variables such as flow to the process or filters affect the performance [2].

Moreover, in water treatment there are observable cycles or episodic events present which cause the process to behave dynamically. The variation in water consumption is one of these, causing changes not only within a day but also within a week and even within a year. Year cycles can be distinguished even more clearly if surface water is treated, because the water temperature is observed to have some effects on the process [7]. In addition, the phenomena existing in the process are usually state dependent, meaning that a certain phenomenon in the process may work differently in different process conditions [8].

As a general tool which can be of assistance in improving water treatment, the modelling of water processes has confronted many challenges. Since the treatment processes involved are physically and chemically heterogeneous [4–6], the water and process parameters are generally complex and their mutual interactions nonlinear [9]. Furthermore, successful applications of traditional mechanistic models are limited to idealized, artificial systems [10], so that the correlation between simulated and experimental data from real processes has been poor and expensive *in situ* testing has been needed [9–11].

A process-oriented approach performs optimizations based on real process data. In practice, the variables used in modelling are derived from archived laboratory or process data resources. At present, data-based multivariate methods such as multiple linear regression (MLR) and artificial neural networks such as multilayer perceptrons (MLPs) are considered advantageous for analysing process data. Many applications have demonstrated that they provide an efficient automated method for modelling industrial process data [12–14]. Data-based modelling has also been used in connection with wastewater treatment [15], water resources [16, 17], water distribution systems [18], and water treatment. The most general applications to water treatment processes involve the prediction of quality parameters such as turbidity, colour [9, 19], or the optimal dosing of flocculation chemicals [9, 11].

MLPs, above all, have proved their efficiency in the modelling of water treatment processes. The method has many advantages: the MLP technique is robust and allows the development of multivariate, nonlinear models without any physical or chemical knowledge of the process [11], which means that it offers a computationally powerful alternative for complex problems in which nonlinearity is present. The drawback with MLP models, however, is that they have more complex mathematical formulae than more explicit models such as those based on linear regression. MLP also requires

substantially more knowledge from the user than do simpler statistical methods. It is therefore reasonable to use this technique only in applications where linear methods have failed.

Traditionally, multivariate analysis methods such as factor analysis and principal component analysis (PCA) have been widely used in analyzing hydrological system. However, the limitations of conventional multivariate statistical methods arising from the challenges mentioned earlier are known [20].

In summary, understanding the complex relationships and phenomena prevailing in large systems is a challenging task. The quality of water in a treatment process, for example, may be affected by several factors which either are not known thoroughly or which have not been verified on an experimental basis. For these reasons, data-based modelling methods, such as MLP, would be preferable for modelling of water treatment processes.

In this paper we employ a multivariate linear regression method (MLR) and a nonlinear modelling method (MLP) to model turbidity and residual aluminium in a water treatment process using both process and laboratory data as model inputs. Because process data typically consist of a large number of variables, we use variable selection as a diagnosis tool to find the most important input variables affecting the outputs. We compare the results of the MLR and MLP models to explore their applicability to real-life modelling purposes.

2. Process and Data

The experimental data were collected from the water treatment plant of Suomen Sokeri in Kirkkonummi, Finland. The plant uses mainly surface water from Lake Humaljärvi or a mixture of this with water from the Pikkala reservoir. The process is a typical chemical process with a coagulation and flocculation unit, flotation, and powdered activated carbon (PAC) filtration (see Figure 1). PAX-14, an aluminium-based coagulation chemical produced by Kemira Kemwater, is used in doses varying between 30 and $80\,g/m^3$. The dose is set as a function of the raw water $KMnO_4$ content, so that the $Al/KMnO_4$ ratio will be between 0.8 and 2 kgAl/kgKMnO$_4$. For most of the time, the ratio is near 1.3. The final decision regarding the dose is in the hands of the process personnel. The process is shown in Figure 1.

The pH value is adjusted to 6.1–6.3 with calcium hydroxide before flocculation, this having been found experimentally to be the optimum pH for removing organic compounds and turbidity. After filtration it is readjusted to 8.2 to be suitable for distribution. Finally, the water is disinfected with UV radiation and by adding sodium hypochlorite.

The data were obtained from process and laboratory measurements over a period of 373 days. The original process data period was 5 minutes, which was averaged to daily data in order to be comparable to the laboratory data. Before modelling, the outliers in the data were filtered out manually and the missing data points filled in by linear interpolation.

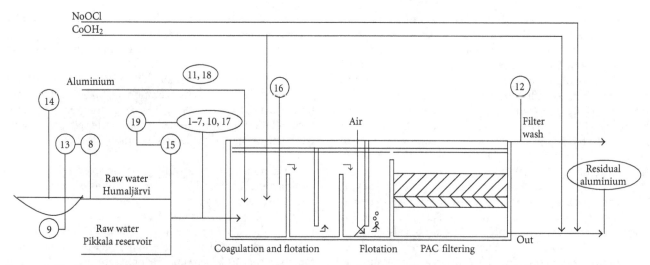

FIGURE 1: The water treatment process used by Suomen Sokeri. The numbers refer to the measuring points for the variables (see Tables 1 and 2).

The raw water and process variables are shown in Tables 1 and 2, Figure respectively.

Some of the process variables were left out before modelling, so that only those variables were chosen which could potentially have an effect on the output when manipulated by the controllers, for example. Consequently, all the variables measured after the output measuring point were omitted, as also were those variables which cannot be converted to on-line measurements. In addition, variables containing data of bad quality (e.g., too many missing data points) were ruled out manually. The measuring points for the process variables are shown in Figure 1.

3. Methods

3.1. Multiple Linear Regression (MLR).
MLR [7] can be used to model the relationship between two or more explanatory variables and a response variable by fitting a linear equation to observed data samples. An MLR model with N observations and P variables is defined by

$$y_i = b_0 + b_1 x_{i1} + b_2 x_{i2} + \cdots + b_P x_{iP} + \varepsilon_i,$$
$$\text{for } i = 1, 2, \ldots, N, \tag{1}$$

where y denotes the value of the response variable, x is the value of the predictor (explanatory) variable, b_0 is a constant, $b_1 \cdots b_P$ equal the unknown coefficients to be estimated, and ε comprises the uncontrolled factors and experimental errors in the model. The fitting is performed by minimizing the sum of the squares of the vertical deviations from each data point to the line that fits best for the observed data, which is known as least squares fitting.

3.2. Multilayer Perceptrons (MLPs).
MLP networks are well-known feed-forward neural networks [12, 14] consisting of processing elements, called neurons, and connections. The neurons are arranged in three or more layers: an input layer,

one or more hidden layers, and an output layer. An MLP network is trained with data samples, leading to a supervised learning procedure. The network input signals are processed forward through successive layers of neurons on a layer-by-layer basis. In the first phase the input layer distributes the inputs to the first hidden layer. Next, the hidden neurons summarize the inputs based on predefined weights, which either weaken or strengthen the effect of each input. The weights are determined by learning from examples (i.e., data samples), which is called supervised learning. Eventually, the inputs are processed by a transfer function, and the result is transferred as a linear combination to the next layer, which is generally the output layer. The performance of the model is then evaluated with an independent validation data set.

MLP neural networks must be trained for each problem separately. A popular MLP training technique is the back-propagation algorithm [21], in which the output values are compared with the proper answer from the original data in order to calculate the value for a predefined error function. Eventually the iterative training procedure defines a set of weights which minimize the error between the actual and expected outputs for all input patterns. In summary, the back-propagation training proceeds in two phases [12].

(1) Forward Phase. The network weights are fixed and the input is forwarded through the network until it reaches the output.

(2) Backward Phase. The output of the network is compared with the desired response to obtain an error signal, which is propagated backwards in the network. In the meantime, the network weights are adjusted successively to minimize the error.

3.3. Selection of Variables.
The enormously increased amount of information available in recent years has caused the selection of variables or reduction of model inputs,

TABLE 1: Raw water variables used for modelling and their correlations with residual Al and turbidity.

	Variable	Unit	Correlation with residual Al	Correlation with turbidity
1	pH of raw water		0.21	0.21
2	$KMnO_4$ of raw water	mg/L O_2	0.18	0.33
3	Hardness of raw water	mmol/L	0.27	0.22
4	Colour of raw water	mg Pt	0.19	0.27
5	Conductivity of raw water	mS/m	0.34	0.38
6	Silicates on raw water	mg/L	0.35	0.28
7	Turbidity of raw water	NTU	0.07	0.06

TABLE 2: Process variables used for modelling and their correlations with residual Al and turbidity.

	Variable	Unit	Correlation with residual Al	Correlation with turbidity
8	Intake from Lake Humaljärvi	m^3/h	−0.16	−0.27
9	Intake from the pikkala reservoir	m^3/h	0.25	0.39
10	Total intake of water	m^3/h	−0.033	−0.07
11	Aluminium feed	L/h	0.11	0.23
12	Filter wash water	m^3/h	−0.36	−0.12
13	Proportion of Lake Humaljärvi/Pikkala reservoir water intake	%	−0.52	−0.38
14	Surface level of Lake Humaljärvi	m	0.28	0.14
15	$KMnO_4$ of raw water	mg/L	0.065	0.44
16	Flocculation pH			
17	Water temperature	°C	−0.72	−0.42
18	Aluminium dose	g/m^3	0.25	0.46
19	Aluminium dose/raw water $KMnO_4$		0.052	−0.08
20	Flow to filter 1	m^3/h	0,078	0.03
21	Flow to filter 2	m^3/h	0,22	0.19
22	Flow to filter 3	m^3/h	−0.097	−0.11
23	Flow to filter 4	m^3/h	0.31	−0.32

to become a relevant part of data analysis [22–25]. The objective of this selection procedure can be to improve the prediction performance of the model, to provide faster processing of the data or to provide a better understanding of the process [24]. When exploiting artificial neural networks for computation purposes, for instance, reducing the number of model inputs may shorten the computing times significantly. With respect to certain tasks such as process diagnostics, however, it is also useful to discover the main factors affecting the physical phenomena.

In practice, the aim is to select a subset p from the set of P variables without appreciably degrading the performance of the model and possibly improving it. Although exhaustive subset selection methods involve the evaluation of a very large number of subsets, the number to be evaluated can be reduced significantly by using suboptimal search procedures [26]. One of these is the *sequential forward selection* method, which was used for the selection of variables in this case.

In sequential forward selection, the variables are included in progressively larger subsets so that the prediction performance of the model is maximized. To select p variables from the set P,

(1) search for the variable that gives the best value for the selected criterion;

(2) search for the variable that gives the best value *with* the variable(s) selected in stage 1;

(3) repeat stage 2 until p variables have been selected;

3.4. Application of Methods. At the first stage variables were selected using multiple linear regression and a sequential forward search. The data were divided into two subsets: a training subset comprising 2/3 of the total number of samples, to be used for training the model, and a validation data set consisting of the remaining 1/3 of the samples, to be used as an independent means of testing the model. The first eight variables that improved the performance of the model most were finally chosen, because in practice the models did not seem to improve beyond this point.

Next, variables were selected using an MLP network with a back-propagation algorithm and a sequential forward search. The data were divided into three subsets: a training

subset, comprising 2/3 of the total number of samples, to be used for training the network, of which a test subset containing 20% of the training data was reserved for back-propagation error calculations and a validation data set, consisting of the remaining 1/3 of the samples, to be used as an independent means of testing the model.

The artificial neural network consisted of the process parameters as inputs, one hidden layer with 5 neurons and the output neuron describing the predicted variable. The parameters of the neural network and the training algorithm were determined experimentally. The radial basis (*radbas*) transfer function was used for the hidden layer and the linear (*purelin*) transfer function for the output layer. The Bayesian regularization back-propagation (*trainbr*) algorithm [27] was exploited in training, and the sum squared error (*sse*) as the error function in training. Matlab (version 7.11) software with the Neural Network Toolbox (version 7.0) was used for the data processing.

4. Results

4.1. Modelling of Turbidity. The variables selected for water turbidity using MLR and MLP are presented in Tables 3 and 4, respectively. Evolution curves for the selecting of variables using the MLR and MLP techniques are shown in Figure 2. The results for predicting the validation data using

TABLE 3: Variables selected for turbidity using multiple linear regression.

Round	Variables	Correlation coefficient (C)
1	Aluminium dose	0.55
2	Intake from the pikkala reservoir	0.62
3	Turbidity of raw water	0.66
4	Proportion of Lake Humaljärvi/Pikkala reservoir water intake	0.70
5	Colour of raw water	0.71
6	KMnO$_4$ of raw water	0.71
7	Flocculation pH	0.71
8	Water temperature	0.71
9	Aluminium dose/raw water KMnO$_4$	0.71
10	Silicates in raw water	0.71

TABLE 4: Variables selected for turbidity using multilayer perceptrons.

Round	Variables	Correlation coefficient (C)
1	Aluminium dose	0.56
2	Intake from the pikkala reservoir	0.66
3	Turbidity of raw water	0.70
4	Proportion of Lake Humaljärvi/Pikkala reservoir water intake	0.75
5	Water temperature	0.75
6	KMnO$_4$ of raw water	0.76
7	Flocculation pH	0.77
8	Intake from Lake Humaljärvi	0.78
9	KMnO$_4$ of raw water	0.76
10	pH of raw water	0.77

MLR and MLP with 8 variables are given in Figures 3 and 4, respectively.

In addition, a two-sample F-test was conducted between the outputs of the MLR and MLP models with 8 variables. The test showed that the null hypothesis cannot be rejected with a P value of 0.5323 using the 0.95 confidence level; that is, there is no significant difference between the linear and nonlinear models.

4.2. Modelling of Residual Aluminium. The variables selected for residual aluminium in the water using MLR and MLP are presented in Tables 5 and 6, respectively. Evolution curves for the selecting of variables using linear regression and the MLP technique are shown in Figure 5. The results for predicting the validation data using MLR and MLP with 8 variables are given in Figures 6 and 7, respectively.

In addition, a two-sample F-test was conducted between the outputs of the MLR and MLP models with the 8 variables. The test showed that the null hypothesis can be rejected with a 0.95 confidence and a P value of 0.0485 that is, there is

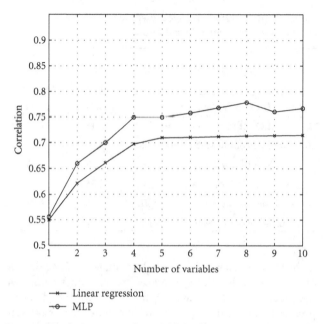

FIGURE 2: Evolution curves for turbidity. The goodness of the model improves at first as variables are added, but then the improvement gradually stops.

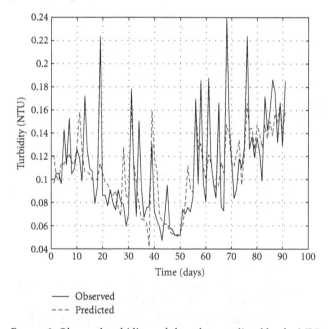

FIGURE 3: Observed turbidity and the values predicted by the MLR model when using the 8 best variables.

a statistically significant difference between the linear and nonlinear models.

5. Discussion

The quality of drinking water is an important matter, because water of low quality may cause health-related and economic problems which have a considerable impact on people's daily lives. Monitoring and controlling water quality is a challenging task; however, as the quality of water in a treatment process may be affected by numerous factors

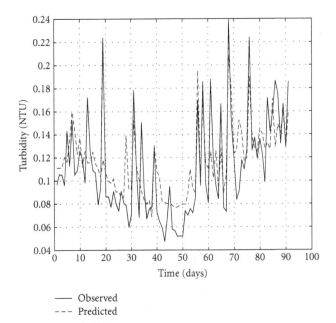

— Observed
--- Predicted

FIGURE 4: Observed turbidity and the values predicted by the MLP model when using the 8 best variables.

TABLE 5: Variables selected for residual aluminium using multiple linear regression (MLR).

Round	Variables	Correlation coefficient (C)
1	Water temperature	0.72
2	Aluminium dose/raw water KMnO$_4$	0.79
3	Silicates in raw water	0.81
4	pH of raw water	0.81
5	Hardness of raw water	0.82
6	Flocculation pH	0.82
7	Conductivity of raw water	0.82
8	Total intake of water	0.82
9	Surface level of Lake Humaljärvi	0.82
10	Colour of raw water	0.82

TABLE 6: Variables selected for residual aluminium using multilayer perceptrons (MLPs).

Round	Variables	Correlation coefficient (C)
1	Water temperature	0.76
2	Aluminium dose/raw water KMnO$_4$	0.86
3	Silicates in raw water	0.88
4	Surface level of Lake Humaljärvi	0.88
5	Hardness of raw water	0.88
6	Turbidity of raw water	0.89
7	Aluminium dose	0.90
8	pH of raw water	0.91
9	KMnO$_4$ of raw water	0.89
10	Aluminium feed	0.91

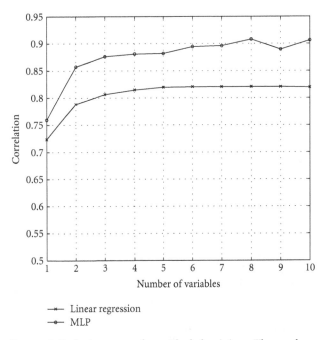

—×— Linear regression
—●— MLP

FIGURE 5: Evolution curves for residual aluminium. The goodness of the model improves at first as variables are added, and then the improvement gradually stops.

which are either not thoroughly known or which have not been verified on an experimental basis. The modelling of water quality has, therefore, become more important in recent years.

Both linear and nonlinear modelling methods were used in this paper to model turbidity and residual aluminium in a water treatment process. The general conclusion is that in both cases the goodness of the nonlinear model was slightly better than that of the linear one, which would indicate that both problems have some nonlinear features. On the other hand, the improvement in the goodness of the model is not great, which seems to suggest that simpler computational methods may be applicable to these problems.

As for turbidity, the results (see Figure 3) show that the linear model is able to predict the generic trend, whereas the majority of the peaks are modelled better by MLP (see Figure 4). It seems, however, that the reasons for some of the sharp peaks remain obscure regardless of the method used. In particular, the F-test test did not show any significant difference between the linear and nonlinear model. Overall, it is reasonable to use the linear method if the objective is only to reveal generic trends and the nonlinear one if the objective is to predict the extreme values as accurately as possible. In addition, MLR is more suitable for applications which require explicit models or fast calculation, for example, in adaptive soft sensors.

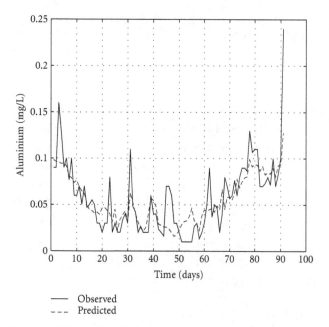

FIGURE 6: Observed residual aluminium and the values predicted by the MLR model when using the 8 best variables.

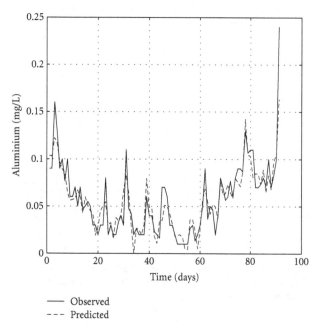

FIGURE 7: Observed residual aluminium and the values predicted by the MLP model when using the 8 best variables.

Slightly better models can be achieved for residual aluminium (see Table 5). In fact, the fit of the nonlinear model for aluminium ($C \approx 0.9$) is very good. Beside producing more accurate estimates, MLP also seems to be superior to the linear method because it is able to predict both the generic trend and the concentration peaks, whereas the linear method cannot find the reasons for the peaks, as can be seen in Figures 6 and 7. In addition, the F-test showed a statistically significant difference between the models. MLP

may, therefore, be regarded as the preferable method for modelling residual aluminium.

The results of variable selection indicate that most of the phenomena behind residual aluminium could be explained with two of the best correlating variables (temperature and Al dose/$KMnO_4$ ratio), whereas aluminium dose, intake from the Pikkala reservoir, and turbidity of raw water were the best variables for explaining the turbidity. In the sense of water chemistry, the most important process parameters are usually Al dose and pH [2]. According to our results, the Al dose (or Al/$KMnO_4$ ratio) is an important variable, because it was selected in the second round of variable selection. This implies that there could be potential for optimizing the dosing of Al, for example, by making a more sophisticated controller for dosing. In contrast, the pH value was not among the most important variables, which implies that the pH value would be already optimized in the process.

Furthermore, it is worth remembering that the selected variables are not necessarily the same as those which have the best correlations with turbidity or residual aluminium (see Tables 1 and 2). This is because the variable selected in each round is always the one that adds most information to the model in the particular round. In other words, the procedure for selecting variables takes multivariate interactions into account, whereas calculating the simple correlations does not.

According to the literature [9, 11, 17], water hydrology and water treatment processes have a nonlinear nature, so nonlinear methods should be used in the modelling. However, the results show no significant difference in the turbidity case, and only a small difference in the residual aluminium case between the linear and nonlinear models. One possible explanation would be phenomena such as seasonality or episodic events affecting the process. In this case such phenomena would be water temperature (strong seasonal dependence) and intake from Pikkala (episodic event). This is supported by the fact that it has been shown earlier that seasonality or episodic events also have a strong influence on the water treatment processes [7, 8]. Sometimes nonlinear models may give better results than linear ones, but a large part of the nonlinearity may arise from the seasonality and/or episodic events and, on the other hand, from the multivariate interactions between the variables connected with these phenomena. In this case, we could find the variables explaining these phenomena using a linear multivariate method, and the resulting model could capture most of this behaviour, so that especially in the case of turbidity the difference between the two methods used was not significant. Thus, nonlinear models are not always needed, although they can somewhat improve the goodness of models.

The results show that the approach used here has several benefits. The approach itself is evidently flexible regardless of the computational method, and it has a high computing power. Trained with real process data, the method is also able to adapt to exceptional situations in the process. In addition, the approach is suitable for cases where the physical processes are not well known or are highly complex. Generally speaking, although the resulting models assimilated good prediction abilities, they could have been improved later by adding more data samples or some process variables that were not used on this occasion.

Some limitations in the performance of the approach may follow from the fact that the variable selection was implemented by adding variables to the model one by one. This means that all the possible combinatorial effects were not evaluated as they would be in more sophisticated approaches. It is, therefore, possible that there may be two or more variables whose mutual interaction may have a considerable effect on the concentration, although their individual effects on the model may be insignificant. On the other hand, the forward selection method makes variable selection robust with regard to interdependences between the variables. It would certainly be possible to model the influence of all combinations of variables, but in reality the computing time required for that would be long, especially in processes involving a large number of variables, and this would obviously reduce the usability of the method in any real-world process applications. The correlations observed here are nevertheless of the same order as those observed by [9], who did not use variable selection in their approach.

Data-based modelling has been used in various water treatment applications in recent years, for example, for predicting raw water quality parameters, optimal flocculation dosages, or the quality parameters of treated water [11, 17]. This study shows that data-based modelling combined with variable selection provides an efficient tool for analysing specific problems affecting water treatment processes. In addition, it shows that online data and process data can be combined in the same data set for these purposes. Furthermore, there is no need to select the variables to be included in the model manually, because they can be selected during modelling by the procedure of variable selection. In addition, this study shows that nonlinear models are not always necessary if simpler and more explicit linear multivariate models perform well enough.

The method has many potential applications. First of all, regression models can be used as real-time prediction models for estimating water quality parameters. In addition, predictive models can be used for proactive management of the process and for forecasting or evaluating water quality and the risks related to it. Process diagnostics is another potential field of application. The selecting of variables, for example, provides valuable information on the factors affecting water quality. Moreover, it is possible to construct a data-based soft sensor for water quality parameters which could be used further for control or fault detection purposes.

When used off-line, the model can help to evaluate quality and/or risk aspects of water safety in different scenarios, including the accumulation of aluminium in consumers. Using virtual process interfaces, it is possible to obtain a better understanding of these things and to conduct scenario analyses based on process histories. The variable selection technique allows the most efficient variables to be selected for the piloting phase, which will reduce the number of pilot tests. Laboratory tests may still be needed after modelling, but the number of variables can be limited to the most effective ones. Overall, the approach as introduced

here provides a simple and economical tool for analysing and optimizing water treatment processes and a fruitful way of investigating interactions between the variables affecting these processes.

6. Conclusions

As drinking water quality guidelines continue to become more stringent, modelling methods which utilize process histories will offer valuable tools for process modelling and control in water treatment plants and provide an alternative to conventional methodologies. Moreover, these modelling techniques allow such utilities to increase their process knowledge and, therefore, facilitate process control. The results are promising as far as the wider use of the data-driven selection of variables and modelling in water treatment processes is concerned, and the approach used here undoubtedly has considerable potential.

Acknowledgments

The writing of this paper was supported by Maa- Ja Vesitekniikan Tuki Ry. The material was produced in the POLARIS project financed by the Finnish Funding Agency for Technology and Innovation (Tekes). The authors gratefully acknowledge this financial support.

References

[1] World Health Organization, *Guidelines for drinking-water quality*, vol. 1, Recommendations, 3rd edition, 2006.

[2] R. D. Letterman, Ed., *Water Quality & Treatment, Handbook of Community Water Supplies*, AWWA, 1999.

[3] A. Campell, "The role of aluminium and copper on neuroinflammation and Alzheimer's disease," *Journal of Alzheimer's Disease*, vol. 10, pp. 165–172, 2006.

[4] J. E. Van Benschoten and J. K. Edzwald, "Chemical aspects of coagulation using aluminum salts - I. Hydrolytic reactions of alum and polyaluminum chloride," *Water Research*, vol. 24, no. 12, pp. 1519–1526, 1990.

[5] J. E. Van Benschoten and J. K. Edzwald, "Chemical aspects of coagulation using aluminum salts - II. Coagulation of fulvic acid using alum and polyaluminum chloride," *Water Research*, vol. 24, no. 12, pp. 1527–1535, 1990.

[6] C. Huang and H. Shiu, "Interactions between alum and organics in coagulation," *Colloids and Surfaces A*, vol. 113, no. 1-2, pp. 155–163, 1996.

[7] P. Juntunen, M. Liukkonen, M. Lehtola, and Y. Hiltunen, "Cluster analysis of a water treatment process by self-organizing maps," in *Proceedings of the 8th IWA Symposium on Systems Analysis and Integrated Assessment*, E. Ayesa and I. Rodríquez-Roda, Eds., pp. 553–558, WATERMATEX, 2011.

[8] P. Juntunen, M. Liukkonen, M. Lehtola, and Y. Hiltunen, "Dynamic modelling approach for detecting turbidity in drinking water," in *Proceedings of the 52nd International Conference of Scandinavian Simulation Society*, E. Dahlquist, Ed., 2011.

[9] C. W. Baxter, Q. Zhang, S. J. Stanley, R. Shariff, R. R. T. Tupas, and H. L. Stark, "Drinking water quality and treatment: the

use of artificial neural networks," *Canadian Journal of Civil Engineering*, vol. 28, supplement 1, pp. 26–35, 2001.

[10] D. N. Thomas, S. J. Judd, and N. Fawcett, "Flocculation modelling: a review," *Water Research*, vol. 33, no. 7, pp. 1579–1592, 1999.

[11] H. R. Maier, N. Morgan, and C. W. K. Chow, "Use of artificial neural networks for predicting optimal alum doses and treated water quality parameters," *Environmental Modelling and Software*, vol. 19, no. 5, pp. 485–494, 2004.

[12] S. Haykin, *Neural Networks and Learning Machines*, Pearson Education, Upper Saddle River, NJ, USA, 3rd edition, 2009.

[13] P. Kadlec, B. Gabrys, and S. Strandt, "Data-driven Soft Sensors in the process industry," *Computers and Chemical Engineering*, vol. 33, no. 4, pp. 795–814, 2009.

[14] M. R. G. Meireles, P. E. M. Almeida, and M. G. Simões, "A comprehensive review for industrial applicability of artificial neural networks," *IEEE Transactions on Industrial Electronics*, vol. 50, no. 3, pp. 585–601, 2003.

[15] M. Heikkinen, H. Poutiainen, M. Liukkonen, T. Heikkinen, and Y. Hiltunen, "Self-organizing maps in the analysis of an industrial wastewater treatment process," *Mathematics and Computers in Simulation*, vol. 82, no. 3, pp. 450–459, 2011.

[16] A. M. Kalteh, P. Hjorth, and R. Berndtsson, "Review of the self-organizing map (SOM) approach in water resources: analysis, modelling and application," *Environmental Modelling and Software*, vol. 23, no. 7, pp. 835–845, 2008.

[17] H. R. Maier and G. C. Dandy, "Neural networks for the prediction and forecasting of water resources variables: a review of modelling issues and applications," *Environmental Modelling and Software*, vol. 15, no. 1, pp. 101–124, 2000.

[18] M. S. Gibbs, G. C. Dandy, and H. R. Maier, "Calibration and optimization of the pumping and disinfection of a real water supply system," *Journal of Water Resources Planning and Management*, vol. 136, no. 4, Article ID 023003QWR, pp. 493–501, 2010.

[19] C. W. Baxter, S. J. Stanley, and Q. Zhang, "Development of a full-scale artificial neural network model for the removal of natural organic matter by enhanced coagulation," *Journal of Water Supply: AQUA*, vol. 48, no. 4, pp. 129–136, 1999.

[20] J. L. Giraudel and S. Lek, "A comparison of self-organizing map algorithm and some conventional statistical methods for ecological community ordination," *Ecological Modelling*, vol. 146, no. 1–3, pp. 329–339, 2001.

[21] P. J. Werbos, *Beyond regression: new tools for prediction and analysis in the behavioral sciences*, Doctoral thesis, Harvard University, Cambridge, Mass, USA, 1974.

[22] A. K. Jain, R. P. W. Duin, and J. Mao, "Statistical pattern recognition: a review," *IEEE Transactions on Pattern Analysis and Machine Intelligence*, vol. 22, no. 1, pp. 4–37, 2000.

[23] A. L. Blum and P. Langley, "Selection of relevant features and examples in machine learning," *Artificial Intelligence*, vol. 97, no. 1-2, pp. 245–271, 1997.

[24] I. Guyon and A. Elisseeff, "An introduction to variable and feature selection," *Journal of Machine Learning Research*, vol. 3, pp. 1157–1182, 2003.

[25] H. Liu and H. Motoda, Eds., *Computational Methods of Feature Selection*, Chapman & Hall, Boca Raton, Fla, USA, 2008.

[26] A. W. Whitney, "Direct method of nonparametric measurement selection," *IEEE Transactions on Computers*, vol. C-20, no. 9, pp. 1100–1103, 1971.

[27] D. J. C. MacKay, "A practical bayesian framework for backpropagation networks," *Neural Computation*, vol. 4, no. 3, pp. 448–472, 1992.

20

The Use of Artificial-Intelligence-Based Ensembles for Intrusion Detection: A Review

Gulshan Kumar[1] and Krishan Kumar[2]

[1] Department of Computer Application, Shaheed Bhagat Singh State Technical Campus, Ferozepur, Punjab 152004, India
[2] Department of Computer Science & Engineering, Punjab Institute of Technology, Kapurthala, Punjab 144601, India

Correspondence should be addressed to Gulshan Kumar, gulshanahuja@gmail.com

Academic Editor: Farid Melgani

In supervised learning-based classification, ensembles have been successfully employed to different application domains. In the literature, many researchers have proposed different ensembles by considering different combination methods, training datasets, base classifiers, and many other factors. Artificial-intelligence-(AI-) based techniques play prominent role in development of ensemble for intrusion detection (ID) and have many benefits over other techniques. However, there is no comprehensive review of ensembles in general and AI-based ensembles for ID to examine and understand their current research status to solve the ID problem. Here, an updated review of ensembles and their taxonomies has been presented in general. The paper also presents the updated review of various AI-based ensembles for ID (in particular) during last decade. The related studies of AI-based ensembles are compared by set of evaluation metrics driven from (1) architecture & approach followed; (2) different methods utilized in different phases of ensemble learning; (3) other measures used to evaluate classification performance of the ensembles. The paper also provides the future directions of the research in this area. The paper will help the better understanding of different directions in which research of ensembles has been done in general and specifically: field of intrusion detection systems (IDSs).

1. Introduction

The threat of Internet attacks is quite real and frequent so this has increased a need for securing information on any network on the Internet. The objective of information security includes confidentiality, authentication, integrity, availability, and nonrepudiation [1]. The set of activities that violates security objectives is called intrusion. Thus secure information requires the phases that provide (1) protection: automatic protection from intrusions; (2) detection: automatic detection of intrusions; (3) reaction: automatic reaction or alarm when system is intruded; (4) recovery: repair or recovery of loss caused due to intrusion [2]. Out of these phases, the perfect detection of an intrusion is the most important. As only after correct detection of intrusion, correct reaction and recovery phase of information security can be implemented. In the literature, many IDSs have been developed implementing various techniques

from different disciplines like statistical techniques, AI techniques, and so forth. Some IDSs have been developed based on single-classification technique while other IDSs (called hybrid/ensemble IDS) implement more-than-one-classfication technique. Ensemble-based IDSs have many advantages over the IDS implementing single technique (refer to Section 2). Many researchers have proposed different ensembles for ID by exploiting the different characteristics of weak classifiers and datasets. To cover various aspects of ensembles, many researchers proposed different taxonomies for ensembles. Keeping the advantages of AI-based techniques over other techniques and ensembles, many researchers proposed AI-based ensembles for ID. However, there exists no comprehensive review of taxonomies of ensembles (in general) and AI-based ensembles for intrusion detection (ID) (in specific).

The objective of this paper is threefold. First objective is to present an updated review of ensembles and their taxonomies in general for supervised classification. Second objective is to present an updated review of different AI-based ensemble/hybrid classifiers proposed for ID during last decade and compare them by set of evaluation metrics which derives from (1) architecture & approach followed; (2) different methods utilized in different phases of ensemble learning; (3) other measures used to evaluate classification performance of the ensembles. Third objective is to highlight research gaps and directions in developing efficient ensemble for ID.

Paper Overview. The rest of paper is organized as follows. Section 2 highlights the state of art, need, advantages, and disadvantages of AI-based techniques and their ensembles for ID. Section 3 lists the reasons and benefits for combining multiple base classifiers. Various taxonomies proposed in the literature are presented in Section 4. The section also describes various methods used at different levels to generate ensembles. Section 5 highlights various AI-based ensembles proposed for ID during the last decade. Related studies are compared by various evaluation metrics. Finally, Section 6 concludes the paper and presents future research directions.

2. Intrusion Detection

An intrusion detection system (IDS) defined as "an effective security technology, which can detect, prevent and possibly react to the computer attacks" is one of the standard components in security infrastructures. It monitors target sources of activities, such as audit and network traffic data in computer or network systems and then deploys various techniques in order to provide security services. The main objective of IDS is to classify intrusive and nonintrusive network activities in an efficient manner. The process of intrusion detection involves the tasks: (1) data acquisition/collection; (2) data Preprocessing & feature selection; (3) model selection for data analysis; (4) classification and result analysis [3]. To handle these tasks, IDS comprises of different modules for efficient ID. The modules are network to monitor, Data collection & storage unit, Data analysis & processing unit, and signal [4, 5] as depicted in Figure 1.

Based upon these modules, IDSs can be categorized into different classes like host-based IDS (HIDS) versus network-based IDS (NIDS), misuse- or signature-based IDS versus anomaly-based IDS, Passive IDS versus Active IDS, and so forth [5]. HIDSs are developed to monitor the activities of a host system and state, while NIDSs monitor the network traffic for multiple hosts. HIDSs and NIDSs have been designed to perform misuse detection and anomaly detection. Anomaly based ID allows detecting unknown attacks for which the signatures have not yet been extracted [2]. In practice, anomaly detectors generate false alarms due, in large part, to the limited data used for training and to the complexity of underlying data distributions that may change dynamically over time. Since it is very difficult to collect and label representative data to design and validate an anomaly detection system, its internal model of normal behavior

will tend to diverge from the underlying data distribution. Further details can be studied in [4, 5].

Since the first introduction, IDSs have been evaluated using a number of different ways based upon evaluation datasets [6]. Various features of IDS can be evaluated, which may range from performance and correctness to usability. However, in the literature most tests that have been performed have mainly focused on measuring the accuracy and effectiveness of IDS, that is, the false alarm rate and the percentage of attacks that are successfully detected. Several other metrics are utilized by researchers to measure the performance of IDS. These metrics can be divided into three classes: threshold, ranking, and probability metrics [7, 8]. Threshold metrics include classification rate (CR), F-measure (FM), and cost per example (CPE). It is not important how close a prediction is to a threshold, only if it is above or below threshold. The value of threshold metrics lies in range from 0 to 1. Ranking metrics include false-positive rate (FPR), detection rate (DR), precision (PR), and area under ROC curve (ROC). The value of ranking metrics lies in range from 0 to 1. These metrics depend on the ordering of the cases, not the actual predicted values. As long as ordering is preserved, it makes no difference. These metrics measure how well the attack instances are ordered before normal instances and can be viewed as a summary of model performance across all possible thresholds. Probability metrics include root mean square error (RMSE). Value of RMSE lies in range from 0 to 1. The metric is minimized when the predicted value for each attack class coincides with the true conditional probability of that class being normal class. Generally, these metrics are computed from confusion matrix.

The performance of IDS is generally evaluated based upon audit data containing mix of legitimate traffic and attacks. The IDSs are evaluated by comparing the true-positive rate (i.e., the percentage of attacks that were correctly recognized) and the false-positive rate (i.e., the percentage of legitimate traffic flagged as an attack). Many researchers tried to collect evaluation audit data. The important audit data available as benchmarked dataset are (1) DARPA evaluation dataset collected at MIT Lincoln Laboratory in year 1998, 1999, and 2000 [9]; (2) KDD cup 1999 dataset [10]; (3) UNM dataset of systems calls [11]; (4) DEFCON 9 capture the flag (CTF) dataset [12]; (5) ITOC dataset [13]; (6) many more datasets collected for realistic evaluation from specific organization. The details can be further explored in [7]. KDD cup 1999 dataset is most popular publically available evaluation benchmarked dataset. But, the dataset is critically discussed in the literature for being nowadays outdated due to the type of attacks and background traffic used and for the methodology implemented for building it [14].

However, in real world, intrusion detection process involves processing of high dimensions of network & system data. Processing of high-dimensional data for ID is highly computationally expensive. This cause may lose real-time capability of IDS. The computation overhead may be reduced by applying feature reduction techniques, which can be further explored in [15, 16]. The distribution of data is also dynamically changing with passage of time having new

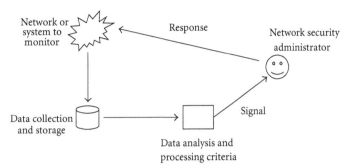

FIGURE 1: Architecture of IDS.

patterns of novel attacks. Nonavailability of signatures of novel attacks in databases leads to high false alarm rate and low detection accuracy. In fact, practitioners as well as researchers have observed that IDSs can easily trigger thousands of alarms per day, upto 99% of which are false positives (i.e., alarms that were mistakenly triggered by benign events) [17]. Most of attacks are likely to generate multiple related alarms. This flood of mostly false alarms makes it very difficult to identify the hidden true positives (i.e., those alarms that correctly flag attacks) [17]. Current intrusion-detection systems do not make it easy for network administrator to logically group related alerts. Another problem with current intrusion detection is scalability as it is difficult to achieve large-scale deployment [18]. The most appealing way to reduce false alarms is to develop better IDSs that generate fewer false alarms. The process of reducing the false alarms is very challenging because the false alarms are the result of many problems. The major problems includes (1) lack of suitable training dataset; (2) significant real-time requirements; (3) ambiguous events which cannot be decided to constitute intrusion easily (for example, failed login); (4) inherent problem of writing correct patterns for ID; (5) current IDSs do not properly aggregate and correlate the alarms that lead to flood of false alarms for network administrator [18].

These causes require IDS to be faster, flexible (instead of strict thresholds), and adaptive (instead of fixed rules), and dynamic learning of new patterns and aggregate logically corelated false alarms to identify root cause of alarms. The efficient IDS would have to address all these issues including reduction of false positives and fast processing of high volume of network traffic and be adaptive to changing environment for novel attacks.

Various classification techniques (classifiers) from different disciplines have been applied to detect the intrusions efficiently. Examples of these techniques include statistical techniques, artificial-intelligence- (AI-) based techniques, and its subfield techniques [5, 19, 20]. Here AI-based techniques include techniques like decision-tree-based techniques, rule-based techniques, data mining-techniques, genetic-algorithm-based techniques, machine-learning techniques (Neural network, SVM, Bayesian network, etc.), pattern recognition techniques and so forth. [5]. Recent advances in the field of AI led many researchers to apply AI-based techniques for ID successfully. Potential benefits

of AI-based techniques over other conventional techniques includes (1) flexibility (versus threshold definition of conventional techniques); (2) adaptability (versus specific rules of conventional techniques); (3) pattern recognition (and detection of new patterns); (4) fast computing (faster than humans); (4) learning capabilities [21]. AI-based techniques help meet the following research issues on IDSs [22]: (1) these techniques has the capability of learning by example that helps to generalize from a representative set of examples and allows detecting new types of intrusion; (2) with learning by example approaches attack "signatures" can be extracted automatically from labeled traffic data, thus allowing to overcome the subjectivity of human interpretation of intrusive behavior, the latter being implemented in many current IDSs; (3) learning by example approaches is able to adapt to new threats. The major difference between AI-based and traditional IDSs is that only AIs can learn new rules automatically, whereas in traditional systems the security administrator must add new rules for each new attack type or each new allowed program. In AI-based systems, it is possible to train the system by examples rather than rules.

Many researchers applied and evaluated AI-based techniques using different evaluation datasets for ID. They reported many challenges related to AI-based techniques and dataset for ID. The challenges related to techniques include: (1) no single-classification technique is capable enough to detect all classes of attacks to acceptable false alarm rate and detection accuracy [23, 24]; (2) some of the existing techniques fall into local minima, for global minima, these techniques are computationally expensive; (3) existing techniques are not capable to model correct hypothesis space of problem [25]; (4) some existing techniques are unstable in nature such as neural networks that show different results with different initializations due to the randomness inherent in the training procedure; (5) different techniques trained on the same data may not only differ in their global performances, but they also may show strong local differences. Each technique may have its own region in the feature space where it performs the best [26]. Related evaluation dataset challenges include (1) lack of sufficient amount of quality training data; (2) class imbalance of training data causes the results of classifiers to be biased towards majority class.

In order to solve these problems, many researchers utilized AI-based ensembles for ID successfully. They proved that AI-based ensembles can improve detection performance over a single technique/classifier [27–29]. The concept of ensemble is to employ multiple base classifiers and their individual predictions are combined in some way to obtain reliable and more accurate predictions [17, 25]. Employment of ensemble and combination of multiple predictions are mainly motivated by three aspects which characterize the intrusion detection domain [3]: (a) relevant information may be present at multiple abstraction levels, (b) the information may be collected from multiple sources, and (c) this information needs to be represented at the human level of understanding.

No doubt, AI-based ensemble/hybrid classifiers improved the performance over single classifier [23, 28–45]. But, still some research issues exist. The major issues include diversity among the base classifiers, ensemble size, computational overhead, input feature space, and combining strategy.

3. Ensemble Classifiers

The ensembles involve the employment of multiple base classifiers and combine their predictions to obtain reliable and more accurate predictions. Dietterich [25] listed three specific reasons for benefits of ensembles: statistical, computational, and representational reason. Other reasons for combining different classifiers include [26] the following. (1) a designer may have access to a number of different classifiers, each developed in a different context and for an entirely different representation/description of the same problem. An example is the identification of persons by their voice, face, and handwriting. (2) Some times more than a single training set is available, each collected at a different time or in a different environment. These training sets may even use different features. (3) Different classifiers trained on the same data may not only differ in their global performances, but they also may show strong local differences. Each classifier may have its own region in the feature space where it performs the best. (4) Some unstable classifiers like neural networks show different results with different initializations due to the randomness inherent in the training procedure. Instead of selecting the best network and discarding the others, one can combine various networks. Different combination strategies can be applied either to classify combination or to correlate alerts [3]. The former approach involves the use of different classifiers to take a unique decision about the data pattern typically related to a single network packet whereas the later approach is mainly aimed at providing a high-level description of the detected pattern/attack by using the outputs of different classifiers/IDS.

Ensemble helps to meet the following challenges of ID (refer to Section 2 for ID challenges). (1) Ensemble comprise of multiple weak classifiers instead of single classifier. The multiple classifiers complement weaknesses of each other and hence improve the performance. (2) Ensembles use the combined knowledge to model the hypothesis of the problem upon different subset of dataset or feature subspace. The combined knowledge of weak classifiers helps to improve the performance even in lack sufficient amount of quality training data. (3) Since ensemble use the multiple classifiers, so it helps to find the global solution that leads to reduce the false alarm rate and increase the detection accuracy. (4) Unstable base classifiers help to generate the diverse set of base classifiers for efficient ensemble. (5) Classifiers trained with same dataset showing different performance help to maintain diversity among the base classifiers.

In nutshell, by using combined knowledge of multiple classifiers trained by different dataset and exploiting different characteristics of problems, ensembles are capable to improve the performance (in terms of increased detection accuracy and decreasing false-positive rate) even in lack of sufficient amount of quality training data. But, computations of multiple predictions in ensembles increase computational overhead. Many researchers and practitioners advocate ensemble classifiers by keeping following points in mind. (1) The availability of enormous computational power (to cope up computational overhead of ensemble classifiers); (2) lack of quality training data for realistic evaluation; (3) improved performance (over single classifier) of ensembles. An important factor affecting the efficiency of ensemble is the diversity among base classifiers [46–48]. The diversity in ensembles refers to different errors made by different base classifiers on data records. In order to produce diverse classifiers, researchers used two types of methods: (1) *Implicit*; (2) *Explicit* [47, 49]. Implicit methods do not involve any direct measure of diversity whereas explicit method does. Kuncheva and Whitaker [50] proposed different metrics to measure diversity. The diversity in ensembles can be obtained by using different (1) starting point in hypothesis space; (2) set of accessible hypotheses; (3) traversal of hypothesis space [47]. The general observation in ensemble construction is to combine multiple diverse classifiers.

By keeping the benefits of AI techniques and performance enhancement by using ensemble approach in mind (refer to Section 2), AI-based ensembles have been successfully applied to improve the performance of classifier in many fields (e.g., finance [51]), bioinformatics [52], medicine [53], information security [28, 33, 54] information retrieval [55], and so forth, many researchers report that ensembles often outperform the individual best base classifier [5, 33, 47, 51, 56–58]. They proposed different concepts to describe the improved performance, reduced generalization error, and successful applications of ensembles to different fields over individual classifier. For example, Allwein et al. [59] interpreted the improved performance in the framework of large margin classifiers, Kleinberg in the reference of Stochastic Discrimination theory [60], and Breiman in the terms of the bias variance analysis [61].

In spite of much research on AI-based ensembles, many research questions still remain unanswered, for example, how many base classifiers should be combined, how base classifiers should be combined, how to generate diverse set of base classifiers, how instances of training dataset should be partitioned to generate base classifiers, how feature space should be partitioned and in particular for ID quality training dataset, and so forth.

4. Taxonomy

Ensemble learning process has three phases: (1) ensemble generation; (2) ensemble selection; (3) ensemble integration. *Ensemble generation* is homogenous if the same induction algorithm is used to generate all the classifiers of the ensemble, otherwise it is said to be heterogeneous. In ensemble generation phase, a pool of diverse base classifiers are generated. This can be done by using (1) different initialization parameters of base classifiers; or (2) different subsets of feature space (feature level); or (3) different data subsets (data level) to train the base classifiers. *Ensemble selection* requires selection of classifiers from pool of diverse base classifiers. Here different methods can be utilized to combine the pool of base classifiers obtained in ensemble generation phase: (1) combine all base classifiers; (2) combine smaller subsets according to clustering; (3) combine reduced sets of base classifiers that exceed specific thresholds on performance (i.e., overproduce and choose strategy) [33]. *Ensemble integration* involves the combination of predictions of set of base classifiers selected in ensemble selection phase. It can use two different methods: (1) combination (also called fusion); or (2) selection [46]. The combination method consists in the combination of the predictions obtained by the different classifiers in the ensemble to obtain the final prediction. The selection approach, specially its dynamic form, selects one (or more) classifier from the ensemble according to the prediction performance of these classifiers on similar data from the validation set. The ensemble integration phase involves many strategies to combine multiple predictions because these strategies have performance variability when tackling different problems. According to No Panacea Theorem for classifier combination, there is always a situation in which, under certain hypotheses, a combination strategy gives very bad performance [62]. This proves that there is neither a perfect combination strategy, nor one generally outperforming each other. This statement can be used as theoretical guideline for a malicious user to disrupt or evade the system, once combination strategy implemented is known to them.

In nutshell, we may have different feature sets, different training sets, different classification methods, or different training sessions, all resulting in a set of classifiers, whose outputs may be combined, with the hope of improving the overall classification performance [26]. If this set of classifiers is fixed, the problem focuses on the ensemble integration phase. It is also possible to use a fixed combiner and optimize the set of input classifiers; the problem focuses on the generation and selection phases.

Keeping in view, the popularity and successful applications of ensembles in different fields, various methods are proposed in the literature for creating ensembles. Researchers have proposed different taxonomies to categorize ensembles. Since research of ensemble is continuously evolving, there is no existing taxonomy that covers every aspect of ensembles. The literature review of important taxonomies is as follows.

Jain et al. [26] grouped different classifier combination schemes into three main categories according to their architecture: (1) parallel; (2) cascading (or serial combination);

(3) hierarchical (tree like). In the parallel architecture, all the individual classifiers are invoked independently, and their results are then combined by a combiner. Most combination schemes in the literature belong to this category. In the gated parallel variant, the outputs of individual classifiers are selected or weighted by a gating device before they are combined. In the cascading architecture, individual classifiers are invoked in a linear sequence. The number of possible classes for a given pattern is gradually reduced as more classifiers in the sequence have been invoked. For the sake of efficiency, inaccurate but cheap classifiers (low computational and measurement demands) are considered first, followed by more accurate and expensive classifiers. In the hierarchical architecture, individual classifiers are combined into a structure, which is similar to that of a decision tree classifier. The tree nodes, however, may now be associated with complex classifiers demanding a large number of features. The advantage of this architecture is the high efficiency and flexibility exploiting the discriminant power of different types of features. Using these three basic architectures, we can build even more complicated classifier combination systems. He listed eighteen different methods for classifier combination and divided them into different categories according to their trainability, adaptivity, and requirement on the output of individual classifiers. The combination methods include (1) voting; (2) sum, mean, median; (3) product, min, max; (4) generalized ensemble; (5) adaptive weighting; (6) stacking; (7) Borda count; (8) logistic regression; (9) class set reduction; (10) Dempster Shafer; (11) fuzzy integral; (12) mixture of local experts (MLE); (13) hierarchical MLE; (14) associative switch; (15) bagging; (16) boosting; (17) random space; (18) neural tree.

Sharkey [63] proposed a three-dimensional taxonomy that include (1) selection or combination of the multiple base classifiers; the ensemble member can be competitive or cooperative: in competitive mode, a single member is selected to provide the final prediction whereas in cooperative mode the predictions of all members are combined; (2) methods based or not on the direct combination of base classifier outputs; there can be top-down or bottom-up ensembles, in top-down mode, the combination method is based on something other than the individual predictions, whereas bottom-up techniques take predictions of the members into account in their combination method, bottom up approach is further divided into two methods, namely, fixed methods (e.g., voting) and dynamic methods (e.g., stacking); (3) methods based on pure ensembles or modular systems. The pure ensemble systems combine a set of classifiers, each of which solves the same original task. On the other hand, the purpose of modular systems is to break down a complex problem into several subproblems so that each learning algorithm either solves a different task or trained by different training set. The taxonomy proposed by Sharkey [63] was further extended by Rokach [64]. He proposed taxonomy based on combiner usage, classifier dependency, diversity generation, ensemble size, and the capability of ensemble methods to be applied with different base learning algorithms.

Kuncheva [46] proposed a basic taxonomy for generating a diverse pool of classifiers. She proposed that diverse classifiers can be generated by using various methods at four different levels, namely, (1) combination level; (2) classifier level; (3) feature level; (4) data level. At combination level, she emphasized the combination rules to accumulate multiple classifiers, distinguishing between fusion methods that combine the outputs of the base classifiers and selection methods, by which a single classifier is selected among the set of available base classifiers. Classifier level may consider different models and may design base learners for specific ensemble methods. At third level, different subsets of features can be used for the classifiers. Finally, different data subsets, so that each base classifier in the ensemble is trained on its own data, can be used to build up the committee of learning machines. She also proposed that there are two types of methods to develop ensembles.

(1) *Decision optimization*: it refers to methods to choose and optimize the combiner for a fixed ensemble of base classifiers. This method corresponds to level A (combination level as described above),

(2) *Coverage optimization*: it refers to methods for creating diverse base classifiers assuming a fixed combiner. This method corresponds to level B, C, and D.

Researchers also proposed that there are trainable and nontrainable ensembles. Trainable ensembles need additional training to create the ensemble (either during the base classifier training or after all base classifiers is trained) [33]. On the other hand, nontrainable ensembles do not need training after the base classifiers have been induced [55, 65].

Witten and Frank [66] provided four methods to generate multiple models: (1) bagging; (2) boosting; (3) stacking; (4) error-correcting code.

Bishop [67] proposed five methods for combining the individual classifiers. The methods are Bayesian model averaging, committees, boosting, tree-based models, and conditional mixture models. Boosting is further divided into two types: (1) minimizing exponential error; (2) error functions for boosting.

Marsland [68] suggested boosting, bagging, and the mixture of experts method as methods for ensembles.

Alpaydin [69] proposed seven methods of combining multiple learning algorithms: (1) voting; (2) error-correcting output codes; (3) bagging; (4) boosting; (5) mixtures of experts (6) stacked generalization; (7) cascading.

Langin and Rahimi [31] proposed three different strategies to combine base classifiers, namely, (1) consecutive combination: a consecutive combination uses methods in order, first one, and then the next; (2) ensemble combinations: an ensemble combination has methods which run in parallel with an additional method at the end which provides a single output from multiple potential outputs; (3) hybrid combinations: a hybrid combination is an offspring of two different parents which implies an interaction of some sort as opposed to being consecutive or parallel. A hybrid strategy can loop back and forth multiple times between methods or can embed one method within another method.

In this study, we adopted and presented the taxonomy proposed by Kuncheva [46] and additional aspects borrowed from Jain et al. [26]. The basic reason for adopting this taxonomy is its simplicity, popularity, and it covers basic aspects for building diverse pool of base classifiers. The author highlighted that diverse pool of classifiers can be generated by using different methods at four levels. The levels are as follows.

4.1. Combination Level. This level focuses on ensemble integration phase of ensemble learning process. Here, predictions of base classifiers are combined in some way to improve the performance of ensemble. The researchers proposed that there are three main ways in combining classifiers, namely, fusion, selection, and Mixture of expert systems [33]. In classifier fusion, each ensemble member is supposed to have knowledge of the whole feature space. Here, each member is trained by the same dataset with all features. To determine final prediction of ensemble, the combiner applies some method to combine the predictions of ensemble members in certain way to get final ensemble prediction, for example, average or majority vote (most popular) method. In classifier selection, each ensemble member is supposed to know well a part of the feature space and be responsible for objects in this part. Here, each member is trained by different dataset. Ensemble output is determined by one classifier.

In nutshell, fusion based combination methods combine all the outputs of the base classifiers, whereas selection based combination methods try to choose the best classifiers among the set of the available base classifiers. Fusion strategy generally falls under coverage optimization, whereas selection strategy falls under decision optimization [33, 46].

4.1.1. Fusion-Based Combination Methods. These methods combine the predictions of the base classifiers to determine ensemble prediction. The major methods proposed in literature are described below.

(i) *Majority Voting Method.* In majority voting ensemble, each base classifier votes for specific class and the class that collects majority of vote is predicted as ensemble final prediction [70–72].

(ii) *Threshold Plurality Vote Method.* This method is further generalization of majority vote method proposed by Xu et al. [73]. This method works by imposing a threshold on the number of votes to select the class, we may move from a unanimity vote rule, by which a class is chosen if all the base classifiers agree on that particular class label, for intermediate cases are considered by moving the threshold of votes, at the expenses of some possible unclassified instances.

(iii) *Naïve Bayes Decision Method:* This method assumes the conditional independence between classifiers. The method selects the class with the highest posterior probability computed through the estimated class conditional probabilities and Bayes' theorem [74, 75].

(iv) *Fuzzy Theory Method.* Many researchers proposed fuzzy set theory to combine base classifiers using fuzzy aggregation connectives to determine ensemble prediction [76, 77]. Fuzzy combination methods are effective as they measure the strength of every subset of classifiers. Thus to determine the class of any unclassified instance is the decision of ensemble which is based upon competence of every subset of based classifiers [50].

(v) *Decision Template Method*. The main concept of decision template is to compare a prototypical answer of ensemble for prediction of class of a given instance. The method may use different similarity measure to evaluate the matching between matrix of classifiers output and matrix of templates. The method can be applied to combine multiple classifier predictions to determine ensemble prediction [78].

(vi) *Metalearning Method*. The method employs a second level of combiner to fuse the predictions of base classifiers for determining final ensemble prediction, for example, stacking. In stacking, the predictions of base classifiers are fed to an intermediate combiner to perform trained combinations of predictions of base classifiers [79]. Another example of metalearning method is to use an arbiter or a combiner to finalize recursively in a hierarchically structured input space on the basis of the predictions made by the base classifiers. The objective of this method is to offer an alternative classification when base classifiers disagree (arbiter tree) or to combine the predictions of base classifiers by learning their relationships with the correct class labels (combiner trees) [80, 81].

(vii) *Hierarchically Structured Method*. The methods are in general characterized by a two step approach: first, at learning of the classes as a set of independent classification problems; second, at combination of the predictions by exploiting the associations between classes that describe the hierarchy. These methods ensure an increment in precision with respect to other flat methods, but this is achieved at cost of the overall recall [82, 83].

(viii) *Boolean Combination (BC) Methods*. Boolean functions especially the conjunction AND and disjunction OR operations have recently been investigated to combine predictions of different classifiers within the ROC space [2]. These methods were shown to improve performance. The methods are based upon assumption that the classifiers are conditionally independent and their respective ROC is smooth and proper. Khreich et al. [2] proposed an iterative Boolean combination (IBC) method to efficiently fuse the predictions from multiple classifiers. The IBC efficiently exploits all Boolean functions applied to the ROC curves and requires no prior assumptions about conditional independence of classifiers or convexity of ROC curves.

4.1.2. Selection-Based Combination Methods. These methods try to choose the best classifiers among the set of the available base classifiers. The final prediction of ensemble is the prediction of selected base classifier or fused prediction of subset of base classifiers as described in aforementioned text. In order to design selection-based ensemble classifier, individual base classifier and its competence on specific input and selection approach must be decided [46]. Important methods proposed in the literature are described in the following section.

(i) *The Test and Select Method*. This method describes a greedy method which adds a new classifier to ensemble if it reduces the squared error [71]. The method can be assisted by different optimization approaches like genetic algorithms [84].

(ii) *Cascading Classifiers Method*. In this method, different base classifiers are employed sequentially to unclassified instance and confidence level of first classifier is recorded. If its level is high enough then its prediction is the ensemble final prediction. Otherwise prediction of next available base classifier is required. This process is recursively repeated [85].

(iii) *Dynamic Classifier Selection Method*. This method measure the competence of each base classifier to determine the prediction of ensemble classifier. The competence of base classifier can be determined dynamically either by using prior information about base classifiers or by posterior information produced by them in terms of their predictions [86, 87]. Limitation of this method is that the measurement of competence of base classifiers is computationally expensive.

(iv) *Clustering-Based Selection Method*. This method employs clustering technique to search subset of base classifiers which perform similar predictions about the unclassified instance. Then the method selects a model from each cluster to select subset of available base classifiers. These methods also help to improve diversity of ensemble [17, 45, 88]. Many researchers also used these methods to reduce the false alarms by correlating similar alarms [18, 88]. These methods are employed to analyze root cause of false alarms [17].

(v) *Statistical Selection Method*. Statistical method can be employed to heterogeneous ensemble. The method selects those base classifiers which perform better performance than others. Then the method combines the selected base classifiers through majority voting method (described in previous section) [89].

4.1.3. Mixture of Expert Systems. This method is a general method similar to ensemble selection [90]. In this method, the recombination of the base classifiers is governed by a supervisor classifier. Supervisor classifier selects the most suitable member of the ensemble on the basis of the available input data. Two additional components are incorporated in mixture of expert's model: (1) a gating network; (2) selector. Gating network receives the same input vectors as the classifiers in the ensemble, but its function is to calculate probabilities for each classifier as to how competent they are to classify the given input. These probabilities, accompanied by the predictions of each of the classifiers, are passed on to the selector, which then determines the final output. These probabilities can be used to stochastically select the expert, or to choose the expert according to a winner-takes-all paradigm, or as weights to combine the outputs of the multiple base classifiers [33, 46].

Discussion 1. The different methods cited in the above section can be summarized in Table 1. Fusion is the simples and popular method to combine different base classifiers. This method works on the assumption that all base classifiers are of same importance but practically it may not be true, whereas in selection method, generally, only one classifier is chosen to label an unclassified instance. Thus selection method requires that the ensemble classifier is further trained to obtain mechanisms for deciding which base classifier should be chosen to label a given unclassified instance [33]). Selection is guaranteed by design to give at least the same training accuracy as the best individual classifier. However, the model might overtrain, giving a deceptively low training error. To guard against overtraining we may use confidence intervals and nominate a classifier only when it is significantly better than the others [46].

4.2. Classifier Level. This level focuses on ensemble selection phase of ensemble learning process. It determines which base classifiers are used to constitute the ensemble prediction. Many researchers investigated the combination of base classifiers at this level very advantageous particularly for ID [23, 28–30, 32–44]. It is supported due to fact that different base classifiers perform differently upon different categories of intrusions (e.g., DoS, Probe, U2R, R2L, etc.). Selection of base classifiers may be done from pool of classifiers, which are trained using different induction algorithms (called heterogeneous ensembles) or the same induction algorithm (called homogeneous ensembles). Many researcher generated ensemble by selecting heterogeneous base classifiers [23, 24, 27–29, 36]. For example, Mukkamalla et al. [27] studied the SVM, ANNs (artificial neural networks), LGPs (linear genetic programs), and MARSs (Multivariate Adaptive Regression Splines) for classification of KDD dataset into five classes. As these classifiers obtained better performance over the others to detect different classes of intrusion in terms of detection accuracy, attack severity, training & testing time (scalability). The author reported that classifier combination improves the performance of system. Similar approach of multiclassifier systems is also advocated by Sabhnani and Serpen [23] by combining three different machine learning techniques, namely, an ANN, k-means clustering, and a Gaussian classifier. However, they do not provide further implementation details about training the classifiers, nor about determining output of the ensemble. However, they proved that the classifier combination approach improved the classification rates. Many techniques generate a pool of homogeneous base classifiers, for examples, genetic algorithms. Although in ensembles, the combined knowledge is important, it is very computationally expensive to combine

a large number of classifiers from the whole population [33]. So, efficient selection and combination of smaller set of base classifiers help to reduce computational overhead without significant lose in the performance. The smaller subset of classifiers may be selected according to clustering [91] or by selecting the classifiers whose performance exceeds specific threshold values. However, in the general literature on classifier combination, it is observed that there is no evidence supporting the use of base classifiers of the same type or different types [33, 46].

4.3. Feature Level. This level focuses on ensemble generation phase of ensemble learning process. Here, pool of classifiers is generated by using different feature subsets of dataset for the training of the base classifiers. Basic reason behind this level is to improve the computational efficiency of the ensemble and to increase the accuracy [46]. By reducing the number of input features of the base classifiers, we can gap the effects of the classical curse of dimensionality problem that characterize high-dimensional and sparse data [102]. Many feature selection techniques for ensemble classifiers are proposed in the literature which can be further investigated in [15, 16, 103].

4.4. Data Level. This level focuses on ensemble generation phase of ensemble learning process. Here, different data subsets are used to train the pool of base classifiers. This level decides which data subset is used to train each base classifier. Most of popular ensemble methods proposed and implemented in the literature utilize data level. These methods are used to generate different training sets and a learning algorithm, which can be applied to the obtained subsets of data in order to produce multiple hypotheses. Various methods have been proposed in literature as described below.

(i) *Bagging.* Bagging (bootstrap aggregating) is originally proposed by Breiman [61]. The method is dependent on the instability of the base classifiers. The instability of base classifiers refers to sensitivity to configuration of base classifier and/or training data. Bagging creates individual classifiers for its ensemble by training each classifier on a random redistribution of the training dataset. Each classifier's training set is generated by randomly drawing, with replacement, N examples—where N is the size of the original training dataset; many of the original examples may be repeated in the resulting training set while others may be left out. Each individual classifier in the ensemble is generated with a different random sampling of the training set. Final prediction of ensemble is generated by fusing different predictions of individual base classifiers. Generally fusion of predictions is performed by using majority voting method. However, this is not always possible due to the size of the dataset. Therefore, the different training subsets are sampled with replacement (bootstrap replicates) from the original training set. Bagging works well if classifier predictions of base classifiers were independent and classifiers had the same individual accuracy, and then

TABLE 1: Summary of ensembles.

Optimization level	Ensemble learning phase	Ensemble level	Strategy adopted	Method employed
Decision optimization	Ensemble integration	Combination level	Fusion	Majority voting method [70–72]
				Threshold plurality vote method [73]
				Naïve Bayes method [74, 75]
				Fuzzy theory method [76, 77]
				Decision template method [78]
				Metalearning method [79]
				Hierarchically structured method [82, 83]
			Selection	Boolean combination method [2]
				The test and select method [71]
				Cascading classifiers method [85]
				Dynamic classifier selection method [86, 87]
				Clustering-based selection method [17, 45, 88, 91]
				Statistical selection method [89]
			Mixture of expert systems	Stochastic selection method [46]
				Winner-takes-all method [46]
				Weighting method [46]
Coverage optimization	Ensemble selection	Classifier level	Homogenous	Clustering-based selection method [17, 45, 88, 91]
				Threshold-based selection method [86]
			Heterogeneous	—
	Ensemble generation	Feature level	Feature selection/reduction	Random subspace method [46]
				The input decimation method [90]
				Genetic algorithms [92]
				Markov blanket BN [28]
				Principal component analysis [93]
				Information theory [16]
		Data level	Resampling	Bagging [61]
				Wagging [94]
				Random forest [95]
				Boosting [96]
				Stacking [79]
			Output code method	One per class (OPC) [97]
				Pairwise coupling [98]
				Correcting classifiers [99]
				Pairwise coupling correcting classifiers [99]
				Error-correcting output coding [100]
				Data-driven ECOC [101]

the majority vote is guaranteed to improve on the individual performance [46].

(ii) *Wagging*. Wagging method is a variant of bagging. This method based on a nonuniform probability to extract instances from the training dataset [94]. While in bagging each instance is drawn with equal probability from the available training dataset, in wagging each instance is extracted according to a weight stochastically assigned.

(iii) *Random Forest (RF)*. This method is a version of bagging which comprised of decision trees (DTs) [95]. Just like bagging, each DT is trained on different random sampling from dataset, or by sampling from the feature set, or from both. The predictions are combined by a majority vote. The performance of RF is comparable to AdaBoost, but is more robust to noise [57, 95].

(iv) *Boosting*. Boosting [96] is popular meta-algorithm for generating ensemble [33]. It is a meta-algorithm which can be viewed as a model averaging method and one of the most powerful learning ideas introduced in the last twenty years [104]. In this method, the ensembles are populated one classifier at the time. Each classifier is trained on selective subset of data from the original dataset. For the first base classifier, the data is selected uniformly. For successive classifiers, the sampling distribution is continuously updated so that instances that are more difficult to classify are selected more often than those that are easy to classify. This method places the highest weight on the examples most often misclassified by the previous base classifier. In this way the base classifier focuses on the hardest instances. Then the boosting algorithm combines the base rules taking a weighted majority vote of the base classifiers which are based on the accuracy of the classifiers [46].

Major difference in bagging and boosting is that in bagging, the resampling of the training set is not dependent on the performance of the earlier classifiers, whereas Boosting attempts to produce new classifiers that are better able to predict examples for which the current ensemble's performance is poor.

(v) *Stacking*. This (also called stacked generalization) is a way of combining multiple classifiers using the concept of a metalearner [79]. Unlike bagging and boosting, stacking may be utilized to combine classifiers of different types. The method involves the following steps: (1) split the training dataset into two disjoint subsets; (2) train several base classifiers on the first part; (3) test the base classifier on the second part; (4) using the predictions from step (3) as the inputs, and the correct responses as the outputs, train a higher level classifier. Note that steps (1) to (3) are the same as cross-validation, but instead of using a winner-takes-all approach, the base learners are combined, possibly non linearly.

(vi) *Output Code Method*. Output code method works by manipulating the coding of classes in multi-class classification problems. Here ensembles are designed to partially correct errors performed by the base classifiers by exploiting the redundancy in the bit-string representation of the classes [25, 105]. More correctly, output coding (OC) methods decompose a multiclass problem in a set of two-class subproblems and then recompose the original problem combining them to achieve the class label.

An equivalent way of thinking about these methods consists in encoding each class as a bit string (named codeword) and in training a different two-class base classifier in order to separately learn each codeword bit. When the classifiers are applied to classify new points, a suitable measure of dissimilarity between the codeword computed by the ensemble and the codeword classes is used to predict the class (e.g., Hamming distance) [100]. Various decomposition schemes have been proposed in the literature: in the one-per-class (OPC) decomposition [97], pairwise coupling (PWC) decomposition [98], the correcting classifiers (CC) and the pairwise coupling correcting classifiers (PWC-CC) [99]. Error-correcting Output Coding (ECOC) [100], and data-driven ECOC [101].

(vii) *Troika*. Troika is an improvement to stacking proposed by Menahem et al. [106]. The method involves three stages to combine the classifiers. In the first stage it combines all base classifiers using specialist classifiers which have a dichotomous model. Second stage contains k metaclassifiers which are used to learn the prediction characteristics of the specialist classifiers. Each metaclassifier is in charge of one class only and will combine all the specialist classifiers which are able to classify their own particular class. The third stage contains only one classifier: the super classifier. The goal of this stage is to produce Troika's final prediction. The inputs of the super classifier are the outputs produced by the metaclassifiers from the previous stage. In the training phase, the super classifier learns the conditions which enable one or more of the metaclassifiers to predict correctly or incorrectly. The super classifier's output is a vector of probabilities (one value for each class) which form the final decision of the Troika ensemble scheme. The authors reported superior performance of Troika over other stacking methods.

Discussion 2. Which is better bagging or boosting? Many researchers compared the two methods including some large-scale experiments [56, 57, 107, 108]. The general consent is that boosting reaches lower testing error. Boosting methods have been crowned as the most accurate available off-the-shelf classifiers on a wide variety of datasets [107]. But, it is observed that boosting methods are sensitive to noise and outliers, especially for small datasets [46, 56, 107]. Bagging is effective with noisy data efforts on noisy data whereas boosting is quite sensitive to noise [57]. Another benefit of bagging methods is that they are parallel in nature in both the training and classification phases, whereas the boosting method is sequential in nature [33].

Details of ensembles are summarized in Table 1.

5. AI Based Ensembles for ID

Many researchers employed AI-based ensembles and hybrid approaches to improve performance of IDS. The focus is on the combination of classifiers and correlating the alerts to reduce the alarms for network security administrator [3]. Combination of classifiers involves development of ensemble at generation and selection phases of learning, whereas ensemble integration phase involve combination of different predictions of multiple classifiers. In the following paragraphs, we presented important AI-based ensembles studies proposed in the last decade and compared them by various evaluation metrics.

Giacinto and Roli [45] proposed an approach based on multiple classifier systems for ID. The approach is based on the motivation that human experts use different feature sets to detect different kinds of attacks. They generated different neural network-based classifiers by training them using different feature subsets of KDD cup 99 dataset, namely, intrinsic, content, and traffic features. The predictions of trained classifiers are fused together to produce final prediction of ensemble by using the methods like the majority voting rule, the average rule, and the belief function. They found that these multistrategy techniques, particularly the belief function, performed better than all three neural nets individually. The overall performance was also comparable to or better than a single neural net trained on the entire feature set; however, the single neural net did a better job identifying previously unseen attacks. Similar experiments are also performed by Didaci et al. [22].

Sabhnani and Serpen [23] proposed a multi-classifier approach to detect intrusions. They utilized different classifiers, namely, an ANN, k-means clustering, and a Gaussian classifier to classify different classes of intrusions by using KDD 1999 dataset. Multiple classifiers were generated by training from all features of training dataset. The classifiers obtained highest accuracies on different categories of intrusions are used to detect corresponding category of intrusions. They reported that classifier combination results the improvement of classification performance. They reported that probability of detection of 88.7%, 97.3%, 29.8%, and 9.6% with 0.4% false alarm rate for Probe, DoS, U2R, and 0.1% for R2L attack classes, respectively.

Chebrolu et al. [28] proposed a hybrid approach to detect intrusions. They utilized Bayesian networks (BNs) and classification and regression trees (CARTs) and their ensemble to generate hybrid system. They empirically proved that CART performed best for Normal, Probe, and U2R and the ensemble approach worked best for R2L and DoS. The heterogeneous ensemble was generated by training the individual classifiers from reduced KDD cup 99 dataset. In the ensemble approach, the final output was decided as follows: each classifier's output is given a weight (0-1 scale) depending on the generalization accuracy. If both classifiers agree then the output is decided accordingly. If there is a conflict then the decision given by the classifier with the highest weight is taken into account. By using hybrid approach, the authors reported that Normal, Probe, and DOS could be detected with 100% accuracy and U2R and R2L with 84% and 99.47% accuracies, respectively.

Abraham and Thomas [43] proposed an ensemble of DT, SVM, and hybrid system consisting of DT and SVM. The classifiers are generated by using training on KDD99 dataset.

They observed in the experiments that different models provided complementary information about the patterns to be classified. The final prediction of ensemble is computed based upon highest score of base classifiers. The score of classifiers is computed by weights assigned according to training performance and their individual predictions. So, for a particular instance to be classified if all of them have different opinions, then their scores are considered. The classifier having the highest score is declared as winner and used to predict the final output of the ensemble. They reported 100% detection of Probe attack class and 99.92%, 68%, and 97.16% detection of DoS, U2R, and R2L attack classes', respectively, using ensemble approach.

Kruegel et al. [109] proposed a multimodel approach that uses a number of different anomaly detection techniques (Bayesian technique) to detect attacks against web servers and web-based applications. The multimodels help to reduce the vulnerability of the detection process with respect to mimicry attacks. The system works by analyzing client queries that reference server side programs. Different models are generated by using a wide range of different features of client queries. The system derives automatically the parameter profiles associated with web applications (e.g., length and structure of parameters) and relationships between queries (e.g., access times and sequences) from the analyzed data. The system takes as input web server log files that conform to the common log format (CLF) and produces an anomaly score for each web request. The task of a model is to assign a probability value to either a query as a whole or one of the query's attributes. This probability value reflects the probability of the occurrence of the given feature value with regards to an established profile. Based on the model outputs, a query is either reported as a potential attack or as normal. This decision is reached by calculating a number of anomaly scores: one for the query itself and one for each attribute. A query is reported as anomalous if at least one of these anomaly scores is above the corresponding detection threshold. The anomaly score is calculated using a weighted sum of model's output and its probability value. The system was tested on data gathered at Google, Inc. and two universities in USA and Europe, showing promising results. However, they used anomaly detection technique (Bayesian technique) to model attribute inputs without taking into account typical semantic differences between classes of characters (alphabetic, numeric, and non-alphanumeric), which usually determine their meaning. Moreover, the authors definitely did not exploit the power of such a model, because they rounded every nonzero probability value to one. Finally, they assumed that the training set is without attacks, by filtering it with a signature-based IDS, in order to throw out at least known attacks.

Similar approach was also proposed by Corona et al. [110]. Here, the authors addressed the problem related to the presence of noise (i.e., attacks) in the training set. The proposed model composed of a set of (independent) application-specific modules. Each module, composed by multiple HMM ensembles, is trained using queries on a specific web application and, during the operational phase, outputs a probability value for each query on this web application. Furthermore, a decision module classifies the query as suspicious (a possible attack) or legitimate, applying a threshold to this probability value. Thresholds are fixed independently for each application-specific module.

Perdisci et al. [88] proposed a clustering-based fusion module to combine multiple alarms that help to reduce the volume of alarms produced by IDSs. The produced meta-alarms provide the system administrator with a concise high-level description of the attack. They suggested assigning different alarms to predefine set of attack classes, called meta-alarms. Many definitions exist to evaluate similarity between an alarm and a meta-alarm. In fact, the distance between an alarm and a meta-alarm is defined in terms of correlation between them, which is in turn defined as an application of a distance function to features characterizing each of the raised alarms.

Hwang et al. [42] proposed a 3-tier hybrid approach to detect intrusions. First tier of system is a signature-based approach to filter the known attacks using black list concept. Second tier of system is anomaly detector that uses the white list concept to distinguish the normal and attack traffic that has by passed first tier. The third tier component of system uses the SVM to classify the unknown attack traffic into five classes, that is, Normal, Probe, DoS, U2R, and R2L. KDD dataset was used to train and test the system. They claimed 94.71% detection accuracy with 3.8% of false alarm rate of old as well as new attacks.

Chen et al. [41] suggested a hybrid flexible neural-tree-based IDS based on flexible neural tree, evolutionary algorithm, and particle swarm optimization (PSO). They focus on improving the ID performance by reducing the input features and hybrid approaches for combining base classifiers. The classifiers are generated by using different feature subset of training dataset. They proved empirically that result of the proposed method is improved. They performed experiments by using 41 features and 12 features of KDD dataset. They reported 98.39%, 98.75%, 99.70%, and 99.09% detection of Probe, DoS, U2R, and R2L attack classes using 41 features of KDD dataset.

Khan et al. [40] suggested a hybrid of SVM and clustering to cut down the training time. A hierarchical clustering algorithm is engaged to establish boundary points in the data that best separate the two classes. These boundary points are used to train the SVM. This is an iterative process, in which the SVM is trained on every new level of cluster nodes in the tree that is being built. Iteratively, support vectors are calculated and the SVM is tested against a stopping criterion to determine if a desirable threshold of accuracy has been achieved. Otherwise the iterative process continues. The authors reported 91%, 97%, 23%, and 43% detection of Probe, DoS, U2R, and R2L attack classes.

Toosi and Kahani [39] proposed IDS by using neurofuzzy classifiers to classify KDD cup 99 dataset into five classes, namely, Normal, Probe, DoS, U2R, and R2L. The proposed system includes two layers. In the first layer, there are five ANFIS modules which are trained to explore the intrusive activity from the input data. Each ANFIS module belongs to one of the classes in the dataset each providing an output which specifies the degree of relativity of the data to the specific class. Second, a fuzzy inference module, based on empirical knowledge, is employed to make the final decision for recognition. The fuzzy inference module implements nonlinear mappings from the outputs of the neurofuzzy classifiers of the pervious layer to the final output space which specifies if the input data are normal or intrusive. The genetic algorithm is used to optimize the structure of neurofuzzy engine. A great time consuming of the system may be a big problem. The authors reported 84.1%, 99.5%, 14.1%, and 31.5% detection of Probe, DoS, U2R, and R2L attack classes.

Yan and Hao [111] presented ensemble of neural network for ID based upon improved MOGA (improvement of NSGA-II). They used improved MOGA to select relevant feature subsets of dataset. Selected subsets of feature are used to train accurate and diverse base classifiers. Final ensemble is constructed by using ensemble selection method. They reported improvement of ID in terms of detection rate and false-positive rate over other related approaches. The authors reported 98.96%, 99.98%, 99.95%, and 98.51% detection of Probe, DoS, U2R, and R2L attack classes with 0.38%, 0.03%, 0.11%, and 8.91% false-positive rate, respectively.

Xiang et al. [36] proposed a hierarchical hybrid system involving multiple-level hybrid classifier, which combines the supervised decision tree classifiers and unsupervised Bayesian clustering to detect intrusions. It was able to achieve a higher true positive rate than previously reported in the literature on the original training and test sets of the KDD Cup 99 dataset. However, this was at the expense of a higher false-positive rate.

Hu et al. [112] suggested an AdaBoost algorithm-based ensemble which in turn uses decision stump as base classifiers. They utilized continuous and categorical features separately without any forced conversion. The proposed system was evaluated using KDD cup 99 dataset. They reported 90.04%–90.88% of detection rate with false alarm rate of 0.31%–1.79%. The proposed system suffers from limitation of incremental learning. It requires continuous retraining for changing environment.

Cretu et al. [113] proposed a micromodel-based ensemble of anomaly sensors to sanitize the training data. Here, different models are generated to produce provisional labels for each training input, and models are combined in a voting scheme to determine which parts of the training data may represent attacks. The models are trained by partitioning the original training dataset.

Zainal et al. [35] proposed heterogeneous ensemble of linear genetic programming (LGP), adaptive neural fuzzy inference system (ANFIS), and random forest (RF) for ID. Base classifiers are generated by using class-specific features of KDD cup 99 dataset. They utilized rough-discrete particle swarm optimization (Rough-BPSO) to select significant features for specific class. Final ensemble prediction is the weighted voting of base classifiers. They empirically proved that by assigning proper weights to classifiers in ensemble approach improves the detection accuracy of all classes of network traffic than individual classifier.

Menahem et al. [106] proposed metalearning-based approach. They utilized multiple classifiers and tried to exploit their strengths. They used C4.5 decision tree [114], Naïve Bayes [115], k-NN clustering [116], VFI-voting feature intervals [34], and OneR [117] classifiers as base classifiers over five malware datasets. Each classifier belongs to different family of classifiers. They proposed to partition the original dataset into two subsets. The first subset is reserved to form the metadataset and the second subset is used to build the base-level classifiers. This classifier (Metaclassifier) combines the different predictions into a final one. They improved the classifiers performance by using Troika [106] over other stacking methods. Troika combines base classifiers in three stages: specialists level, metaclassifiers, and super classifier. In order to conclude which ensemble performs best over multiple datasets, they followed the procedure proposed in [118].

Wang et al. [32] proposed an approach, called FC-ANN, based on ANN and fuzzy clustering, to solve the problem and help IDS achieve higher detection rate, less false-positive rate, and stronger stability. They used fuzzy clustering technique to generate different homogeneous training subsets from heterogeneous training set, which are further used to ANN models as base models. Finally, a metalearner, fuzzy aggregation module, was employed to aggregate these results. They reported the improvement of proposed approach over BPNN and other well-known methods such as decision tree and the Naïve Bayes in terms of detection precision and detection stability.

Khreich et al. [2] proposed an iterative Boolean combination (IBC) technique for efficient fusion of the responses from any crisp or soft detector trained on fixed-size datasets in the ROC space. The proposed technique applies all Boolean functions to combine the ROC curves corresponding to multiple classifiers. It requires no prior assumptions, and its time complexity is linear with the number of classifiers. They generated HMMs models as base classifiers by training them using different number of HMM states and random initializations. They applied multiple HMM to dataset and final prediction is computed by exploiting all Boolean functions applied to the ROC curves. At each iteration, the proposed technique selects those combinations that improve the ROC convex hull and recombines them with the original ROC curves until the ROC convex hull ceases to improve. The results of computer simulations conducted on both synthetic (UNM intrusion detection dataset of system calls) and real-world host-based intrusion detection data indicate that the IBC of responses from multiple HMMs can achieve a significantly higher level of performance than the Boolean conjunction and disjunction combinations, especially when training data are limited and imbalanced. However, IBC does not allow to efficiently adapt a fusion function over time when new data becomes available, since it requires a fixed number of classifiers. The IBC technique was further improved as incremental Boolean combination (incrBC) by the authors [119]. The incrBC is a ROC-based system to efficiently adapt ensemble of HMM (EoHMMs) over time, from new training data, according to a learn-and-combine approach without multiple iterations. Given new training data, a new pool of HMMs is generated from newly acquired data using different HMM states

and initializations. The responses from these newly trained HMMs are then combined with those of the previously trained HMMs in ROC space using the incremental Boolean combination (incrBC) technique.

Govindarajan and Chandrasekaran [30] presented hybrid architecture of multilayer perceptron and radial basis function and their ensemble for ID. Different ensemble members were generated by training from reduced dataset. The final outputs were decided as follows: each classifier's output is given a weight (0-1 scale) depending on the generalization performance during the training process. If both classifiers agree then the output is decided accordingly. If there was a conflict then the decision given by the classifier with the highest weight is taken into account. They showed that the performance of the proposed method is superior to that of single usage of base classification methods. Additionally it has been found that ensemble of multilayer perceptron is superior to ensemble of radial basis function classifier for normal behavior and reverse is the case for abnormal behavior. They reported that the proposed method provides significant improvement of prediction accuracy in ID.

Muda et al. [120] proposed a combined approach of clustering and classification. The clustering is performed by using K-means algorithm to form groups of similar data in earlier stage. Next, in second stage, clustered data is classified by attack category using Naïve Bayes classifier. They reported the better performance of proposed hybrid approach over single Naïve Bayes classifier over KDD 1999 dataset. But the proposed method suffers from limitation that it is unable to detect similar attacks like U2R and R2L.

These related studies can be compared by following a set of evaluation metrics which derives from: (1) architecture & approach followed; (2) different methods utilized in different phases of ensemble learning; (3) other measures used to evaluate classification performance of the ensembles as depicted in Table 2. Here, architecture of system can be parallel, cascading, or hierarchical [35], the classifiers can be combined by ensemble- or hybrid-combining approach. Ensemble level refers to different levels (combination level, classifier level, feature level, or data level as proposed in [46]) used in different ensemble learning phases (ensemble generation, ensemble selection, and ensemble integration). Diversity among the base classifiers can be measured by implicit or explicit methods [47, 49]. In order to evaluate the performance, different performance metrics can be computed based upon benchmarked datasets.

6. Discussion

Over the past decade, ID based upon ensemble approaches has been a widely studied topic, being able to satisfy the growing demand of reliable and intelligent IDS. In our view, these approaches contribute to intrusion detection in different ways. These approaches combine complementary multiple classifiers. They use combined knowledge to meet the challenges of ID-like high false alarm rate,

TABLE 2: Comparison of AI based ensembles for ID.

Study	Architecture	Combining approach	Ensemble learning phase and ensemble level			Combining method employed	Metric	Dataset	Diversity	Base classifier
			Generation	Selection	Integration					
Giacinto and Roli [45]	Parallel	Ensemble	Feature level	—	Fusion	Majority voting, average rule, belief function	Error rate, FPR, cost	KDD 99	Implicit	NN
Sabhnani and Serpen [23]	—	Hybrid	—	Classifier level	—	Multi-classifiers method	DR, FPR	KDD 99	—	NN, KM, GC
Chebrolu et al. [28]	Parallel	Ensemble	—	Classifier level	Selection	Weighting method	CA	KDD 99	Implicit	BN, CART
Abraham et al. [43]	Parallel	Ensemble	Feature level	Classifier level	Selection	Weighting method	CA	KDD 99	Implicit	DT, SVM
Kruegel et al. [109]	Parallel	Ensemble	Feature and data level	—	Fusion	Score-and probability-based method	FPR	Real world dataset	Implicit	BN
Perdisci et al. [88]	—	Ensemble	—	—	Fusion	Clustering	—	Real world dataset	—	—
Hwang et al. [42]	Cascading	Hybrid	—	—	—	Consecutive combination	DR, FPR	KDD 99	—	SVM
Chen et al. [41]	Hierarchical	Hybrid	Feature level	—	—	Multi-classifiers method	DR, FNR, FPR	KDD 99	—	FNT
Khan et al. [40]	Cascading	Hybrid	—	—	—	Clustering + classification	CA, training time, FP, FN	KDD 99	—	SVM, clustering
Toosi and kahani [39]	Parallel	Ensemble	—	Classifier level	Fusion	Fuzzy theory method	CA, DR, FPR, CPE	KDD 99	Implicit	NN, fuzzy logic
Yan and Hao [111]	Parallel	Ensemble	Feature level	—	Selection		DR, FPR	KDD 99	Implicit	NN
Xiang et al. [36]	Cascading	Hybrid	Data level	Classifier level	—	Clustering + classification	TP, FP	KDD 99	—	DT, BC
Cretu et al. [113]	Parallel	Ensemble	Data level	—	Fusion	Voting method	FP, TP	Real world data	—	Anagram, Payl
Hu et al. [112]	Parallel	Ensemble	Feature level	—	—	Mixture of expert systems	DR, FAR, computation time	KDD 99	Implicit	DS
Corona et al. [110]	Parallel	Ensemble	Feature and data level	—	Fusion	Threshold probability method	FPR, DR	Real world dataset	Implicit	HMM
Zainal et al. [35]	Parallel	Ensemble	Feature level	Classifier level	Fusion	Weighted voting method	CA, TP, FP	KDD 99	Implicit	LGP, ANFIS, RF
Menahem et al. [106]	Parallel	Ensemble	Data level	Classifier level	Fusion	Meta learning	CA, area under the ROC curve, training time	Real-time network traffic	Implicit	DT, NB, K-NN, VFI, OneR
Wang et al. [32]	Parallel	Ensemble	Data level	—	Fusion	Meta learning	Precision, recall, F-measure	KDD 99	Implicit	NN, fuzzy logic, clustering

TABLE 2: Continued.

Study	Architecture	Combining approach	Ensemble learning phase and ensemble level			Combining method employed	Metric	Dataset	Diversity	Base classifier
			Generation	Selection	Integration					
Khreich et al. [2]	Parallel	Ensemble	—	—	Fusion	Iterative Boolean combination method	ROC space	UNM dataset, real world dataset Immune system	Implicit	HMM
Govindarajan and Chandrasekaran [30]	Parallel	Ensemble	Data level	—	Fusion	Weighted method	CA	dataset from University of New Mexico	Implicit	MLP, RBF
Muda et al. [120]	Cascading	Hybrid	Data level	—	—	Clustering + classification	CA, DR, FPR	KDD 99	—	KM, NB

Abbreviations—NN: neural network; KM: K-means clustering; GC: Gaussian classifier; BN: Bayesian network; CART: classification and regression trees; DT: decision tree; SVM: support vector machine; FNT: fuzzy neural tree; BC: bayesian clustering; DS: decision stump; LGP: linear genetic programming; ANFIS: adaptive neural fuzzy inference system; RF: random forest; NB: Naïve Bayes; K-NN: K-nearest neighbor; VFI: voting feature intervals; MLP: multilayer perceptron; RBF: radial basis function; HMM: hidden Markov model.

low detection accuracy, and better performance in lack of sufficient amount of quality training dataset. The results of ensemble approach are proved to be improved than single best classifier. Researchers focused heterogeneous as well homogeneous ensembles. Heterogeneous ensembles exploit the characteristics of different classifiers to improve the results over single classifier. It is supported by the fact that different base classifiers perform differently upon different categories of intrusions (e.g., DoS, Probe, U2R, R2L, etc.) [8]. The performance variation of various classifiers for different intrusions may be described by two aspects. The first aspect is the different design principles of classifiers which work to optimize different parameters. For example, SVM is designed to minimize structural risk based upon statistical theory whereas ANN to minimize empirical risk in which classification function is derived by minimizing the mean square error over the training dataset. The second aspect is that detection of intrusions depends upon specific features of dataset. But, availability of irrelevant and redundant feature affects detection performance of classifiers. Homogeneous ensembles focus on different features of training dataset and/or different training subsets and/or other ways to generate diverse base classifiers. Applications of the AI-based ensembles revealed that they have pros and cons. Hence, ensemble approach couples the base classifiers together in a way that they supplement each other favorably. The resulting synergy has been shown to be an effective way for building IDSs with improved performance in terms of detection accuracy and false-positive rate. It is observed that successful employment of ensemble for ID depends upon many factors including size of training dataset, modification of dataset for training of different base classifiers, choice of accurate and diverse base classifiers, ability of base classifiers to detect different intrusions, and choice of level for generating ensemble of base classifiers, for example, combination, classifier, feature, or data level. It may be concluded that by considering appropriate base classifiers, training sample size & combination method, the performance of hybrid classifier/ensemble can be improved.

We compared the related AI-based ensemble studies for ID in terms of variety of aspects as shown in Table 2. Majority of research works described here were trained & tested on KDD cup 1999 dataset. Since these works are evaluated in different environments using different training and test datasets extracted from KDD cup 1999 dataset, these studies cannot be critically analyzed based upon these reported results. But, it is clear from results presented in Section 4 that all researches did not perform well for minority attack classes of U2R and R2L attacks. The reason may be either class imbalance in training dataset or 11 attack types in these two classes only appear in the test dataset, not the training set, and they constitute more than 50% of the data. However, ensembles utilized the combined knowledge of multiple classifiers to improve the performance in these minority attacks classes. But, still there is a need to generate diverse set of base classifiers that perform well on majority and minority attack classes. Many researchers proposed use of population-based approaches to generate diverse set of classifiers.

Although some promising results have been achieved by current AI-based ensembles to IDSs, there are still challenges that lie ahead for researchers in this area. First and foremost, high-quality benchmark datasets for network intrusion detection are needed. The KDD 99 derived from DARPA 1998 & 1999 datasets are main benchmarks used to evaluate the performance of network intrusion detection systems. However, they are suffering from a fatal drawback: failing to realistically simulate a real-world network [102, 121]. An IDS trained and tested on these datasets may demonstrate unacceptable performance in real environments. In order to validate the evaluation results of IDS on a simulated dataset, one has to develop a methodology to quantify the similarity of simulated and real network traces. KDD cup 1999 dataset and its original form possess some special features, such as huge volume, high dimension, and highly skewed data distribution. Similar properties are not generally found in other benchmark dataset, so they have been usually used for challenging and evaluating learning algorithms in both supervised and unsupervised mode. However, this purpose of dataset is also under criticism [121]. The major criticisms are that DARPA datasets include irregularities, like differences in the TTL for attacks versus normal traffic, so that even a basic IDS could attain an excellent performance [121] and the KDD99 training and test datasets have dissimilar target hypotheses for U2R and R2L classes [23]. Therefore, using these datasets only is not sufficient to reveal the efficiency of a learning algorithm. So, new and good quality benchmark datasets need to be developed for realistic evaluation of IDS. While developing new dataset, payload, and temporal locality information along with header information may be considered and beneficial for realistic evaluation of IDS.

Second challenge to tackle in AI-based ensembles is the enormous amount of audit data that make it difficult to build effective IDS. The processing of enormous amount of data increases computational overhead and causes delay in detection of intrusions. The delay in detection of intrusions leads to loss of real-time capability of IDS. Many researchers suggested the use of feature selection/reduction techniques [16, 122]. These techniques help remove irrelevant and redundant features and identify appropriate features for intrusion detection. The reduction in features reduces the amount of audit data for effective IDS. A focus on feature reduction/selection technique is highly recommended to reduce computational overhead of ensembles. Some researchers proposed to use a distributed environment in which each node is assigned a part of dataset. An ensemble method was used to fuse or select predictions.

Thirdly, an important feature of IDS is the capability to adapt to dynamic behavior of intrusive and normal traffic. If the IDSs are not flexible enough to cope with behavioral changes, detection performance will noticeably decline. AI-based techniques and their ensembles can help to address this important issue, but still only a small number of researchers have focused it so far.

Most of the methods discussed in this paper have their roots in the ensemble learning process. The process has three phases, namely, generation of base classifiers, selection of classifiers from base classifiers, and integration of different predictions from selected classifiers. The paper clearly shows that some researchers have applied their knowledge to address different issues at these phases for intrusion detection. But still there is a need to focus more on issues of each phase of ensemble learning. It is expected that new discoveries and a deepened understanding of different techniques suitable for different phases in ensemble learning of ID problem will be the subject of future work.

7. Conclusive Remarks

AI-based techniques and their ensembles are presently attracting considerable attention from the research community for intrusion detection. Their features, such as flexibility, adaptability, new pattern recognition, fault tolerance, learning capabilities, high computational speed, and error resilience for noisy data, fit the prerequisite of building effective IDS. Ensemble approach imitates our second nature to look for several opinions before making an essential decision. The basic principle is to evaluate several individual pattern classifiers, and integrate them in order to reach a classification that is better than the one obtained by each of them separately.

Our overview focused on supervised AI-based ensemble for intrusion detection proposed in last decade, since historically these were the first to be studied and applied to several application domains. More precisely, in this paper a general taxonomy, distinguishing between decision and coverage optimization ensembles, important AI-based ensembles for intrusion detection proposed in last decade has been described, considering the different ways supervised base classifiers can be generated or combined together.

However, the practice of AI-based classifiers reveals that each of them has advantages and disadvantages for intrusion detection. Ensemble has the power to combine the strengths of these classifiers in such a way that their disadvantages will be compensated, thus offering better solutions. We therefore included ensemble learning as a topic in this paper. The findings of research work in each study are systematically summarized and compared, which allows us to clearly identify existing research challenges for intrusion detection and underline research directions. It is expected that this paper can serve as a practical channel through the maze of the literature.

References

[1] J. McCumber, "Information system security: a comprehensive model," in *Proceedings of the 14th National Computer Security Conference*, Baltimore, Md, USA, 1991.

[2] W. Khreich, E. Granger, A. Miri, and R. Sabourin, "Iterative Boolean combination of classifiers in the ROC space: an application to anomaly detection with HMMs," *Pattern Recognition*, vol. 43, no. 8, pp. 2732–2752, 2010.

[3] I. Corona, G. Giacinto, C. Mazzariello, F. Roli, and C. Sansone, "Information fusion for computer security: state of the art and open issues," *Information Fusion*, vol. 10, no. 4, pp. 274–284, 2009.

[4] S. Axelsson, "Research in intrusion detection system—a survey," Tech. Rep. CMU/SEI, 1999.

[5] G. Kumar, K. Kumar, and M. Sachdeva, "The use of artificial intelligence based techniques for intrusion detection—a review," *Artificial Intelligence Review*, vol. 34, no. 4, pp. 369–387, 2010.

[6] C. Kruegel, F. Valeur, and G. Vigna, *Intrusion Detection and Correlation, Challenges and Solution, Advances in Information Security*, Springer, 2005.

[7] R. Caruana and A. Niculescu-Mizil, "Data mining in metric space: an empirical analysis of supervised learning performance criteria," in *Proceedings of the 10th ACM SIGMOD International Conference on Knowledge Discovery and Data Mining (KDD-2004)*, pp. 69–78, ACM Press, August 2004.

[8] G. Kumar and K. Kumar, "AI based supervised classifiers an analysis for intrusion detection," in *Proceedings of the International Conference on Advances in Computing and Artificial Intelligence (ACAI '11)*, pp. 170–174, ACM Digital Library, Chitkara, India, July 2011.

[9] J. W. Haines, R. P. Lippmann, D. J. Fried, E. Tran, S. Boswell, and M. A. Zissman, "DARPA intrusion detection system evaluation: design and procedures," Tech. Rep., MIT Lincoln Laboratory, 1999.

[10] KDDCup, "The Third International Knowledge Discovery and Data Mining Tools Competition," 1999, http://kdd.ics.uci.edu/databases/kddcup99/kddcup99.html.

[11] UNM dataset, http://www.cs.unm.edu/immsec/systemcalls.htm.

[12] DEFCON 9, http://ictf.cs.ucsb.edu/data/defcon_ctf_09/.

[13] ITOC dataset, http://www.itoc.usma.edu/research/dataset/.

[14] J. McHugh, "Testing intrusion detection systems: a critique of the 1998 and 1999 DARPA intrusion detection system evaluations as performed by Lincoln laboratory," *ACM Transactions on Information and System Security*, vol. 3-4, pp. 262–294, 2000.

[15] G. Kumar, K. Kumar, and M. Sachdeva, "An empirical comparative analysis of feature reduction methods for intrusion detection," *International Journal of Information and Telecommunication*, vol. 1, pp. 44–51, 2010.

[16] G. Kumar and K. Kumar, "An information theoretic approach for feature selection," *Security and Communication Networks*, vol. 5, pp. 178–185, 2012.

[17] K. Julisch, "Clustering intrusion detection alarms to support root cause analysis," *ACM Transactions on Information and System Security*, vol. 6, no. 4, pp. 443–471, 2003.

[18] H. Debar and A. Wespi, "Aggregation and correlation of intrusion-detection alerts, recent advances in intrusion detection," *Lecture Notes in Computer Science*, vol. 2212, pp. 85–103, 2001.

[19] A. Patcha and J. M. Park, "An overview of anomaly detection techniques: existing solutions and latest technological trends," *Computer Networks*, vol. 51, no. 12, pp. 3448–3470, 2007.

[20] P. García-Teodoro, J. Díaz-Verdejo, G. Maciá-Fernández, and E. Vázquez, "Anomaly-based network intrusion detection: techniques, systems and challenges," *Computers & Security*, vol. 28, no. 1-2, pp. 18–28, 2009.

[21] M. C. Ponce, "Intrusion detection system with artificial intelligence," in *Proceedings of the FIST Conference*, Universidad Pontificia Comillas de Madrid, 2004, edition: 1/28 .

[22] L. Didaci, G. Giacinto, and F. Roli, "Ensemble learning for intrusion detection in computer networks," in *Proceedings*

of the 8th Conference of the Italian Association of Artificial Intelligence (AIAA '02), Siena, Italy, 2002.

[23] M. Sabhnani and G. Serpen, "Application of machine learning algorithms to KDD intrusion detection dataset within misuse detection context," in *Proceedings of the International Conference on Machine Learning; Models, Technologies and Applications (MLMTA '03)*, pp. 209–215, June 2003.

[24] M. Panda and M. R. Patra, "A comparative study of data mining algorithms for network intrusion detection," in *Proceedings of the 1st International Conference on Emerging Trends in Engineering and Technology (ICETET '08)*, pp. 504–507, IEEE Computer Society, July 2008.

[25] T. G. Dietterich, "Ensemble methods in machine learning," in *Proceedings of the Multiple Classifier Systems. First International Workshop (MCS '00)*, J. Kittler and F. Roli, Eds., vol. 1857 of *Lecture Notes in Computer Science*, pp. 1–15, Cagliari, Italy, 2000.

[26] A. K. Jain, R. P. W. Duin, and J. Mao, "Statistical pattern recognition: a review," *IEEE Transactions on Pattern Analysis and Machine Intelligence*, vol. 22, no. 1, pp. 4–37, 2000.

[27] S. Mukkamala, A. H. Sung, and A. Abraham, "Intrusion detection using an ensemble of intelligent paradigms," *Journal of Network and Computer Applications*, vol. 28, no. 2, pp. 167–182, 2005.

[28] S. Chebrolu, A. Abraham, and J. P. Thomas, "Feature deduction and ensemble design of intrusion detection systems," *Computers and Security*, vol. 24, no. 4, pp. 295–307, 2005.

[29] S. Peddabachigari, A. Abraham, C. Grosan, and J. Thomas, "Modeling intrusion detection system using hybrid intelligent systems," *Journal of Network and Computer Applications*, vol. 30, no. 1, pp. 114–132, 2007.

[30] M. Govindarajan and R. M. Chandrasekaran, "Intrusion detection using neural based hybrid classification methods," *Computer Networks*, vol. 55, no. 8, pp. 1662–1671, 2011.

[31] C. Langin and S. Rahimi, "Soft computing in intrusion detection: the state of the art," *Journal of Ambient Intelligence and Humanized Computing*, vol. 1, no. 2, pp. 133–145, 2010.

[32] G. Wang, H. Jinxing, M. Jian, and H. Lihua, "A new approach to intrusion detection using Artificial Neural Networks and fuzzy clustering," *Expert Systems with Applications*, vol. 37, no. 9, pp. 6225–6232, 2010.

[33] V. Engen, *Machine learning for network based intrusion detection [Ph.D. thesis]*, Bournemouth University, June 2010.

[34] G. D. Guvenir, "Classification by voting feature intervals," in *Proceedings of the European Conference on Machine Learning*, pp. 85–92, 1997.

[35] A. Zainal, M. A. Maarof, and S. M. Shamsuddin, "Ensemble classifiers for network intrusion detection system," *Journal of Information Assurance and Security*, vol. 4, pp. 217–225, 2009.

[36] C. Xiang, P. C. Yong, and L. S. Meng, "Design of multiple-level hybrid classifier for intrusion detection system using Bayesian clustering and decision trees," *Pattern Recognition Letters*, vol. 29, no. 7, pp. 918–924, 2008.

[37] N. B. Anuar, H. Sallehudin, A. Gani, and O. Zakari, "Identifying false alarm for network intrusion detection system using hybrid data mining and decision tree," *Malaysian Journal of Computer Science*, vol. 21, no. 2, pp. 101–115, 2008.

[38] F. Gharibian and A. A. Ghorbani, "Comparative study of supervised machine learning techniques for intrusion detection," in *Proceedings of the 5th Annual Conference on Communication Networks and Services Research (CNSR '07)*, pp. 350–358, Washington, DC, USA, May 2007.

[39] A. N. Toosi and M. Kahani, "A new approach to intrusion detection based on an evolutionary soft computing model using neuro-fuzzy classifiers," *Computer Communications*, vol. 30, no. 10, pp. 2201–2212, 2007.

[40] L. Khan, M. Awad, and B. Thuraisingham, "A new intrusion detection system using support vector machines and hierarchical clustering," *The International Journal on Very Large Data Bases*, vol. 16, no. 4, pp. 507–521, 2007.

[41] Y. Chen, A. Abraham, and B. Yang, "Hybrid flexible neural-tree-based intrusion detection systems," *International Journal of Intelligent Systems*, vol. 22, no. 4, pp. 337–352, 2007.

[42] T. S. Hwang, T.-J. Lee, and Y.-J. Lee, "A three-tier IDS via data mining approach," in *Proceedings of the 3rd Annual ACM Workshop on Mining Network Data (MineNet '07)*, pp. 1–6, June 2007.

[43] A. Abraham and J. Thomas, "Distributed intrusion detection systems: a computational intelligence approach," in *Applications of Information Systems to Homeland Security and Defense*, H. Abbass and D. Essam, Eds., pp. 105–135, Idea Group, New York, NY, USA, 2005, chapter 5.

[44] Z. S. Pan, S. C. Chen, G. B. Hu, and D. Q. Zhang, "Hybrid neural network and C4.5 for misuse detection," in *Proceedings of the International Conference on Machine Learning and Cybernetics*, pp. 2463–2467, November 2003.

[45] G. Giacinto and F. Roli, "An approach to the automatic design of multiple classifier systems," *Pattern Recognition Letters*, vol. 22, no. 1, pp. 25–33, 2001.

[46] L. I. Kuncheva, *Combining Pattern Classifiers: Methods and Algorithms*, Wiley-Interscience, New York, NY, USA, 2004.

[47] G. Brown, J. Wyatt, R. Harris, and X. Yao, "Diversity creation methods: a survey and categorisation," *Journal of Information Fusion*, vol. 6, no. 1, pp. 5–20, 2005.

[48] L. K. Hansen and P. Salamon, "Neural network ensembles," *IEEE Transactions on Pattern Analysis and Machine Intelligence*, vol. 12, no. 10, pp. 993–1001, 1990.

[49] E. K. Tang, P. N. Suganthan, and X. Yao, "An analysis of diversity measures," *Machine Learning*, vol. 65, no. 1, pp. 247–271, 2006.

[50] L. I. Kuncheva and C. J. Whitaker, "Measures of diversity in classifier ensembles and their relationship with the ensemble accuracy," *Machine Learning*, vol. 51, no. 2, pp. 181–207, 2003.

[51] W. Leigh, R. Purvis, and J. M. Ragusa, "Forecasting the NYSE composite index with technical analysis, pattern recognizer, neural network, and genetic algorithm: a case study in romantic decision support," *Decision Support Systems*, vol. 32, no. 4, pp. 361–377, 2002.

[52] A. C. Tan, D. Gilbert, and Y. Deville, "Multi-class protein fold classification using a New Ensemble Machine Learning Approach," *Genome Informatics*, vol. 14, pp. 206–217, 2003.

[53] P. Mangiameli, D. West, and R. Rampal, "Model selection for medical diagnosis decision support systems," *Decision Support Systems*, vol. 36, no. 3, pp. 247–259, 2004.

[54] R. Moskovitch, Y. Elovici, and L. Rokach, "Detection of unknown computer worms based on behavioral classification of the host," *Computational Statistics and Data Analysis*, vol. 52, no. 9, pp. 4544–4566, 2008.

[55] R. P. W. Duin, "The combining classifier: to train or not to train?" in *Proceedings of 16th International Conference on Pattern Recognition (ICPR' 02)*, pp. 765–770, Quebec City, Canada, 2002.

[56] E. Bauer and R. Kohavi, "Empirical comparison of voting classification algorithms: bagging, boosting, and variants," *Machine Learning*, vol. 36, no. 1, pp. 105–139, 1999.

[57] T. G. Dietterich, "An experimental comparison of three methods for constructing ensembles of decision trees: bagging, boosting, and randomization," *Machine Learning*, vol. 40, no. 2, pp. 139–157, 2000.

[58] R. E. Banfield, L. O. Hall, K. W. Bowyer, and W. P. Kegelmeyer, "A comparison of decision tree ensemble creation techniques," *IEEE Transactions on Pattern Analysis and Machine Intelligence*, vol. 29, no. 1, pp. 173–180, 2007.

[59] E. L. Allwein, R. E. Schapire, and Y. Singer, "Reducing multiclass to binary: a unifying approach for margin classifiers," *Journal of Machine Learning Research*, vol. 1, no. 2, pp. 113–141, 2001.

[60] E. M. Kleinberg, "On the algorithmic implementation of stochastic discrimination," *IEEE Transactions on Pattern Analysis and Machine Intelligence*, vol. 22, no. 5, pp. 473–490, 2000.

[61] L. Breiman, "Bias, variance and arcing classifiers," Tech. Rep. TR 460, Statistics Department, University of California, Berkeley, Calif, USA, 1996.

[62] R. Hu and R. I. Damper, "A "No Panacea Theorem" for classifier combination," *Pattern Recognition*, vol. 41, no. 8, pp. 2665–2673, 2008.

[63] A. Sharkey, "Types of multi-ney systems," in *Multiple Classifier Systems, Third International Workshop (MCS '02)*, F. Roli and J. Kittler, Eds., vol. 2364 of *Lecture Notes in Computer Science*, pp. 108–117, 2002.

[64] L. Rokach, "Taxonomy for characterizing ensemble methods in classification tasks: a review and annotated bibliography," *Computational Statistics and Data Analysis*, vol. 53, no. 12, pp. 4046–4072, 2009.

[65] M. S. Kamel and N. M. Wanas, "Data dependence in combining classifiers," in *Proceedings of 4th International Workshop on Multiple Classifier Systems (MCS '03)*, T. Windeattand and F. Roli, Eds., vol. 2709 of *Lecture Notes in Computer Science*, pp. 1–14, Guildford, UK, 2003.

[66] I. H. Witten and E. Frank, *Data Mining: Practical Machine Learning Tools and Techniques*, The Morgan Kaufmann Series in Data Management Systems, Morgan Kaufmann, San Francisco, Calif, USA, 2nd edition, 2005.

[67] C. M. Bishop, *Pattern Recognition and Machine Learning*, Information Science and Statistics, Springer, New York, NY, USA, 2006.

[68] S. Marsland, *Machine Learning: An Algorithmic Perspective*, Chapman & Hall/CRC Machine Learning & Pattern Recognition, CRC Press, Boca Raton, Fla, USA, 2009.

[69] E. Alpaydin, *Introduction to Machine Learning*, Adaptive Computation and Machine Learning, The MIT Press, Cambridge, Mass, USA, 2nd edition, 2010.

[70] F. Kimura and M. Shridhar, "Handwritten numerical recognition based on multiple algorithms," *Pattern Recognition*, vol. 24, no. 10, pp. 969–983, 1991.

[71] M. P. Perrone and L. N. Cooper, "When networks disagree: ensemble methods for hybrid neural networks," in *Artificial Neural Networks for Speech and Vision*, R. J. Mammone, Ed., pp. 126–142, Chapman & Hall, London, UK, 1993.

[72] L. Lam and C. Y. Suen, "Application of majority voting to pattern recognition: an analysis of its behavior and performance," *IEEE Transactions on Systems, Man, and Cybernetics A*, vol. 27, no. 5, pp. 553–568, 1997.

[73] L. Xu, A. Krzyzak, and C. Y. Suen, "Methods of combining multiple classifiers and their applications to handwriting recognition," *IEEE Transactions on Systems, Man and Cybernetics*, vol. 22, no. 3, pp. 418–435, 1992.

[74] P. Domingos and M. Pazzani, "On the optimality of the simple Bayesian classifier under zero-one loss," *Machine Learning*, vol. 29, no. 2-3, pp. 103–130, 1997.

[75] R. O. Duda, P. E. Hart, and D. G. Stork, *Pattern Classification*, John Wiley & Sons, New York, NY, USA, 2nd edition, 2001.

[76] S. B. Cho and J. H. Kim, "Combining multiple neural networks by fuzzy integral for robust classification," *IEEE Transactions on Systems, Man and Cybernetics*, vol. 25, no. 2, pp. 380–384, 1995.

[77] A. Verikas, A. Lipnickas, K. Malmqvist, M. Bacauskiene, and A. Gelzinis, "Soft combination of neural classifiers: a comparative study," *Pattern Recognition Letters*, vol. 20, no. 4, pp. 429–444, 1999.

[78] M. Re and G. Valentini, "Integration of heterogeneous data sources for gene function prediction using decision templates and ensembles of learning machines," *Neurocomputing*, vol. 73, no. 7–9, pp. 1533–1537, 2010.

[79] D. H. Wolpert, "Stacked generalization," *Neural Networks*, vol. 5, no. 2, pp. 241–259, 1992.

[80] P. K. Chan and S. J. Stolfo, "On the accuracy of meta-learning for scalable data mining," *Journal of Intelligent Information Systems*, vol. 8, no. 1, pp. 5–28, 1997.

[81] T. Hothorn and B. Lausen, "Bundling classifiers by bagging trees," *Computational Statistics and Data Analysis*, vol. 49, no. 4, pp. 1068–1078, 2005.

[82] Y. Guan, C. L. Myers, D. C. Hess, Z. Barutcuoglu, A. A. Caudy, and O. G. Troyanskaya, "Predicting gene function in a hierarchical context with an ensemble of classifiers," *Genome Biology*, vol. 9, supplement 1, article S3, 2008.

[83] G. Obozinski, G. Lanckriet, C. Grant, M. I. Jordan, and W. S. Noble, "Consistent probabilistic outputs for protein function prediction," *Genome Biology*, vol. 9, supplement 1, article S6, 2008.

[84] W. B. Langdon and B. F. Buxton, "Genetic programming for improved receiver operating characteristics," in *Proceedings of the 2nd International Conference on Multiple Classifier System*, J. Kittler and F. Roli, Eds., pp. 68–77, Cambridge, UK, 2001.

[85] E. Alpaydin and C. Kaynak, "Cascading classifiers," *Kybernetika*, vol. 34, no. 4, pp. 369–374, 1998.

[86] G. Giacinto and F. Roli, "Dynamic classifier fusion," in *Proceedings of the Multiple Classifier Systems. First International Workshop (MCS '00)*, J. Kittler and F. Roli, Eds., vol. 1857 of *Lecture Notes in Computer Science*, pp. 177–189, Springer, Cagliari, Italy, 2000.

[87] E. M. Dos Santos, R. Sabourin, and P. Maupin, "A dynamic overproduce-and-choose strategy for the selection of classifier ensembles," *Pattern Recognition*, vol. 41, no. 10, pp. 2993–3009, 2008.

[88] R. Perdisci, G. Giacinto, and F. Roli, "Alarm clustering for intrusion detection systems in computer networks," *Engineering Applications of Artificial Intelligence*, vol. 19, no. 4, pp. 429–438, 2006.

[89] G. Tsoumakas, L. Angelis, and I. Vlahavas, "Selective fusion of heterogeneous classifiers," *Intelligent Data Analysis*, vol. 9, no. 6, pp. 511–525, 2005.

[90] R. A. Jacobs, "Methods for combining experts' probability assessments," *Neural Computation*, vol. 7, no. 5, pp. 867–888, 1995.

[91] X. Yao and M. Md. Islam, "Evolving artificial neural network ensembles," *IEEE Computational Intelligence Magazine*, vol. 3, pp. 31–42, 2008.

[92] M. Y. Su, K. C. Chang, H. F. Wei, and C. Y. Lin, "Feature weighting and selection for a real-time network intrusion detection system based on GA with KNN," *Intelligence and Security Informatics*, vol. 5075, pp. 195–204, 2008.

[93] J. Xiao and H. Song, "A novel intrusion detection method based on adaptive resonance theory and principal component analysis," in *Proceedings of the International Conference on Communications and Mobile Computing (CMC '09)*, pp. 445–449, January 2009.

[94] R. Valentini, *Ensemble Methods: A Review*, CRC press, 2001.

[95] L. Breiman, "Random forests," *Machine Learning*, vol. 45, no. 1, pp. 5–32, 2001.

[96] Y. Freund and R. E. Schapire, "Experiments with a new boosting algorithm," in *Proceedings of the 30th International Conference on Machine Learning*, pp. 148–156, San Francisco, Calif, USA, 1996.

[97] R. Anand, K. Mehrotra, C. K. Mohan, and S. Ranka, "Efficient classification for multiclass problems using modular neural networks," *IEEE Transactions on Neural Networks*, vol. 6, no. 1, pp. 117–124, 1995.

[98] T. Hastie and R. Tibshirani, "Classification by pairwise coupling," *The Annals of Statistics*, vol. 26, no. 1, pp. 451–471, 1998.

[99] M. Moreira and E. Mayoraz, "Improved pairwise coupling classification with correcting classifiers," in *Proceedings of the 10th European Conference on Machine Learning*, C. Nedellec and C. Rouveirol, Eds., vol. 1398 of *Lecture Notes in Computer Science*, pp. 160–171, Berlin, Germany, 1998.

[100] T. G. Dietterich and G. Bakiri, "Error—correcting output codes: a general method for improving multiclass inductive learning programs," in *Proceedings of the 9th AAAI National Conference on Artificial Intelligence*, pp. 572–577, 1991.

[101] J. Zhou, H. Peng, and C. Y. Suen, "Data-driven decomposition for multi-class classification," *Pattern Recognition*, vol. 41, no. 1, pp. 67–76, 2008.

[102] J. Friedman and P. Hall, "On bagging and nonlinear estimation," Tech. Rep., Statistics Department, University of Stanford, Palo Alto, Calif, USA, 2000.

[103] L. I. Kuncheva, F. Roli, G. L. Marcialis, and C. A. Shipp, "Complexity of data subsets generated by the random subspace method: an experimental investigation," in *Multiple Classi_er Systems. Second International Workshop (MCS '01)*, J. Kittler and F. Roli, Eds., pp. 349–358, Cambridge, UK, 2001.

[104] M. Sewell, "Ensemble Learning," Research Note RN/11/02, UCL department of computer science, 2011.

[105] E. Mayoraz and M. Moreira, "On the decomposition of polychotomies into dichotomies," in *Proceedings of the XIV International Conference on Machine Learning*, pp. 219–226, Nashville, Tenn, USA, July 1997.

[106] E. Menahem, L. Rokach, and Y. Elovici, "Troika—an improved stacking schema for classification tasks," *Information Sciences*, vol. 179, no. 24, pp. 4097–4122, 2009.

[107] L. Breiman, "Arcing classifiers," *The Annals of Statistics*, vol. 26, no. 3, pp. 801–849, 1998.

[108] G. Valentini, *Ensemble methods based on bias-variance analysis [Ph.D. thesis]*, University of Genova, Genova, Italy, 2003.

[109] C. Kruegel, G. Vigna, and W. Robertson, "A multi-model approach to the detection of web-based attacks," *Computer Networks*, vol. 48, no. 5, pp. 717–738, 2005.

[110] I. Corona, D. Ariu, and G. Giacinto, "HMM-web: a framework for the detection of attacks against web applications," in *Proceedings of the IEEE International Conference on Communications (ICC '09)*, June 2009.

[111] Y. Yan and H. Hao, "An ensemble approach to intrusion detection based on improved multi-objective genetic algorithm," *Journal of Software*, vol. 18, no. 6, pp. 1369–1378, 2007.

[112] W. M. Hu, W. Hu, and S. Maybank, "AdaBoost-based algorithm for network intrusion detection," *IEEE Transactions on Systems, Man, and Cybernetics B*, vol. 38, no. 2, pp. 577–583, 2008.

[113] G. F. Cretu, A. Stavrou, M. E. Locasto, S. J. Stolfo, and A. D. Keromytis, "Casting out demons: sanitizing training data for anomaly sensors," in *Proceedings of the IEEE Symposium on Security and Privacy (SP '08)*, pp. 81–95, IEEE Computer Society, May 2008.

[114] J. R. Quinlan, *C4.5 Programs for Machine Learning*, Morgan Kaufmann, San Mateo, Calif, USA, 1997.

[115] G. H. John and P. Langley, "Estimating continuous distributions in Bayesian classifiers," in *Proceedings of the Conference on Uncertainty in Artificial Intelligence*, pp. 338–345, 1995.

[116] D. W. Aha, D. Kibler, and M. K. Albert, "Instance-based learning algorithms," *Machine Learning*, vol. 6, no. 1, pp. 37–66, 1991.

[117] R. C. Holte, "Very simple classification rules perform well on most commonly used datasets," *Machine Learning*, vol. 11, no. 1, pp. 63–91, 1993.

[118] J. Demšar, "Statistical comparisons of classifiers over multiple data sets," *Journal of Machine Learning Research*, vol. 7, pp. 1–30, 2006.

[119] W. Khreich, E. Granger, A. Miri, and R. Sabourin, "Adaptive ROC-based ensembles of HMMs applied to anomaly detection," *Pattern Recognition*, vol. 45, no. 1, pp. 208–230, 2012.

[120] Z. Muda, W. Yassin, M. N. Sulaiman, and N. I. Udzir, "A K-Means and Naive Bayes learning approach for better intrusion detection," *Information Technology Journal*, vol. 10, no. 3, pp. 648–655, 2011.

[121] M. V. Mahoney and P. K. Chan, "An analysis of the 1999 DARPA/Lincoln laboratory evaluation data for network anomaly detection," Tech. Rep. CS-200302, Computer Science Department, Florida Institute of Technology, 2003.

[122] G. Kumar and K. Kumar, "A novel evaluation function for feature selection based upon information theory," in *Proceedings of the IEEE International Conference on Electrical and Computer Engineering (CCECE '11)*, pp. 000395–000399, Niagara Falls, Canada, May 2011.

Permissions

The contributors of this book come from diverse backgrounds, making this book a truly international effort. This book will bring forth new frontiers with its revolutionizing research information and detailed analysis of the nascent developments around the world.

We would like to thank all the contributing authors for lending their expertise to make the book truly unique. They have played a crucial role in the development of this book. Without their invaluable contributions this book wouldn't have been possible. They have made vital efforts to compile up to date information on the varied aspects of this subject to make this book a valuable addition to the collection of many professionals and students.

This book was conceptualized with the vision of imparting up-to-date information and advanced data in this field. To ensure the same, a matchless editorial board was set up. Every individual on the board went through rigorous rounds of assessment to prove their worth. After which they invested a large part of their time researching and compiling the most relevant data for our readers. Conferences and sessions were held from time to time between the editorial board and the contributing authors to present the data in the most comprehensible form. The editorial team has worked tirelessly to provide valuable and valid information to help people across the globe.

Every chapter published in this book has been scrutinized by our experts. Their significance has been extensively debated. The topics covered herein carry significant findings which will fuel the growth of the discipline. They may even be implemented as practical applications or may be referred to as a beginning point for another development. Chapters in this book were first published by Hindawi Publishing Corporation; hereby published with permission under the Creative Commons Attribution License or equivalent.

The editorial board has been involved in producing this book since its inception. They have spent rigorous hours researching and exploring the diverse topics which have resulted in the successful publishing of this book. They have passed on their knowledge of decades through this book. To expedite this challenging task, the publisher supported the team at every step. A small team of assistant editors was also appointed to further simplify the editing procedure and attain best results for the readers.

Our editorial team has been hand-picked from every corner of the world. Their multi-ethnicity adds dynamic inputs to the discussions which result in innovative outcomes. These outcomes are then further discussed with the researchers and contributors who give their valuable feedback and opinion regarding the same. The feedback is then collaborated with the researches and they are edited in a comprehensive manner to aid the understanding of the subject.

Apart from the editorial board, the designing team has also invested a significant amount of their time in understanding the subject and creating the most relevant covers. They scrutinized every image to scout for the most suitable representation of the subject and create an appropriate cover for the book.

The publishing team has been involved in this book since its early stages. They were actively engaged in every process, be it collecting the data, connecting with the contributors or procuring relevant information. The team has been an ardent support to the editorial, designing and production team. Their endless efforts to recruit the best for this project, has resulted in the accomplishment of this book. They are a veteran in the field of academics and their pool of knowledge is as vast as their experience in printing. Their expertise and guidance has proved useful at every step. Their uncompromising quality standards have made this book an exceptional effort. Their encouragement from time to time has been an inspiration for everyone.

The publisher and the editorial board hope that this book will prove to be a valuable piece of knowledge for researchers, students, practitioners and scholars across the globe.

List of Contributors

Ibtissem Chiha
Ensi Enim, Monastir, Rabat, Tunisia

Noureddine Liouane
Ensi Enim, Tunisia

Pierre Borne
National Cancer Institute, 92513 Boulogne Billan Court Cedex, France

Ferhat Ucan
Center of Research for Advanced Technologies of Informatics and Security (TU¨BI˙TAK BILGEM), 41470 Kocaeli, Turkey

D. Turgay Altılar
Computer Engineering Department, Istanbul Technical University, 34469 Istanbul, Turkey

Xiuming Yu, Meijing Li and Taewook Kim
Database and Bioinformatics Laboratory, Chungbuk National University, Cheongju 361-763, Republic of Korea

Seon-phil Jeong
Division of Science and Technology, BNU-HKBU United International College, Zhuhai 519-085, China

Keun Ho Ryu
Database and Bioinformatics Laboratory, Chungbuk National University, Cheongju 361-763, Republic of Korea
Division of Science and Technology, BNU-HKBU United International College, Zhuhai 519-085, China
Multimedia Systems Laboratory, School of Computer Science and Engineering, The University of Aizu, Aizu-Wakamatsu, Fukushima 965-8580, Japan

Xuan Guo, Yoshiyuki Toyoda, Jie Huang, Shuxue Ding and Yong Liu
Graduate Department of Computer and Information Systems, Graduate School of Computer Science and Engineering, The University of Aizu, Aizu-Wakamatsu 965-8580, Japan

Huankang Li
Department of Computer Science and Engineering, Shanghai Jiaotong University, 200240 Shanghai, China

M. Gorji-Bandpy and A. Mozaffari
Department of Mechanical Engineering, Babol University of Technology, P.O. Box 484, Babol, Iran

Farzad Hashemzadeh
Faculty of Electrical Engineering, Sarab Islamic Azad University, Sarab 54716-376, Iran

Yufang Qin, Junzhong Ji and Chunnian Liu
Beijing Municipal Key Laboratory of Multimedia and Intelligent Software Technology, College of Computer Science and Technology, Beijing University of Technology, Beijing 100124, China

Aminreza Noghrehabadi, Mohammad Ghalambaz and Afshin Ghanbarzadeh
Department of Mechanical Engineering, Shahid Chamran University of Ahvaz, 6135743337 Ahvaz, Iran

Mehdi Ghalambaz
Engineering Part of Iman Madar Naslaha Co. (IMEN), Ahvaz, Iran

Khaled Chahine
Department of Electrical and Electronics Engineering, Lebanese International University, Mazraa, Beirut 146404, Lebanon

Khalil El Khamlichi Drissi
Pascal Institute, UMR 6602, 24 Avenue des Landais, 63177 Aubiere Cedex, France

Ozlem Terzi
Faculty of Technical Education, Suleyman Demirel University, 32260 Isparta, Turkey

Sanjay K. Boddhu and John C. Gallagher
Department of Computer Science and Engineering, Wright State University, Dayton, OH 45435, USA

Lei Jiang and Suhuai Luo
School of DCIT, University of Newcastle, Callaghan, NSW 2308, Australia

Jiaming Li
ICT Centre, Commonwealth Scientific and Industrial Research Organization, Clayton South, VIC 3169, Australia

Sam West and Glenn Platt
Energy Technology Division, Commonwealth Scientific and Industrial Research Organization, Clayton South, VIC 3169, Australia

Yasuji Sawada
Tohoku Institute of Technology, 35-1 Yagiyama-Kasumi, Taihaku, Sendai 982-8577, Japan

G. Casalino
Dipartimento di Informatica, Universita di Bari, Via E. Orabona 4, I-70125 Bari, Italy

N. Del Buono
Dipartimento di Matematica, Universita di Bari, Via E. Orabona 4, I-70125 Bari, Italy

M. Minervini
Computer Science and Engineering Ph.D Division, Institute for Advanced Studies Lucca (IMT), Piazza S. Ponziano 6, 55100 Lucca, Italy

Shigeaki Sakurai
Business Intelligence Laboratory and Advanced IT Laboratory, Toshiba Solutions Corporation, Tokyo 183-8512, Japan
Department of Computational Intelligence and Systems Science, Interdisciplinary Graduate School of Science and Engineering, Tokyo Institute of Technology, Kanagawa 226-8502, Japan

King Hann Lim
Electrical and Computer Department, School of Engineering and Science, Curtin University, Sarawak Malaysia, CDT 250, 98009 Miri Sarawak, Malaysia

Kah Phooi Seng
School of Computer Technology, Sunway University, No. 5, Jalan Universiti, Bandar Sunway, Selangor Darul Ehsan, 46150 Petaling, Malaysia

Li-Minn Ang
Centre for Communications Engineering Research, Edith Cowan University, Joondalup, WA 6027, Australia

A. Belayneh and J. Adamowski
Department of Bioresource Engineering, Faculty of Agricultural and Environmental Sciences, McGill University, QC, Canada

Eric Sakk and Ayanna Alexander
Department of Computer Science, Morgan State University, Baltimore, MD 21251, USA

Petri Juntunen, Mika Liukkonen, Markku J. Lehtola and Yrjo Hiltunen
Department of Environmental Science, University of Eastern Finland, P.O. Box 1627, 70211 Kuopio, Finland

Marja Pelo
Finnsugar Ltd., Sokeritehtaantie 20, 02460 Kantvik, Finland

Gulshan Kumar

Department of Computer Application, Shaheed Bhagat Singh State Technical Campus, Ferozepur, Punjab 152004, India

Krishan Kumar

Department of Computer Science & Engineering, Punjab Institute of Technology, Kapurthala, Punjab 144601, India

Printed in the USA
CPSIA information can be obtained
at www.ICGtesting.com
JSHW052022301024
72690JS00004B/141

9 781632 403308